The Untouchables, who number some 150 million, are among the most subordinated and poorest people in India. In a sensitive and compelling account of the lives of those at the very bottom of Indian society, Oliver Mendelsohn and Marika Vicziany explore the construction of the Untouchables as a social and political category, the historical background which led to such a definition and their position in Indian society today. The authors argue that despite efforts to ameliorate their condition on the part of the state, and on the part of the new generation of political leaders who represent them, a considerable edifice of discrimination persists on the basis of a tradition of ritual subordination. Even now, therefore, at the end of the twentieth century, it still makes sense to categorise these people as 'Untouchables'.

As the most comprehensive account available of the phenomenon of Untouchability, this book promises to make a major contribution to the literature, and in particular to the current social and economic debates on poverty within the global context. Its wide-ranging perspectives will ensure an interdisciplinary readership from historians of South Asia, to students of politics and economics, religion and sociology.

Contemporary South Asia

The Untouchables

Contemporary South Asia 4

Contemporary South Asia has been established to publish books on
the politics, society and culture of South Asia since 1947. In accessible
and comprehensive studies, authors who are already engaged in
researching specific aspects of South Asian society explore a wide
variety of broad-ranging and topical themes. The series will be of
interest to anyone who is concerned with the study of South Asia and
with the legacy of its colonial past.

1 Ayesha Jalal *Democracy and Authoritarianism in South Asia: A
   Comparative and Historical Perspective*
2 Jan Breman, *Footloose Labour: Working in India's Informal Economy*
3 Roger Jeffery and Patricia Jeffery, *Population, Gender and Politics:
   Demographic Change in Rural North India*

The Untouchables

Subordination, poverty and the state in modern India

Oliver Mendelsohn

La Trobe University

and

Marika Vicziany

Monash University

CAMBRIDGE
UNIVERSITY PRESS

CAMBRIDGE UNIVERSITY PRESS
Cambridge, New York, Melbourne, Madrid, Cape Town, Singapore, São Paulo

Cambridge University Press
The Edinburgh Building, Cambridge CB2 2RU, UK

Published in the United States of America by Cambridge University Press, New York

www.cambridge.org
Information on this title: www.cambridge.org/9780521553629

First published 1998

A catalogue record for this publication is available from the British Library

ISBN-13 978-0-521-55362-9 hardback
ISBN-10 0-521-55362-8 hardback

ISBN-13 978-0-521-55671-2 paperback
ISBN-10 0-521-55671-6 paperback

Transferred to digital printing 2006

For RM and RM

Contents

Tables

Glossary of Indian or special terms

Note: Some foreign terms explained in the text and used only on that page have been omitted from this glossary

achuta	Hindi word translatable as 'outcaste' or 'Untouchable'
adi	original
Adi-Andhra	literally (lit.), the original people of Andhra; used by some Untouchables of Andhra Pradesh to identify themselves
Ad Dharm	lit., the original religion; a sect established in Punjab in the 1920s
Adi-Dravida	lit., the original people among the Dravidians of south India; used as self-identification by some of the Untouchables of Tamilnadu
Adi-Karnataka	lit., the original people of Karnataka; used as self-identification by some of the Untouchables of Karnataka
Ahar	see *Ahir*
Ahir	also *Ahar* and *Yadav;* a peasant caste of Uttar Pradesh, Bihar and other regions of north India
Ande Koraga	Untouchable caste of Tamilnadu
Ayurveda	a traditional Indian system of medicine
Babasaheb	honorific term devised for B. R. Ambedkar
Babri Masjid	the mosque alleged to have been built on the site of a pre-existing Hindu temple at Ayodya in Uttar Pradesh
Backward Castes	low (Shudra) castes that are immediately above the Untouchables in the ritual hierarchy
Balai	Untouchable caste of weavers in Rajasthan
Bania	a general term for commercial castes
bargadar	Bengali term for sharecropper
bataidar	Hindi term for sharecropper

Bauri	Untouchable caste of West Bengal, Orissa and Bihar
bhakta	a poet of the *bhakti* movement
bhakti	a medieval and later revivalist movement of Hindu worship that stressed devotion rather than learning
Bhangi	Untouchable sweeper caste of northern India; see *Valmiki*
bhoodan movement	a movement to bring about land reform by voluntary divestment
Bhoomi Sena	private army of the Kurmi landlords of Bihar
Bhumihar	landowning caste that is particularly strong in central Bihar
bidi	traditional Indian leaf cigarette
Brahmarshi Sena	private army of the Bhumihar landlords of Bihar
Brahmin	the highest (in the sense of most reputed) caste
Brahminwadi	derogatory term used by the followers of Kanshi Ram and Mayawati to identify attitudes or behaviour claimed to embody Brahminical prejudice against Dalits
C(h)andala	Sanskrit word translatable as 'polluting' or 'Untouchable'
Chamar	Untouchable caste of northern and western India with a traditional occupational connection to leather work; the largest Untouchable caste
Chambhar	Maharashtra variant of 'Chamar'
charpai	a portable bed strung with rope
Chu(h)ra	Untouchable sweeper caste of Himachal Pradesh and adjacent regions
Dalit	a Marathi word for Untouchables; originally used for the followers of Ambedkar, but now one of the most common terms identifying Untouchables as a whole; sometimes used for oppressed people in general
darshan	to pay respect, to seek blessing (usually of gods)
deshmukh	village landlord
Dhanak	Untouchable caste of Rajasthan employed as servants and village watchmen
dharma	duty/religion/law
dharna	sit-in as a form of protest
Dhobi	caste of washerfolk, Untouchable in many regions of India
diku	term employed for outside oppressors of tribal people

dindi	the human clusters which form the pilgrimage to Pandhapur, western India
Diwali	Hindu New Year celebrated by the lighting of lamps and associated rituals
Dom	Untouchable caste which traditionally worked in cremation grounds, scavenged, wove baskets and beat drums
Dusadh	also *Paswan,* the second largest Untouchable caste of Bihar, which traditionally worked as servants and village watchmen
Emergency	the period from 1975 to 1977 when Prime Minister Indira Gandhi invoked a Constitutional Emergency which suspended the ordinary democratic and civil liberties
Ezhava (also *Tiyyar*)	once mildly Untouchable (but not Scheduled) caste of Kerala
Garibi Hatao	lit., Banish Poverty!; Indira Gandhi's election slogan in 1971
Gariya luhars	the travelling blacksmiths of Rajasthan
Green revolution	the introduction of high-yielding varieties of wheat and later rice into Indian agriculture from the late 1960s, and consequential changes in agricultural technologies
Gujars	peasant caste of north India
Gurukul	Arya Samaj monastery
Hari	Untouchable caste associated with cremation grounds
Harijan	lit., People of God; used by Gandhi to identify Untouchables
Harijan Sevak Sangh	welfare organisation established by Gandhi to persuade caste Hindus to abolish Untouchability
hartal	closure of shops or other facilities as a protest
hookah	communal tobacco pipe
Holeya	large Untouchable caste of village servants in Karnataka
Jains	community variously treated as a caste or as a religious community
jamadar	sub-contractor of labour
jan sewa	service to the people
Jatav	segment of Chamars located in western Uttar Pradesh
jati	one of the constituents of 'caste'; endogamous (in-

	marrying) units of which there are thousands throughout India
jhopris	huts
julaha	Muslim weaver
Kabir panth	Hindu sect which follows the teachings of the *bhakta* Kabir
karma	a tenet of mainstream Hindu philosophy whereby one's deeds/condition (including caste) will determine lives yet-to-be lived; the doctrine is often seen to discriminate against Untouchables
Kayastha	an unusually literate caste of northern India, now conceived as 'high-caste', whatever its origins
Khatik	Untouchable north Indian caste of shepherds and butchers
Koiri	peasant caste, particularly strong in Bihar
Kshatriya	the second *varna* of Hindu society; their occupation is traditionally conceived as that of ruler and warrior
kullarh	disposable earthenware pot
Kurmi	peasant caste of Uttar Pradesh and Bihar
Lalbegi	variant name for *Bhangi*
lassi	buttermilk
Lal Sena	lit., Red Army; armed Naxalite revolutionaries in Bihar
Lingayat	dominant landlord caste of Karnataka
Lorik Sena	private army of the Yadav landlords of Bihar
Madiga	particularly deprived Untouchable caste in Andhra Pradesh
mahasabha	association
Mahar	Untouchable caste of village servants in Marahrashtra; Ambedkar's caste
Mahatma	term of honour (lit., Great Soul) for M. K. Gandhi
Mala	Untouchable caste of village servants in Andhra Pradesh
Mali	peasant caste of northern and western India
Mallaha	fisherfolk of Uttar Pradesh and Bihar
mandal	association or society
Mang	large Untouchable caste of Maharashtra
mantra	repetition of words of prayer
Manusmriti	the laws according to Manu, a medieval text writer
Manuwadi	derogatory term used by Kanshi Ram and Mayawati's followers to identify behaviour claimed

	to embody high-caste prejudice against Dalits; see also *Brahminwadi*
Maratha	large and powerful caste in Maharashtra
maya	Sanskrit word often translated as 'illusion'
Mazhabi Sikh	Untouchable sweeper converts to Sikhism
Mehtar	another word for *Bhangi*
mela	celebration, festival or gathering
mukkadam	jobber/labour contractor; variant of *jamadar*
Musahar	the third largest (after Chamar and Dusadh) Untouchable caste of Bihar, and particularly poor
Nadars	once mildly Untouchable (but not Scheduled) caste of Tamilnadu; similar to the *Ezhava*
Namas(h)udra	large Untouchable caste of Bengal
Naxalites	insurrectionary Marxists of West Bengal and later Bihar
nirguna bhatki	the more radical branch of *bhakti*
Operation Barga	the program to register the rights of sharecroppers in West Bengal during the 1970s and 1980s
Other Backward Classes (or Castes) (OBC)	see *Backward Castes;* socially and educationally deprived (but not Untouchable) castes in relation to whom the Constitution also authorises remedial action
Panchama	Sanskrit term suggesting that the Untouchables are 'really' the fifth category of the *varna* order
panchayat	village or caste council (*panch* meaning 'five', hence lit., council of five)
Pandit	Brahmin, particularly a Brahmin scholar
Paraiyan	Untouchable caste of Tamilnadu
Pasi	Untouchable caste of hereditary brewers in Bihar
Paswan	variant of *Dusadh*
Patel	dominant landlord caste of Gujarat
patwari	junior revenue official
pradhan	head of panchayat or council
pukka	ripe, finished; of buildings: construction with brick or stone rather than less permanent materials
Pulaya	Untouchable caste of Kerala; the classic 'slave caste' as late as the nineteenth century
Purada Vannan	Untouchable caste of south India
Raedasi Sikh	Chamars of Punjab who converted to Sikhism
Raegar	north Indian Untouchable caste closely related to Chamars
Rajbanshi	large Untouchable caste of Bengal

saddhu	Hindu holyman
saguna bhakti	the less radical stream of *bhakti*
samaj	association
sant	Hindu saint
sarpanch	head of *panchayat*
satyagraha	a particular form of non-violent struggle that Gandhi developed
Scheduled Caste	the official term for the castes named by legal instrument so as to qualify them for special benefits at national and state levels; largely synonomous with the terms 'Untouchable caste' or 'Untouchables'
S(h)udra	the lowest of the four categories of the *varna* representation of Hindu society, their traditional occupation being to 'serve' in a wide variety of manual tasks
sufi	devotional cults of Islam
Sunri	Untouchable caste of brewers, agricultural labourers and small businessmen in West Bengal
Sweepers	occupational term for a number of Indian castes whose traditional job it is to sweep public spaces and collect nightsoil and garbage
tehsildar	revenue official
Telegu	the regional language of Andhra Pradesh
toddy	country liquor distilled from the coconut tree
twice-born	the first three categories of the *varna* order whose males are entitled to wear the 'sacred thread' after a ceremony of early manhood; hence, a general term for 'upper-caste'
Vaishya	the third category of the *varna* order of Hindu society; their traditional occupation was that of traders
Valmiki	the now usually preferred name for the Bhangi or sweeper community which follows the teachings of the saint Valmiki
Vankar	Untouchable weaver caste of Gujarat
varna	the four categories (lit., colours) into which classical Hindu texts divide society
Vedas	ancient texts of great reverence within Hinduism
Yadav	see *Ahir*
zamindars	revenue intermediaries and landlords under the British

Preface

Our primary debt in the preparation of this work is to the people who form its subject. We have talked to many hundreds of them over the years, and they have been marvellously trusting and generous with their time. Only one of them ever complained – we had tried his patience that day, and he wanted to get on with his work. His name is Amee Chand, a Bhangi (Valmiki) tailor in Alwar District of Rajasthan, and over many years he has been simply our very best source of knowledge. We hope that this book is sufficient justification for the trouble to which we put Amee Chand and so many others.

We cannot hope to thank all the people in official, academic and journalism circles who have given us assistance. Indeed, many of the officials must not be named for fear of embarrassing them. But the following are some of the people who were invaluable in gathering the material for this book. Swami Agnivesh has become a friend as well as a person whom we have written about, and his assistance has been crucial. Inder Mohan also helped us in understanding the situation of the new urban poor such as the rag pickers and the quarry workers. Bhagwan Das provided some early insight into the Ambedkarite movement, and L. G. Havanur gave us a copy of his influential report (and a memorable lunch in Bangalore). Raghavan, then of *The Times of India*, Jakapanavar, Indudan Honnapur and Professor Parvathamma were also specially useful in Bangalore and Mysore. Smita Gupta of *The Times of India* provided invaluable assistance in the research on Kanshi Ram, as did Manohara Prasad of the Dr Ambedkar Foundation. Our Friends S. D. and Anuradha Muni were invariably hospitable in Delhi.

In Trivandrum, V. K. Narayanan and Professor Jayakumar were particularly helpful. Among people in Bihar, we can single out I. D. Sharma, Arun Sinha, Nirmal Sengupta, K. B. Saxena, A. R. Bandyopadhyaya, and the general assistance of the A. N. Sinha Institute for Social Studies, Patna. In New Delhi and Calcutta, Bikram Sarkar was most helpful.

One of the nice things about engagement in serious academic work is that one realises the substance of the phrase 'community of scholars'. We owe particular gratitude to Bernard Cohn for sponsoring our visit to the University of Chicago for a number of months in 1989. We benefited greatly from this visit, including from the comments at a seminar we gave at the Centre for South Asian Studies, and from our immersion in the wonderful Indian collection in the Regenstein Library under the friendly guidance of Jim Nye. During this same period we tested some of our ideas in seminars at the University of Pennsylvania and Tufts University. At many turns Marc Galanter has been a great help.

As to comments on drafts of our writing, we can thank Professors D. A. Low, M. N. Pearson and Dharma Kumar. David Ludden took particular care to offer critical commentary, and the book is better for this (though we are certain we will not have satisfied his criticisms). We also owe much to two anonymous reviewers for Cambridge University Press. Professor Upendra Baxi read the whole manuscript and offered valuable comments.

Ronald Mendelsohn read the manuscript with immense care and offered innumerable suggestions on matters of style, logic and comprehensibility to non-specialists.

Financial assistance with research for this work has come from La Trobe and Monash Universities, and from the Australian Research Grants Scheme. We freely acknowledge this support in an era of declining sympathy for research that is not more obviously 'useful'.

A version of chapter 6 has been published in the *Journal of Commonwealth and Comparative Politics*, 29(1), 1991, 44–71; and parts of chapter 8 appeared in *Economic and Political Weekly*, 21(12), 1986, 501–09.

Finally, though it belongs to a different universe of logic, we need to recognise the marvellous openness of Indian society that has made the present work possible. We are not writing about the most congenial aspects of India, and yet our work has been tolerated and even welcomed. Since we count ourselves friends of India, we are immensely grateful for the understanding that our theme is a human and not a national one.

1   Who are the Untouchables?

This book is about a grouping of some 150 million people who belong to particular castes at the very bottom of Indian society. Although caste identity is the basis on which the subject has been constructed, this is only incidentally a work about caste as a cultural phenomenon. Our main preoccupations are with subordination and poverty, class, politics (including violent politics), the state and public policy. But equally, it is not possible to understand the situation of the Untouchables by exclusive reference to broad categories of analysis that treat them as simply one of many cases of subordination within India or elsewhere. The Untouchables may be capable of comparison with other social groupings but they remain a highly distinctive cultural and moral community.

Two broad propositions are fundamental to the present work. The first is that the Untouchables are among the very bottom elements of Indian society in both status and economic terms; and the second is that they have undergone a profound change in their view of themselves and the society around them. Whatever the truth of past assertions that the Untouchables accepted their own inferiority, it is our view that in recent years there has been a greatly enhanced mood of assertiveness about their human and political rights. A large part of this book will be taken up with expounding the basis of these two judgments.

But before this is done, we need to justify our construction of the subject itself. It has to be said that the basis on which this work is constructed is not currently fashionable. For some years the mainstream of fresh scholarship on India has tended to attack the centrality of caste in Indian life, and to argue that it was the British rulers and their fellow-traveller scholars who installed caste into an Orientalist and exaggeratedly central position within Indian civilisation (Inden 1990: 56–66; Dirks 1987: 7–8). The essentialism of an earlier scholarship has been laid bare, whereby exotic and seemingly novel Indian structures were wrongly seen to be the intellectual basis for too sharp a counterposition of India and the West. Louis Dumont (1970) has been seen as the apotheosis of this approach, with his rigorous insistence that India is the land of *homo hierarchicus* as against the individualism characteristic of the modern West (Das 1995: 34–41; Dirks 1987: 4).

The present writers find themselves comfortable with much of the attack on old and not-so-old Orientalist scholarship on India. And we will be at considerable pains in this book to develop the argument that the Untouchables were in a sense 'constructed' or 'invented' in the late colonial period, mainly the twentieth century, rather than existing as an entity for centuries past. But equally, and indeed more profoundly, they were fashioned as a political grouping from clay that was many hundreds of years old. They were not conjured out of thin air. Our argument is that the Untouchables were a subordinated people long before twentieth-century politics transformed them into a category of political relevance. There is a danger that this view will be forgotten in following the admittedly fascinating process whereby the Untouchables ceased being merely a dispersed and highly fragmented congeries of subordinated communities and became a unitary category covering the sub-continent as a whole.

It will assist in locating the themes of this book to say a word about the way in which the research unfolded. This research is now of some years' duration, and originated in an interest in the violence that appeared to be suffusing much of the Indian countryside – the State of Bihar above all – from the late 1970s. It rapidly became apparent that the subject of violence was both too broad and too narrow a focus of study. Much of the violence surrounded the Untouchables or what were then still usually called 'Harijans'. It became clear that a proper understanding of the 'Harijan atrocity' could only arise from a deeper understanding of the whole situation of the Untouchables. So a particular problem led backwards and sideways into what has become a general study of the Untouchables in the twentieth century, with considerable reference to earlier history. The subject of violence is now discussed at length in only one of the chapters of this work, and violence is taken to be an important dimension rather than the epitome of the lives of Untouchables today. At the same time, the heart of this book lies in the attempt to sum up a condition of social subordination which we take to be deeply entrenched even today.

What's in a name?

Aside from the empirical difficulty of a project which attempts to say something about so large a human population, the subject immediately opens up a set of intellectual problems surrounding the personal and social identity of the people in question. The first issue is one of nomenclature. We have chosen to use the term 'Untouchables' as general identifier of the people about whom we are writing, but this choice is hedged about with difficulties. The most powerful count *against* this term is that almost no one identifies him/herself by reference to it. Presumably a primary ground of this *non*-use is that the word encapsulates the subordinated condition that the people in question are seeking to escape from. Why would one identify oneself by reference to an odious condition imposed by others? Unfortunately, there is no generally acceptable alternative for the people in question or for sympathetic observers such as ourselves. The possibilities fall into several different categories.

The first category is names of a clearly political character. While the two leading terms are 'Harijan' and 'Dalit', as early as 1917 the prefix 'Adi' or 'Original' was employed by Untouchable leaders seeking to assert a status as a people subordinated by later Aryan immigrants to India (Omvedt 1994: 118). So the terms 'Adi-Dravida', 'Adi-Karnataka' and 'Adi-Andhra' are still used as self-description by large numbers of Untouchables in the different States of south India. But this language is too localised to be generally employable across India, and in any case it embodies a questionable thesis (the claim to 'originality') as to the history of Indian settlement.

The term 'Harijan' was adopted by Mahatma Gandhi in 1933 as the winning entry in a national competition for a suitable name to replace the terms noted in the second category below. Gandhi's object was to invent a name which identified the relevant people without fixing them with an inferior status – 'Harijan' is translatable as 'People of God'. This term was widely adopted in the general population and also by Untouchables themselves, but in recent years the name has lost support. To many the word appears as a patronising and ultimately meaningless exercise: what does it mean to say that traditionally despised communities are people of God? Thus the term has come to be seen as a symbol of the non-radical integrationist politics of Gandhi and his followers. As early as the 1930s the word became something of an epithet among Untouchables themselves – 'he is a Harijan' was sometimes used pejoratively by militant activists to denote a person who had internalised attitudes of inferiority and had an accepting view of his place in the Hindu world. For these reasons it has seemed inappropriate to employ the term in this book, except in specialised contexts. Thus we make considerable use of the widely used term 'Harijan atrocity' in relation to the upsurge in violence suffered by Untouchables from the period of the late 1970s.

The word 'Dalit' is now fast supplanting the other generic names for persons descended from the old Untouchable castes. This is a word in the Marathi language of western India, and is apparently derived from Sanskrit. In an 1831 dictionary the word is defined as 'ground' or 'broken or reduced to pieces generally' (Molesworth's Marathi–English Dictionary 1831). It was seemingly first used in the context of caste oppression by the great nineteenth-century reformer Phule, but its modern history dates from the early 1970s among activists from the Untouchable Mahar caste (Zelliot 1992: 267, 271). By now the term has spread to Karnataka and increasingly throughout India. Like 'Harijan' the term is intensely political, but the politics this time are more assertive and self-directed, sometimes separatist. While use of the term might seem to express an appropriate solidarity with the contemporary face of Untouchable politics, there remain major problems in adopting it as the generic term. Although the word is now quite widespread, it still has deep roots in a tradition of political radicalism inspired by the figure of B. R. Ambedkar. Until it loses this association the term will wrongly tend to suggest that the huge Untouchable population of India has been swept up into a single radical politics. Connected with this problem, in very large regions like Bihar, West Bengal and most of Uttar Pradesh, 'Dalit' is still not widely used as an expression of self-identity. But since the term is undoubtedly gaining ground among Untouchables and even in the media, we will have frequent occasion to employ it when we are analysing contemporary political movements (particularly in chapter 7).

The second category is a cluster of terms devised mainly in British bureaucratic contexts – above all the Census – from late in the nineteenth century to the 1930s. These terms included 'Outcastes', 'Depressed Castes' and 'Exterior Castes'. The endpoint of this line of verbal/conceptual development is the term 'Scheduled Castes', now the official identifier of what we are calling the Untouchables. The so-called Schedule is a list of castes entitled to parliamentary seats, public employment and special educational benefits. This Schedule was originally promulgated by the British Goverment of India in 1936 but the term 'Scheduled Castes' only became widely used after Independence. While the term has a useful moral neutrality, it is essentially legal in nature: the people in question have been transformed into a special legal class of citizens for certain purposes of the state. We will need to use the term frequently when dealing with provisions of government, but it is inappropriate for more general use.

Perhaps the least attractive term is 'ex-untouchable', often used in the early years after Independence and still to be found today. The term is legally sound – Untouchability was abolished by the Constitution of India – and also appears to distance the practitioner from the morality of Untouchability. But the term is sociologically false, if one takes the view that Untouchability has not in fact been dismantled.

This brings us back to our general preference for the term 'Untouchable'. The word is of early twentieth-century origin and it can variably be viewed as an invented term belonging to the second category above (together with terms like 'Outcastes'), or as a free translation of vernacular words such as *achuta* in Hindi. 'Untouchable' is perhaps a reasonable translation of achuta, though translation begs the questions we are seeking to uncover. Our own reasons for using the term as a general identifier are several. First, it is both sufficiently broad and sufficiently specific to identify all the people we seek to discuss in this work. Secondly, it is not so obviously political in nature as is 'Harijan' or 'Dalit', and so by its very use it does not commit the writers to one, perhaps partisan, view of the whole problem. In this sense 'Untouchable' is more neutral than these obviously political words, though we do not make the mistake of believing that the word is neutral in the sense of value-free. Indeed, thirdly, the word 'Untouchable' is highly evocative of a condition which we see as one of the more pernicious forms of subordination to be encountered anywhere. Its very evocativeness – the idea that some people are so degraded as to be physically and morally 'untouchable' – has established the word as clearly the best known of all the terms. Outside India this is the word people know. On the other hand, we are acutely aware that the term is less than congenial in that it identifies people by reference to a morally unacceptable structure. This awareness leads us to assert a small amount of critical distance by generally capitalising the term ('Untouchable'), thereby seeking to hint that here is a term that is not 'natural', morally appropriate or devised by the subjects of the term themselves. Capitalisation seems particularly appropriate in that the practice of ritual Untouchability is now unlawful. Finally, we need to reiterate that our own context is a special one. We are not political actors, and we are not seeking to legislate the use of language in this area. Our object has simply been to arrive at a term that best suits the purposes of the present exercise.

The Untouchables and Hindu orthodoxy

Untouchables have for many centuries occupied a deeply ambiguous place within Indian society. From the standpoint of the Great Tradition represented by the *Vedas*, Untouchables have no place at all. What much later became known as Hindu society was divided by the Vedas into four categories or *varnas* associated with particular social occupations: Brahmin (priest and teacher), Kshatriya (ruler and warrior), Vaishya (trader) and Sudra (servant). These varnas are often, but quite misleadingly, called 'caste' (which itself is the translation of a Portuguese word, rather than being of Indian origin). The absence of Untouchables from the varna scheme may arise simply from the later emergence of this social condition: the weight of opinion suggests that Untouchability only crystallised in the second century of the common era, whereas the varna principle seems to have been established over one thousand years earlier. But since the varna classification has persisted as a representation of the whole Hindu order, the position of Untouchables as Hindus has been contradictory. Their presence cannot be denied, but they have no legitimate place in the order.

In everyday life, particularly in the villages, the operative conception of caste is *jati* rather than varna. There are thousands of jatis in India, the largest containing many millions of persons and the smallest perhaps only hundreds. Jatis are endogamous (in-marrying) units with individual traditions and rules as to personal conduct. The existence of jatis is often reconciled with the Great Tradition by asserting that they are simply an elaboration of the four varnas. But just one of the problems of this approach is that Untouchables are organised in jatis just as other Hindus are. Chamar, Bhangi, Dhobi, Pulaya, Paswan, Madagi are some of the many hundreds of Untouchable jatis scattered through every region of India. At the local level everyone knows that there are particular Untouchable castes rather than Untouchables in general. And yet because of their absence from the varna scheme, the Untouchables are often depicted as being 'outcastes' or without caste. They are seen as a lower grouping to be distinguished from 'caste Hindus'.

But in another sense Untouchables can be analytically represented to be at the very core of Hinduism. Thus the most influential (also the most contested) recent account of caste locates its essence in the counterposition of Brahmin and Untouchable (Dumont 1970: 33–64). This is the most perfect representation of the dichotomy between purity (the Brahmin) and pollution (the Untouchable), a dichotomy that Dumont argues to be the basis of the whole caste hierarchy and thus Indian civilisation as a whole. For Dumont this jati hierarchy constitutes 'the caste system', though it derives some of its strength from the existence of the parallel but incomplete varna hierarchy.

For most Hindus impurity is either a temporary or a limited affair. Thus women are polluted during menstruation, and on this account may not cook food for their family (Dumont 1970: 53). Daily pollution arises from the secretions of the body, and the left hand is permanently polluted by its use in cleaning the body. Birth and death engender great pollution, and the new mother must be sequestered for a period of some days before she will be fit to be seen and touched. Texts such as Manu and Jataka – difficult to date, they seem to have been written early in the present era – lay down the duties and sins of the varnas, paying particular attention to

Brahmins. 'A Candala [Untouchable] and a boar, a cock and also a dog, and a woman in her courses and an eunuch, may not see the Brahmans eating' (Manu 1884: III, verse 239). But pollution from an Untouchable is particularly serious. So the Jataka tells the tale of a famished young Brahmin who shares the food of a Candala, and then goes off to die in despair in the forest (Dumont 1970: 53). This degree of expiation is perhaps hortatory: the normal mode prescribed for reinstating purity is to bathe oneself.

Alone, the Untouchables are a permanently polluted people. Their status is said to arise from the work they perform, such as skinning animal carcasses, tanning leather and making shoes; playing in musical bands; butchery of animals; fishing; removal of human waste; attendance at cremation grounds; washing clothes; coconut harvesting and the brewing of toddy, to name some of the principal grounds of permanent pollution. Ostensibly, then, today's Untouchables – all 150 million of them – are descended from persons polluted by their unclean work.

Just why either the varna system or Untouchability developed in India is far from clear, but perhaps it had something to do with the incursion of 'Aryans' who migrated from Europe and established themselves in India. One persistent line of thought is that the varnas represent the efforts of the Aryans to create a social order in which they came to terms with pre-Aryan (including Dravidian) India but simultaneously asserted their apartness and moral, political and economic superiority. On this view, the higher varnas are either composed of or have some favourable connection with the Aryans. Conversely the Sudras were at the bottom of the status hierarchy and were also the people who did much of the hard physical labour of society. Later, in ways that are even less satisfactorily explained than the origins of varna, the still more lowly Untouchables were constituted. Gandhi and many other Indian thinkers have sought to argue that varna was originally a benign division of labour without attribution of differential moral worth, and that it was only later corrupted by the development of moral hierarchy and Untouchability in particular. But there is no evidence for this, and it seems inherently implausible. Rather, the early convergence of what might be called status and class in India lends credence to analytical approaches that proceed from a presumption of exploitation.

A simple ritual basis for Untouchability is rendered problematical by the lack of identity between Untouchable status and employment in polluting occupations. Today, most Untouchables do not perform the work that is the polluting mark of their caste. So among Chamars, the largest Untouchable caste in India, only a small minority are employed in connection with their hereditary and polluting work with skins and leather. Chamars are above all agricultural labourers. Some important Untouchable castes, including the Dusadhs of Bihar and the Mahars of Maharashtra, traditionally performed work that was mostly non-polluting. The Mahars had no specialised skills but were general village servants and messengers, though they did sometimes collect the skins of fallen animals. And the Dusadhs were field labourers and servants to individual high-caste families. Just why such castes came to be Untouchable is therefore a matter of some conjecture. It is scarcely plausible that 150 million people are all descended from people who were once employed in the comparatively small number of deeply polluting occupations. The difficulty of this explanation again points to the likelihood that exploitation entered into the very construction of the phenomenon of Untouchability.

These remarks do something to locate the social landscape of the Untouchables, and they lead us to a couple of more sharply defined questions. First, just how distinct are Untouchables from other Indians both today and historically? And, as a corollary of this question, how subordinated are Untouchables relative to other socially depressed communities? These questions have received radically divergent answers from both Indians and foreigners.

Untouchability as a contemporary condition

No serious observer doubts that a large proportion of those now identified as Untouchables are descended from people who suffered severe oppression in the past. But what is no longer universally agreed is that there is today, or even historically, a body of people who are so ill-treated and so distinct from other Indians that they should be separated out and labelled 'Untouchables' or some synonymous term. We can run together a number of observations in writing or speech over a period of years to produce a composite that is broadly representative of objections to such an approach:

The 'Untouchables' are a regular part of Indian society, which has always been an aggregation of multiple compartments or statuses varying over both region or culture group and time. People from the castes called 'Untouchable' are distinguished by being generally poor and of very low status, but not so low that they should be identified as a collective grouping opposed to the remainder of higher-status society. The old Untouchable castes are not the only lowly people in India: there are many other communities that are desparately poor and subject to significant discrimination by their ritual and economic superiors. In so sharply distinguishing Untouchables from others the flaw is twofold: first, the approach asserts a false unity among Untouchables, who are just as divided from each other along caste, regional, linguistic and general cultural lines as they are from the rest of Indian society. And secondly, the barrier ignores the truth that beneath all the differences among Hindus there is a profound unity which binds the highest to the lowest. This unity is one of belief and social inter-dependence. As to the practice of ritual Untouchability, reform is now well under way. There remains some discrimination in various parts of India against the Untouchables, and others too, but this is only anachronistic residue. As the economic condition of the Untouchables improves, so this residue will tend to dry up.

Although no single thinker has articulated this whole package of views so neatly, the account is no straw man. The various positions within this composite narrative have commanded considerable support from both political actors and critics, as will become apparent in the next section and in later parts of the book.

While the present writers do not share the above approach, it is not without plausibility. Thus quite clearly the Untouchables are not a people of any single ethnic or cultural identity. They speak the language of their region. Their forms of worship conform to a common Indian pattern, albeit that they are skewed towards local folk traditions and often stripped of discriminatory concepts like *karma* (which justifies present degraded status by reference to misdeeds in previous life). And crucially, Untouchables are divided into castes which are organised on a regional basis: they know little or nothing of comparable castes in other regions.

In economic terms many Untouchables are field labourers or workers in a large number of so-called unskilled occupations. Increasingly they look like a particularly downtrodden proletariat, sometimes lumpenproletariat. But they share this situation with many millions of Indians from different religious and caste communities, and sometimes *class* seems the most appropriate concept with which to approach this broadly experienced condition. Even within the logic of *caste*, the Untouchables fail to emerge as the single subordinated element. Backward elements among what the varna order calls 'Sudras' are also clearly subordinated today. The Constitution of India terms these groups the 'socially and educationally backward classes', and authorises government to provide them (as well as the Scheduled Castes and Tribes) with special benefits to help them overcome their disabilities. One of the central political thrusts of recent years has been to increase the provision of such benefits to the relevant castes who constitute the 'backward classes'. More generally, the present writers are not attracted to the task of constructing a hierarchy of misery and oppression, such that the subjects of our own work are invariably to be depicted as occupying the very bottom rungs of society.

It is also easy to show that the orthodox account of the Untouchables as a comprehensively polluted people cannot serve as a complete description of their place in village society. That place is, and always has been, a complicated affair. Even in the matter of religious and cultural life, where ritual discrimination is greatest, the Untouchables are not so comprehensively shut out as orthodox ideology would suggest. For example, in some regions of India Untouchables have long participated in the important festival of Holi. This is the egalitarian festival whereby villagers are allowed to throw colour at each other without regard to caste, age or other status, and it has been argued that this playful setting aside of hierarchy and ritualised respect is an annual safety valve against festering resentments (Marriott 1971: 211).

Untouchables are also widely seen to have a special connection with the dark forces that flow through life, and they are often enlisted to propitiate these forces. The Untouchable midwife, for example, is sometimes invested with supernatural powers that can work for good or evil. In Maharashtra, it is said that a fort built by the warrior king Shivaji failed to remain standing; the solution was to bury alive a young Mahar couple in a wall of the fort (Dandekar 1983: 397–8). And Moffatt reports Untouchable participation in the elaborate annual festivities for the god Selliyamman in Tamilnadu (Moffatt 1979: 270–89). The task of this god is to mediate between the village and evil spirits, and this disreputable connection is the cause of her low status among gods of the region. This taint is also the key to the important role played by Untouchables in actual worship of the god: 'they are intermediaries downward in the worship of Selliyamman, intermediaries on behalf of other, higher humans and on behalf of the goddess herself' (Moffatt 1979: 271). In the annual re-enactment of the marriage of the god Untouchables play the part of the groom's family while the complementary part of the bride's family is played by the higher castes. The Untouchables bring as gifts a sari, comb, mirror, flower garlands, fruits and sweets, and the crucial marriage necklace. If the Untouchables were not present the celebration of Selliyamman would break down and the god would be unreliable as a shield against the forces of darkness. These and other examples provide ready evidence to the effect that Untouchables are a functioning part, albeit a distinctive part, of the Indian cultural community. But just what can be concluded from this circumstance is an issue taken up in the next section.

The world of work has also habitually thrown Untouchables together with Indians of higher status. If Untouchables are employed on a casual basis (as bandsmen, for example) or if their goods (such as leather items and woven material) are purchased, then the engagement or commerce will necessarily entail a measure of social intercourse. During the British and post-Independence periods, and presumably before this too, many Untouchable men, women and children have been attached to particular landholding families as permanent or semi-permanent labourers. Again, such relationships must have entailed considerable exchange with their employers/masters. An agricultural labourer, for example, needs to meet with his or her overseer on perhaps a daily basis.

Another tension between orthodoxy and social practice is represented by the exploitation of Untouchable women by their high-caste masters: evidence from our own time suggests that this practice has been habitual rather than merely occasional. Not the least contradictory aspect of such connection is that the Untouchable woman was never so degraded or ritually polluted as to be sexually unapproachable: Untouchability was always a curse, never a protection.

In sum, it is wrong to imagine that the idea of 'Untouchability' has entailed a systematic division of society into the people marked by this condition and all the rest. Moreover, whatever the situation in, say, the middle of the nineteenth century, by now amelioration has softened the historic oppression. To give just one example of what is discussed at length later, particularly in chapter 4, Untouchable children now go to school in large numbers and are generally free of the grosser forms of humiliation that were practised on them in the early years when schooling became a possibility. In many regions of India it is poverty rather than social oppression that presents itself as the principal disability of people from the Untouchable castes, and this has frequently led to claims that at least in those regions the very concept of Untouchability is no longer apposite.

But while it is now possible to imagine a social world that will no longer be disfigured by Untouchability, that world is not yet in place. The view argued here is that 'the Untouchables' remain a distinctive grouping within Indian society conceived as a whole. It is a mistake to believe that unless there is *systematic* oppression deriving from the status of ritual Untouchability, then the latter concept no longer makes sense. Untouchables still tend to suffer from multiple and severe discriminations and from poverty, and it is no comment on this statement to assert (correctly) that other Indian groupings – the specially 'backward' castes, tribals, from some perspectives even 'women' – also suffer disproportionately from such treatment and circumstances. Our argument is that the basis of the subordination of these other groupings is not identical to that which constitutes the Untouchables as inferior. It is also important to say that the Untouchables are by far the most numerous of discrete groupings of Indians – 'women' are surely not an easily comparable category – subjected to cumulative subordination.

The distinction in the previous paragraph between the physical and the analytical eye is in some ways the key to an accurate estimation of the position of Untouchables in India today. Thus it is not possible to provide a single account – some kind of 'pen portrait' – of the lived experience of the many millions of Untouchables, and almost certainly it has never been possible. Such an account would overstate commonalities among Untouchables, and understate convergences with higher society. Moreover, and increasingly today, many of the barriers against Untouchables are not immediately and physically visible. But none of this is to deny the existence of a fault line that runs through Indian society, a line that divides Untouchables from the other elements. Now, as in the past, the analytical basis of Untouchability is the ideology of purity and pollution. This ideology has functioned as the prime support of a moral economy which has maintained most Untouchables in a peculiarly inferior position. The empirical task then becomes one of bringing forward evidence that tends to establish the existence of the fault. That evidence is no longer so pronounced as it once was, but it is still there. For the moment we will leave aside the matter of poverty, because of its ambiguity. Thus although we want to argue that poverty is one of the defining marks of the status of being Untouchable, we have to recognise that this is a mark of other whole communities too. So in order to quieten any doubts that may exist as to the existence of Untouchability as a contemporary syndrome rather than a mere cluster of historically constructed castes, we need to point to circumstances or treatment that are more particular to Untouchables. The least ambiguous pieces of evidence are gross acts of discrimination and physical violence.

Chapter 2 is devoted to the matter of violence, and we argue from many examples that there is a species of violence that has its roots in ritually based distaste for Untouchables. Much of this violence does not arise from the straightforward imposition of high-caste authority but as a high-caste reaction to initiatives of Untouchables to slough off their historic condition and to rise in the world. To know this is to explain at least in part the seeming increase in such violence that first became apparent in the late 1970s. The more Untouchables have *resisted* their subordination, the more savage has been the reaction they have engendered. This competition for resources, both material and social, can be portrayed as acting upon the ideological fault line that runs through Indian society.

Aside from the particular issue of violence there remains a great flow of oppressive behaviour towards Untouchables. Thus it is still common to find situations where Untouchables are not allowed to use the common village well or to drink from cups used by others in public teashops. But these public situations do not lay bare the full extent of discrimination.

Although evidence is more difficult to come by – it must be gathered formally through interview and survey – it is clear that Untouchables are avoided, even shunned, in a range of domestic, 'private', situations surrounding food, drink and general social life. Much research work still needs to be done about the interaction of Untouchables and other villagers through the gamut of their lives. But clearly Untouchables remain profoundly unequal in the moral world of the Indian village and also the Indian town and institution. A culture of condescension, discrimination and sometimes downright oppression tends to reinforce the material poverty that afflicts a large proportion of the Untouchable population. True, there are now many individuals who manage to escape this culture and take advantage of institutional preferences that lead to middle-class status. But again, this is not a problem for the argument presented in this book. We are talking about *tendencies* rather than monolithic uniformities.

Our argument, then, is that it continues to make sense – at least for the time being – to talk in terms of a grouping called 'Untouchables', 'Harijans', 'Dalits' or other comparable term. The primary constituent of this grouping is the common experience of a particular and severe form of social oppression. At the same time, common experience has also given rise to a certain sense of shared social place among the victims. The best historical evidence of common feeling is the medieval *bhakti* movement (discussed below), which was in part a lament against Untouchability. But only in the present century has any sense of common Untouchable destiny firmed into something like political solidarity across caste and regional lines. For some three-quarters of a century, as a direct result of British interventions, there has been considerable, if episodic and always fragmentary, political mobilisation of Untouchables *qua* Untouchables. Despite the attention that has been paid to the historical figure of Gandhi, it has been Untouchables themselves who have brought about this mobilisation. With great difficulty a number of Dalit leaders have sought to build broad constituencies from among the tens of millions of Untouchables across India. By far the most significant of these leaders was B. R. Ambedkar (1891-1956), while the two leading figures of the present period are Kanshi Ram and Ram Vilas Paswan. All three of these leaders have sought to maximise their support amongst Untouchables while simultaneously appealing to other Indians sympathetic to a relatively radical attack on high-caste privilege. This political project has involved two distinct tasks. First, they have tried to transcend the primary support base of their own caste community so as to be acknowledged as a leader of Untouchables in general. And secondly, they have sought to reach out to a wider, non-Untouchable, constituency. So Ambedkar oscillated throughout the 1930s and 1940s between organising his several political parties around caste and Untouchability on the one hand, and around the idea of class and economic subordination on the other. Ambedkar's political dilemmas reflected the defeating variety of culture and outlook among Untouchables, and also the difficulty of attracting non-Untouchables to a banner raised by an Untouchable leader. But despite such problems and the limited success that any of the Untouchable leaders have had, over time there has been a developing consciousness and mood of resistance among Untouchables as a whole. It may remain a practical impossibility to organise Untouchables as a single, all-India, political force, but as a whole Dalits are now more committed than ever before to what they increasingly recognise as their common struggle. Moreover, political events have moved in their direction. With the disintegration of the old dominance of the Congress Party, Dalit issues are now closer to centre stage than at any time since their brief moment of glory almost seventy years ago. Dalits are now beginning to be accorded a political presence more consistent with their huge population.

Divergent views on the identity of the Untouchables

Despite the complexity and deep ambiguity of Untouchable identity over a period of centuries, what became a conventional account of them emerged under the spur of British imperium in the years between 1870 and 1930. By about 1930 all the major political protagonists, Gandhi included, were prepared to agree that Untouchables were both a distinctive and an oppressed segment of the Indian population. This agreement was the basis upon which a huge machinery of institutional privilege was erected so as to right the historic wrongs. But the consensus masked powerful differences as to the distinctiveness of the Untouchables, and these differences were progressively articulated in later years. Thus while Gandhi had never had any doubt as to the oppression suffered by groups such as the Sweepers, he was highly resistant to any conception that purported to divide off Harijans from the wider Hindu community. For Gandhi Untouchability was an historical corruption of Hinduism which could be corrected by right-minded caste Hindus. Against this the Untouchable leader Ambedkar came to regard Untouchability as intrinsic to the whole construction of Hinduism by Brahmins; his ultimate act was to stage a mass conversion of his followers to Buddhism. Nehru, nationalist leader and first Prime Minister, took a more 'modern', materialist, position than either Gandhi or Ambedkar. For the socialist-minded Nehru the problem was overwhelmingly economic. As poverty abated, so the discrimination too would dry up (Nehru, CAD 1949: VIII, 331).

The half-century since the achievement of Indian Independence has seen far less preoccupation with either the practical problem or the underlying nature of Untouchability than during the earlier years of the twentieth century. This might be attributed to the waning severity of the condition of Untouchability itself, but in our own view it is not. For the first three decades after 1947 it was politically convenient rather than realistic to imagine that the condition of Untouchability had been sufficiently confronted through criminal legislation and a quantitatively impressive scheme of compensatory institutional advantage for the old victims of Untouchability. But while the issue was relegated to the margins of post-Independence politics, a cluster of writers – some of them Indian, some foreign – continued to be concerned with the place and the prospects of Untouchable Indians. This interest was more prominent in the first couple of decades after Independence, when issues such as the compatibility of caste and democracy were taken seriously. Later, from the late 1970s, there was new concern with the matter of violence done to Untouchables. It is only now, at the very end of the twentieth century, that the larger issue of identity has re-emerged in the context of a transformed political scene in India. In the present section our interest is mostly concentrated on relatively recent academic writings on the whole character of Untouchability.

The major academic debate of recent years has revolved around the old question of the distinctiveness of Untouchables relative to other Indians. A major issue has been the extent to which Untouchables can be seen to have accepted the orthodox version of Hinduism which so degrades them. Dumont's book on caste (1970) served to crystallise this debate, with its representation of Hinduism as a moral hierarchy deeply accepted even by the most subordinated elements. Berreman labelled Dumont's scheme 'the Brahminical view of caste' for its suggested blindness to the tyranny exerted over those at the bottom of the order:

Dumont fails almost totally to recognise caste for what it is on an empirical level: institutionalized inequality; guaranteed differential access to the valued things in life. Let there be no mistake. The human meaning of caste for those who live it is power and vulnerability, privilege and oppression, honor and denigration, plenty and want, reward and deprivation, security and anxiety. As an anthropological document, a description of caste which fails to convey this is a travesty... (Berreman 1979: 159).

So for Berreman, Dumont was concentrating on the wrong matter. The appropriate issue was not whether Untouchables were part of and accepted the Hindu order, but how an inhuman order of domination and subordination could be broken.

Dumont soon found an ardent champion in Michael Moffatt (1979).

On the basis of his own empirical study of a south Indian Untouchable community, Moffatt argued that the Untouchables do indeed belong to a single Hindu community marked by a high degree of cultural consensus. Moffatt aligned himself with the third of three models or theories of Untouchables he identified. The first portrays the Untouchables as an 'outcast' people possessed of a distinct culture and a freer spirit (in sexuality, for example) than the high-caste guardians of Hinduism. Although there are differences between them, he associates Berreman, Kathleen Gough and Joan Mencher with this model.

The second theoretical grouping is said to be those who approach the Untouchables through an emphasis on 'diversity', a view associated with Bernard Cohn, Pauline Kolenda and others. Like the first grouping, these observers concentrate on the contrasts between Untouchables and the higher castes. But they differ in declining to posit an outright rejection of the dominant culture by the Untouchables, and instead discern an adaptation of that culture to the particular needs of Untouchable communities. Kolenda, for example, accepts that the basic themes of the Sweepers' religion are common to both higher-caste religion as it is practised and also the Sanskrit texts. But she shows that the Sweepers have also expunged from their beliefs the discriminatory doctrines of karma and *dharma*, with their implication that the Sweepers' degraded status arises from their misdeeds in a previous life (Moffatt 1979: 15–16).

Moffatt identifies a third 'unity' model in the work of Dumont and the ethnosociological approach of Marriott, Inden (in a former incarnation) and Nicholas. What these writers and Moffatt himself share is a focus on ideology and culture and an insistence that these are not reducible to more universal phenomena like stratification, power or oppression. Untouchables are a regular part of Hinduism and share in its common culture and ideology. Subordination and oppression of those at the bottom of the system should not obscure the essential unity of Hindu society, which is to be viewed on its own rather than in comparative terms. So, oppression of low-caste Hindus should not be treated as a phenomenon comparable with, say, racism directed to African-Americans. That racism stands as contradiction to the egalitarian principles of American society, whereas the principle of hierarchy is intrinsic to Hindu society. For Moffatt it is Dumont who has most clearly seen the centrality and the universal acceptance of hierarchy within the Hindu caste order (Moffatt 1979: 21–31).

Moffat's formulation reflects a dominant preoccupation of American sociology of the period, viz. the question of whether particular societies could be said to be marked primarily by 'consensus' or by 'conflict'. Berreman, for example, clearly stands on the side of 'conflict', whereas

Moffat is able to discern a pervasive common culture or 'consensus' in India.

More recently, the debate about the Untouchables has sometimes been subsumed in a larger debate about the significance of caste itself. A post-structural and post-colonial scholarship has paid new attention to the way in which the British rulers 'invented' or 'constructed' India through Orientalist conceptions such as their version of caste. The argument is not that caste did not exist prior to British rule, but rather that the British exaggerated out of all proportion the importance and unchangeability of caste within Indian society. For the British, caste is said to have become the 'essence' of an India which was profoundly different from European society.

Ronald Inden is one of the writers to have promoted this critical view with great determination. Inden has now repudiated the views he expressed in an earlier collaboration with McKim Marriott (Marriott and Inden 1974), when he was 'lured' by the 'siren' of caste (Inden 1990: 82). He now regards 'kingship' and 'polity' as more constitutive of Indian society than caste. The British obsession with caste is seen to have created an 'essentialist' India, a 'pre-enlightened world where superstition and darkness reign, with poverty, exploitation, and political chaos as the result'. This essentialism robbed Indians of their 'agency', treating them as trapped in an unchangeable world of extremes (Inden 1990: 83–4).

It might be thought that Inden has successfully transcended the debate about the Untouchables. Why should one attempt to work out the relation of the Untouchables to the higher castes, if it is the British obsession with caste itself that has encouraged this false problematic? But Inden cannot escape so easily. In the 'old' piece written with Marriott, Inden is concerned to assert the unity of Hindu society (Marriott and Inden 1974). This theoretical position enables the two to write a long essay on caste without any substantial discussion of the Untouchables. When Inden comes to write his own theoretical work after loudly abandoning the ethnosociology of McKim Marriott, he fails even to mention the Untouchables (by this name or any other) (Inden 1990). His basis for the omission is again unstated but it seems to be that the Untouchables, like Caste with a capital 'C', did not really exist before the British invented them. This view is both historically dubious and implicitly protective of the present order, since it has no inherent sympathy with political struggles on behalf of subordinated communities.

The question of Untouchable identity raised by Berreman, Kolenda, Cohn and many others was not created by the British, and nor will it go away if outsiders now ignore it. Rather, the crucial British influence came about through acting on an historically long-lived social situation. The

British did not 'imagine' the Untouchables into existence. Rather, they helped create (whether consciously or not) the conditions whereby an Untouchable leadership could attempt to assert an independent political presence united across caste and region for the first time. These baldly stated judgments will be elaborated in this and subsequent chapters.

Nonetheless, Inden is in possession of some solid ground on which to mount a denial of the existence of the Untouchables as a single people. Any such categorical postulate has to be set beside the manifest disunity to be found across the multitude of separate Untouchable castes. How can it be said, then, that all the non-Untouchable castes represent one category, and the Untouchable castes another? Are there soft bars, as it were, between the non-Untouchable castes, and a hard bar between all of these castes as a unity and the Untouchables as the other? As an extension of this question, is it to be said that the Untouchables are at best a unit of external observation and analysis rather than one of social action?

The latter view (more often expressed in conversation than print) fails to make appropriate distinctions. Thus there is no doubt that the status of being Untouchable is ascribed to particular communities by others, rather than being chosen by themselves. In this sense it can reasonably be asserted that the Untouchables are not a community or nation comparable with other far-flung communities. The Jews, for example, are a widespread people who share religious beliefs, sympathy and a certain amount of culture, as well as historical discrimination. Common culture cannot so obviously be claimed for the Untouchable castes. But if we are to compare Untouchables with other formations such as those of class and gender, it may be that they emerge with quite a lot in common.

For us, the crucial question is whether the Untouchables share a social situation that is sufficiently common to be the basis or potential basis for their mobilisation as a distinct unit for some important purposes. This is a complicated empirical, not a priori, question about both consciousness and action, and our effort to answer it will occupy large parts of this work. For the moment we will simply state our position that there is indeed something of a 'hard bar' separating Untouchables from the rest of Indian society, and that Untouchables themselves have come to see that bar as the basis for a certain amount of common consciousness and action.

To return to Moffatt's characterisation of the debate, Berreman is surely right to place the dehumanising aspects of caste at the very centre of its study. But to endorse this position is not to deny value in a number of less directed accounts – those of Cohn and Kolenda, for example – of what is a highly complex social condition. Thus surely it must be true that Untouchables accept a great deal of the common Indian culture; indeed, we have difficulty imagining how this could not be the case. But we are equally sure that Untouchables do not today take the view that they are morally inferior to high-caste Indians and that they deserve their degraded life. It is Moffatt himself who has promoted this view more than any other writer, and his major evidence is that Untouchable castes rank each other according to the same standard of purity and pollution that consigns them collectively to the very bottom of the status ladder. *Ergo*, they accept the moral basis of their own inferiority.

Moffatt's evidence would be a problem for any argument that the Untouchables are an entirely distinct people who have declined to internalise some of the principal aspects of Indian civilisation. But we doubt that anyone has taken such an extreme view as this. Moffatt's central error is to have left out the crucial perspective of the Untouchables as individual human beings in favour of an account driven wholly by structural theory. Other recent work on the Untouchables and also on comparable situations outside India is a surer guide to this interior world. James Scott's work (1985) is an important example. Scott argues that poor Malay villagers habitually resist their own subordination, but that they do so in subtle rather than confrontational ways. They fashion their own social weapons, the 'weapons of the weak', rather than confront their more powerful oppressors on *their* terms. While we should resist the implication that all subordinated people are by definition in a state of resistance, Scott has captured the crucial insight that resistance is not an all-or-nothing state to be discovered only in rebellion or other brazenly assertive behaviour.

The most instructive story of an 'ordinary' Untouchable has been told by James Freeman (1979). *Untouchable* is a biography of Muli, a man of the Bauri community of Orissa. Muli is far from a typical human being of any community, but his life and outlook do epitomise a great deal of the Untouchable condition. His life has been a marginal one both within his own community and relative to the high castes. Muli makes his way in the world through procuring Untouchable women for sexual liaisons with high-caste men. He sees this as an easier way of life than breaking stones in a quarry, the occupation of most other Bauri men of his village.

Muli's life and outlook are not neatly to be encapsulated in any of Moffatt's three categories. He is a bundle of contradictory attitudes. On the one hand he has contempt for a society which treats him as degraded and polluting, and bitterly resents the savage discrimination that he and all the Bauris suffer at the hands of high-caste Hindus. He mockingly describes the efforts of high-caste women to avoid his presence and how teashop owners do not let him enter their shop. High-caste men are equally scorned for their bare tolerance of him on account of his utility as a source of Untouchable women. He frequently breaks caste taboos by eating and drinking with high-caste men. But at the same time Muli seems to have internalised many of the norms of pollution. He refused to touch a Brahmin in taking an oath, saying that he was afraid to commit this particular sin. And along with his whole community, he treats Washermen as an inferior Untouchable community which must be ritually avoided. Similarly, his community practises elaborate rituals derived from the high castes in order to get rid of pollution following a death in the family (Freeman 1979: 125–7, 205, 377, 383). All of this, and much else, suggests that at a deep level Muli accepts the order of pollution within orthodox Hindusim.

Contradictoriness and ambivalence within Muli's internal world are surely to be expected. The Hinduism that he and the other Bauris experience consists in the Untouchability system which so devalues and impoverishes them, but also in a loftier and less overtly discriminatory world of thoughts, images and idols. It would be surprising indeed if poor and exploited Untouchables were able to make a clean intellectual and psychological break from this system on the ground that it condemned them to a clearly subordinate position. But equally, both historically and far more so today, we find it impossible to adopt the idea that the Untouchables accepted their own systematic inferiority. This flies in the face of both evidence and human logic. It is precisely the complex, degraded and contradictory experience of Untouchables that has made it so difficult for outside observers to epitomise their situation.

If we return to Louis Dumont's monumental work on caste, it can justly be criticised for its lack of attention to the view from the bottom of the order. In a sense Berreman is right to say that Dumont has given us the 'Brahminical view of caste'. But it is also true that this Brahminical view has had the greatest influence on the character the caste order has developed. Within the order of caste as ritual hierarchy the Brahmin view is supreme. And as we understand it, this is the predominant Untouchable view of caste as much as the Brahmin view. Thus if one compares the writings of Ambedkar with those of Dumont, there are striking parallels. It is the idea (as well as the injustice) of Brahmin-inspired pollution that dominates Ambedkar's writings, particularly *Who Were the Shudras?* (1946) and *The Untouchables* (1948). Ambedkar does not set out to assert any systematic rejection of the varna system by the Untouchables: there is no basis at all for classifying his writings as committed to an idea of the Untouchables as a distinct culture group. Ambedkar was positively obsessed with Brahmins, whom he sought to devalue as a way of discrediting the texts upon which he saw their own dominance of Hindu society to be built. Correctly or not, Ambedkar took the view that in previous centuries Untouchables had been by-and-large compliant if not complicit in their own subordination by Brahminism.

Political developments over the last decade or so have by now overtaken the earlier (somewhat bloodless) debate over the relation of Untouchables to wider Indian society. Untouchables have not been at the centre of either of the two principal developments of this period, but they have been enlisted to both. The first development has been the articulation of a national politics of resistance to high-caste privilege and advantage. This politics took shape from 1990 around the issue of adoption of the Mandal Committee's recommendations that compensatory discrimination be extended at the national level to a wider category of 'Backward' or 'Sudra' beneficiaries. While this proposal did not directly concern the Scheduled Castes, it was the basis of attempts to create a broad coalition of the disadvantaged that encompassed Dalits as a central element; the present national Government led by the Janata Dal grows out of this initiative. The second development is the rise of the Bharatiya Janata Party (BJP), now by far the largest individual party in the national Parliament. Its rise has been fuelled by articulating a coherent conception of India as 'Hindutva' or essentially Hindu. This conception has been self-consciously directed against Muslims both at home and abroad, and is essentially a high-caste view of the world. But for reasons of broader electoral appeal the BJP has seen a strategic advantage in trying to tap into the huge Untouchable population. So in its confrontation with Islam the forces of Hindutva have been more than happy to treat Dalits as unproblematical 'Hindus'. In 1997 the BJP went so far as to form a coalition Government in the huge State of Uttar Pradesh with the Bahujana Samaj Party led by the radical Dalit Kanshi Ram. It is still too early to make a mature assessment of the effect of these two broad developments on Untouchable identity and the relation of Untouchables to the broader Indian population. But the likelihood is that both developments will work towards greater integration and also more power for Dalits.

A major theme of the present chapter is that the Untouchables have not been a smooth and regular part of Hindu society, against the view of writers such as Moffatt (or the opportunistic manœuvrings of the BJP). Our argument is that the whole problem represented by Untouchables has been profoundly transformed over the last century or so, and that during this period the pace of change has been accelerating. In a word, Untouchables have become greatly more self-conscious and assertive. But even before these changes took hold there is hard evidence that Untouchability was not simply accepted without reflection or protest by its victims. The best evidence is from the medieval bhakti period.

The evidence from the bhakti tradition

If literary evidence suggests that Untouchability had entrenched itself by the second century of the present era, the detail of Untouchables' lives is remarkably sketchy until the modern period. But some of the best indications of the internal world of Untouchables emerge from the literature of bhakti, a so-called 'devotional' movement sometimes dated as far back as the seventh century but whose main influence was exerted for some 500 years from the eleventh century. Bhakti sought to renew faith on the basis of principle rather than resort to textual authority by passionless Brahmins (Pandits). Consider these words of the great Kabir, a *bhakta* (poet) from the Varanasi region in the mid-fifteenth century (Hess 1983: 25):

> Pandits sat and read the law
> babbled of what they never saw

The continental sweep of bhakti, its longevity, and the social diversity of its contributors, ensured that the movement did not stand for any unified doctrine. Since a great many of the bhakti poets were themselves from low-caste and Untouchable situations, their poetry is often imbued with a sense of a common humanity in the eyes of God. This has led some commentators to claim that bhakti was a systematic attack on the caste order. Again we can attend to Kabir (Hess 1983: 19):

> It's all one skin and bone
> one piss and shit
> one blood, one meat.
> From one drop, a universe.
> Who's Brahmin? Who's Shudra?

Crudeness is one of Kabir's verbal techniques to confront empty custom. Sometimes he paints more positive images, as in these words addressed directly to a Brahmin (Hess 1983: 55):

> Pandit, look in your heart for knowledge
> Tell me where untouchability
> came from, since you believe in it.
> Mix red juice, white juice and air -
> a body bakes in a body.
> As soon as the eight lotuses
> are ready, it comes
> into the world. Then what's
> untouchable?
> Eighty-four hundred thousand vessels
> decay into dust, while the potter
> keeps slapping clay

on the wheel, and with a touch
cuts each one off.
We eat by touching, we wash
by touching, from a touch
the world was born.
So who's untouched? asks Kabir
Only he
who has no taint of Maya.

These are only two of a great many passages that demonstrate Kabir's absolute commitment to the idea of human equality and his denial of caste as a measure of human worth. But just how radical a force were Kabir and the bhakti poets in general?

To answer this question we need first to distinguish between two different traditions of bhakti, viz. the *nirguna bhakti* (of Kabir among others) and the *saguna* tradition prevalent in southern and western India. Saguna bhakti was the less confrontational and maintained a commitment to traditional belief and worship, including the adoration of idols. Untouchables may not have been excluded from ritual participation in this tradition, but they were subjected to the already entrenched discriminations. Consider the case of Choka Mela, an Untouchable Mahar and also one of the principal saguna bhaktas. Choka Mela belonged to a multi-caste sect, whose activities included a twice-annual pilgrimage to the temple of Pandhapur. This pilgrimage continues to the present day, and even now the pilgrims walk in separate *dindi* or clusters determined on the basis of ritual hierarchy (Karve 1988: 150, 170). Choka Mela's bones are buried at the site, but because of his ritual unfitness they are located at a suitable distance from the temple walls (Deleury 1960: 61).

Choka Mela's compliance with orthodox custom was perhaps partly a case of simple pragmatism, but clearly it was also an acceptance of his own station in life as a humble Mahar (Gokhale 1993: 42):

Johar maybap johar[1]
I am your Mahar's Mahar
I am hungry
For your leftovers
I am hopeful
I am the servant of your slaves
For your leavings
I've brought my basket

---

[1] The expression 'Johar maybap johar' was a traditional greeting given by Mahars to their masters. The idea is that the Johar or master is 'maybap' or mother-father, the world, to the humble Mahar.

This is the expression of feeling at once infinitely sad and utterly compliant. Many Mahar Dalits of our own time have for this reason rejected Choka Mela as a worthy exemplar (Gokhale 1993: 43). But on another level he was indeed asserting a claim to equality. He was prepared to accept a postponement of equality to the time when spirit was divorced from body.

Although a follower of his illustrious father, Choka's son Karma Mela could be blunter and more bitter (Gokhale-Turner 1981: 32):

> You made us impure
> I don't know why Lord
> We've eaten leftovers all our life
> Doesn't that trouble you
> Our house is stocked with rice and yogurt
> How do you refuse it
> Chokha's Karma Mela asks
> Why did you give me birth.

This is a several-layered lament about discrimination. Karma Mela notes that he and his people have eaten 'leftovers' all their life, by which he means the inferior and often ritually polluting handouts of food that were recompense for the Mahar's labour. But the major cry of the verse concerns the refusal of temple authorities to accept gifts of pristine food (the rice and yoghurt) as a way of currying favour with the gods. The last line questions whether so degraded a human life has any real value. This is not a lament about poverty: indeed, material wellbeing is celebrated by proclaiming that the household is 'stocked' with foods appropriate as gifts to the gods.

The temper of Choka and even Karma Mela is demonstrably less refractory than that of Kabir or Ravidas, both practitioners of nirguna bhakti. This stream represented a more thoroughgoing rejection of traditional worship and beliefs, including the worship of idols. God was conceived to be without form, to be approached without aid of physical props. This theological boldness spilled over into the social thinking of bhaktas like Kabir, but it is not possible to make out a strong case for their constituting a revolutionary movement. It was not any tameness of ideology that limited their impact; rather, bhakti was to a large extent appropriated and assimilated into orthodox Hinduism (Friedlander 1987; Lorenzen 1981a).

The process of cooptation can be seen in the historical fate suffered by Kabir, and it entailed the manipulation of his ambiguous social origins. Kabir was born into what is generally described as a family of Untouchable Muslim *julahas* or weavers (Hess 1983: 143). The seeming contradiction whereby Kabir's family was apparently both Untouchable

Hindu and also Muslim has not proved to be the basis of the tangled historical construction of Kabir, since neither the Untouchables nor the Muslims have been successful in claiming Kabir as their own. Rather, the Kabir legend has been appropriated and variably reconstructed by Brahmins and low-caste Hindus.

There are a number of Brahminical versions that compete with the seemingly straightforward truth that Kabir was born into a family of Muslim weavers. One story is that Kabir was 'really' the orphan of a Brahmin widow and was then reared by adoptive parents, whose social identity is irrelevant to his own social position. In more mythic vein, another Brahminical tale is that Kabir was actually an incarnation of the god Vishnu and was conceived immaculately; again, the accident of his human family becomes an irrelevance. Other legends have placed Kabir as a disciple of a south Indian Brahmin, Ramanand (Lorenzen 1981a: 156–9). It is unlikely that such accounts are simply a Brahmin effort to appropriate a cherished religious figure. Kabir's message was, after all, deeply subversive of Brahminical pretensions to superiority. But it is one thing, albeit regrettable, for a Brahmin to employ such 'rough rhetoric' (Hess 1983: 143), and quite another for the rude words of derision and sarcasm to come from an Untouchable weaver. If Kabir could be seen as a Brahmin, then his challenging words would only be those of a reformer within the Great Tradition. As an exemplar of Brahminical broadmindedness Kabir could be drained of any revolutionary potential.

Brahmins may have been the first Hindus to lay successful claim to the legacy of Kabir, but in subsequent centuries an even stronger claim has been staked by 'clean' but low castes concerned to improve or Sanskritise their position in the caste hierarchy. In north Indian States like Bihar the powerful *Kabir panth* has over the centuries built numerous monasteries, often standing in attached tracts of agricultural land. Naturally, these lands tend even today to be worked by exploited Untouchables and other lowly labourers. So in these different ways the powerful, potentially revolutionary, voice of Kabir has been systematically appropriated by communities that have narrow self-interest and not great social change as their object (Lorenzen 1981b: 274–8).

This short account of the bhakti movement has had several objects. First, the movement is particularly valuable for giving the lie to less balanced accounts of our own time which seem to suggest that Untouchability was not a major structure of Indian society before the British intrusion. Frankly, it is nothing more than loose thinking to maintain such a proposition. Secondly, the bhakti material makes clear that the most severe aspects of caste, including Untouchability, have not been accepted without challenge in centuries past. More particularly, the fact that many of the bhaktas were either Untouchable or of low caste suggests that accounts such as those of Moffatt are historically blind to the degree of resistance from below that has characterised Indian society. But conversely, the bhakti experience also points to the tenacity of orthodox Hinduism in either absorbing and smothering, or limiting by way of containment, radical schools of thought that challenged the control of the high castes.

For several centuries after bhakti's medieval highpoint, the historical record on Untouchables can be seen to have dwindled to the level of stray reference and occasional temple inscription. One possible inference from the renewed silence is that Untouchable consciousness and resistance had been overwhelmed. Our own view is that such inference is unwarranted. The feelings that welled up in Untouchable and low-caste communities during the most productive phase of bhakti can surely not have simply ceased to exist. But what we can say is that it was not until developments of the British period that a fresh ideological attack could be mounted against the principles sustaining Untouchability. This new challenge enjoyed circumstances far more favourable than those of the bhakti poets.

The British impact on Untouchable identity

Although the principle of Untouchability strikes the modern mind as an anathema, this was not the position of the British in India. In 1916 M. B. Dadabhoy, an Indian nationalist, epitomised British policy towards the Untouchables as one of 'benevolent indifference' (Home Proceedings [Dadabhoy] 1920: 761). The term is apt. The British never took up the Untouchables as a cause, but at the same time they were not drawn into positively endorsing a social system which they could recognise as morally dubious.

Until the 1920s British and wider European interest in the Untouchables was for the most part left to Christian missionaries. These had been active in India from early in the eighteenth century, and they gathered impressive numbers of adherents in the south and west of India. But there is no evidence of any special Christian interest in the Untouchables until the last third of the nineteenth century. At that time the European missionaries did begin to turn a more interested eye to the condition of Untouchables. A trickle of such people gained some modest education in missionary schools, and the Untouchables came to be viewed as specially likely objects of conversion.

Much of the British impact on Untouchables arose from holding a mirror to Indian society, thereby presenting freshly sharp images to modernising Hindus and to Untouchables themselves. For the British, India was not merely a land to be conquered and exploited; it was also a society to be puzzled over. Aspects of society that were taken for granted by Indians themselves could excite a special kind of applied scholarship in the administrators of the raj. Caste, tribe and religion were the very centrepiece of these inquiries, and they converged on the issue of the Untouchables.

The vehicle of much of this administrative scholarship was the Census, which began on an India-wide basis in 1871–2. British Census officials became obsessed with the question of whether Untouchables were properly classifiable as Hindus, or whether they were a people *sui generis*. This may well have been the very first time such a question was asked. Until Indian civilisation was defined relative to the world outside, there was no need for a concept of 'Hindu' at all. That word and to some extent the very concept of the Hindu seem to have been supplied by Persians, Europeans and Central Asians rather than Indians themselves. And while Brahminical ritual supremacy served to constitute Untouchable castes as profoundly 'other', it did not constitute them as belonging to another non-Hindu religious community. Nor did the Muslim conquerors have much impact on the matter. The Muslims succeeded in rapidly building a large religious community through both immigration and conversion, but they displayed little interest in engineering relations among the non-Muslim population. It was the era of the British that sharpened all the deep ambiguities and tensions of Untouchable life in India.

From the first to the last British Census of India, the census takers worried over just who the Untouchables were and what relation they had to other Indian communities. So in 1871–2 the Chamars, long since recognised as the largest Untouchable caste of India, were in the province of Bengal lumped into a category called 'Semi-Hinduised Aborigines'. In other provinces Untouchable castes including the Mahars and Pariahs were placed with Buddhists and Jains, religious communities, into a category called 'Outcastes or Not Recognising Caste' (Census 1871–2: Gen. Report 22, 26).

The British Census officers saw themselves as simply trying to answer the question of just who was a Hindu. In their own mind their job was made harder by the attitudes of their assistants. In the 1881 Census the British superintendent of one province complained in these terms:

Many of the more bigoted high caste Hindoos employed as census enumerators or supervisors objected to record such low persons as of the Hindoo religion. This was illustrated in numerous instances brought to my notice of such persons having been recorded as of the Dher, Mang or Chandal religion by mere repetition of their caste in the column for religion. Possibly some out of their humility and ignorance may not have claimed to be of the Hindoo religion. More probably they were not even asked. In my office these people have all been tabulated as of the Hindoo religion. (Census 1881: Gen. Report 17)

The complaint here is that high-caste Hindus did not want to recognise Untouchable castes as belonging to the Hindu religious community at all, and the same kind of British observation was again made in the Censuses of 1891 and 1901. By 1911 the British noticed that a complete reversal had occurred, whereby the self-styled leaders of Hinduism were adamant that the Untouchable castes were a regular part of Hinduism (Mukerji 1909: 78–9). The spur to the change was the arithmetic of parliamentary representation that was begun under the Morely-Minto reforms of 1909–10: the Muslim League had sought to argue that the Hindu population was artificially inflated by inclusion of the Untouchables, and in response the Hindus now laid vehement claim to these people.

Gait, Census Commissioner in 1911, issued a preparatory circular to his provincial commissioners on the question of drawing the border between Hindus and others who were dubiously Hindu. He listed the efforts of his predecessors in this matter, and then proposed more exact criteria of his own. Communities could be regarded as Hindu if there were appropriate answers to the following six questions:

1. Do the members of the caste or tribe worship the great Hindu Gods?
2. Are they allowed to enter Hindu temples or to make offerings at the shrine?
3. Will good Brahmins act as their priests?
4. Will degraded Brahmins do so? In that case are they recognised as Brahmins by persons outside the caste, or are they Brahmins only in name?
5. Will clean castes take water from them?
6. Do they cause pollution, (a) by touch; (b) by proximity?
    (*The Tribune:* 12 November 1910)

When Gait's circular of July 1910 found its way into the newspapers, it caused consternation among Hindu leaders. They believed – on good evidence, it has to be said – that Gait's attention had been directed to this matter by the newly formed Muslim League. Gait later claimed that he had always intended to count the Untouchable castes as Hindus but that he also intended to add 'an explanatory memorandum that the figures for Hindus included certain depressed classes who cannot be regarded as such, but who have been so classed at the Census for want of a better alternative' (*The Tribune*: 19 December 1910).

G. S. Ghurye's view is that 'the intellectual curiosity of some of the early officials is mostly responsible for the treatment of caste given to it in the Census'. This is not a view favourable to the British, since Ghurye regards the curiosity as gratuitous and resulting in 'a livening up of the caste-spirit' (Ghurye 1957: 193). No doubt a number of motivations fed the burgeoning Census enterprise, but 'intellectual curiosity' is a useful term to locate some of them.

What the Census Commissioners accomplished, on the other hand, was to carve out an ideological space that could accommodate the collective 'Depressed Classes', 'Exterior Castes' (as they became in the 1931 Census) or what we are calling the Untouchables. It is difficult to exaggerate the importance of this approach for the success of Ambedkar's political strategy in the late 1920s and 1930s. The Census Commissioners had established the Untouchables as a legitimate social category, and it was then a matter of political concession rather than ideological imagination to treat them as entitled to the kind of advantages bestowed on other groupings – the Muslims, above all. Whereas Kabir and the other great bhakti thinkers had looked towards an ultimate equality of all individuals in the eyes of God, the Anglo-Indian state had created a more practical basis for Untouchable progress. The British had provided the instruments with which the Untouchables could assert themselves as a political collectivity, rather than merely pressing their moral worth as individuals.

So far the discussion has revolved around the place of the Untouchables in Indian society, and we have stated a case for seeing the Untouchables as a grouping that is in important respects distinct from the rest of Indian society. What we have not yet done is provide direct evidence of the extent to which the Untouchables are not merely a distinct people but also a *subordinated* one. Thus we now turn to a discussion of what we have called the twin bases of this subordination, viz. the poverty of the Untouchables and the discrimination that has been and still continues to be practised against them.

The Untouchables and poverty

In India, itself a poor country, the standard measure of poverty is simply that of income sufficient to allow the ingestion of a base number of food calories daily – 2,400 calories for rural Indians, 2,100 for urban. During the late 1970s and early 80s some useful work was produced on Untouchable and tribal poverty according to this measure. This work is now out-of-date – no comparable surveys have been undertaken recently – but the results are still suggestive. In 1977–8 about 70 per cent of the Untouchable population was rated 'poor', relative to some 56 per cent of the overall population (the latter figure being inflated by inclusion of the Untouchables themselves). Even more telling, the lower the calorie consumption line was drawn the greater was the proportion of Untouchables in the category. So when the calorie figure was halved, almost one-quarter (24.37 per cent) of these ultra-poor were

Untouchables. At the time, Untouchables were 14.6 per cent of the population (Census 1971, I, II-A(ii), xx). The proportion (as opposed to absolute number) of Untouchables who are 'poor' has probably declined along with that of the general population since the late 1970s, but we would not expect any great difference in the Untouchable share of the poor or ultra-poor.[2]

Calorie intake is only one of many possible measures of poverty, and it can yield only limited insight into the Untouchable condition. For the present purposes Indian poverty can more usefully be defined as the sum of low standards of nutrition, health, housing, general material consumption and formal education. These, in turn, lead to a lack of social and political effectiveness. By these criteria, the Untouchables are overwhelmingly a poor people.

The principal source, as opposed to the measure, of Untouchables' poverty is their relationship with agricultural land. There is a relentless logic that flows from their being an agrarian people without strong land assets. Indian villagers who do not own land are generally worse off than those who do, while at the same time the urban population of India is better off than the rural. Some 81 per cent of Untouchables live in villages, compared with about 74 per cent of the overall population (Census 1991, I (I) 1993: 3). Not all villagers without land are poor – there are landless Brahmins, for example, whose status and education have pro-

---

[2] The quantification in this paragraph is derived from S. P. Gupta, K. L. Datta and Padam Singh (1983). The figures analysed in this article are drawn from the 32nd round of the National Sample Survey, the first sampling exercise to separate out Scheduled Caste persons. Figures provided to the authors in February 1988 by Dr Padam Singh, ex-Member, Planning Commission, New Delhi, suggest that by 1983–4 the percentage of Scheduled Caste persons below the poverty line had fallen by some 10 per cent. All of these figures are no more than broadly indicative, since this is not a statistical area of high precision.

There are other suggestive approaches to measuring poverty or 'backwardness'. For example, in the context of preparing lists of 'Backward Classes' for the purpose of official preference as 'Other Backward Classes' two major surveys of the relative prosperity of all castes in the State of Karnataka were undertaken in 1972–5 and then in 1984 (Government of Karnataka [Havanur] 1975; [Venkatswamy] 1986). The criteria for measuring 'backwardness' in the second of these surveys were possession of a house or house site; whether the house was made of permanent materials; land ownership; level of income; proportion of agricultural labourers; illiteracy rate; proportion of population in urban residence; numbers in government employment; students studying at senior school (Venkatswamy 1986: II, 190). Of course, the Scheduled Castes duly emerged from the survey as backward. This was no special condition, since for political reasons most of the State's population was judged 'backward'. But the Scheduled Castes (counted as a single entity and not separated into castes) were 'backward' on more criteria than was any other caste (Venkatswamy 1986: II, 190–2). Only in their share of Class IV government employment – the menial grade which includes sweepers, a position monopolised by Untouchables because of its traditionally polluting character – were the Scheduled Castes counted as 'forward'.

tected them from poverty. And it is far from true that all poverty is rural; chapter 6 looks at a new population serving urban aggregations. But even the new urban poor tend to be rural poor at a later time: they have often been pushed out of one form of poverty into another.

It is true that there is a scattering of land ownership throughout the Untouchable population. This is sometimes of considerable antiquity, perhaps arising from the gift of a grateful rural magnate. In Maharashtra Mahars served as village servants and were entitled to a collective portion of land (though much of this land may no longer be in Mahar hands). More recently, many small plots of land have been distributed to Untouchable and other labourers as part of post-Independence land reforms. Most of these transfers did not not take place through the mechanism of confiscation and redistribution, but rather by hiving off small plots from village commons. The plots were almost always far too small to sustain a family. And in a great many cases, the beneficiaries have ended up losing the land to more secure farmers. Overall, only a very small proportion of Untouchable families own sufficient land to support themselves.

We have already observed that the majority of Untouchables never perform the 'traditional' work that is the presumptive basis of their Untouchability. Almost exactly half (49.06 per cent) of what the Census calls 'main' (as opposed to more occasional) Scheduled Caste workers are agricultural labourers (Census 1991, I (1) 1993: 18). The next highest classification is 'cultivators', who constitute 25.4 per cent of these main workers. Along with other minor classifications, a total of 77.1 per cent of Scheduled Caste main workers are in the primary sector. Only 9.8 per cent are in the 'secondary' or manufacturing and allied sector (including traditional crafts such as shoe-making and basket-weaving), and 13 per cent in the tertiary services sector (which comprises trade and commerce, and transport).

The occupational category that needs most explanation is that of 'cultivator'. It cannot be assumed that such persons are simply self-employed farmers. The Census definition makes clear that the category includes sharecroppers, and we can assume that a very high proportion of the Scheduled Caste 'cultivators' are indeed sharecroppers. The sharecropping system is practised widely in West Bengal, Bihar and the eastern areas of Uttar Pradesh, but not in most of the rest of the country. These three States alone comprise 44 per cent of the total Untouchable population of India, and we know from observation that a great many of the sharecroppers are Untouchables. So it is logical to think that the sharecroppers account for a high proportion of the Scheduled Caste 'cultivator' category in the Census. Sharecropping in north-eastern India is closer to agricultural labour than land ownership. The 'traditional' arrangement is that sharecropper and owner share the crop on a 50:50 basis, where the sharecropper supplies all labour and inputs. In the event that there is irrigation or other input provided by the owner, the worker's share declines to as little as a third of the crop. The sharecropper generally has no security of tenure. And importantly, sharecroppers tend also to work for wages or for payment in kind on other plots of land.

Their position as agricultural labourers or sharecroppers in weak agricultural zones condemns the great majority of Untouchables to a grossly inferior life for the forseeable future. With only a few regional exceptions, it is quite impossible to use the meagre wages or crop share as the basis of social advancement for the next generation. At best, the field labour of adults or near-adults can keep a family in basic food, clothing and shelter. But social disaster can result from even a minor change of circumstance or health. Only in zones of capitalist agriculture and labour shortage, notably Punjab and neighbouring regions, are the rates of pay such as to enable field labourers to think in terms of family ambitions. In the less productive and more populous regions, there is no likelihood that field labourers will achieve any dramatic increase in their present share of production. The difficulties are not merely the arduousness of organising rural workers and the existence of strong opposing interests, but also chronic low productivity. In this situation claims for higher wages are the stuff of bitter, even violent, conflict.

The consequence of the characteristic condition of complete or near-landlessness among Untouchables is not to be measured only in material poverty. Land is many things in a peasant society such as India, including social and political power. The failure to redistribute more land to the tillers of the soil has effectively forestalled the possibility of the Untouchables taking a more powerful part in decision making in rural India. One of the worst aspects of this relative powerlessness is a lack of influence on the local manifestations of the state, including police and welfare officials. Instead of a sympathetic bureaucracy dedicated to the promotion of the welfare of the poorest Indians, those at the bottom often encounter a positively hostile state apparatus.

Although there is considerable variation in the incidence of Untouchable poverty between the various States, this may be less than one might expect. In one set of now quite old calculations made in the Planning Commission for the period 1977–8, only the 'green revolution' States of Punjab (26 per cent) and Haryana (33 per cent) had an incidence of Untouchable poverty less than half that of the total Untouchables within the State. On the other hand Maharashtra (66 per cent) emerged as having as much Untouchable poverty as did Uttar Pradesh (63 per cent), despite its being a far more prosperous State. Apparently the rural prosperity of Punjab and Haryana filters down more rapidly to Untouchables than does the more urban prosperity of Maharashtra. But it is still true that with the exception of Punjab and Haryana, urban Untouchables experience somewhat less poverty than do their rural counterparts: this parallels the experience of the general population.

A different perspective on the problem can be gained by looking at the composition of a social category quite different from that of 'the poor', viz. the 'middle class' or more broadly, the 'new consumers'. It is currently fashionable to talk of an emerging middle class of much larger and more diverse character than older conceptions of such a class. While there are no firmly agreed criteria for identifying this larger middle class, the most common criteria have to do with the availability of disposable income within family units. Whatever the validity of such vague criteria, it is thoroughly clear that in both towns and villages the capacity to purchase consumer products has been growing fast. This is undoubtedly a highly important development within the Indian economy. In the present context, the question is just how many Untouchables are represented in the new consumers.

A recent survey has divided the Indian population into five categories on the basis of their income: Low (58.5 per cent), Lower Middle (25.4 per cent), Middle (10.4 per cent), Upper Middle (3.7 per cent) and High (2 per cent) (Rao and Natarajan 1994: 4–5). These percentages are calculated for the year 1992–3. The 'Low' category includes people both below and above the official poverty line: a Planning Commission study for the period 1987–8 states that 39.34 per cent of the Indian population were below the poverty line – around 330 million people in over 60 million households. Rao and Natarajan argue that the 'Low' category has been shrinking relative to the higher categories; the 'Lower Middle' category is almost stable; and the three highest categories are growing fast (Rao and Natarajan 1994: 6). While consumption is obviously greatest among the wealthier categories, even the 'Low' category is now consuming items such as radios, black and white televisions, watches, bicycles, torches, pressure cookers and electric fans.

We can make some good guesses as to where the Untouchables fit within this schema. Most of them must be in the 'Low' category. We can assume that Untouchables are still disproportionately represented among the poor (measured by calorie intake). Almost by definition, the Indian poor have virtually no power of discretionary expenditure. Those Untouchables who are not 'poor' are still likely to be found in the 'Low' rather than one of the higher categories. This seems to follow from the knowledge that as a whole category Untouchables continue to suffer from a lack of occupational mobility. Their most prized way out of agricultural labour and/or the occupation traditional to their caste is to acquire a reserved position in government service under the scheme of compensatory preference. But as we will argue in chapter 4, this route is available only to a tiny proportion of the eligible beneficiaries. Except for the most menial public-sector positions – sweeper, peon and so on – the actual beneficiaries of the preferential scheme are bound to come from that small portion of the Untouchable population that is already relatively advanced. And it is only these higher government service positions that can help propel a family into the loftier consumer categories.

Most of the fast-growing number of Untouchables who have migrated for work outside their village are to be found on building sites and roads in the towns and cities, quarrying rock and making bricks, pulling rickshaws and handcarts, scavenging for waste materials or occasionally performing some acquired but low-prestige skill such as repairing motor vehicles. Other new opportunities have opened up in 'traditional' occupations. Thus a large number of Untouchable labourers from Bihar have been seasonal migrants to Punjab and Haryana, where they have been in great demand for their skills in developing rice production as a cash crop. And sweepers have found a ready market for their needed but despised skills in the growing cities and towns. These people will at best find a place in Rao and Natarajan's 'Low' economic rank, not higher. At worst, and this is frequently the case, they have exchanged one form of misery for another. If the principal occupants of the middle ranks are landed agriculturalists, persons in secure government or private employment, or the myriad small business families, then there can be remarkably few Untouchable families to be found in such relative ease. While the Census records 13 per cent of the Untouchable workers as being in the 'tertiary' sector of commerce and transport, it is difficult to believe that more than a fragment of these are upwardly mobile business people. It is still rare, with perhaps the exception of West Bengal, to find a small trader (in food, cloth, medicinal drugs and so on) who is an Untouchable. Perhaps running a rickshaw 'business' qualifies one as a member of the tertiary sector.

Clearly the Untouchables are far from unique among Indians in their poverty or near-poverty. Indeed, there are whole other communities that are terribly poor. The tribals are an obvious example: their poverty seems to be growing rather than diminishing, as they are increasingly plunged into a new disappropriation of their land in many regions of India. There are also other desperately poor communities like the Gariya Luhars or travelling blacksmiths of Rajasthan and the Mallahas or fisherfolk of Uttar Pradesh and Bihar. And there are a vast number of individuals from virtually every community in India who are poor. It would be pointless, indeed offensive, to seek to downgrade the sometimes abject poverty of these people in order to assert a claim that Untouchables are the most wretched of all. On the other hand, there is no other discrete grouping of poor Indians that approaches the size of the Untouchables.

The picture of Untouchable progress is not entirely gloomy. In the past, one of the major measures of the backwardness of Untouchables was their illiteracy. This is now changing. In 1971 only 15 per cent of the total Untouchable population was literate; in 1981 the figure had grown to 21 per cent, and in 1991 it reached over 37 per cent. The rate of increase for Untouchable women is particularly steep: it rose from a mere 6 per cent in 1971, through 11 percent in 1981, to reach almost 24 per cent by 1991. Moreover the gap between the Untouchables and the general population is closing: in 1971 the Untouchables struggled to a literacy rate achieved by the general population twenty years earlier, whereas in 1991 the Untouchable figure (including for women) was roughly that of the general figure only ten years earlier. Literacy tends to bestow multiple benefits on its practitioners, but above all it lends confidence and expands mental horizons. It leads to a more assertive, less compliant, community. Acquisition of literacy by girls provides a base for more equal communication between husbands and wives. This, in turn, can lead to changes in reproductive behaviour.

There are many other positive indicators. The poorest Indians, including Untouchables, are not being killed by famine or epidemic to the extent that they were a hundred years ago. Emergency relief measures, including food for work programs, have provided an important safety net. New public employment has made a difference, and even the meanest labouring opportunities have afforded a way out of absolute destitution for many. And there are the beginnings of welfare measures such as aged pensions in most States. These are changes of the greatest importance. But there also more disquieting indications.

Some of these pointers can be found in the regions where Untouchables have done best in recent years. Thus Kerala has done more than any other State to meet the basic health, housing and education needs of its poorest people, Untouchables included. But at the same time, the Untouchables of Kerala seem now to be fixed in a mould of poverty and menial labour. Their performance in higher education is weak and they appear to have poor prospects of raising their children to a life of greater amenity and higher status. In Punjab, Haryana and a number of other regions of northern India, the Untouchables have achieved higher income from a more prosperous agricultural sector than in Kerala. Their social amenities have not been as good, though on the indicators of literacy, health and infant mortality they score well relative to most of the less prosperous zones. But like their counterparts in Kerala, the Untouchables of these relatively well-to-do regions seem unable to escape from the socially subordinate condition that is the mark of agricultural labour. They remain structurally at the bottom of society, with little indication that they will be able to bridge the new gaps of sophistication that are opening up at the end of the twentieth century.

Adverse discrimination

Historically, so far as one can tell, poverty and ritual debasement went hand-in-hand in the case of the Untouchables. We have suggested further that the ideology of Untouchability may well have developed, at least in part, as rationalisation of material exploitation. It seems to follow that if the ideology were now destroyed, the poverty of the former Untouchable castes could be addressed without regard to discriminations of a ritual character. But this is only hypothesis, since the ideology of Untouchability has clearly not been destroyed. There has been progress in this direction, perhaps more progress than in the struggle against poverty. But like caste itself, Untouchability has changed character as well as lost some of its intensity.

In order to discuss what has happened to ritual Untouchability we can usefully proceed from the benchmark represented by the Schedule of 1936, the instrument which specified a list of castes according to certain nominated criteria. The basic test for inclusion in the Schedule was the 'Untouchability' of a given caste, though a sprinkling of castes deemed specially backward in educational and social terms may have been incorporated without their being strictly 'Untouchable' (Galanter 1984: 130). Conversely a few castes – the Ezhavas of Travancore, for example – had suffered at least a mild Untouchability in the past but were considered too socially advanced to be placed in a Schedule which would guarantee preferential treatment by the state.

The conception of Untouchability had been rehearsed in the various Censuses over a period of half a century. By the time of J. H. Hutton's Census in 1931, the object was no longer to inquire into whether the Untouchables were Hindus but to identify 'exterior' castes that merited beneficial treatment by the state. Hutton's criteria were considerably more detailed and inclusive than those of Gait in 1911. But for Hutton the most important test was the right to use roads, wells and schools; religious disabilities and social 'difficulties' were only 'contributory' indications (Hutton 1963: 195). Presumably Hutton was thinking in terms of a strict public/private divide, where merely social or religious restrictions (including temple entry) were properly speaking a matter for civil society rather than the state.

Hutton was well aware that the particular treatment of the lowest castes varied greatly between different regions. But he was determined to push past the demands for recognising only the 'purest' kind of Untouchability. So many of the northern castes included in the Schedule did not suffer the same ritual disabilities that had been the mark of Untouchability in the south.[3] What can be said is that the Schedule was composed of castes that were socially the very lowest in the reputational hierarchies of their particular province (Dushkin in Galanter 1984: 130). This is the explanation for the seeming anomaly whereby West Bengal has perhaps the mildest recent history of Untouchability and close to the highest proportion of Scheduled Castes (23.6 per cent in 1991).

What was special to southern and to some extent western India was the history of restriction of Untouchable movement through public space, though reform was well under way by the time the Schedule was promulgated. In many parts of the south Untouchables had previously had to maintain prescribed distances – they varied with the lowliness of the caste – from clean Hindus. Should the shadow of an Untouchable fall upon a Brahmin, major pollution had taken place. Sometimes Untouchables had had to ring a bell to announce their polluting arrival, and to wear spittoons (in the case, for example, of the Ande Koragas of Madras and the Mahars of Maharashtra) so as to catch any polluting spittle that might drop from their lips (Census 1931 'Exterior Castes': 483; Robertson 1938: 16, 37). There was said to be a caste of 'unseeables', the Purada Vannans of Tinnevelly District, who washed the clothes of other Untouchables at night and hid their polluting presence by day (Census 1931 'Exterior Castes': 483). Since there was a close connection between ritual and economic subordination, some of the worst cases of economic exploitation had also been in the south. So in Travancore, now part of Kerala, until well into the nineteenth century the Pulaya labourers had been bound to their masters in a form of slavery that entailed being heritable and transferable. But the survey material available to Hutton was of limited and variable quality, and it is not clear whether the south was markedly more discriminatory than other parts of India by the late 1930s.

It was clear that in the north distance pollution did not exist at the time

---

[3] Some of the earlier lists had contained very few northern castes. See, for example, the minute of dissent in the Indian Franchise Committee 1932: 728–33. Three members of the Committee signed this minute and estimated that there were only 600,000 Untouchables in the United Provinces and 70,000 in Bengal. The majority of the Committee did not opt for a final figure for the United Provinces, but estimated the numbers for Bengal at about 7.5 million (Indian Franchise Committee 1932: 621).

the Schedule was formulated. There were no public prescriptions as to the distance that any Untouchable had to preserve between himself – seemingly a male pollutes more than a female, except a female giving birth or at time of menstruation! – and a Brahmin or any other Hindu. Nor did pollution by actual touch provoke the same consternation and obligatory purification as it did in the south. Only the castes of scavengers and sweepers – the Bhangis, Doms, Mehtars and so on (these are largely functional equivalents located in different regions) – were comprehensively shunned in a physical sense. These are the castes whose work is undeniably dirty, even if the result of their labours is to make public space cleaner for everyone. The Bhangis are uniquely despised across northern India, even by the other Untouchable castes. None but the most determined modernist will even now take water or food from their hand.

For the other Untouchable castes, pollution by actual touch has been a more complicated affair in the north. Thus Jagjivan Ram, the Chamar who rose to be Deputy Prime Minister, states that already during his childhood the Chamars were able to use the common wells in his own Bihari village (Interview: 5 January 1983). Bengal was also relatively relaxed. Perhaps it is a pointer to this comparative liberality that Bengali Brahmins eat fish along with the rest of the population of the region, whereas all other Brahmins treat fish as a species of polluting flesh.[4] In the matter of access to roads and water, the regional report of the Census of 1931 had this to say:

In Bengal nowhere is any caste excluded from a public road merely on account of the position of the caste. In certain areas the very lowest classes of scavengers, sweepers, etc., are not allowed, as in Malda and Hooghly, to use the public wells, but in most cases the restriction does not exist at all, and where it exists, it is either dependent upon the size or nature of the well or is overcome by some form of adjustment between the classes. In some districts, for instance, members of the sweeper classes are not allowed to use *kaccha* (earth) wells but may use masonry wells, or they are excluded from wells with a diameter less than a certain distance (say 6 feet) but are permitted to use larger wells than these. In some cases the higher castes, in a manner of speaking, take the disability upon themselves and voluntarily leave certain wells exclusively to the lower castes; or the lower castes, when they wish to draw water, will not let down their own vessels or touch the vessel used for drawing the water by higher castes but will wait beside the well till one of the higher castes fills their vessels. (Census of 1931, V (1), Bengal: 496–7)

From this it is clear that discrimination and ritual pollution remained a motif of Bengali society sixty-five years ago. But it seems that Untouchability was no longer a dominating ideology, and the grossest

---

[4] But it is anomalous that the occupation of fishing is the presumptive basis for the Untouchability of a number of castes in Bengal, as elsewhere.

displays seem to have been residual rather than routine. So Untouchable children were already freely admissable to the schools, though the children of the lowest castes were still infrequently to be found there. Some Untouchable castes were already making substantial economic progress and simultaneously seeking to slough off their reputation as ritually unclean. The Namasudras and Rajabanshis, the two largest Untouchable castes in contemporary West Bengal, were the leading examples of this phenomenon. By 1931 these castes already had lawyers among their ranks. They had considerable misgivings about being classified as Untouchable, though they could also see their interest in acquiring any advantage that might flow from this. Thus at their own motion the Rajabanshis were not counted an 'exterior' caste in the Census of 1931, but conversely they were admitted to the 1936 Schedule which promised to deliver them tangible benefits.

If we turn now to what has happened to Untouchability since the 1930s, the picture is varied. Arguably one of the very worst cases has become just about the best. So except in two northern Districts bordering Karnataka, gross displays of discrimination are no longer a part of the life of Kerala. We have seen that the Pulayas and other Untouchables of Kerala remain poor, but they are not now the objects of overt discrimination. Some of them complain that discrimination is still practised in covert ways, and this is instinctively believable. Surely it passes comprehension that a region so steeped in dehumanising ritual hierarchy could have banished it without trace within a couple of generations. But this kind of discriminatory residue is a world away from the horrors of the Pulayas' existence 100 years ago. The rest of the south is not so free of discriminatory behaviour as is Kerala, but the most distinctive southern discriminations of old are now gone. In particular, distance pollution appears no longer to be practised.

For India as a whole it is possible to say that the areas of social life most securely opened up to Untouchables are those directly under the auspices of the state. Undoubtedly the most important of these is the education system. Untouchable children are provided access to all government schools in India, and apparently with rare exceptions they are now treated without formal segregation within the schoolroom. There is also no barrier against them – indeed, they are given some compensatory preference – in institutions of higher education. The same scheme of preference has provided access to public employment for Untouchables, and by now – it was different in the early years – there is no routine practice of the grossest discrimination against them in the course of this employment. Similarly, Untouchables are now freely admissable into public hospitals. And in both urban and rural areas Untouchables can now travel in a bus or train with people of whatever caste background. These are changes of the greatest importance.

In the major cities the new culture of accommodation goes considerably further than this. Pragmatism (rather than a self-conscious spirit of reform) has given rise to a culture that is seemingly careless of the demands of orthodoxy. A Bombay Brahmin cannot afford to be choosy about who is next to him in a queue – whether it is in the post office, the bank or a fast-food outlet. After all, to be prepared to eat fast-food is already to have stepped quite outside the bounds of caste orthodoxy. But this is by no means the whole of the story. Beneath the cosmopolitan carelessness of Bombay, say, there are deep-seated separations. The factor of class ensures that higher-status people will come into no more than highly limited contact with Untouchables, who tend to be at the bottom of both class and caste orders. So as a matter of logic it is quite possible for public civility to coexist with the maintenance of deep prejudice against Untouchables. In cities such as Bombay and Delhi it is difficult to know just how pronounced such feelings are. We do know from numerous anecdotal and survey accounts that in institutional settings such as colleges there is usually quite a small degree of personal interaction, let alone friendship, between Untouchable students and their higher-caste colleagues. It is true that separations on the basis of class, ethnicity, culture and gender are common in institutional settings throughout the world. But in the case of the Untouchables there is a whole pattern of separations that points to an underlying discrimination. To give one important example, Untouchables are scarcely ever employed in private businesses other than in a menial capacity.

Perhaps the best survey of the modern incidence of ritual Untouchability was conducted by I. P. Desai in rural Gujarat, now almost twenty-five years ago (Desai 1976). Gujarat is an economically progressive region, but Desai found that the practice of Untouchability was still widespread in the villages he surveyed. It was least practised in what he calls the 'public' situations of bus travel, seating arrangements in schools and post office service. He calls these 'public' matters because they are directly regulated by statute. So Desai found that in only one village out of fifty-nine was there discrimination in the arrangement of seating in a school classroom: it is probably safe to assume that not even this single instance would be encountered today. Postal discrimination was higher: only 4 per cent of post offices discriminated against Untouchables in the sale of stamps and like matters, but 17 per cent of postmen displayed discriminatory attitudes during their delivery of mail. The one 'public' area of high discrimination was in seating arrangements at statutory *panchayat* meetings (Desai 1976: 258).

In the so-called 'private' sphere, the incidence of discrimination soared. In 90 per cent of the villages Untouchables were not allowed into the houses of caste Hindus. An even higher percentage of barbers did not serve Untouchables: barbers are themselves of low rather than Untouchable caste, and presumably their concern is less with their own pollution and more with the certain loss of high-caste patronage. Sixty per cent of village shopkeepers took care to avoid directly touching anything to do with Untouchables, even their money, in conducting transactions. Seventy per cent of the potters did not allow the Untouchables to touch pots while going about their purchases, and in 89 per cent of the villages Untouchables were prohibited from entering temples frequented by caste Hindus.

For Desai the heart of the Untouchability question is whether water sources are treated as polluted by Untouchables' use. The water question is clearly more relevant than any question about food pollution, since the latter occurs in multiple Hindu social situations that do not involve Untouchables. Denial of access to common water sources seems to be a discrimination particular to Untouchables, though it is possible to find the denial affecting some tribals too. So in view of the overall 'conservatism' of his respondents, Desai found it 'surprising' that 26 per cent of the villages allowed Untouchables access to common water sources (Desai 1976: 62–3). In 10 per cent of villages the water source was considered polluted if used by Untouchables, and here Untouchables were dependent on the grace and favour of caste Hindu users to acquire water. Untouchables had to wait near the well until someone agreed to pour water into their containers, taking care that the two containers did not touch. (If a clay vessel was touched, it became irredeemably polluted and had to be thrown away or given to an Untouchable.) But in the largest number of villages, 64 per cent, the whole problem was side-stepped through the provision of separate water facilities for Untouchables. These villages were not more benevolent in their outlook, merely better provided with wells. Overall it appears that Bengali Untouchables had better access to water facilities in 1931 than Gujarati Untouchables in I. P. Desai's survey some forty years later.

Desai's findings demonstrate that the transformation we have identified has left intact a great edifice of discrimination. What Desai discovered was an increasingly subtle behavioural system able to accommodate radically opposed ideological systems by confining them to different social sites. In this way it is possible for a Brahmin child to sit next to an Untouchable child in the classroom, while the Untouchable continues to be denied access to the well from which the Brahmin draws water. There is no doubt that compartmentalisation is greatly to be preferred to comprehensive Untouchability. It provides space for a measure of material and social comfort, and breaks the cycle of relentless subordination. But equally, the underlying discrimination severely qualifies the life chances of its victims.

Desai's results probably hold good for large parts of rural India, but clearly they do not apply everywhere. The practice of ritual Untouchability has moderated further in those States where it was already mildest sixty years ago. In West Bengal, for example, ritual Untouchability would seem to be no more than a minor factor in rural life today. The vestiges of water pollution sketched in the Census of 1931 have presumably disappeared. And clearly there is no gross discrimination in the schools. We know these things negatively, as it were, from the absence of reports to the contrary in sources such as the annual reports of the Commissioner for Scheduled Castes and Tribes. Positive information is hard to come by, partly because of the nature of political culture in West Bengal. The State has now had a Government formed by Communist Parties for a couple of decades, and the pervasive Marxist discourse has moulded the way in which social issues are discussed. In a word, this culture is hostile to analysis of problems as arising from *caste* society. The Government has been sympathetic and active in the promotion of the rights of *bargadars* (sharecroppers) defined by their position in the productive process, and many of these bargadars happen to be Untouchables. But the Government has persistently fallen short, and is seemingly careless, of the mandatory quotas of Scheduled Castes that it must employ in public services. It follows that the upper castes which control the Party and the Government have been the beneficiaries of this lack of diligence. They continue to rule the State (and the Party) as they have always done.[5] A similar kind of carelessness is evident in Kerala, also ruled for many years by the same Communist Parties. These two Governments cannot be said to have sanctioned the continuance of Untouchability, but they can be faulted for failing to promote the policies of compensatory discrimination. In West Bengal, with the exception of a couple of the larger castes, the Untouchables remain firmly at the bottom of the economic and therefore the social heap.

As a final example, we can take the State of Bihar. We have noted that prior to Independence Bengal and Bihar had a common mildness in their Untouchability regime, but over the last two decades these two States have diverged sharply. Bihar has become the most endemically conflictual

---

[5] Ross Mallick, himself a Bengali Untouchable, has delivered (1993) an extended and scathing attack on the Marxist Governments of West Bengal. He is particularly critical of the proposition that West Bengal does not practise Untouchability today and that the CPI(M) Government is blind to considerations of caste and Untouchability.

State of the Union, and the Untouchables are at the centre of the very worst conflict. Much of this can be characterised as 'class' rather than 'caste' conflict, because it is over land. But the conflict also arises from the movement for what is called in Bihar 'social respect', including the cessation of sexual offences against Untouchable women and the repudiation of higher-caste behaviour ranging from arrogance to straight-out oppression. Even the land conflict immediately becomes caught up in the whole history of ritual and hierarchical relations between Untouchables and caste Hindus, rather than being simply a class affair. This is a prime reason for the violent direction taken by so much of agrarian conflict in contemporary Bihar. What cannot be tolerated by many villagers is that such despised people as the Untouchables – even the particularly degraded Musahars – are standing up and demanding their rights. Old-fashioned ritual Untouchability may not be in issue, but clearly a particularly pernicious 'casteism' is at work here. The compartmentalisation we talked about earlier has broken down. In circumstances of stress, old and oppressive attitudes quickly rise to the surface.

2 The question of the 'Harijan atrocity'

For thirty years after Independence the Untouchables were no more than a marginal issue in India. Then, almost immediately after the cessation of Indira Gandhi's Emergency in 1977, the matter of their connection with violence suddenly became the stuff of front-page news. A series of particularly gruesome 'Harijan atrocities' genuinely shocked national opinion makers. In the present context we need to ask whether these incidents, and the routinely high level of violence apparently suffered by Untouchables, is the summation of age-old subordination or whether it arises from a new consciousness and resistance on their part. In trying to answer these questions we are setting out to present just one more image, albeit an important one, of the contemporary condition of Untouchables. We should resist the temptation to see this violence as the distilled essence of the whole historical system of Untouchability. But at the same time, violence may be able to point us towards powerful currents moving beneath the surface of Indian life.

Reportage of violence done to Untouchables is a recent affair, as can be seen from the reports of the Commissioner for Scheduled Castes and Scheduled Tribes (RCSCST). As the Constitutional authority charged with measuring the progress of the Scheduled Castes (Article 338), the Commissioner has been reporting on 'complaints' since the Sixth Report of 1956–7. In that Report the Commissioner provided six examples of what he considered to be justified complaints in the scant two pages he devoted to the topic. But he also included five cases where the facts were 'exaggerated and distorted', and with studied concern for impartiality he reported more generally on the difficulty of judging 'whether the complaints of harassment, etc., made to me are genuine or false' (RCSCST 1956–7: 21). By the time of the twenty-first Report of 1971–3, perceptions had changed. The much larger complaints section was restyled 'Cases of Atrocities and Harassment', a nomenclature which seemed to fit mounting concern about violence done to Untouchables. In the variant form 'Harijan atrocity', this was a term that quickly slipped into the vernacular of Indian newspaper reportage and official documents as an omnibus identifier of the frequent violence suffered by Untouchables. Over the following two decades the term 'Harijan atrocity' became scarcely more emotive in impact than the language it replaced. The term was routinised and bureaucratised at a time when wider political developments suggested that India as a whole was an increasingly violent society and therefore that the Untouchables were not such exceptional victims. So despite occasional thunderings from politicians or bureaucrats, India, if not the Untouchables themselves, had learnt to live with 'Harijan atrocities'.

It is not easy to say just how prevalent such violence is, or what the trends are. The best run of figures is the annual survey published in the Commissioner's Report, and this shows a major increase in acts of violence over the years: typically there are now thousands of cases registered each year. But periodically the Reports also say that their own figures are not to be believed because of variable administrative and hence reporting regimes at the provincial level (RCSCST 1971–3: 162) and changing definitions of what is to be recorded as a 'Harijan atrocity' (RCSCST 1983–4: 52). Another Report notes major deviations in the incidence of violence from year to year, 'if statistics relating to atrocities on Scheduled Castes and Scheduled Tribes are any indication' (RCSCST 1979–81: 340). In short, it would be unwise to make any precise claims about incidence and trends.

This said, it is highly likely that the incidence of violence involving Untouchables has indeed increased significantly over the post-Independence period. Beyond the evidence represented by figures and the far greater reportage of such matters over the last two decades, this trend is suggested by the actual nature of the violence. This can be divided into two broad categories: first, 'traditional' violence; and secondly, that which flows from modern forms of resistance on the part of Untouchables or is a caste Hindu response to the changing situation of Untouchables. The second category is now dominant, and it tends to revolve around a new and still emerging social and political identity constructed over the period of the present century. Nowadays violence is by and large not being visited upon Dalits as totally passive victims, but rather comes about as a reaction to demands they are making or their uptake of benefits provided by the state.

'Traditional' violence against Untouchables

Clearly violence against Untouchables is not a new phenomenon, despite the silence of the historical record. Their vulnerability arose partly from their utter dependence on their masters: it defies belief to think that a slave, for example, was always free from the physical wrath of a brutish master. The position of women must have been particularly weak, say, 200 years ago. Women were easy sexual prey, either in return for some inducement (Briggs 1920: 43) or through sheer force. Continuing cases of abuse of Untouchable women have fuelled the campaigns for 'social respectability' waged by radical groups in regions like Bihar. Nowadays it is more likely that a 'traditional' act of violence like rape of an Untouchable woman will at least be reported to the authorities, though not necessarily pursued with any seriousness. Still, there are a disturbing number of references to exploitative liaisons and prostitution of Untouchable women in our own period. Very clearly, this will become a major focus of inquiry, debate and resistance in the years to come.[1]

It is possible to find other recent examples of 'traditional' violence against Untouchables. Thus there are reports of violence or at least force being applied to Untouchables on the basis of their association in the caste Hindu mind with the dark forces of life: they are taken to embody and have power over evil spirits. So in a village in the Saurashtra region of Gujarat State the people (presumably caste Hindus) believed that the Untouchables were the cause of disease being suffered by cattle of the village. They went in a mob to an Untouchable house and forced a woman and her daughter to go to the cattle and remove the curse upon them by stretching their hands over the beasts and eating an offering of coconut (RCSCST 1957–8: 23).

Similarly, in a village in Saharsa District of Bihar a boy from a lower-caste family died of snake bite in August 1973. After the body was brought back from the hospital his family was persuaded that the tragedy had come about from the witchcraft of an aged Untouchable woman. Four women and the male head of an Untouchable family physically isolated from the other Untouchables of the village were dragged from their house to the home of the dead boy, and the women were ordered to chant *mantras* to bring the boy back to life. The women pleaded their ignorance of witchcraft and the furious caste Hindus stripped, kicked and beat them. When this produced no results, 'iron sickles were heated in front of the women and their feet, arms and other delicate parts were branded' (RCSCST 1971–3: 165–6).

Whether or not there were contributing circumstances to these events, there is no doubt that a belief in the dark powers of Untouchables is an important aspect of folk culture throughout India. For example, in Maharashtra the Mahars are typically the guardians of Mariai, the

---

[1] If official figures are to be believed, the incidence of sexual assaults against Untouchable women is not disproportionate to that for the population as a whole (RCSCST 1979–81: 353). Unfortunately, official figures must always be taken with extreme caution and it is quite possible that sexual assault on such women is specially under-reported.

goddess of cholera, and her shrine is located in their colony (Robertson 1938: 23). At times such Untouchable potency may work to offset customary oppression. For example, a survey of the practice of Untouchability conducted by the Commissioner for Scheduled Castes and Scheduled Tribes during the year 1958–9 (unsurprisingly) found that Untouchability was practised in the Siva temple of a suburban village of Azamgarh District, Uttar Pradesh: the Untouchables had to gain *darshan* from outside, and could offer money but not flowers or edible items. But this discrimination was relieved at certain times of the year: 'During the Dashahara and Bhagwati Puja, when the goddess is propitiated to ward off an epidemic like small-pox, no caste discrimination is observed' (RCSCST 1958–9: 35). So the potency of Untouchables in warding off evil spirits gains them some temporary favour from custodians of the temple.

The importance of the above examples should not be minimised, not least because they provide a glimpse of an important dimension of caste Hindu attitudes towards the Untouchables. At the same time, and with the crucial exception of sexual assaults/coercion of women, we can say that most contemporary acts of violence against Untouchables should not be classified as 'traditional'. Rather, to repeat, they arise in the context of the new and still emerging identity of the Dalits. Sometimes violence is directly provoked by their claims, whereas at other times there is caste Hindu backlash against new government benefits or rising economic and status levels enjoyed by Untouchables. Perhaps most disturbing of all, there is abundant evidence of severe mistreatment and often violence visited upon Untouchables by the very government agencies supposed to protect them – notably the police. No doubt the poor have always been mistreated by the state – in this sense violence from this source could also be regarded as 'traditional'. But clearly the problem has been getting far worse as battle lines have been drawn by both rising and falling elements in civil society. The behaviour of state officials is directly linked to power relations in society at large.

If we concentrate on the demands of the Untouchables themselves, these can be discussed under two major headings: first, objections to discrimination arising from the practice of ritual Untouchability, together with more general claims to social respect; and secondly, claims to agricultural land, housing sites, and payment of statutory minimum wages. The second of these categories encompasses far more of the violent confrontations that have broken out in recent years. But the two categories have in common an attitude which can usefully be termed *resistance*. Sometimes the particular claims are made by individuals or groups acting outside any organised political context. At other times they are encouraged by political parties or even revolutionary organisations (the so-called Naxalites). The nature and context of the claims will become apparent through discussion of a number of concrete examples.

Violence arising from resistance to ritual Untouchability

Removal of dead cattle

On the first occasion the Commissioner of Scheduled Castes and Scheduled Tribes discussed 'complaints', he reported that a 'Harijan' family was harassed and beaten because of 'their refusal to lift the dead cattle' (RCSCST 1956–7: 20). We are not told anything more about the nature of the conflict, save that the people doing the harassment were Gujars and that local authorities took the case to court and that the accused 'were brought to book'. It is possible to flesh out this story from what we know about similar disputes, many of which have been detailed in official reports and press accounts over the years.

The Harijans referred to in the Report were probably Chamars, who represent the largest Untouchable caste in India (and the second largest caste overall, behind the Brahmins). The occupation of the Chamars, or their equivalents in other parts of India, includes the removal of carcasses of dead cattle and all dealing in hides, including skinning and tanning, and the fabrication of leather articles, such as shoes, saddles and leather buckets for wells. Some Chamars perform only particular elements of this broad occupational connection with leather: for example, particular Chamar sub-castes or at least occupational communities will work with finished leather but not engage in the lower-status activity of tanning. Some will remove the carcasses of camels and horses but not cattle, whereas other communities will do the reverse. But despite the overall identification of Chamars with hides and leather, this involvement represents a strictly minority occupation for them. Overwhelmingly the Chamars are agricultural labourers, often working for high-caste landholders for whom ploughing is a sin (Briggs 1920: 22, 24, 56–57; Kolenda 1978: 54).

Particular sub-castes or religious communities among the Chamars have foresworn all contact with hides or leather, in order to try to increase the status of the group by ridding it of low-status activities which are the presumptive basis of Untouchability. But, of course, this leaves caste Hindus with a problem. Contact with dead cows is unthinkable to a high-caste person, and involvement with any other dead animals is scarcely much better. The animal is valuable for its meat and skin, but only if someone processes it. In the meantime, fallen animals will foul the air. So the violent incident mentioned by the Commissioner in his sixth Report begins to be more comprehensible. The Gujars are a peasant rather than high caste, but clearly they would not welcome the dilemma into which the local Chamars had thrust them.

Admittedly the above is not a simple case of the practice of ritual Untouchability. What is at issue is the cessation of a task which is the suggested basis of a particular community's ritual Untouchability. It could be argued that the Gujars are only seeking to enforce the traditional industrial order of the village. Who could easily be recruited to perform the task vacated by the Chamars? On the other hand, the case makes no sense outside the context of Untouchability: if the task did not involve ritual pollution, the Gujars would no doubt have been willing to do it themselves. While putting hand to plough is a sin for Brahmins, here we are dealing with a task that is rejected by all Hindus within the varna order. So it seems appropriate to regard the attempt to force the Chamars back to their job of carcass disposal as an effort to enforce the order of Untouchability.

Again and again, in different locations across India, the same issue has been fought throughout the present century. Chakravarti reports a case from his field-work village in Rajasthan (1975: 59–61). A Raegar (closely related to the Chamars) refused to remove a fallen buffalo in 1952, in conformity with a decision of his caste fellows in the village and in the wider Jaipur region. This provoked a major crisis for the Rajput landholders of the village, and they delivered a heavy beating to the dissenting Raegar. He was forced to resume his traditional duty, and it was not until a couple of years later that the Raegars of the village managed to make their ban stick. In a village near Lucknow a case with the same essential ingredients resulted in a mass attack by some forty armed Ahirs; thirteen Untouchables were hospitalised (RCSCST 1973–4: 190). The severity of this incident seemed to arise from a considerable history of tension over the issue. Even in West Bengal – supposedly free from ritual Untouchability today – it is possible to find reports of the very same conflicts (RCSCST 1975–7: 45).

Access to water

The question of access to water by Untouchables continues to be a source of discord and sometimes violent conflict. The Commissioner reported on a case from Gujarat in 1974 which involved the murder of two Untouchables and the injury of a number of others (RCSCST 1973–4: 186–8). Water had dried up in the wells used by the Untouchables, so they had to take recourse to the common wells of the village.

The Patels, presumably the dominant landholders of the villager, objected to this. The Dalits approached the authorities for assistance, and the police duly registered a case under the *Untouchability Offences Act* 1955. Two low-level policemen were also assigned to the village to keep the peace. But several weeks later the conflict broke out in earnest again, this time between women from the two communities. The Patel men were summoned and they obliged by beating up the police and then ransacking houses of the Dalits and severely beating a number of them, in two cases leading to death.

This case is by no means singular as an example of discrimination against Untouchables in the matter of access to common water sources. As we noted in chapter 1, I. P. Desai's survey of villages in South Gujarat some twenty-five years ago found such discrimination to be the norm. But to a large extent it was masked by the widespread government policy (no doubt correct) of providing wells and taps within Untouchable settlements. The problem in the above case, of course, was that the Dalits' own wells had run dry. In the past they would have had to hang around waiting for caste Hindus to draw water and pour it into their buckets – no doubt the caste Hindus saw the extra work as a small price to pay (by women!) for perpetuating dominance – but clearly they were no longer prepared to do this. Given such a generational development of resistance on the part of Dalits, it is only massive efforts in sinking wells dedicated to Untouchables that have limited the violence.

Teashops

There are widespread reports of Untouchability continuing to be practised in teashops in various parts of India; clearly this problem is more likely to occur in villages or small towns where the identity of customers will be known (for example, Desai 1976: 255–6). One such case exploded into a major incident at the town of Hathras, Aligarh District of Uttar Pradesh, in May 1980. Five young men from the Valmiki (Bhangi or Sweeper) community 'who happened to be under the influence of drinks' asked for *lassi* (buttermilk) at a tea stall in the town. As was apparently the custom in the shop, they were served the drink in *kullarhs* or disposable earthenware pots. The men became angry at being served in this way and demanded that the drink be served in glasses. The issue quickly ignited into a major confrontation involving supporters of the Valmikis and the caste Hindu shopkeeper. Before the issue died down three days later, there had been vigorous stone throwing with attendant injuries, the burning of tens of houses of the Untouchables, strikes by Valmiki municipal sweepers and reciprocal *hartals* or closure of shops by caste Hindus. In the view of the investigating team sent out by the Commissioner, the context of the incident was an Assembly election which inflamed a pre-existing political conflict. The incident arose as 'a result of pre-planned political manœuvrings and to some extent infightings between two groups of a political party'. Once the Assembly elections were over, the caste tension started receding (RCSCST 1979–81: 367).

Assuming that the above judgment is correct, clearly the Valmikis had pressed the right button to provoke a conflict with their caste Hindu opponents. What they had done was nothing more than set aside the avoidance strategy that we have referred to as ubiquitous in contemporary India. The issue of Untouchability in the teashops of Hathras had been side-stepped by usually, though apparently not invariably, serving tea in disposable containers rather than reusable glasses (which it also had). By a simple device the shopkeepers had shrouded the question of Untouchability in a fog of ambiguity, apparently satisfying both Untouchables and caste Hindus. Clearly this was an advance over the past, when Untouchables would have been refused service altogether. But for once it did not suit the Untouchables to put up with the ambiguity, since they believed that it did in fact mask the persistence of discrimination on the basis of the ideology of Untouchability.

Marriage processions

The reports are dotted with cases that seem peculiarly rooted in another era. Thus there are a number of violent incidents that arise from wedding processions. Violence has broken out in response to the assumption by Untouchables of traditions previously monopolised by caste Hindus, including the groom's riding of a white horse or being borne in a palanquin during wedding processions. The most serious report of this kind comes from the mountainous Almora District of Uttar Pradesh, an incident in which fourteen Untouchables were killed in May 1980 (RCSCST 1979–81: 361–4). It began when caste Hindus demanded that the groom dismount from the palanquin at the entrance to a village which lay on the path to the marriage party's destination. This was required, the caste Hindus said, to show reverence to the deity located in a temple at the other end of the village. A week earlier the very same situation had arisen, and the Untouchables had given in. But apparently this time the 'youths' were determined to press ahead. A scuffle broke out and one of the caste Hindus was stabbed to death. The infuriated caste Hindus regrouped and chased some of their opponents into a house, which was torched with the loss of six lives. Another eight Untouchables were stoned and clubbed to death.

The Commissioner's investigation was unable to make a conclusive determination between the rival accounts of village tradition. It was asserted by the Untouchables that they were being discriminated against *qua* Untouchables, and that there was no general policy that required the groom to dismount outside the village as opposed to in the immediate vicinity of the temple. They said they had every intention to dismount and offer prayer to the deity at the appropriate point in the procession. The alternative view from the caste Hindu side was that everyone, and not merely Untouchables, was obliged to dismount from a palanquin at the entrance to the village (RCSCST 1979–81: 362). Whatever the truth of the matter, the Commissioner had no doubt that the affair was the outcome of 'caste animosities and hatred'. 'Some of the Scheduled Castes persons educated and living outside in places like Delhi have imbibed an urge to do away with all social discrimination' (RCSCST 1979–81: 363).

This incident is revealing for several reasons. First, the incapacity of the Commissioner's investigators, albeit on a very short visit, to discern the 'truth' about conventional behaviour relative to the village deity is not surprising. This question would presumably have been overlaid with multiple and inconsistent perceptions among the different communities. We can assume that there was indeed discrimination in the village on the basis of Untouchability, though we have no knowledge of its form or its severity. Certainly we know as a general matter that where Untouchables stand, squat or ride relative to caste Hindus has always been a major point of division. Untouchables were by tradition obliged to be physically lower than caste Hindus if the two were in some proximity, and they can never have been allowed to ride in ceremonial style through a caste Hindu quarter.[2] As to the Untouchables' state of mind, it is quite plausible that their consciousness had been progressively transformed. Many of the Untouchables are said to have had experience in the world outside their remote region, particularly in the city of Delhi. In short, the Untouchables may have been becoming more militant. This may have predisposed them to believe that in the matter of wedding processions they were being subjected to discriminations that did not apply to the high-caste population. So even if it could be sustained that there was something of a convention among high-caste people that they did in fact dismount from

[2] In the near past this was readily apparent to everyone, including one of the present writers doing field-work in Alwar District of Rajasthan in the early 1970s. An old Chamar man resolutely declined to sit on the *charpai* while telling his story in the presence of Brahmins of the village. It was more trouble than it was worth for him to do this, though during the conversation he provoked some derisory laughter by contrasting the politeness of the foreigner's language with the roughness of the Brahmins' address.

a horse or palanquin well before coming to the temple, any Untouchable failure to observe this convention might not have been wilful.

Secondly, the sheer brutality of this incident is striking. How is the murder of so many Untouchables to be explained? Undoubtedly it has something to do with the event that a high-caste man had been killed before any Untouchables had been so dealt with. The thread of extravagant revenge runs through a number of the cases of multiple murder of Untouchables: it runs through the *Pipra* incident discussed below, for example. Revenge is not a difficult emotion to understand, but extravagant revenge has another element in its constitution. In the present case we need to explain the massing together of large numbers of high-caste men and their *premeditated* orgy of violence – the burning and the beating.

Mass violence in the Indian sub-continent is scarcely limited to attacks on Untouchables. The greatest recent scenes of uncontrolled carnage have been enacted in conflicts between Hindus and Muslims at the time of partition and even in post-partition India. Hindu-Muslim communalism and mass mobilisation against Untouchables spring from different sources, but what the two have in common is belief in the *otherness* of the object of their violence. This same sense is present in exacerbated racism, in whatever national or international context this presents itself. In India, such a sense goes some distance towards explaining the sheer passion that enables mobilisation of numbers of people and the willingness to exceed ordinary social bounds.

What is special to incidents like the Almora palanquin case or Belchi or Pipra is the outrage that is felt when those most lowly raise their heads – in the palanquin case, literally. It is bad enough when the Untouchables assert rights to equal treatment. But when they go so far as to spill the first blood, the sense of outraged hierarchy bursts its bounds. So the worst Harijan atrocity cases consist in large numbers of caste Hindus – sometimes many hundreds – pursuing Untouchables in vengeful retribution for a wrong, perhaps a death, done to one of them. Invariably in such cases, there is a great asymmetry between the organised caste Hindu mob – this is no spontaneous passion – and the terrified Untouchable rabble who flee before *force majeure*.

Land, wages and social oppression

The most severe conflict of a routine kind that now involves Untouchables is over land. This phenomenon is a comparatively new development, predominantly confined to the last two decades. Sometimes the dispute is over ownership of land; more often it is over the level of wages paid to Untouchables for working the land. This issue in a sense brings

the Untouchables into conformity with the rest of the agrarian population. For rural India as a whole, land has been the predominant issue in
dispute for the whole of the modern period. Throughout both the British
and post-Independence periods, for example, the criminal jurisdiction
has been dominated by incidents that arise from underlying disputes over
land between individual farmers. Thus land disputes are the most
common cause of assaults (including murder) and allegations of theft
(deriving from disputed ownership of crops) (Mendelsohn 1981: 837–8).
But such disputes almost never involved Untouchables, who were by-
standers to conflicts between caste Hindus or other landholders in the
countryside. Untouchables, after all, were generally landless.

The change has taken place in the post-Independence period, indeed
over the last two decades. In a subsequent chapter we will discuss the most
telling failure of post-Independence policy affecting the Untouchables,
viz. the failure of so-called land reform to deliver land to the tiller. This
failure of policy has entailed an absence of any large-scale transfer of land
ownership across the country from landed to landless people, and by far
the most numerous single grouping of the landless is the Untouchables. At
the same time, the Government of India has been consistently committed
at the rhetorical and to some extent behavioural level to redistributive
policies (most notably, the scheme of compensatory discrimination for
Scheduled Castes and Tribes). And there has continued to be some
emphasis on redistribution of land. This reached its most recent peak in
Indira Gandhi's Emergency of 1975–7, during which there was some little
redistribution of land accomplished even in States where none had been
done previously – Bihar, for one. The continual rhetorical and occasionally behavioural commitment to land reform has had a marked effect on
the consciousness of landless people – they have come to believe that they
are entitled to land which is surplus to 'ceiling' levels fixed by the State
governments. Similarly, they are now ready to claim plots of land which
have for one reason or another reverted to the ownership of the state.

As part of a whole regime of progressive labour regulation, the Union
and State governments have also enacted minimum wages legislation.
This legislation is conspicuous for its non-implementation, but it too has
brought about changes in consciousness and is the focus of widespread
agitation for enforcement. In the agrarian sphere, the call for enforcement
of statutory minimum wages legislation is properly conceived as an aspect
of the wider campaign for land reform. If the fruits of land are spread
more evenly among those who are conceded to have a legitimate interest
in it, then a measure of (admittedly non-radical) reform has been accomplished. Together, the claims for land and higher wages have provoked
major agrarian confrontations in many parts of India. Some of the most

severe conflicts have been in Bihar, and we will concentrate on this State for a more detailed discussion of the matter.

The case of Bihar

Bihar is the second largest State in India, with a population of over 86 million in the 1991 Census. It is also one of the poorest and least developed States, despite the fertility of its land and its concentration of mineral resources. In the 1991 Census Bihar's literacy level of under 39 per cent was the lowest of all the States of India. The contemporary political character of Bihar has taken shape in the context of rapidly changing social relations and an economy that is barely growing. Nowadays Bihar gives the impression of being racked by social warfare which is variously characterised as caste conflict, class conflict or violence fomented by Naxalites (revolutionary communists). We need to try to sort out the character of the conflict in order to understand the contemporary condition of Untouchables in Bihar.

With some simplification, it is possible to think of Bihari society as composed of three strata defined according to both caste and class criteria. The top stratum is composed of Brahmins, Rajputs and Bhumihars – all 'twice-born' (high) castes which have historically controlled the land and been by far the wealthiest communities in the region. A fourth caste, the Kayasthas, also became part of this upper stratum during the British period, though they may not be strictly 'twice-born' and certainly did not acquire the same degree of landed property as the other castes. This upper stratum supplied the overwhelming preponderance of *zamindars* (revenue intermediaries) under the Permanent Settlement, which so shaped the economic life of the province for a century-and-a-half. Most of these people have never worked the land by their own hand: indeed for Brahmins, to put hand to plough is a positive sin. Rather, they managed the farming of 'their' land through a variety of arrangements. Sometimes they had tenants, some of whom (the so-called occupancy tenants) had legally protected tenure under the Permanent Settlement. Often, particularly in North Bihar, land was given out to *bataidars* or sharecroppers. In other instances, these high-caste zamindars operated the land with paid labour of a continuing or daily nature. The size of holdings varied greatly among this upper stratum of Bihari society, and there was a general divide between the regions north and south of the Ganges: the northern Districts contained zamindaris of far greater size than the holdings south of the river in central Bihar. (There is a further region to the south which is the so-called tribal belt; this region is not discussed here.)

The middle stratum of Bihari society is mainly composed of 'backward' or peasant castes, the most numerous of which are Yadavs (or Ahirs), Kurmis and Koiris. Characteristically but far from universally, these people are now peasant proprietors with holdings which in Indian terms are classifiable as small-to-medium. During the British period these farmers were usually the tenants of high-caste zamindars. In terms of population, this is the largest grouping within Bihari society.

At the bottom are the landless people, the largest component of which is some 14 million Untouchables. Not all Untouchables are landless, and not all the landless are Untouchables. Many among the 'backward' castes of Bihar are also landless, particularly among what are known as the 'backward backwards': the boating and fishing community of Mallahas, for example, is desperately poor and probably quite as landless as the Untouchables.[3] Perhaps the least homogenous caste is the Yadavs, apparently the largest caste of the State. The Yadavs are usually and quite reasonably characterised as a core element of the rising middle castes of Bihari society, but many Yadavs are in fact poor and landless labourers.

In very broad terms, the great agrarian winner of the post-Independence era has been the middle stratum. The abolition of the zamindari system whereby relations between tenants and the state were mediated by a landlord class, served to convert a great many of this stratum into a newly independent peasantry. They have not merely contrived to hold onto their land but have greatly expanded their total holdings through purchases from the upper stratum. There are no figures available on the extent of this redistribution through the marketplace, but it has clearly been a major phenomenon over the last several decades. The corollary is that the upper castes' grip on the countryside has been slipping. They have been forced to sell agricultural land for family expenses such as dowry, the higher education of their sons and even daughters, and the construction of urban houses as they progressively realign their ambitions in an urban direction. Relations between the upper and middle strata have become increasingly tense as the peasant castes grow in self-confidence and are concerned to challenge their hereditary masters in every area of economic, social and political life. The Yadavs have been at the very centre of this conflict; their relations with the Bhumihars, who are the predominant upper caste south of the Ganges, have been particularly embittered. A measure of the progress made by the Yadavs since Independence is Lalloo Prasad Yadav's occupancy of the Chief Minister's position from 1991 to 1997.

[3] This became apparent to us during a field trip to East Champaran District in 1980. The Mallahas of this District were demonstrably among the poorest of Indians. We visited households in which there were simply no possessions at all – no items of a personal or a domestic nature.

For the first thirty years after Independence it was not possible to think of the bottom stratum of Bihari society as a political actor in any sense comparable with the other two broad groupings. Over the last twenty years this situation has changed. There is still no question of treating the bottom stratum as a serious pretender to power in the State. But to the surprise of almost all observers, this stratum – and the Untouchables in particular – have begun to assert themselves with considerable political force. The violence they have both suffered and dealt out since the late seventies can now be seen as predominantly political violence.

A table produced by the Commissioner for Scheduled Castes and Scheduled Tribes in the Report for 1979–81 shows that Bihar was not among the twelve States with the highest number of 'Harijan atrocities' between 1967 and 1974. Suddenly in that year Bihar made its first appearance as the sixth worst case; in 1974 it was ranked fourth, and then third for the four years from 1976 to 1979. In subsequent years Bihar has remained near the top of the table. But by the Commissioner's own admissions such figures are unreliable. Conceivably, the reporting regime in Bihar improved suddenly in the mid-seventies to reveal the dimensions of a problem that had existed previously. But it is also likely that as the political situation in Bihar became more embattled and particularly as Untouchables began to resist as never before, their new situation began to be reflected in the statistics on violence.

On one reading of what has been happening to the Untouchables, they have been sucked into the vortex of violent and utterly primordial caste-ism that is seen to have overtaken Bihar. In this account, each of the major Untouchable castes – the three largest are the Chamars, the Dusadhs and the Musahars – is taken to be acting in a corporate manner that imitates the behaviour of the other castes in the State. Evidence for this perspective is quite easy to find. There can be no doubt that there is a high degree of group political consciousness among individual castes in Bihar, including Untouchable castes, and that if possible they tend to act in ways calculated to advance their common good. Thus one of the more sinister developments of recent years is the mushrooming of *Senas* or armies as the enforcers of caste interest in the increasingly bloody Bihari country-side. So there is the *Bhoomi Sena* as the armed force of the Kurmis, the *Lorik Sena* as an arm of the Yadavs, the *Brahmarshi Sena* of the Bhumihars, and so on. Although there is no Dusadh or Chamar Sena, there is the *Lal Sena* (Red Army) organised by Naxalite revolutionaries and dedicated to and partly composed of Untouchables. So the proposition is sometimes put that radical political activity of Untouchables is really only Bihari caste politics in a different guise.

Clearly there is some truth in the account of Bihar as an atavistic war between the castes, but in the end this image distorts more than it illuminates. There is a great deal of irrationality in Bihar, and sometimes a frightening lack of ordinary social cooperativeness between the castes. But there is also more rational calculation than may sometimes appear, and a powerful class as well as caste logic in Bihari behaviour. This is our basis for dividing Bihari society into the three broad strata described above. So the primary political struggle since Independence has been between those castes which have dominated Bihar for centuries and the castes which have been immediately inferior to them in economic and social terms. This is a class struggle as much as it is a struggle between castes. Although there is great traditional rivalry between the upper castes of Bihar, and an early post-Independence history of intense competition between them within Congress, there is not the edge of bitterness or violence that often characterises relations between, say, the Bhumihars of the upper stratum and the Yadavs of the middle. The latter struggle is a complex of status, class and cultural antagonisms fed by the weight of history.

In the case of the castes which lie in the bottom stratum of Bihari society, particularly the Untouchables, they too are acting out of a class as well as a caste logic. So their enemies are far from constant in terms of caste identity: Untouchables have violently clashed with Kurmis and Yadavs from the middle stratum, and Bhumihars, Rajputs and Brahmins from the upper stratum. The key characteristic of their opponents has not been caste identity but rather land control: in the particular region where violent conflict has become endemic, Untouchables have tended to come into conflict with those castes which happen to control the land. Nor is this a merely Bihari phenomenon: throughout India there have been reports of Untouchables coming into conflict with newly rising peasant communities, rather than simply their traditional exploiters from upper castes. The focus on land control rather than caste identity helps explain how it is possible that (landowning and exploitative) Yadavs can be the bitter enemies of Untouchables in one situation, whereas (poor and landless) Yadavs can fight beside Untouchables elsewhere. Sometimes caste feeling works to weld together Yadavs of different class positions, but often it does not.

There is at least one other general explanation which competes with the idea of Bihari casteism to account for the aggressive grassroots political action in Bihar south of the Ganges. In this account the violent activity around the particular issues of land and social respect is part of a broader insurrectionary movement systematically organised by professional revolutionaries and calculated to appeal to Untouchables and various backward class elements. This is a view that gained much credence in official and police circles in both Patna and New Delhi, particularly during the 1970s and early 1980s. But in a variant form it is sometimes the view of the revolutionaries themselves (Anon. 1986). Again, the view has considerable plausibility. The most striking piece of evidence in its favour is that political action taken by Untouchables and other radical backward caste groups against harsh landlords is heavily concentrated in those Districts south of the Ganges where revolutionary parties have invested their major organisational efforts. Although arguments of a cultural, structural and historical nature are frequently advanced to account for the disparity in radical action and overall violence between north and south Bihar, the most plausible explanation is that there has simply been more Naxalite organisation south of the Ganges than to the north.

In order to understand more fully what has been happening in south Bihar, something of the wider context needs to be sketched in. First, the appearance of the so-called Naxalites should be explained. The name comes from an insurrectionary movement beginning in 1967 around the small town of Naxalbari in West Bengal. Inspired by the strategies of Mao Tse-tung as interpreted by veteran communist Charu Mazumadar, a band of mostly upper-caste young Bengalis sought to create a revolutionary base in the countryside of West Bengal. The movement in Naxalbari was brutally suppressed within several months and Charu Mazumdar died in custody in 1972 (Banerjee 1980: 422). Thereafter the revolutionary mantle was monopolised in Bengal by the two mainstream communist parties. But Mazumdar's Communist Party of India (Marxist-Leninist) or CPI(ML) was not altogether killed in Naxalbari. Its spirit and perhaps a little of its organisation too was resurrected in Bihar. The first site of Naxalite organisation in Bihar was in Bhojpur District (Mukherjee and Yadav 1980: 7; Das 1983: 245–54). From the beginning Naxalism in Bihar was marked by the participation of leaders from a number of backward and Untouchable castes, and was closely centred on the situation of Untouchables. The height of the insurrectionary activities in Bhojpur was reached in 1975, when Indira Gandhi imposed her State of Emergency. 'Operation Thunder', a police operation of the State government during the Emergency, appears to have struck a decisive blow against Naxalite activities in Bhojpur (Frankel 1989: 120). But even before then the movement had spilled over into adjoining Districts.

But to concede the crucial role played by Naxalite revolutionaries in the continuing struggle over economic and social issues in south Bihar is not to suggest that there is anything like a revolutionary situation in that area. A better characterisation is that a small band of revolutionary activists has been able to organise a still relatively small number of active supporters in south Bihar. But to an extent that was not generally predicted, the

Naxalites have also contrived over a period now of many years to influence – or, at the very least, not to alienate – mainstream opinion among Untouchables and other landless people. The Naxalites began with direct and sometimes violent action – an early Naxalite slogan was that the appropriate response to oppressive landlords was *che inch chote kardenge* (literally translated, to lower them by six inches – by beheading). But already in 1982 the Indian People's Front (IPF) had been set up as an above-ground organisation designed to attract mass support, and in the late eighties and early nineties this organisation contested State and national elections (Hauser 1993: 351) and even published a quite sophisticated book in 1986 setting their movement in context (*Report from the Flaming Fields of Bihar*). The IPF went so far as to win a seat in the Parliamentary election of 1989, as well as a number of State seats. In short, the Naxalites have proceeded from the politics of insurrection to a predominantly, though not exclusively, lawful approach to political action.

The State of Emergency was a major factor in the emergence of the violent politics of contemporary Bihar. This period was notable not merely for right-wing authoritarianism exemplified by Operation Thunder, but also a left authoritarianism in the form of efforts to bring about land reform. (There were other anti-poverty and social reform measures that were part of the '20 Point Programme'of the Emergency, including the ending of bonded labour – a matter which mostly affected Untouchables and tribals.) Prior to the Emergency in Bihar, not a single acre of land had been resumed and redistributed to the landless under the existing land ceiling legislation. Under strict instructions from New Delhi, some 225,000 acres were redistributed during the Emergency. Of course, this figure was pitiful relative to the overall need for redistribution 'to the tiller'. Even worse, in the ensuing years most of this land was clawed back by the owners through court action. Nonetheless, for the first time land was changing hands at the behest of the state, and it was mainly Untouchables who were the beneficiaries. Such action contributed to a long-term heightening of consciousness among Untouchables that their lot in life was not merely to accept their own landlessness.

Another precipitating factor in the new violence involving Untouchables was the outcome of the election at the end of the Emergency in 1977. Karpoori Thakur's Janata Government was the first non-Congress government elected in Bihar, and also the first to be led by a person from the 'backward' castes (though the Untouchable Bhole Paswan Shastri had had short periods as Chief Minister in Congress governments). Thakur was from the small and ritually low barber caste, and he was a long-time socialist by conviction and career. His most decisive act as Chief Minister was to extend the system of reservation of government jobs so as to include not merely the Scheduled Castes and Tribes but also 'backwards'. This policy was explosive in the already strained relations between the upper and middle strata of Bihari society. Suddenly in 1978 it seemed that Bihar was utterly split between 'backwards' and 'forwards' – with the Untouchables standing uneasily beside this divide, since they were already beneficiaries of reservation and therefore had nothing to gain from the policy change. The conflicts in Bihar in the late seventies were a perfect foretaste of the reaction engendered by the V. P. Singh Government when it sought to enact the same policy at the Centre in 1990.

The period of Karpoori Thakur's Chief Ministership from 1977 to 1980 marked the beginning of a major upsurge in the number of 'Harijan atrocities' reported from Bihar. There remains doubt as to the extent to which Thakur's own actions precipitated the upsurge. Thus part of the explanation for the increased violence at this time was that the legacy of the Emergency was being contested in relation to land that had been at least notionally reassigned by the State to Untouchables and other land-less people. Sometimes the land so assigned was 'wasteland' used as a common grazing resource for the village as a whole. On other occasions the land had been resumed from individual landlords as being surplus to the enacted ceiling on land ownership. In both situations, typically the new assignment of land was bitterly resented and was the direct cause of many violent clashes between dominant landholding communities and Untouchables. The first notorious 'Harijan atrocity' of this kind was Belchi, which occurred in May 1977 – after the ending of the Emergency but before the election which delivered power to Karpoori Thakur.

Karpoori Thakur could become indignant at suggestions that he himself should bear any responsibility for violence against Untouchables – indeed, he denied the factual premise of such increase. He was able to point to a long record of support for Harijans, as they continue to be called in Bihar, and to his particular and highly controversial articulation of the desirability that Harijans arm themselves in order to fight their oppressors in the countryside (Interview: May 10 1985). But this very call was one of the factors that raised the temperature of politics in Bihar, and so may have further contributed to the phenomenon he was seeking to curb. Above all, Karpoori Thakur's regime provided the opportunity for radical groups to organise the countryside in a way that had been impossi-ble during the Emergency. It was during his time that the Naxalites first made their strong presence felt outside their original Bihari base in Bhojpur District.

Although we have characterised the rising level of violence surrounding Untouchables in Bihar as a consequence of increased assertiveness of the

Untouchables themselves, far more often than not it is they who have been the major victims of the violence. True, in the early period there were 'executions' of oppressive landlords undertaken by the Naxalites – and on some occasions the 'executioners' may have been Untouchable members of the underground organisation that ordered the killing. And more generally, Bihari Untouchables have learnt to dispense as well as suffer violence – country guns made from bicycle pumps have become almost a motif of Untouchable resistance. But inevitably Untouchables have literally and figuratively been outgunned. They have had to contend not merely with the forces of the village but also with the might of the state, particularly in the form of the police. This can be seen in a number of major Harijan atrocities since the late 1970s.

Pipra

The Pipra event was the third large-scale massacre of Untouchables in Bihar carried out by Kurmis in a period of two-and-a-half years: the earlier ones were in Belchi in 1977, and Bishrampur in 1978 (A. N. Sinha Institute nd: 9). We have singled out this rather than any of the other events simply because there is a credible published account of the background to the event. Pipra is a village in Punpun Division of Patna District, and on the night of 25/26 February 1980 four men, four women, three boys and three girls from two families of the Chamar community were shot dead by a mob of some five hundred people apparently organised by a couple of Kurmi landlords. The bodies were set on fire, along with houses and cattle in the Chamar hamlet some 100 metres from the main village occupied by the caste Hindus; the pall of smoke could be seen for many miles. When the police van arrived on the scene at about 4 am, the mob vanished.

There was a considerable history of conflict which led to this massacre. The fundamental dispute was over land, but these bad relations were ramified by other serious differences. Conflict over land goes back to partition, at which time much of the land of Pipra was owned by Muslims. It seems that during the communal clashes of 1947 the Chamars had given protection to some Muslims, and their story is that they were rewarded with the gift of 4 bighas of land when the Muslims left the village. This land has been the subject of dispute ever since. In the subsequent period and through mechanisms that are not clear, the Kurmis have succeeded to virtually all other lands under the village: the Chamars have tiny plots of land other than the land in dispute. The Kurmis' status has changed from being predominantly labourers on lands owned by the Muslim landlords to employers of labour on their own land (A. N. Sinha

Institute nd: 8–9). As to the disputed land, particular Kurmis have continuously asserted that they bought it from the departing Muslims. The dispute has been promoted in the courts, including the High Court of Bihar, for many years. Allegedly unlawfully, the disputed land had been occupied by Bhola Singh (since murdered) with the help of other Kurmis of the village.

Meanwhile, there was a long-standing sexual scandal. Taramani, a divorced Chamar woman, had entered into a long-term liaison with Radhika Singh, one of the Kurmi landowners of Pipra. The Chamars were very angry about this affair, which they took to be a slur on their honour. Some three months before the massacre, Taramani had finally been forced out of Pipra – apparently to the fury of Radhika Singh (A. N. Sinha Institute: nd 26).

The village disputes were fed by the surrounding political conflict general to Punpun Division, a centre of Naxalite activities in Bihar both before and after the Pipra massacre. This conflict had included land grab movements, campaigns for social respect and, above all, the push for payment of statutory minimum wages. There had been a strike over the wages issue in Pipra followed by permanent withdrawal of labour by many of the Chamars: at the time of the massacre there were only a few labourers left working for the Kurmis of the village. The Chamars of Pipra are said to have had contact and considerable sympathy with the Naxalite movement.

The most potent factor which precipitated the massacre was the murder of two prominent Kurmi landlords of nearby villages in December 1979 and January 1980. Bhola Singh was Chairman and Deonandan Singh Treasurer of the Kisan Suraksha Sangh, an organisation of peasant caste landholders established to promote their common interest in the conflictual politics of Punpun Division. Given this history of conflict, the Kurmis of Pipra suspected that it was the Chamars of their village who had committed the murder of at least Bhola Singh; he had been an employer of Untouchable labour in Pipra. Indeed the police account was that the massacre was revenge for the death of the landlords. Between the time of the murder of the Kurmis and the mass murder of the Chamars there was continuing conflict in the form of theft of standing crops in fields owned by the Kurmis.

It is possible but by no means certain on the public evidence that the Chamars of Pipra killed the two Kurmi landlords. But the question of just who performed the murders is not strictly pertinent here. It is perceptions that matter, and clearly the Kurmis of Pipra believed that the deaths and all the other aggravation they were suffering were the responsibility of the Chamars of Pipra. Assuming that revenge and a political show of strength were the dominant motives of the Kurmis, what again impresses an observer is the planning of the affair and its scale. The event was clearly premeditated and carefully organised so as to mass together 500 Kurmis from a number of villages (A. N. Sinha Institute nd: 29). Given such organisation, it is difficult to conceive that the killing of women and children was simply the action of a mob that ran out of control. There may not have been a concrete ambition to kill, say, children, but it must have been the case that ordinary feelings of restraint had been set aside before the attack began. The killing of obviously innocent parties then follows as a matter of course. Perhaps it is instructive to note that the shoe is almost never on the other foot – we have come across no comparable instance of heedless massacre done by, rather than to, Untouchables.

Arwal

The massacre at Arwal in Jehanabad District, 19 April 1986, was an affair of a different character. Twenty-one Untouchables were shot dead by armed police. The venue was a confined space next to a library, and the savagery and one-sidedness of the affair have given rise to comparisons with the Jallianwallabagh massacre – one of the most potent symbols of the oppressiveness of British rule in India. In this case the underlying issue was a dispute between two Untouchable parties over proprietorship of certain land in a village close to the township of Arwal. This land is said to have originally been waste land but proprietorship had been assigned by officials to one Rameshwar Rajak; he is apparently a relatively prosperous person from an unnamed Untouchable caste (People's Union for Civil Liberties 1986: 2). The land had been simultaneously claimed by nine poorer Untouchable families whose houses adjoined the area. In ways that are far from clear, this dispute had been transformed into a major local issue. The Mazdoor Kisan Sangram Samiti (MKSS) – one of several Naxalite groups operating in the region – had become involved, and on 19 April it organised a rally variously estimated in size at between 500 and 800 persons. It seems that the crowd was very largely composed of Untouchables, some of them women and children.

The procession of protesters first demolished the mud wall built by Rameshwar to enclose the disputed land, and then they made their way to a field in front of the local library. This field borders the police station, and there are only two paths out of the field if one is not to trespass into the police precinct (PUCL nd: 3). A large contingent of police and armed constabulary, including Gurkhas, had been assembled to confront the gathering organised by the MKSS. Naturally, the police and the protesters' versions of what happened differ. The police allege provocation, but the investigating team from the People's Union for Civil Liberties (PUCL) – a voluntary civil liberties organisation – found no evidence of this. These investigators could find no documentation of any injuries suffered by the police. The police confiscated several country-made fire-arms, but there was said to be no evidence that they were used in the affair. The meeting was judged to have been peaceful, 'though strong worded speeches might have been delivered' (PUCL nd: 14). The PUCL team concluded that 'it is not believable that the crowd holding a few country made pistols and a riketty (sic) rifle will indulge in the sheer madness and open fire on police armed with rifles and stenguns' (PUCL nd: 13).

Despite the peaceful, if angry, nature of the assembly, the police are said to have fired fifty-three rounds of bullets, killing twenty-one persons. The PUCL team found that:

the general hostility of the police towards the so called Naxalites or Extremists and their hurt ego in their failure to protect the compound wall of Rameshwar Rajak were the main inspiring factors for the police to engage in inhuman and barbaric killing of the people. (PUCL nd: 14)

A subsequent and more authoritative Report of the Indian People's Human Rights Tribunal (including two former State Chief Justices) said:

This brutal and indiscriminate firing was mainly the result of state guidelines issued on April 6, 1986 for the police to treat the agitations arising out of the imbalanced economical structure of society as a purely 'law and order' problem and to ensure more positive and forward policing. (IPHRT 1987: 79–80, quoted in Hauser 1993: 345)

The Arwal tragedy is a specially dramatic case of violent repression of protesters organised under the banner of a proscribed Naxalite organisation. But as the two Reports cited above make clear, it is really a story of the repression of poor people, mainly Untouchables, by the forces of the state. It is only the somewhat hysterical identification of ordinary villagers as Naxalite extremists that allows such a massacre to take place. The Untouchables at Arwal were flocking to the banner of one of the radical organisations which have gained the confidence of poor people, in the face of the manifest failure of mainstream parties to further their interests or protect them. Like the above Reports, we too find incredible the idea that the assembly that day was of Naxalite extremists. The assembly had been organised by the MKSS, which can, not unreasonably, be called 'Naxalite'. But clearly most of the participants were ordinary poor people trying to protest what they saw to be an injustice. Perhaps it might be argued that they were being used to stage-manage a political event, but they were clearly far from a dangerous revolutionary rabble that needed to be brutally fired upon.

The Arwal massacre is scarcely a typical event even for Bihar, but nor is it to be cast aside as an aberration. It is a particularly dramatic example of the way in which the state is routinely, if not universally, arraigned against those at the bottom of Indian society. The police, in particular, are very often the oppressors rather than protectors of poor people. What is different about this particular case is that the police were closely following government orders to confront with severity the forces of 'extremism' in the region. Ordinarily police oppression of the poor arises not so directly from official and public policy but from the interaction of local power and public administration at the local and regional levels. Clearly Arwal is not a case of Untouchables being persecuted *qua* Untouchables – after all, the land dispute that provoked the assembly was between two parties of Untouchables. But the poverty of Untouchables is an integral part of their makeup as a people, so it matters little whether they are being oppressed by police as Untouchables or merely as poor people trying to find a political path denied them by the regular parties. As Karpoori Thakur said in what turned out to be the last interview of his life, what shocked him most about contemporary Bihar was the extent to which the state had become the positive enemy of the people (Mendelsohn 1988).

Pipra and Arwal are, then, two sides of the one coin. They represent both civil power and the power of the state arraigned against Untouchables asserting their rights. It is impossible to judge the merits of the land disputes that figured in these two particular conflicts, but we can say that Untouchables have generally been fighting for what is theirs by clear moral and legal right. This is clearly true of their pursuit of 'social respect' and the receipt of wage levels prescribed in the minimum wages legislation. But in the present condition of society in Bihar, such demands provoke violent resistance. Pipra may be one of the worst examples of such violence, but it remains an accurate pointer to what is happening on almost a daily basis in south Bihar.

Any assessment of the gains to have been made by Untouchable resistance in Bihar is problematic. In the matter of wage rates in Bihar, Government of India figures suggest that these have risen over the last two decades; indeed, they have risen considerably more than productivity (Jose 1988: Table 13). But even if these figures are reliable, there is currently too little evidence to attribute the rise to the political activity we have been describing. Wage rates for agricultural labour are highly variable as between the various States of India (Jose 1988: A-49; see below, chapter 5). There is some correlation between labour productivity and wages, such that the highest wage rates are in the most productive States of Punjab and Haryana. But the less productive State of Kerala enjoys wage rates (as opposed to income) not much inferior to those of Punjab and Haryana, and the usual explanation is couched in terms of more effective labour organisation and the intervention of Governments sympathetic to rural labour (Jose 1988: Table 6B). It is possible that in Bihar too, and despite a hostile government, wage rates for labourers have been rising in response to pressure exerted by the labourers. But Bihar is not the only State in which official figures show wage rises to have considerably outstripped productivity gains, so any such conclusion would need to be sustained by a great deal of empirical work.

In any case, there is real doubt as to the accuracy of available figures on wage rates. One prominent observer of Bihar reported the results of an emprical study of a number of villages thus:

There are large variations in wage rates (wage received per person-day) from village to village, from one season to another and even from person to person. The mode of payment involves cash, grains, land, meals, breakfast and any combination of these. In 12 villages there were as many as 71 types of such wages per person-day. When these were converted to money values using prices of grains prevailing in different villages of the sample, there were 210 wage rates. (Prasad 1987: 849)

Our own observations bear out this view. We were able to get a detailed account of wages in one particular village of what is now Jehanabad District, one of the regions most convulsed by political conflict. The visit was in May 1984 and there had been a strike (lasting a mere one day) by labourers of the village earlier that year. Because this action followed many strikes in surrounding villages, employers quickly conceded some ground to the labourers. But the concrete outcome of the strike was equivocal. Apparently the major gain was that the going rate for casual daily labour rose from 1 kg of grain plus the supply of breakfast of 250 grams weight and a main meal of 500 grams (a total of 1.75 kg) to a figure of 1.5 kg of grain plus the two meals (a total of 2.25 kg). At the same time the amount of land given for cultivation to tied labourers (as opposed to 'free' labourers who are not attached to a particular family for a fixed period) was reduced: this was to offset a reduction in the number of days of unpaid labour extracted from tied labourers, and was connected to technological change surrounding the introduction of a winter crop. At the time of our visit to the village very few of the employers were actually paying the new rate. No employer was paying enhanced wages to tied as opposed to free labour – a large proportion of the workforce. And even in the case of free labourers, apparently few of them were benefiting from the enhanced rate. One of our informants (an academic from the dominant Bhumihar community) even doubted whether payment of the new rates would actually represent an advance for the labourers, given the complexity of the whole employment package.

This short discussion on wage rates is designed simply to impart a sense of how difficult it is to measure payment to agricultural labourers, and therefore to plot improvements in wages and overall income. Only after this is achieved with some accuracy will it be possible to address seriously the question of causes for any increases.

But even without evidence of significant redistribution of the fruits of agriculture, the new political movements of south Bihar clearly represent a major social turning point. What stands out again and again is the surprising boldness of the Untouchables. The tribals have long had a reputation for physical resistance to their *diku* or outsider oppressors (Guha 1983: 64–5), but the Untouchables had seemingly been more downtrodden and fearful in their landlessness. This has now changed once-and-for all, at least in 'the Naxalite affected belt'. The intensity and longevity of the struggle has surprised everyone; it has now been proceeding for some two decades, and has assumed the status of a constantly simmering local insurrection. This phenomenon does not seem to fit perceptions about the quiescence and sheer backwardness of Untouchables in this abjectly poor region. To some the symbol of the insurrection has become the Musahars, the most downtrodden of all Untouchables castes in Bihar: their previous identity in the Bihari mind was an association with the field rats they catch and eat as a delicacy during the rainy season. The Musahars have been at the very centre of Untouchable resistance.

Of course, it is far from true that all Untouchables even in the half-dozen 'disturbed' Districts are militant. Old patterns of deference persist: the Chamar leader of the strike in the Jehanabad village described above recounted his story while squatting on the ground in front of a charpai on which one of us and a high-caste person sat. If the Chamar had asserted a right to sit next to us on the charpai, no doubt it would have been bitterly resented by high-caste people. But it is also significant that the Chamar leader was a middle-aged man – young men find such enforced deference increasingly irksome. Nor should traditional patterns of outward deference deflect an appreciation of the sea-change in outlook even among older Untouchables throughout India. What was clearly more significant in this particular situation was the militancy of the Chamar strike leader – his history of action and his declarations about future action – rather than his adherence to old forms of physical deference.

In short, the positive side to the unrest and violence in Bihar is its rootedness in the more assertive stance of Untouchables. Since Untouchable assertiveness is bound to provoke resentment and opposition on the part of the privileged classes, tension and even some violence is no doubt to be expected. But equally, it has to be recognised that the Untouchables continue to be predominantly the victims of the violence in which they are parties. Any glorification of the violence – suggested, for example, in the revolutionary romanticism of the Indian People's Front's book title, *Report from the Flaming Fields of Bihar* – is shallow. And always the painful modesty of the claims advanced by and on behalf of Untouchables needs to be recalled, half a century after Indian Independence.

Karnataka

There is sometimes a tendency to see Bihar – or perhaps Bihar plus eastern Uttar Pradesh – as a case by itself. The work of scholars like Pradhan Prasad has fed this tendency, with his insistence that Bihar is mired in a state of 'semi-feudalism' as against the capitalist relations that mark many other regions of rural India (Prasad 1987: 852). We will return to the theme of regional comparison in chapter 5, but for the moment we can observe that although the cumulative situation in Bihar and nearby districts is uniquely conflictual many aspects of the embattled circumstances of Bihari Untouchables are present throughout India. A couple of examples taken from Karnataka are instructive on this issue. Karnataka is perhaps the best example of a 'moderate' Indian State. It is on the poorer end of the scale of States, though it has a significant high-tech industrial establishment in the city of Bangalore. The abjectness of poverty in Bihar or West Bengal or Uttar Pradesh is said not to be characteristic of Karnataka. It has had relatively progressive Congress and non-Congress governments which have had credible, if far from wholly successful, anti-poverty strategies. Karnataka does not have a national reputation for violence. But the following incidents show that there is serious violence involving Untouchables in Karnataka.

The two cases described here came to our attention during field-work in Karnataka. Only one of them can be said to have involved a 'Harijan atrocity', and even this was not a major case such as that of Pipra. The second case is one of avoidance of violence, but much can be learnt from the unfolding of this conflict too. In the first case the act of violence consisted in a group of Dalits (and a caste Hindu who was caught up in the affair) being forced to consume human faeces. The event took place in a village in Belgaum District during August 1987, and we examined it in January 1988 on the basis of reports and interviews with some of the participants in the village.[4]

There were a number of factors in the chain that led to this 'Harijan

---

[4] Interviews with Holeyas and the Lingayat *pradhan* in Bendegeri Village, Belgaum District, 14 January 1988.

atrocity'. The first factor was an election in 1987 for the statutory *pan-chayats* or local government bodies, which at the time were being clothed with much greater power to disburse development funds. The electoral system had also been recently changed to provide for reservation of seats for Scheduled Castes and Tribes and for women. In the village in question the three seats on the panchayat were all won by the Janata party against fierce opposition from a locally based peasant party. The position of pradhan or head of the panchayat was taken by a Lingayat, the most powerful caste in Karnataka, and the Scheduled Caste seat went to an Holeya (a large Untouchable caste). The unsuccessful candidate for pradhan was also from the dominant Lingayat caste, and this man was said to be the main organiser of the atrocity. One of the victims was the son of the successful Dalit candidate. Apparently the defeated Lingayat blamed the Holeyas for his defeat, and there had been many bitter words after the election.

A second destabilising factor was the Integrated Rural Development Program (IRDP). In the present case the successful Dalit in the election had received IRDP assistance to buy a milch buffalo. But the advent of the buffalo increased as well as reduced the Dalit's dependence on high-caste farmers. The new owners did not have sufficient agricultural land to feed the buffalo, so they were dependent on caste Hindus and the Lingayats in particular to allow them to cut green fodder from their fields. Presumably there were reciprocal arrangements whereby the fodder was paid for in labour.

On the day in question Subhash, son of the newly elected Dalit, had gone to the fields with three other Dalits and a Maratha (caste Hindu) friend to cut some fodder for the buffalo. Night was beginning to fall and it had started to rain. Out of prior agreement, mischief making or simple laziness – the version varies with the witness – they began to cut fodder from a field belonging to someone in the unsuccessful Lingayat candidate's family. The latter were furious and managed to capture the five young men and herd them to the chief accused's house. Along the way the Lingayats forced Subhash to pick up some human faeces that lay by the roadside and carry it in a piece of paper. When they got to the accused's house, Subhash and his friends were forced to eat the faeces. They had to comply for fear of death at the point of a scythe.

The victims told us that they wanted to commit suicide out of a sense of shame for what they had been forced to do. Feelings were greatly inflamed in the village – particularly among the Marathas, since one of their number had by chance been caught up in the affair – but no general violence had broken out. The incident had become a major issue throughout Karnataka, and the Dalit Sangharsh Samiti (the principal Dalit organisation in Karnataka) organised a number of rallies demanding government action against the culprits.[5] In late January the latter were officially expelled from the village pending charges being heard in a court.

This incident is instructive on a number of counts. Of course, the grotesque action was quite out of proportion to any provocation caused by the fodder cutting. Even when the aggravated feelings following the election are taken into account, there is a gap in reconstructing causation. That gap cannot be filled, we believe, by more empirical material on the incident itself – there would always remain an empirical gap. The degrading incident can only be understood by reference to the outraged feelings of people such as these particular Lingayats at the rise of Untouchables in the village. How dare they own buffalo, contest and win elections and act against the interests of their moral superiors! Who do these people think they are?

There is a great deal of powerful anecdotal evidence to the effect that any rising prosperity of Untouchables is usually greeted with hostility from caste Hindus. Of course, social envy is scarcely an unusual emotion. What is significant about such feeling relative to Untouchables is that they remain a peculiarly vulnerable people and as such are more easily damaged and deterred from activities that promote their own welfare. We came across another situation in Belgaum District of Karnataka which exemplifies this. This is not a case of 'Harijan atrocity' but rather of the avoidance of any serious violence. But the sheer arduousness of such avoidance suggests the dimensions of the problem.

The conflict in this instance was between the dominant Jain landholders in a particular village and Holeya Untouchables: there were said to be 400–500 Jain families and 82 Holeya households, together with a number of other castes in smaller numbers. The problem presented itself to the outside world in October 1985, when the Holeyas staged a *dharna* or sit-in outside the office of the local *tehsildar* (a minor official). They said they were being oppressed in their village and wished to be relocated to a safer environment. When they declined to return to their village, the District Commissioner, the head official, had to be called in. In his own telling the Commissioner had a reluctance to intervene. He thought it could be the beginning of a movement which would present a major problem of public order; he did not wish to encourage this. If the situation did get out of hand because of his own sympathy with the Untouchables, a black mark would be placed against his name and his career might be permanently ruined. It would be far easier to get them to go home.

---

[5] Press handout by the State Convenor of the Karnataka Dalitha Sangharsha Samithi, Bangalore, nd (*c* 18 January 1988).

But despite these forebodings, the Commissioner felt he had to take seriously the Holeyas' claim that they could not be protected in the village. So he inspected the village and found the situation to be much as they had painted it. The Holeyas were living in miserable houses on a flood plain of the Krishna river – when it burst its banks, many of their houses were flooded. Their predominant occupation was that of labourers for the Jain landholders, whose major crop was sugar cane. Very slowly, the Holeyas were bettering their condition. Some of them had acquired a cow or two, and they were managing to sell a bit of milk to a nearby dairy. Five of the Holeyas were employed in the dairy, two of them as permanent employees earning 900 rupees a month. So their utter dependence on the Jains had slightly waned.

At the same time the Holeyas' acquisition of a few cows had set up a new dependence on the landholders for fodder. They had been permitted to crop some of the waste leaves of the sugar cane, but there had been minor skirmishes over this – the allegation was that they were cutting new leaves and therefore damaging the crop. One day a Holeya boy was driven off when he sought to cut fodder. Out of their new spirit of boldness, the Holeyas forced the Jains into a dialogue on the matter – after all, the Jains needed the Holeyas as much as the Holeyas needed the work. The rich Jains are said to have been greatly displeased at having to talk to the lowly Holeyas as if they were equals, and the result of the dialogue was not a happy one for the Holeyas. They were authorised to cut fodder for their animals but their daily wages were reduced from 10 to 8 rupees. This was the last straw for the Holeyas and led to their dharna before the authorities.

Since the Commissioner judged that the village situation was oppressive and intractable, he agreed to help the Holeyas relocate if they could find a suitable place. They were duly transported to a likely village, but within a short period of time were driven off as unwelcome. The Commissioner was finally able to settle them on part of a tract of some 450 acres which had been resumed under land reform legislation from the control of a temple. The land had been earmarked for a sugar factory but it was now judged that both uses could be accommodated. Our visit in 1988 showed the Holeyas to have been been successfully settled with decent housing, clean water and sufficient land to till.

Already the Holeyas' story has become something of a fable among Dalit activists in Karnataka. But as a fable it has no capacity to provide guidance in comparable struggles: the conjunction of a large tract of vacant land and an unusually dedicated District Officer will be rare indeed. The case is more instructive on the question of contemporary strains arising from the most modest of improvements in the condition of Untouchables, and on the particular nature of the stress points that are developing. In comparable cases of endemic conflict over wages, social exploitation and land use, there are more likely to be 'Harijan atrocities' than magnificent resolutions.

The riots over renaming Marathwada University

Later in this work (chapter 7) we will discuss the activities of the Mahar movement of Maharashtra in the era following Ambedkar's death. For the moment all we need say is that despite the movement's overall failure, from time to time a particular issue excites sufficient passion to mobilise large numbers of Mahars and to provoke violent backlash from caste Hindus. The event that provoked the greatest violence in recent times was the seemingly innocuous effort to change the name of 'Marathwada University' in the city of Aurangabad to 'Dr Babasaheb Ambedkar Marathwada University'. As the great figure of Untouchable history in the modern period, Ambedkar's inspirational status has been steadily growing throughout the period of Indian Independence. So on 26 July 1978 Sharad Pawar, Chief Minister of Maharashtra, responded to pressure from the Mahars in Ambedkar's own region and moved a resolution in the State Assembly renaming Marathwada University after the great man (Punalekar 1981: 62). Although the demand was longstanding and controversial, perhaps the Chief Minister thought that he was engaging in little more than parish pump politics. The announcement immediately provoked widespread uproar.

On the very day of the proclamation about 2,000 students from the University marched in protest. They demanded that shops in Aurangabad be closed. The next day violence increased, including the throwing of stones at various targets. On 28 July government cars and rail carriages were burnt, and huge mobs went on the rampage in a number of locations in the state. Despite signs at various times that the mobs were beginning to lose momentum, what happened was only a change of direction. For the first six days the violence was mainly directed against government institutions and property. From 1 August until about 6 August the Untouchables and particularly the Mahars became a major focus of the protesters. Only two Dalits are said to have been killed, but as many as 900 of their households were directly affected by the riots in their villages. For example, in one particular village fifty-five Dalit houses were burnt down; in another, it was forty-three houses; and in a third, forty houses. There was a dreadful orgy of burning and beating by caste Hindu villagers in five Districts of Maharashtra (Punalekar 1981: 72–81, 95, 124; RCSCST 1977–8: II, 129–32).

Punalekar's study is directed to just why such an outpouring of violence occurred in rural Maharashtra, as opposed to the intrinsically more understandable rioting of students directly affected by the symbolic name change. He pursued this object by asking questions in a number of villages affected by the riots. Punalekar reports a deep resentment fuelled by the growing independence, resoluteness and modest improvement in the economic and social circumstances of the Mahars. He quotes one Mahar to this effect: 'It is a common tendency among Savarnas [upper castes], rich or poor, to pull back the Mahars from any advancement. They will constantly wish to keep them backward and behind them' (129).

There have been strains caused by disputes over access to water, elections, the withdrawal of external social deference, the celebration of Ambedkar Jayanti (birthday), the practice of Buddhist rather than Hindu rituals, the relative prosperity of Mahars who have studied and entered professions such as medicine through the reservation system, and so on. The Mahars are compared unfavourably with the other large Untouchable caste of Maharashtra, the Mangs. A caste Hindu is quoted as saying: 'Look at the Mangs. How obedient and submissive they are to the villagers. They follow the traditions of our village society better. Their behaviour is also restrained. They are not defiant like the Mahars' (152).

Punalekar's explanation for the Marathwada riots, then, is that the tinder of resentment built up in the caste Hindu (predominantly middle-caste landowners') mind was ignited by the symbolic change of name to 'Dr Babasaheb Ambedkar Marathwada University'. All the resentment that had been building up for many years exploded in the Districts surrounding the University.

This explanation is consistent with the material commented on throughout this chapter. The theme of resentment at what we have called Untouchable *resistance* emerges strongly throughout India. Much of the violence suffered by Untouchables represents a bitter outpouring of cumulative resentment which is triggered by an event of relative significance. The violence of the reaction is usually incomprehensible without the larger context of anger at the changing outlook and behaviour of Untouchables. Significantly, all the cases we have discussed involve the reactions of caste Hindus, middle and high caste, rather than those of other communities. There is far less violence between Untouchables and Muslims.[6] This is partly a result of less involvement between the two

---

[6] There have been a number of serious incidents between Untouchables and Muslims in urban locations of Uttar Pradesh. The trigger for some of these incidents has been the keeping of pigs by particular Untouchable communities. And in other situations Untouchables may have been used by high-caste interests to engage in anti-Muslim action. But tensions between these two large populations in Uttar Pradesh have not been a central dynamic of social life there.

groupings: for example, there appear to be comparatively few Muslim landholders who employ Untouchable labourers. But this is not the whole of the story. There is a ritual dimension to the caste Hindu objection to the changing status of Untouchables.

Conclusion

Our aim in this chapter has not been to encourage an inference that the life of Untouchables is overwhelmingly disfigured by violence in contemporary India. This cannot be said about any region in India, and in some regions there is very little violence. Moreover, while violence is ugly and destructive, it can also be a measure of potentially progressive change in the circumstances or at least the outlook of Untouchables. But again, there can be no simple conclusion that the presence of violence is an indicator of either greater amenity or greater hope for Dalits. Thus there are few complaints of violence in Punjab and West Bengal, yet these are certainly not among the most oppressive social regimes. On a broader geographical basis, south India is far less productive of violence than the north; perhaps the generally more peaceable character of life in the south has something to do with this. But there are also differences within the south: Karnataka reports far more cases than do Tamil Nadu or Andhra Pradesh, possibly because of the influence of Maharashtra culture from the north. Kerala has few cases other than in two of its Districts, Palghat and Kasargod; these border Karnataka, and report a large number of violent incidents. The largest number of cases, both in absolute and per capita terms, is reported from Uttar Pradesh, Madhya Pradesh, Bihar, Gujarat, Maharashtra and Rajasthan (RSCST 1986–7: 229). In at least the first three States, land relations are at the heart of a large proportion of these clashes. But in all six States, dominant interests have fiercely defended the social and economic hierarchy in the face of demands put by an increasingly assertive Untouchable population. Why have West Bengal and Punjab escaped this violence? In the case of West Bengal, the comparatively relaxed attitude towards ritual pollution may have inhibited the development of violent resistance to (the highly moderate) land reforms which benefited many Untouchables in the 1970s and 1980s. The low incidence of violence in Punjab is not so easily accounted for, and probably owes little to the greater prosperity of that State in the recent past. It may be that explanations are to be found in the historical character of agrarian relations in Punjab, where there were few large estates and perhaps less capacity for Untouchables to claim land as legitimately theirs.

This brief consideration of regional variations must warn us against any easy conclusions about the larger causes of violence. But equally, it is utterly transparent that violence done to Untouchables is a serious dimension of social life in India today. From the analysis in this chapter it will be apparent that Untouchables are not suffering the violence as the eternal victims of caste Hindu society. The phenomenon is more complex than this. We have suggested that it is precisely the changing character of Untouchable consciousness that lies behind the increased incidence of violence that broke out from the late 1970s.

3   Religion, politics and the Untouchables from the nineteenth century to 1956

We have argued that the basis of much of the contemporary violence surrounding Untouchables is a conscious resistance to oppression. Consciousness of oppression may well be as old as the system of Untouchability itself, but the conditions for its development into militancy were put in place only during the period of direct British rule after the uprising of 1857. The present chapter sets out to explore this period, particularly the crucial quarter-century before Independence. This was the period dominated by Gandhi and Ambedkar. The narrative is a tangled skein of religion and politics: both Gandhi and Ambedkar ultimately committed themselves to an essentially religious solution to the task of attacking Untouchability. Gandhi was broadly consistent in his attitudes to the Untouchable question throughout his political life, though his commitment and tactics varied. The Untouchability of what Gandhi came to call 'Harijans' or 'People of God' was for him an historical corruption of Hinduism. It would be cured by caste Hindus purging themselves of the immorality that had insinuated itself into the pure body of Hinduism. Untouchables would join their fellow Hindus in a reborn equality.

Ambedkar, on the other hand, moved through several distinct phases in his thinking. One of his first campaigns in the late 1920s was an effort to force Hindu temples in Maharashtra to open their doors to Untouchables. But by the time Gandhi endorsed this strategy in the 1930s, Ambedkar had abandoned it. By then Ambedkar saw Hinduism as irredeemable, as having an essential and not merely an historical association with dehumanising discrimination. First he turned in his mind to Sikhism, but finally he marched millions of his Mahar followers into Buddhism shortly before his death in 1956. In opting for religious conversion Ambedkar had considered and explicitly rejected the materialist analysis of Indian society produced by Marxism. Personal attraction to spirituality had a lot to do with the political choices that Gandhi and Ambedkar made. It is also true that the intertwining of religious and political views is commonplace in India. But beyond this, it was the multi-stranded character of Untouchability that can be seen to have produced a movement of great complexity.

The struggle of Untouchables themselves, as opposed to the efforts of their well-wishers, can be seen to have moved through distinct periods over the last hundred years or so – though objectives dominant in one period have often lapped over into another. The first period of roughly sixty years after the assumption of power by the Crown in 1857 can broadly be characterised as the effort to be accepted on a more equal basis by Hindu society, and it can be divided into two phases. In the first phase Untouchables had no general critique of Hindu society, and were concerned with nothing more than gaining acceptability for themselves within that society. They saw their principal opportunity in the new forces that were at work in India, including the presence of Christianity, and their own willingness to abandon traditional occupations and habits regarded by respectable (read high-caste) Hindu society as dirty and morally objectionable. So different communities, the Mahars for example, gave up eating meat or at least the meat of pigs and cows (Robertson 1938: 33). Some leather-working communities abandoned their hereditary task of skinning fallen cattle. There was widespread emphasis on the need for frequent bathing in order to maintain physical congeniality – as if such matters were the real basis of their low status. Much of this self-improvement can be seen as an aspect of what Srinivas calls Sanskritisation or emulation of the high castes (Srinivas 1955:17), and during the first two decades of the twentieth century this was perhaps the most significant manifestation of social change affecting the Untouchables. But the time lines are not always so neatly defined. For at least one (mildly Untouchable) community, the Nadars or Shanars of Travancore and Tamil country, the process of self-improvement began as early as the first third of the nineteenth century. And on the other hand the movement for behavioural self-improvement is still at work among Untouchables today, though by now it is all too apparent that such reform can more readily enhance self-esteem than the opinion of others. During this first phase it is often difficult to tell whether self-reform is initiated from within the community itself or, as was perhaps more often the case, directly from Indian and European outsiders.

In this first period many Untouchables, particularly in south India, were converted to Christianity. Conversion was simply one response to the great ferment that began to affect Untouchables late in the century. The mass conversion movement began in the 1870s and was largely spent by the early years of the present century. Untouchable converts were not so much trying to opt out of the society they knew as identifying in the churches a way of improving their subordinate social and economic situation. The churches represented a store of instruction as to how Untouchables might better themselves, and during the famines of the 1870s they also proved to be a valuable source of material assistance. By then, as opposed to their earlier stance, the churches were beginning to take up issues of social justice in India. Nor were the beliefs of Christianity so alien as attention to monotheism might suggest. The story and iconography of Jesus proved easily assimilable to Indian forms of belief.

In the second phase of the first period, the 1920s, Untouchables were no longer content to try to win favour by curbing their own allegedly degenerate occupations and habits and allying themselves with foreign churches. Now, particularly in the west and south, they set out to force caste Hindus to accept them by opening up public temples to Untouchable worshippers. Meanwhile in Punjab Mangoo Ram established a new religion which he called *Ad Dharm*. What the Ad Dharmis had in common with the Ambedkarites was a rejection of any need to change their ways in order to deserve acceptance in respectable society. In this phase the break with the bhakti past was clear. Equality was no longer an abstraction but something to be realised at once, by force if necessary. But the vision of equality remained ritual and ethical rather than secular and materialist.

From the moment that Ambedkar gained an influential seat at the Round Table Conferences of 1930–1 and incurred the opposition of Gandhi, the Untouchable struggle was transformed. By then Ambedkar had abandoned temple entry as a fruitless and pointless exercise. He now rested his major hopes in the emerging world of representative politics that the British were prepared to encourage. But the 1930s turned out to be far from the period of political triumph that Ambedkar looked forward to. His own limitations as a political organiser contrasted with Gandhi's genius for political symbolism. Ambedkar and his followers were pushed to an increasingly radical margin. These political failures must be part of the explanation for Ambedkar's gathering determination to seek a religious way out. In 1935 Ambedkar declared at Yeola that he would not die a Hindu, though it took him another two decades to enact this intention.

Measured by conventional criteria, Ambedkar's act of religious conversion was a curiosity. Ambedkar was a worldly man, extraordinarily well educated in India, the US and Britain, and with a deep sympathy for the forms of western constitutionalism. He had recently discharged the historic office of principal draftsman of the Constitution of India. It is only by attending to the depth of his consciousness as an Untouchable that his act of religious conversion makes sense. His conversion was a profoundly political act as well as a personal affirmation of faith. From an external perspective it was also a desperate turning back to the kind of religious separatism that the Ad Dharm movement represented.

It is difficult to categorise the Untouchable struggle in the years after Ambedkar's victories of 1930–1 in a manner consistent with that for the earlier period. This is because Ambedkar's victories were so monumental that they have dwarfed all the later achievements. At the Round Table Conferences, and only marginally pegged back later in the Poona Pact of 1932, Ambedkar was the most prodigious political athlete. Solely by virtue of his athleticism the Untouchables vaulted to centre stage, a position they had never occupied before and have never occupied since. In an important sense the Untouchable struggle has for all the succeeding years been trying to catch up to where Ambedkar stood at that one political moment. What Ambedkar achieved in London was the promise of certain institutional machinery advantageous to the Untouchables. This promise was honoured, albeit with modifications. But neither Ambedkar nor any other Untouchable could convert this institutional advantage into an effective political constituency. Only Gandhi could later claim (at least on the basis of electoral results) to have an Untouchable following right across India. No wonder Ambedkar became so embittered.

Despite the difficulty of categorising the movement after 1932, and despite Ambedkar's own almost quixotic conversion to Buddhism in 1956, the struggle throughout this period can be seen as belonging solidly to the realm of secular politics and institutional advantage rather than to religious and social reform. This is what changed decisively in London in 1930–1, though not for Gandhi: his Harijan movement of the 1930s was already an old-fashioned attempt to bring about religious inclusion. In the 1930s and gathering pace after Independence, Untouchable leaders have sought a modern equality in economic and social life. They have lacked leadership and unity but have nonetheless become increasingly militant. Their struggle was progressively diverted in the 1970s and 1980s from representative institutions to fields and villages, though there are signs that the two are beginning to join together.

The Untouchables from the late nineteenth century to 1930

This section will discuss in some detail the events and movements involving or affecting the Untouchables during the period when their lives began to change significantly. This history is of shorter duration than that of some of the higher-status communities. A significant number of Brahmins, for example, responded to British rule by learning English as early as the first half of the nineteenth century, thereby positioning themselves to dominate the civil services. In eastern India Kayasthas followed the same path. But Untouchables and other socially inferior communities received no such early advantage at the hands of the Anglo-Indian state. The communities that experienced the most extensive involvement with the new British rulers of India underwent the earliest change in culture. For the Untouchables, the whole of the nineteenth century brought no more than marginal change to their circumstances or outlook. Right at the end of the century the beginnings of a new Untouchable leadership began to form in the west and south of the country, but it was not until the second decade of the present century that this leadership began to make any significant impact even within the Untouchable communities them-selves. And it was not until Gandhi's campaigns of the 1930s that the huge Untouchable population of the Hindi-speaking heartland – the present Uttar Pradesh, Bihar, Madhya Pradesh – was touched to any extent by the great ferment.

There were a couple of at least quasi-Untouchable castes that stand out as exceptions. The Nadars of Tamil country and Travancore and the Ezhavas of Travancore are by tradition toddy tappers, and this was the presumptive basis of their very low social status (alcohol being a sub-stance forsworn by Brahmins). Hardgrave describes the Nadars as having occupied at the beginning of the nineteenth century 'a social limbo some-where between the Sudras and the outcaste Untouchables' (Hardgrave 1969: 21). They could walk through the Brahmin quarter of a village but they shared with the Untouchables the power to pollute by proximity. The difference was that the Nadars could only pollute from much closer up than could the Pallans or Paraiyans. Roughly the same status attached to the Ezhavas in Travancore: they suffered from distance pollution but were always much less discriminated against than, say, the Pulayas.

By the end of the nineteenth century the Nadars had largely trans-formed themselves within the new environment established by British rule. The Ezhavas' progress began later, but by the end of the century they too were a community substantially on the rise (Aiyappan 1944). In the case of the Nadars, a large proportion of them had converted to Christianity by the 1840s. Some, including Christians, began to slough off habits of low social esteem. New economic opportunities enabled many among the community, but never all, to abandon tree-climbing for coco-nuts. One section of the community eventually developed considerable wealth as wholesale traders. Others, particularly among the Christians, pursued education sufficient to become teachers, advocates and doctors (Hardgrave 1969: 262–6). All this meant that whatever claim they might have had on the basis of their ambiguous Untouchability, the Nadars were quite too advanced to be placed on the Schedule of Untouchable

Castes in 1936. The same was true for the Ezhavas, and indeed neither community evinced any desire to be placed on a list that would implicitly reduce the status to which they had attained.

At the other extreme among the Untouchables were the slaves, including the notorious example of the Pulayas of Travancore. Slavery was not an isolated phenomenon: it was widespread throughout the south, and had been so for centuries (Kumar 1992: 47–8). To give one example, early in the nineteenth century Buchanan reported that most of the agricultural work in Palghat, now a District of Kerala, was performed by slaves (cherumans). These slaves could be bought and sold, mortgaged and rented out. They were 'very severely treated; and their diminutive stature and squalid appearance show evidently a want of adequate nourishment' (Buchanan in Hjelje 1967: 89–90). Despite their extreme subordination even among Untouchables, the fate of these slaves of south India is in some ways emblematic of the whole history of the Untouchables in the nineteenth century.

In 1843 the Parliament at Westminster passed the Abolition of Slavery Act for India (Act V of 1843), but the ideological boldness of this Act – part of a movement right across the Empire – failed to be matched by the diligence of its enforcement. The only immediate change was that an owner could no longer gain a court order to return a deserting slave. But it was not the weakness of enforcement that accounted for the ineffectiveness of abolition. Rather, the failure was grounded in an absence of alternative employment. Only later in the century were slaves able to escape to plantations that gave them employment (Kumar 1992: 128–43). Hjelje concludes that even if they had really cared about the issue, the British would not have been able to end slavery within a short period. This argument is persuasive, and a reminder of the limits of British power. The British were simply not in a position to engineer sudden transformations of Indian society. But equally, they were never committed to such transformations in the first place.

Some of the best evidence of British treatment of Untouchables relative to caste Hindus comes from case reports of the courts. While the courts emerge as no friend of the Untouchables, nor do they function as the simple enforcers of high-caste power. Thus the courts freely granted injunctions to maintain the exclusivity of temples by restraining particular castes from entering them. Sometimes damages were awarded to compensate for the costs of rites of purification incurred through the polluting presence of Untouchables or other prohibited communities (Galanter 1972: 229). Galanter notes that the cases reveal 'a judicial notion of a single articulated Hindu community in which there were authoritative opinions (supplied by custom and accepted texts) which determined the respective rights of the component groups' (Galanter 1972: 230). At the same time, the courts were less inclined to enforce exclusion in relation to 'secular' public facilities such as schools, wells and roads. And they tried to confine themselves to claims involving civil or property rights as opposed to mere claims for social standing. So they declined to enforce customary discriminations such as failure to dismount from a palanquin. But on the other side the courts did not recognise the enforceability of service relations and so act against secondary boycotts – denial of access to services or facilities – which were a frequent and devastating high-caste response to Untouchable or low-caste recalcitrance (Galanter 1972: 231–4).

A similar equivocation asserted itself in the British approach to education and the labour market (discussed below). As early as 1852 the British staged a public ceremony in Bombay to present Jotirao Phule with a pair of shawls to honour his establishment of the first special school for Untouchables in the 1840s (O'Hanlon 1985: 118). The Brahmins were outraged that Phule, a mere lower-caste Mali, should be honoured in a fashion reserved for highly esteemed Pandits. In 1858 the Government of Bombay continued its reformist tack by declaring that all government-funded schools had to admit students without regard to questions of religion or caste. But such declarations were never honoured. In the face of threatened high-caste boycott, those few Untouchables who might have benefited were routinely denied their opportunity.

The Untouchables and Christianity

It is clearly true, then, that the British were careful to avoid outraging orthodox Indian opinion, even if they did not always act positively to shore it up. But it is also crucial to attend to significant forces connected to British rule that were not so faint-hearted. Thus from early in the nineteenth century there had been a great struggle between Burkean conservatives and several strands of liberals, including Free Traders, Utilitarians and Evangelicals (Stokes 1959: xi–xvi). The conservatives of the East India Company, including Clive and Hastings, were greatly wary of unleashing European ideas and laws in India. Hastings wrote that 'the people of this country do not require our aid to furnish them with a rule for their conduct, or a standard for their property' (Hastings in Stokes 1959: 3). And throughout the nineteenth century this confidence in the sturdiness of Indian society was a recurrent article of faith in what became the dominant stream of British opinion makers.

Ranged against this stream were what Stokes calls the liberal 'assimilationists', men imbued with contempt for Indian civilisation and intent on flooding it with the superior virtues of Europe. James Mill, the great Utilitarian reformer, could sum up no less a population than the whole of China and India in these terms:

Both nations are to nearly an equal degree tainted with the vices of insincerity; dissembling, treacherous, mendacious, to an excess which surpasses even the usual measure of uncultivated society. Both are disposed to excessive exaggeration with regard to every thing relating to themselves. Both are cowardly and unfeeling. Both are in the highest degree conceited of themselves, and full of affected contempt for others. Both are, in the physical sense, disgustingly unclean in their persons and houses. (Mill 1820: II, 195)

Mill had a considerable influence on British policy in India, both directly and through Macaulay, particularly in the matter of providing European education to the Indian elites. But for the present purposes it is the related stance of the Evangelicals that is most relevant – the common strand was an impatience with the traditions and culture of India and a zeal for assimilation. After retiring from their position as advisers to Cornwallis in Bengal, John Shore and Charles Grant joined Wilberforce as prominent constituents of the Clapham Sect of Evangelicals (Stokes 1959: 27). The two great objects of the Clapham Sect were abolition of slavery and the opening up of benighted India to the work of missionaries. For Wilberforce, famed for his crusade against slavery, it was the missionary enterprise that was 'the greatest of all causes, for I really place it before Abolition' (Wilberforce in Stokes 1959: 28). The influence of the Sect in the Commons eventually secured this object in the form of the Charter Act of 1813.

For most of the nineteenth century the Christian missionaries were a distinctly destabilising force, particularly in south India, as they strove to negate on the ground the social conservatism that generally marked the Anglo-Indian state. But the missionaries had initially been wary of too active an involvement with those at the bottom of Indian society, for fear that they would alienate the high castes and therefore limit their overall effectiveness. But by the 1870s the situation had changed. High-caste society was now responding deeply to the challenge of European ideas and institutions, but it was for the most part doing so within the councils of Hinduism. If Christianity were to progress in India, if wicked idolatry and superstition were to be turned back, then the best opportunity lay with those at the bottom of society. The previous insistence on Christian knowledge as a prerequisite to conversion was dropped. In place of the slow accumulation of individual conversions, key figures led larger groups into the embrace of the churches. Families, even whole villages, converted en masse. In the space of a couple of decades the Indian churches quite changed character. From being communities of high-caste converts who continued to practise Hindu discriminations – the Syrian Christians of Travancore, for example – the south Indian churches entered the twentieth century as predominantly rural congregations of low and Untouchable castes.

Once they turned in earnest to the Untouchables, the missionaries mounted a quite powerful challenge to high-caste authority in south India. This emerges strongly from Reverend Clough's account of his American Baptist Mission's activities among the Madigas of Telegu country between the late 1860s and his return to America shortly before his death in 1910 (Clough 1914). Clough was a fearless crusader – he toured the villages of his converts with horse and cart, grabbing all the Hindu idols he could lay hands on and hauling them back to his house. 'My compound was full of the ruins of the past worship of the people' (Clough 1914: 320). He was the scourge of old Madiga rituals like the beating of drums to ward off evil spirits and possession rites, in which idols were paraded through the village and drugged Madigas danced until they gave sign of possession.

[I]t was thought the invisible being represented by the idol was finding expression through them... The intention... was that the Madigas should identify themselves with the fiends and demons on the land, and keep them in check. Then there would be no smallpox, no cholera, no cattle disease and no famine. (Clough 1914: 166)

Clough's activities were by no means welcome to the high castes. They, no less than the Madigas themselves, believed in the potency of Madiga rituals to propitiate the demons:

The caste people, who expect the Madigas to worship and appease the demons who afflict men and cattle, had taken note of all that had happened. They feared the consequences, and took measures of restriction which they thought might satisfy those invisible fiends which they dreaded. The Christians were ostracized. (Clough 1914: 107)

When disease broke out among the cattle, the caste Hindus even enlisted the Anglo-Indian state to enforce the traditional order. The Madigas were marched to the local magistrate and accused of having caused the death of the cattle. But Clough interceded with the magistrate, and the prisoners were discharged (Clough 1914: 107).

Sometimes, from their own ideological perspective, the missionaries contributed to the overall process of Sanskritisation or emulation of the higher castes. For example, from as early as 1814 Nadar Christian women were pressing government to allow them to cover their breasts in a manner previously reserved only to high-caste women such as the Nayars (Hardgrave 1969: 60). Their missionary leaders made strong representations that anything less than full clothing of the upper body was unacceptable to a Christian woman. But the Nayars and Nambudiri Brahmins were angry that such lowly persons could seek to obliterate a major distinction of respectability, and the controversy rolled on for many years. In 1858 and 1859 there were major riots in which Nadar women were forcibly stripped of their breast cloths in the bazaars of Travancore (Hardgrave 1969: 64). What had begun as a demand of the Christian Nadars had by then been adopted by all Nadar women. And in 1915–16 exactly the same issue came to a head for the Pulayas, the largest (discounting the Ezhavas) and most lowly Untouchable community of Travancore. Again the Nayars bitterly confronted the Pulaya women who had covered their breasts and thrown away the bead necklace that was their only sanctioned covering above the waist (Saradmoni 1980: 152–3). Once again the hand of the Christians was at work here – in the Census of 1931 43 per cent of the Pulayas were returned as Christians (Census 1931: 28 (i), 385–8). But 1916 was late in the day to try to protect such ostentatious discrimination, and the Nayars were forced into concession by Ayyankali, the (non-Christian) leader of the Pulayas.

The greatest impact of the Christian missionaries was to introduce small but politically significant numbers of Untouchables to western education. For almost all Untouchables, indeed for most of the Indian population, even rudimentary education had lain beyond the bounds of possibility. In case they should try, it was an article of Brahminical faith that Untouchables be prohibited from approaching the great texts of Sanskrit. In this context, the impact of throwing open schoolroom doors to Untouchables at the end of the nineteenth century was little short of revolutionary. At the time, partly through sheer lack of interest and partly in pursuit of social appeasement, the Government of India had made no substantial effort to admit Untouchables to its own schools. This is the explanation for the predominance of Christian schooling among those who emerged as leaders of the Untouchables in the early part of the twentieth century. Their only other major sources of education in the nineteenth century were schools provided in Indian Army cantonments and by a few maverick princely rulers, notably the Maharajahs of Baroda and Travancore.

The question of conversion to Islam

From the time the British started counting the population of India, the self-appointed leaders of 'Hinduism' (as if that were a simple unity) were panicked by the size and growth of the Muslim population. The issue regularly rose to a crescendo in the period leading up to and following the decennial Census. Hindu leaders were concerned with the allegedly greater fertility of the Muslim population, and conversion to both Christianity and Islam was also blamed for the suggested decline of the Hindus in demographic terms (Mukerji 1909: 6–8). Groups like the Arya Samaj became obsessed with the idea that the seeming egalitarianism of Islam and Christianity was providing an avenue of escape for sub-ordinated Untouchables.

Close attention to the phenomenon of conversion suggests that the Hindu panic was quite misconceived. In particular, there is no evidence of any major conversion of Untouchables to Islam at any period of Indian history. There were instances of the conversion of low Indian castes to Islam – some elements of the Mappilla community of southern Malabar are a case in point (Hardgrave 1977: 59). But such instances seem to have been rare. There is every reason to believe that the Muslim population of (undivided) India was not of predominantly low caste, let alone Untouchable, origins. The best scholarship suggests a number of factors as mostly responsible for the size of the Muslim population of the sub-continent. A major source was migration into India of traders along the coasts (Bayly 1989: 73–96) and of conquerors in the north. There appears also to have been a significant conversion of Buddhist communities, when Buddhism began to disintegrate in India; some of this particular conversion movement may well have swept up low-caste people (Levtzion 1981: 38). As to conversion as a whole, Rizvi nominates five categories of early converts to Islam on the sub-continent: persecuted religious minorities; captive members of the ruling classes; village headmen, tax collectors and the like; artisans dependent on the patronage of Muslim rulers; and the children of slaves kept by Muslims. Of these categories, perhaps only the last contained significant numbers of Untouchables. The primary engine of these early conversions was political pressure and economic incentive, not ideological or physical refuge to subordinated communities like the Untouchables (Rizvi 1981: 59). Where Untouchables did convert to Islam, they may often have done so as part of the entourage of magnates to whom they were attached. In later periods the devotional cult of Sufism had an impact in the sub-continent, but again there is no ground for believing that this impact was mainly exerted on those at the bottom of the Hindu order. Nor did an attraction to Sufism necessarily involve 'conversion' in syncretic India. If one puts the evidence of early conversion beside calculations of population growth rates, there seems no room for conceding any large-scale conversion during modern times. In short, and against the claims of activists like Shraddhananda, there is no solid evidence of Muslims' hiving off large numbers of Untouchables. Conversely, there is an abundance of evidence that many Muslim communities have themselves been energetic practitioners of caste and ritual Untouchability (Ansari 1960: 50–1, 73).

The Untouchables and new employment in colonial India

Untouchables were among the most mobile of Indian communities during the period of British rule, though the occupation of the great majority of them was the same in 1947 as it was at the beginning of British rule. But unlike the movement of other communities such as the Brahmins and Kayasthas, Untouchable mobility was generally not of a kind that laid a foundation for their economic or social advancement. Such progress was to be had in the growing towns and cities of British India, whereas Untouchables often moved from one non-urban situation to another or were temporary or semi-permanent migrants to the edges of urban civilisation or to insecure campments within. And when they did become part of regular urban life, it was usually at the very bottom of society.

Perhaps the most benevolent, albeit occasionally dangerous, employment directly opened up to Untouchables during this period was military service. From the late eighteenth century Mahars were recruited into the Bombay army of the East India Company, and Cohen estimates that they constituted one-sixth of the army up to 1857 (Cohen 1969: 455). In Bihar Dusadhs and Chamars joined in some numbers, as did Paraiyans in Madras. Army service was not unknown to Untouchables prior to the British – Shivaji's army is one example – but the numbers must have been far smaller and it seems likely that they were not able to rise above the meanest rank of foot soldier (Cadell 1938: 12). The experience of army life under the British must have transformed the outlook of many an Untouchable. Someone who had served in the trenches of Flanders was unlikely to accept the order of Untouchability with equanimity. There were also benefits conferred on the families of serving men, not the least of them being education. Ambedkar reported that he himself had been protected from personal experience of Untouchability as a child by living in military cantonments whose society and schools did not take account of caste or religion (Ambedkar c 1980: 65).

But British recruitment into the army proved fickle. By the 1890s army service had become more respectable in the eyes of higher-caste communities, and this coincided with a gathering British conviction that among the Indians there were certain 'martial races' whose recruitment was to be preferred. Forced retirement and little new recruitment of Untouchables was the result (Robertson 1938: 59). The special needs of the British Empire in the two World Wars induced a return to non-discrimination, but only for the duration of the wars (Cohen 1969: 458; Deshpande 1996: 177, 180–3).

Untouchables played some part in the new industrialisation of India in the second half of the nineteenth century. Associated as they were with harsh and uncongenial labour, Untouchables were slotted into the least attractive positions in the new industrial order. They were a primary source of labour for the construction of railways, which began in the 1850s and soon became one of the great emblems of British rule. And once the railways were operating, Untouchables were concentrated in the menial jobs – on one count late in the century, some 46 per cent of them were 'coolies' (goods carters) (Pradhan 1938: 564). In western India, they moved into the textile mills established by the British. The mills were concentrated in the Vidarbha region, especially Nagpur, and in Bombay. In the latter Untouchables comprised only 4 per cent of the population in 1864, and only 1 per cent of the mill workers in 1872 (Gokhale 1993: 48–9). But by 1921 12 per cent of the workforce of the Bombay mills was Untouchable (Morris 1965: 75). As in the railways, Untouchables were concentrated in the least preferred sectors of the mills. Over 72 per cent of Untouchable men were in the ring-spinning department, where they comprised 40 per cent of total male workers, and were almost comprehensively shut out of the higher-status and better-paid weaving departments. The basis of this exclusion has often been argued to be fear of pollution – in the course of joining yarns it was common practice to suck the yarn onto the shuttle, thereby threatening pollution to a caste Hindu down the line. But a simpler explanation may also be true, viz. that the higher castes and Muslims were 'preserving their lucrative monopoly against newcomers' (Morris 1965: 79).

Untouchables were also heavily represented on the docks, and in one area Mahars were fully 98 per cent of the most menial coal labourers (Zelliot 1969: 35–6). But probably the most prominent new employment within the organised sector of colonial India was that of the Sweepers.[1] Under the British, India developed far larger urban concentrations than before, and of course these had to be kept clean. Since the provision of sewerage lagged far behind the growth of towns and cities – it still does – the task of clearing waste had to be left to manual methods. The cleaning of public space and cartage of waste came to be discharged by a number of kindred Untouchable castes. In northern India the core caste was the Bhangis, who had functioned traditionally, though not exclusively, as

---

[1] Sometimes this term is used to include 'scavengers' of human night soil, and sometimes it refers only to actual cleaning in streets and buildings. Unless specified otherwise, we are using the term in the more inclusive sense.

sweeper and scavengers of human waste.[2] In western and southern India there was no caste so specialised in the matter of cleaning, but in several regions there was a large Untouchable caste that functioned as general village servants. The Mahars of western India, the Malas of Telegu country and the Holeyas of the Kannada-speaking region are three major examples. These were the communities that tended to perform the new urban cleaning work in their region.

The Sweepers were uniquely urbanised for an Untouchable community, but a great army of Untouchables was sucked into the towns and the urban fringe from late in the nineteenth century. Some of them became waiters, butlers and maids to British families and clubs (Robertson 1938: 4). But far more of them found employment in the building boom of the nineteenth and early twentieth centuries. A pattern was laid down that persists to the present, whereby the physically hard and so-called unskilled jobs of urban and peri-urban situations are more often than not discharged by Untouchables. Other Untouchables joined the new plantation economy in the hills of north and south India, Ceylon, Fiji and the West Indies. So the agricultural labourers who have been migrating from Bihar to Punjab since the 1960s, and the labourers in thousands of stone quarries and brickworks throughout India, are today carrying on a 'tradition' that is close to a century-and-a-half old. Whether these men and women of a century ago were 'pushed' out of the village or positively 'pulled' into the quarry or plantation is often a question of semantics rather than one of substance. We need to keep in focus the world of the nineteenth-century village as one of gross exploitation, sometimes enslavement, of Untouchables, and of famines as devastating as had ever occurred in India. There was ample reason to leave the village if there was the shadow of an alternative.

True, not all Untouchables were forced into a new drudgery. In the 1920s and 30s it was possible to find in the newly mechanised leather industry of northern India Chamar workers who had had become so prosperous that they adopted the family name *Machinwala* (Machine-

---

[2] The Bhangis also went by a number of other names – for example, Mehtar, Lalbegi and Valmiki (after one of their saints). There were other communities, notably the Doms, whose traditional occupation overlapped with that of the Bhangis. The Doms worked in cremation grounds, removed dead cattle, scavenged, wove baskets, beat drums and so on (Singh 1993: 483). They were also widespread throughout northern India, and perhaps could have been a competitor for the urban work practically monopolised in the north by the Bhangis. None of the above castes was found in anything like the number or spread of other Untouchable castes that were part of the backbone of agriculture – the Chamars, for example. This is because even high-caste people, generally women, tend to clean their own houses and surrounds in village India, even today. And since toilets were present only in large settlements, toilet cleaning (or scavenging) was not a common occupation in village India.

person) (Juergensmeyer 1982: 50). The term was designed to indicate that here was a person in a dynamic modern industry, a person to command some respect. And the Mahars of western India quite rapidly transformed themselves into a community that remained overwhelmingly poor and exploited but with an urban elite of extraordinary achievement, if not of great wealth.

It is appropriate to say something more about the overall situation of the Mahars. Traditionally the Mahars were neither identified with a particular polluting occupation (though they sometimes removed dead cattle), nor functioned primarily as agricultural labourers. They were village servants who performed a variety of quite diverse functions. The Mahars were village watchmen and trackers of thieves; couriers for government officials; messengers (conveying death notices, for example) for other villagers. They swept village roads and repaired wells, and they executed the seemingly high-status task of authoritatively measuring boundaries between disputing villagers. Mahars also staged *tamashas* (entertainments), and even kept the village supplied with coarse woven cloth. In return for these multifarious labours, the Mahars were entitled to certain *inam* or rent-free agricultural lands for their own farming and also to a *baluta* or fixed portion of the produce of the other lands under the village. Together, these rights were called the *watan* (Gokhale 1993: 29–30, 32–3).

The Mahars were unlike most other large Untouchable castes by virtue of not being primarily employed as field labourers on lands controlled by others. But despite the seeming advantage of having their own lands – these tended to be very small relative to those held by the peasant castes – they were no more independent than other Untouchables. Instead of being dependent on individual landowners, they were at the beck-and-call of all their social superiors in the village. Failure in their tasks – for example, the event of a theft during their watch – would lead to drastic punishment (Dangle 1992: *passim*). Under British rule, the value of Mahar services began to decline – the institution of a public postal service was one development that undercut their position. And to some extent, though less than for the Chambhars, they were adversely affected by the opening of leather tanneries, to which landholders began to cede rights of skin collection. This increasing marginalisation within the village economy is no doubt rightly identified as part of the reason for their unusual mobility under British rule. But it cannot be the whole of the explanation why it was the Mahars, and not the Mangs and Chambhars of the region, who moved in large numbers into the army, the mills, the railways and the docks. That explanation remains elusive. The great majority of the Mahar migrants remained poor, if not as poor as those who stayed behind in the village. But service in the army and to a lesser extent in the mills and as sweepers was the basis for the emergence of a small educated elite. It is far from coincidental that the most impressive Untouchable leader emerged from the most mobile and progressive of Untouchable communities.[3]

It follows from this short discussion of changes in employment during the colonial period that nineteenth- and early twentieth-century economic change had generally not created any strong foundation for a new movement of Untouchable liberation. Unlike the also mobile Brahmins, the Untouchables were labouring under cumulative deprivations that inhibited the development of such a leadership.

Hindu reform movements

By the last third of the nineteenth century Hindu society was responding strongly to the multiple challenges that had been posed by British rule, including the spur of the Indian Census. One of the most significant of the social reform movements was the Arya Samaj, formed in 1875 – just after the first Census – to revive Hinduism through purging it of idolatry and equipping it to confront what were seen as the rival faiths of Christianity and Islam. The Arya Samaj was established in Bombay but then spread quite widely, its major strength developing in Punjab. It quickly threw itself into battle with the forces of conversion, by setting out to reclaim as whole members of the Hindu community those Untouchables who had quite recently converted to Christianity or Islam. This was done by adapting the ritual act of *shuddhi*, until then a rarely performed ceremony to purify and readmit persons outcasted for breach of the rules of a particular caste community. During the reconversion ceremony there was much symbolic interdining, touching and singing (Graham 1942: 463). But this acceptance was strictly ceremonial. The Samaj was dominated in the early years by trading castes and Brahmins, and although by 1911 a third of the Punjab membership was Untouchable, none of them was in a leadership position (Jordens 1987: 137). Moreover, the very lowest Untouchable castes – the Sweepers in particular – were virtually shunned as members (Jones 1976: 310). Even at the level of doctrine the Arya Samaj was committed only to a limited equality. Thus the movement insisted that the varna order remain the basis of Hinduism, albeit that the fourfold division was now conceived as

---

[3] Again, we exclude the Ezhavas and Nadars from this statement. Whatever their status at, say, the beginning of the nineteenth century, these communities cannot be said to have been 'Untouchable' in the twentieth century. Since this book is mostly about the twentieth century, the case of the Ezhavas and Nadars is no more than touched upon.

a hierarchy of personal and acquired merit rather than an hereditary status. Jones has noted that Brahmins had no reason to fear from this redefinition 'for they would, if they were pure and properly educated, retain superiority' (p.33). Conversely, the Untouchables would have to travel a long and hard road to acquire merit equal to that of their social superiors.[4]

In short, the Arya Samaj's commitment to the eradication of Untouchability was less than whole-hearted. Its shortcomings were exposed much later in the 1920s by one of its own monks, Swami Shraddhananda, whose preparedness to drop all barriers and dine with Untouchables as a matter of course was quite too radical a posture for his colleagues. The Arya Samaj soon removed him from high office (Jordens 1987: 151). But despite Shraddhananda's undoubted commitment to the cause of abolition, his stand was marked by the same underlying flaw that marred the performance of the Arya Samaj in general. Shraddhananda's major objective was not the purification of Hinduism but the defeat of Islam and Christianity (Shraddhananda 1926). He believed he had fortuitously stumbled upon a giant Muslim conspiracy to convert Untouchables to Islam as a way of subverting the Hindu majority (Jordens 1981: 140–54). Shraddhananda conceived it to be his God-given mission to reclaim the Untouchables for Mother Hinduism. His mission came to an end in 1926 when he was murdered by a Muslim. Just one of the problems of Shraddhananda's approach was that the number of Untouchables converting to Islam had not been great.

When we turn to the non-Brahmin movements of Maharashtra and Madras, we come closer to the concerns of the Untouchables themselves. Jotirao Phule (1827–90) can reasonably be described as the principal founder of the anti-caste movement in India as a whole. His essential proposition was that Maharashtra was a society with a small elite of Aryan Brahmins and other high-caste communities which had used their religious authority and, under the British, their access to western education and government positions to subordinate the great mass of non-Aryan natives (O'Hanlon 1985: 220). As an aspect of his overall position Phule was a determined and consistent critic of Untouchability, and he made a considerable impact on an emerging intelligentsia among the Mahars. Walangkar, one of the most important Mahar politicians before Ambedkar, thought sufficient of Phule to have joined his Satyashodak

---

[4] The most radical wing of the Arya Samaj, the Jat Pat Todak Mandal, was bold enough to invite Ambedkar to give the main address at their annual conference in 1936. But they withdrew their invitation when Ambedkar refused to tone down his criticisms of the *sastras* (orthodox texts) and promised to announce that this was to be his last speech as a Hindu (Graham 1942: 541–2).

Samaj (Truth-seeking Society) (Omvedt 1976: 126–7). But mere opposition to Brahminism as ritual and social power was insufficient to glue together the Untouchables – themselves deeply divided by caste – and the largest peasant communities of the region. The more politically ambitious Phule's movement became, the more it came to represent majority interests and above all the interests of the Marathas as the most ambitious landed caste of the region. In 1890 the separate Mahar movement came into existence, and after this time the Mahars had no organised involvement with the non-Brahmin movement. There was no bitter break, merely the development of organisations with substantially different interests to serve.

Thirty years later the same story was re-enacted in Madras, though this time with greater bitterness. In Madras the major vehicle of the non-Brahmin movement was the Justice Party, formed in 1916 to combat what was seen to be Brahmin dominance of cultural expression and bureaucratic employment under the British (Irshick 1969: 47–9). With the prospect of provincial elections under the Montagu-Chelmsford reforms, the non-Brahmin leadership made overtures to Untouchable leaders who were beginning to make some headway in organising an Untouchable presence in Madras Presidency (Irshick 1969: 70–1; Arnold 1977: 19). But whatever Untouchable support there had been for the Justice Party was rapidly and acrimoniously lost. In 1921 the 'Puliyanthope troubles' arose out of a difficult strike situation at two mills in Madras. The Untouchable workforce returned to work quite quickly, thereby incurring the enmity of caste Hindus determined to maintain the strike. Several caste Hindus were killed in clashes with police, and the organ of the Justice Party blamed the situation partly on the 'pampering' of the Untouchables by the Labour Department. M. C. Rajah, principal representative of the Untouchables in the Legislative Council, was outraged by the charges levelled by Justice Party leaders. In mid-1923 Rajah declared that the 'natural animosity' of the Justice Party was obvious long before the Puliyanthope troubles. 'It is the high-handed poisonous action of members of a party who after inflicting all known and unknown injury on our community shed crocodile tears and pose as friends of the Depressed Classes' (Irshick 1969: 192). Irshick notes that by the time of this conflict the Justice Party had quite departed from its early, more inclusive stand. It had stopped being a genuine reform association and had become a 'broker for government jobs for a few select non-Brahman caste Hindus' (p.193).

The Madras rupture in 1923 brought about a permanent end to unity between organised Untouchables and the 'non-Brahmin' or 'backward classes' movements – unless the political manœuvrings of the 1990s are a rekindling of the earlier spirit. Despite their progressive ideology, the non-Brahmin movements in both Maharashtra and Madras were dominated by the upper strata of lower-caste Hindus who had realistic ambitions to capture state power. It was by no means implausible to argue that the Shudra castes and the Untouchables were conjoint victims of upper-caste, particularly Brahmin, power. But such characterisation also cut across massive differences in wealth, status and power within a category which comprised a large proportion, by some calculations even a majority, of all Indians. As the party leading the Independence movement, the Indian National Congress proved able to construct an ideology which sublimated profound social differences to an overarching nationalism. Likewise in Kerala and West Bengal the Communist Party was much later able to accomplish a comparable integration through Marxist ideology. But anti-Brahminism lacked the positive appeals of nationalism and Marxism, and it rapidly lost the support of any but its central proponents.

If the Arya Samaj and the non-Brahmin movement could not claim to represent mainstream Hindu Indian opinion, clearly the Indian National Congress could. But from the time of its establishment in 1885, Congress deliberately averted its face from issues considered to be internal to Indian society. It conceived of itself as nothing more nor less than the medium through which Indian Independence from Britain could be achieved. Over time, always reluctantly and superficially, Congress was drawn into social issues, including the issue of Untouchability. In 1917 Congress finally adopted a resolution urging upon the people of India

the necessity, justice and righteousness of removing all disabilities imposed by custom on the Depressed Classes, the disabilities being of a most vexatious and oppressive character, subjecting these classes to considerable hardship and inconvenience. (Natarajan 1962: 148)

By the time of this resolution Hindu attention had been focussed on the issue by the interrogations of the Census and the spectre of mass conversions to Islam and Christianity. Congress could no longer avoid the matter altogether. But the limits of the Congress position can be discerned in the views of its President at the time, the Englishwoman Annie Besant. One-time Fabian, now theosophist and enthusiast of Hindu revivalism, Besant's views on the 'Depressed Classes' were scarcely progressive. In 1909 Mrs Besant had written in the *Indian Review* that the depressed classes were of the type found in all societies, 'ignorant, degraded, unclean in language and habits, people who perform many tasks which are necessary for Society, but who are despised and neglected by the very Society to whose needs they minister' (Anon nd: 41). She warmed to her subject. These people are:

drunken and utterly indifferent to cleanliness, whether of food, person or dwelling . . . The children of the depressed classes need, first of all, to be taught cleanliness, outside decency of behaviour, and the earliest rudiments of education, religion and morality. Their bodies, at present, are ill-odorous and foul, with the liquor and strong-smelling foods out of which for generations they have been built up; it will need some generations of purer food and living to make their bodies fit to sit in the close neighbourhood of a school-room with children who have received bodies from an ancestry trained in habits of exquisite personal cleanliness, and fed on pure food-stuffs. We have to raise the depressed classes to a similar level of physical purity, not to drag down the clean to the level of the dirty, and until this is done close association is undesirable. . .

I know now that the conditions do not make the people, but that it is the drunken and dirty people who **cause** the conditions, and that the wastrals before mentioned, born under good conditions, come into these because they are their natural home...(Besant in Anon nd: 46–7, 51)

It might be tempting to write Mrs Besant off as an eccentric English-woman, but what she is giving unusually clear voice to here is a strict version of Brahminism. The latter paragraph is a perfect evocation of the determinist doctrine of karma, amazingly at odds with her old attachment to socialism. But the language of even undeniably progressive leaders of the time now reads as condescending and limited. Thus the Gaekwad (Maharaja) of Baroda, rightly celebrated for his support of Untouchables, concluded an article in 1909 by stating:

the true corrective lies in the hands of the depressed classes themselves – they must improve themselves in every way and assert their claim to just treatment without making themselves troublesome to their neighbours and without neglect-ing their duties, humble though they may be, but on which the health and com-forts of the society depends. (Baroda in Anon nd: 17)

We need not multiply examples further. The conclusion to be drawn is that until the 1920s there was no deep or broad commitment of main-stream Indian opinion to the liberation of the Untouchables. Various organisations were greatly exercised by the problem, particularly by the regrettable proclivity of Untouchables to convert to Christianity and, it was believed, to Islam too. And some high-caste individuals – another is V. R. Shinde, a Brahmin in Bombay – were deeply seized of the moral imperative to transform the lives of what was agreed to be a miserable and large section of the Indian population. But none of this touched the main currents of Indian political life. It was only when Untouchables found their own voice and when political circumstances afforded them a point of entry that they were able to join that broad stream.

Early Untouchable organisation

The modern protest of Untouchable castes can be said to have begun with the (mildly Untouchable) Nadars and the Ezhavas. At a time when Phule was propounding his radical attack on caste in Maharashtra, Sri

Narayana Guru (1857–1928) was developing a comparable but simultaneously religious critique that was widely influential even beyond his own Ezhava community in Travancore. Under his direction the Ezhavas applied their growing wealth in the 1880s to the development of their own schools and temples. By 1891 there were already some 25,000 educated Ezhavas in Travancore, and in 1896 13,176 of them signed a petition to the Maharajah asking that government schools and the civil service be opened up to them (Saradmoni 1980: 135).

Sri Narayana's unitarian doctrine of 'one caste, one religion and one God for man' amounted to a repudiation of caste, and he explicitly sought to include the Pulayas and other Untouchable castes in his movement. But this was too much for his caste fellows, and violence greeted attempts to bring the Ezhavas and the Pulayas together (Saradmoni 1980: 146). It was not until the emergence of Ayyankali (1863–1941) that the Pulayas gained an effective voice. But the speed with which Ayyankali organised his community was an indication of how far the ferment had sapped the vitality of the *ancien régime* and diminished the fear of some of the most subordinated of all Untouchables. By 1900 numerous marches along the thoroughfares of Travancore had secured the Pulayas' right to use most of the public roads of the state, though roads leading to temples remained out of bounds (Saradmoni 1980: 130–2). Ayyankali's role in defending the Pulaya women's right to cover their breasts has been noted above. And at about the same time Ayyankali led perhaps the first strike by agricultural workers in Kerala – not for higher wages, but to insist on the right of Untouchable children to attend school.[5] So within the first two decades of the century the Pulayas had waged a surprisingly aggressive campaign to attack some of the most irksome discriminations against them. Later, they were swept up by Gandhian and then Marxist politics in Kerala.

There was other early militancy in different pockets of India. In 1889 Bombay sweepers, almost all of them Mahars, twice went on strike over demands for higher wages, paid days off, and curbs on the exactions of *mukkadams* or jobbers (Masselos 1983: 102).[6] The strikes were on the whole unsuccessful, but the consciousness that produced them was fresh and impressive. At the time the only Mahar political organisation in existence was V. G. Walangkar's Anarya Dosh Parihar Samaj (Society for the Removal of the Stigma of Untouchability), established in 1886. Walangkar's first major act was a petition in 1890 for the Government of

[5] Saradmoni (1980: 149) dates this strike in 1915, whereas Oommen (1985: 62–3) places it in 1907–8.
[6] In Bombay the sweepers and scavengers were separate industrial categories. The scavengers were almost invariably Bhangis in the 1880s, and they did not go on strike (Masselos 1983: 105).

India to resume recruitment of Mahars and other Untouchables into the army. In the petition he affirmed the loyalty of the Untouchables to the British and a lack of sympathy with Congress agitation, themes which remained constant for the Mahars and most other Untouchables for half a century more (Gokhale 1993: 65–6). This was the first of a number of Mahar organisations formed over the next quarter-century, though they were confined to a very small section of the community: it was only a developed consciousness that Ambedkar was able to build on in the 1920s.

Parallel with concern for access to army and government positions, the great preoccupation of Mahar leaders was with the need for education and the abandonment of disreputable social practices. The following resolution of the Mahar Parishad in 1920 was typical of many such resolutions on the latter theme:

> Be it resolved: Not to eat the flesh of dead cattle nor that of sacrificial chicken and goats; Not to consider dead cats and dogs polluting; Not to drink alcohol at childbirth, wedding, and other ceremonies; Not to give dowries; in case of widow remarriage, to give only Rs. 25; to prohibit the caste council from buying liquor with the monies paid in fines for offences of pollution (vital); Not to use johar as a greeting amongst ourselves, rather, to use Ram Ram or Namaskar; To send children to boarding schools or hostels for their education, not to consider that polluting; Not to bury the dead, but rather to cremate them. (Gokhale 1993: 69)

Here was a slate of reforms that was clearly not of the Mahars' own origination. It was in part a reaction to the sort of orthodox disgust retailed by Annie Besant, and embodied a hope that the abandonment of unacceptable habits (burial, for example) would have an ameliorating effect on discrimination by caste Hindus. But the community was simultaneously asked to abandon practices that constituted too slavish an attachment to the order of pollution and were an impediment to their modernisation. So the Mahars are exhorted not to treat dead dogs and cats as polluting, though it is unclear why this matter should receive any prominence. More importantly, the Mahars are told not to be so orthodox as to regard mixing with other castes in boarding schools as polluting; to maintain such a view was to restrict educational opportunity.

The early Mahar movement before 1920 is comparable in a number of respects with the single-caste movements of the Ezhavas, the Nadars and Pulayas of south India, and also of other communities such as the Namsudras of Bengal. All of these caste-based movements were committed to the goals of ritual self-reform, education and gaining access to employment under the state. And a number of the key leaders of the movements were also committed to a wider solidarity of Untouchables and oppressed low castes. This inclusive position was taken a step further in the movement throughout south India which sought to construct an identity on the basis of the Untouchables as the original, pre-Aryan inhabitants of India (see above, p. 3). But movements of Untouchables constructed around a multi-caste identity have tended to founder on suspicion between the component castes, as have efforts on the part of enlightened leaders of single-caste movements to identify with other Untouchable castes.

Untouchable organisation during the 1920s

The special nature of the British response to Indian nationalism changed the context of Untouchable resistance after 1910 and particularly during the 1920s. In the Morely-Minto reforms of 1909–10 the Government of India began to concede elected as opposed to merely nominated Indian representation to its Legislative Councils, but the basis of representation continued to be interests (landowners, for example) rather than geographical units (Wolpert 1967: 185–6; Brown 1985: 142–4). Crucially, the British now expanded the concept of interest to allow for separate electorates for Muslims. This development had a dual relevance to the Untouchables. First, the communal status of Untouchables had been brought into direct political contention by the self-interested argument of the Muslim League that Hindu numbers were being inflated relative to Muslims through false identification of the 'degraded castes' as Hindus (Muhammed 1980: II, 117). And secondly, the concession of representation to Muslims established a precedent for political representation of other communities.

By 1918 the communities seeking representation included the Sikhs in Punjab; non-Brahmins in Madras; Christians, Anglo-Indians and Europeans throughout India; and the Lingayats of Bombay (Government of Great Britain 1918: 188–9). There was not yet any strong demand from the Untouchables. B. R. Ambedkar, in between his two periods of study in London, asked to make a submission to the Southborough Franchise Committee. But his and his fellow Mahar G. A. Gawai's call for separate electorates for the Depressed Classes was ignored (Keer 1971: 40; Khairmode 1955: II, 277). The Southborough Committee was able to pronounce paternalistically that 'we intend to make the best arrangements we can for their [the Untouchables'] representation, in order that they too may ultimately learn the lesson of self-protection' (Government of Great Britain 1919: para. 155). Under the *Government of India Act* 1919 the Untouchables accordingly emerged with provision for representatives nominated by the Government of India and the Provinces. It was not until the climactic Round Table Conferences of 1930–1 that they were able to secure the promise of elected representation.

The important contests of the 1920s were mostly about the practice of ritual Untouchability, and the first great set-piece was the Vaikom *satyagraha* of 1924–5. This was a campaign to open to Untouchables the road passing a particular temple; such roads, as well as the temples themselves, had not been conceded by the high castes in the earlier contests over road use in Travancore. The campaign was undertaken by the Kerala Congress Committee with the support of Ezhava and Untouchable activists, but with no commitment from the national organisation of Congress. Gandhi was eventually pushed into taking a public stand in support of the protesters, partly because of criticism of his silence from Sri Narayana Guru and Shraddhananda (Jordens 1987: 144–7). His eventual settlement of the conflict was devalued in his own mind by the official declaration that the road was now open to all 'non-Hindus' – the implication was that Untouchables were not Hindus (Desai 1937: 21–2).

The Untouchable victory in Vaikom was greeted enthusiastically by Ambedkar in Bombay, and it was a related issue that marked the beginning of his own notoriety (Keer 1971: 63; Zelliot 1972: 81). Because of his later importance, something needs to be said about the emergence of Ambedkar (1891–1956). He was able to acquire an education – first in army cantonments and then in Bombay – at a time when this was still a great rarity among Mahars. After graduating from Elphinstone College in Bombay in 1912, he was given a scholarship by the Gaekwad of Baroda specifically because he was an Untouchable. From 1913 to 1917 and then from 1920 to 1923 Ambedkar studied at Columbia in New York and at the London School of Economics and the English bar. Seemingly by the time he had finished high school Ambedkar was already more educated than any other Mahar, and his achievements abroad (including two doctorates) were probably unrivalled by another Untouchable for many years. After an abortive attempt to work off his scholarship in the service of Baroda state – as an Untouchable he could not find any rooms to rent in town – he became a college lecturer and practitioner before the Bombay High Court.

These educational attainments seem to have been a prime factor in Ambedkar's rapid political rise in Bombay. As early as 1927 he was officially nominated to the Legislative Council as one of two representatives of the Depressed Classes (Keer 1971: 83). For the next quarter-century Ambedkar played something of a dual role as a figure in official circles and later in government under the British, and as a Mahar political organiser and exemplar for radical Untouchables throughout India. Initially there was nothing novel in his set of goals. The *Bahishkrit*

Hitakarini Sabha (Depressed Classes Benevolent Institute) he formed in
1924 was a social service organisation whose major commitment was to
education. This was by then a standard Mahar goal, though the stance
had shifted from shame at their own lack of education to an insistence
that education was a right wrongly denied to the community (Gokhale
1993: 85–6). Ambedkar also threw himself into three major issues already
exercising the Mahar movement: abolition of the Mahar watan (on the
ground that the system forced the Mahars into a subordinate dependence
within the village), and the campaigns to gain access to common water
sources and public temples (Gokhale 1993: 83).

It was the question of access to water that was raised first in the form of
the Mahad satyagraha of 1927. Some ten thousand people turned up to a
meeting called by Ambedkar and they heard speeches on all the topics of
the day, including a call for Mahar women to wear their saris in the style of
high-caste women so as to avoid stigma (Gokhale 1993: 92). Then, apparently quite without premeditation, Ambedkar's natural radicalism produced his first serious confrontation with orthodoxy. In a spirit of reform
the Mahad municipality had previously declared its Chowdar water tank
open to all people without discrimination, but in fact the tank remained
closed to Untouchables though not to Christians or Muslims. Spurred by
the heat of the day and a shortage of water, Ambedkar determined to lead
a procession to the tank. He himself was the first to draw water.
Orthodoxy was duly outraged; the tank had to be ritually purified; and the
municipal council was induced to reverse its commitment to non-
discrimination (Keer 1971: 69–108). Ambedkar's response was to prepare
for more action, somewhat opportunistically adopting the Gandhian
technique of satyagraha.

At the next gathering in December 1927 Ambedkar took a truly
massive step forward. At the suggestion of one of his Brahmin advisers, he
set fire to a copy of the *Manusmrti*. This document is still portrayed as the
basis of 'Hindu law', the gift of the greatest of the Brahmin law-givers. It is
also a document of profound justification for the idea of pollution and its
most perfect realisation in the form of the *panchama* or Untouchables. Of
course, Ambedkar's act of burning the Manusmrti was utterly explosive.
(When the action was repeated in 1971, the detonation was still almost as
loud.) It was so offensive to the formal body of Hinduism that it alienated
all but the most radical of his caste Hindu supporters (Zelliot 1972: 82). If
much of Ambedkar's previous intervention had been no more than
reformist, here was an act of such defiance that it took him into territory
untrodden by any activist before him.

Despite the power of Ambedkar's symbolism, the satyagraha had to be abandoned for a number of pragmatic reasons. In some ways the whole Mahad affair came to represent the limitations as well as strengths of Ambedkar's style: his interventions were electrifying, and pointed the way to a future that was gloriously opposed to the miserable past. But as a politician on the ground, he often failed to devise strategies that carried the movement unambiguously forward. The same judgment could be made about his relatively brief temple entry movement. In the face of orthodox and violent opposition, there was not a single victory – not in the Thakurdwar temple in Bombay in 1927, the Parvati temple in Poona in 1929, nor the Kalaram temple in Nasik, a struggle which began in 1930 but limped on for the following five years (Keer 1971: 86, 137–8; Pradhan 1986: 123–4; Zelliot 1972: 82–3). Aside from questions of timing and tactics, the crucial weakness of the movement was that it failed to gain the support of more than a handful of caste Hindu reformers. Ambedkar was too uncompromising and intemperate a figure for most people who were not Untouchable.

While Ambedkar was concerning himself with a frontal attack on Hindu orthodoxy in Maharashtra, Mangoo Ram was building his Ad Dharm (Original Religion) organisation in Punjab. Mangoo Ram too had lived for many years outside India, though his experience had been more earthy than that of Ambedkar. Within two years of his return in 1925 he had established his new 'religion'. The central proposition was that the Untouchables were the original (*ad*) inhabitants of India and that they had been pushed into subordination by later arrivals. It followed that a new religious philosophy had to be formulated to resurrect the original identity. As to the chosen name, Mangoo Ram simply added the term 'Dharm' to the 'Adi' which had previously been adopted in the south as a way of asserting Untouchable primacy and independence. Mangoo Ram's religious philosophy never attained to more than a sketch drawn around the teachings of the medieval Chamar bhakta Ravi Das, but his organising powers and ability to gain finance from wealthier Chamars were considerable. Within four years the Ad Dharm movement had mobilised some 400,000 Chamar supporters. He even managed to encourage some Chuhras (Sweepers) to join in, though years later he observed that they were never in the 'inner circle' (Juergensmeyer 1982: 60). Ad Dharm was essentially a transitional social movement between the less assertive organisations of the period before 1920 and Ambedkarite radicalism of the 1930s. The movement had simply faded away as a force by the mid-thirties (Juergensmeyer 1982: 143). In various other parts of the country there was considerable social and political activity too. For example, P. R. Venkatswamy, himself a participant in the movement, has provided rich documentation of activity in the princely state of Hyderabad that began as early as 1912 and gathered pace in the 1920s (Venkatswamy 1955). This activity broadly replicated the concerns for self-reform, education and equality that were being asserted through much of India at the time. But everything changed in Hyderabad too once Ambedkar burst on to the national scene in the early 1930s.

Omvedt has sought to simplify the analysis of Untouchable politics by discerning at least as far back as the 1920s two tendencies among Untouchable leaders, one leaning towards 'autonomy' from mainstream Hindu society and the other towards 'integration' within it (Omvedt 1994: 114). This characterisation has the merit of distinguishing Ambedkar and his followers or sympathisers (plus maverick figures like Mangoo Ram) from those who leant to the integrationist tendency later represented by Gandhi above all. But there are two problems with Omvedt's analysis. First, it is doubtful that such a sharp division existed as early as the 1920s: it was the events of 1930–2 and their elaboration through the rest of that decade that drove a firm wedge between Untouchable leaders. More importantly, Omvedt's binary classification proceeds on the basis of attitudes towards 'Hinduism' rather than willingness to confront oppressors. If one takes, for example, the present and epic struggle of the Musahars in Bihar (see above pp. 55–62), their attitude towards 'Hinduism' does not appear to be a factor at all. It is doubtful that any systematic philosophy (not even Marxism) is guiding the lowly Musahars' resolute efforts to acquire greater social respect and a better economic outcome for themselves. And it certainly makes no sense to claim that these people belong to the school that seeks either 'autonomy from' or 'integration with' Hinduism. That language may place the Ambedkarite position in context, but it will not do service in classifying the variety of Untouchable movements around India over the last three-quarters of a century.

What emerges from the 1920s is the ambiguity and uncertainty of Untouchable politics. On the crucial question of nationalism, the Untouchables were not sure whether they stood with Congress in its demand for an early end to British rule. They could easily recognise the lack of British commitment to the cause of Untouchable liberation, and they were as capable as any other Indian of feeling a sense of outraged nationalism over the continuing British presence. But the period of British rule had also wrought more beneficial change to the Untouchable condition than had occurred over many centuries; many of the Untouchable leaders had gained their education and prospects as a direct result of British rule. And on the other side, Congress was dominated by high-caste Hindus who hung back from commitment to the Untouchable cause. Worse, some of them were deeply hostile to Untouchables. Only Gandhi

declared himself fully committed, but his prescriptions were mostly hortatory rather than confrontational and always subordinated in the twenties
to the goal of maintaining nationalist unity. In some ways the dilemma
remained the same during the 1930s, but by then the great conflict
between Gandhi and Ambedkar had ensured that not even mainstream
political forces could continue to ignore the issue of Untouchability.

Ambedkar and Gandhi after 1930

The Round Table Conferences and the Poona Pact

If we are to believe Gandhi's secretary, Gandhi was under the impression
that Ambedkar was a radical Brahmin until they met in London at the
second Round Table Conference of 1931 (Desai 1953: 52). Whether or
not this account is accurate – the two had actually met previously – the
very claim reveals something of the prevailing political climate. In 1930
Ambedkar was not a figure of national prominence. And for his part,
Gandhi was certainly not on the lookout for Untouchable leaders.
Already he saw carriage of the Untouchable issue as his alone.

The great set-piece between Gandhi and Ambedkar is so well known
that we need only sketch it lightly here. Ambedkar's first victory arose
from the Simon Commission of 1929–30, which adopted as policy his
'golden mean' of multi-member joint electorates with seats reserved for
representatives of the Depressed Classes. The matter was referred to the
Round Table Conference to be held in London in 1930. On the strength
of his showing before the Simon Commission Ambedkar was invited to
the new Conference as one of two representatives of the Untouchables.
He now reverted to his earlier position, and argued for wholly separate
electorates for Untouchables. In the absence of Gandhi – the Congress
leaders were in gaol because of their non-cooperation movement – this
position was accepted by the British, as it was for the Muslims and several
other smaller 'minorities'.

Gandhi was never more passionate than in his rejection of this position
at the second Round Table Conference in 1931: 'I can understand the
claims advanced by other minorities, but the claims advanced on behalf of
the Untouchables, that to me is "the unkindest cut of all".' The fault lay in
politicisation of the social problem that was Untouchability: 'Those who
speak of political rights of Untouchables do not know their India...' There
was, after all, 'a body of Hindu reformers who... are pledged to remove
this blot of Untouchability . . . I would far rather that Hinduism die than
that Untouchability lived'. And Gandhi made it perfectly plain just who
was leading the Untouchables: 'I claim myself in my own person to repre-

sent the vast mass of the Untouchables...' As for Ambedkar, his 'bitter experiences' had 'warped his judgment'. He could not claim to represent the Untouchables, and was threatening the unity of Hinduism itself (Government of Great Britain 1932: 544). The Conference broke up in bitter disagreement.

During the Conference Ambedkar had enjoyed the support of the other Untouchable representative, M. C. Rajah from Madras. But afterwards Rajah was anxious to avoid what he foresaw to be a damaging conflict for the Untouchables, and entered into a pact with Munje, President of the Hindu Mahasabha, calling for joint rather than separate electorates for Untouchables. The Rajah-Munje pact immediately divided Untouchable leaders down the middle (Pradhan 1986: 160–7). Ambedkar was supported by the majority of Mahar leaders and by a number of other organisations, including the Ad Dharm Mandal and one of the organs of the Bengali Namasudras. Rajah's supporters included the important Chamar leaders of Ambedkar's Maharashtra, one of them P. N. Rajbhoj. Bitter and even violent exchanges took place between the two sides over the succeeding months.

The conflict reached maturity in India the following year, when the British proceeded as part of their Communal Award to declare in favour of separate electorates for Untouchables. Gandhi's response was to enter into perhaps the most famous of his 'fasts unto death' on 20 September 1932. Faced with the martyrdom of the great Mahatma, Ambedkar had no choice but to back down.[7] He agreed in the Poona Pact to scrapping of separate electorates for Untouchable voters in return for a substantial increase in the number of general seats to be reserved for candidates from the Untouchable castes.

By most reckonings Gandhi had won the contest (Kumar 1985: 27). He had fended off an institutional arrangement premised on the position that the Untouchables were as distinct from the regular Hindu community as were the Muslims. The concession of an even larger number of parliamentary seats to Untouchables than had been contemplated by the British was a high price for Gandhi to pay, but it was worth paying if it could be insisted that the arrangement was simply a way of making sure that Untouchable Hindus were afforded opportunities for accelerated advancement in the new India. The principle that Untouchables were Hindus had successfully been defended. But while Ambedkar may have given way to Gandhi in Poona, he too could be seen to have had great success during the struggle of some three years' duration. He had transformed the Untouchability question from a moral problem dominated by

[7] This account has drawn on Zelliot 1969: 174–91.

reformist Hindus into a matter of political rights for a subordinated segment of Indian society. And the promise of a large number of parliamentary seats seemed to guarantee that a strong Untouchable voice would now be heard in Indian public life. Ambedkar, after all, had been a comparatively recent convert to the principle of separate Untouchable electorates. It was only much later, after his own electoral failures and the perceived weakness of Untouchables within Congress, that Ambedkar came to see Poona as the moment when Gandhi deprived them of machinery that could have constituted a political base independent of Hindu India (Ambedkar 1945, 1991: 102).

Gandhi's Harijan campaign and the 1937 and 1946 elections

Gandhi threw himself into a new campaign against Untouchability almost the moment the Poona Pact was concluded. His motivation was utterly high-minded, but it was also far from irrelevant that the Untouchables were now an important electorate of the future as well as a great social cause. Gandhi's principal focus became the right of Untouchables to worship in public temples, the very issue he had previously avoided as too inflammatory. Aside from its divisiveness, this was a natural issue for Gandhi to adopt as the self-styled purifier and saviour of Hinduism. The first campaign he joined was the effort that began late in 1932 to open up the Guruvayur temple in Cochin. He condemned the earlier tactics of the Ambedkarites: there was to be no storming of gates or vigorous chanting or displays of great enthusiasm (Gandhi 1934: 99–101). The wishes of even devout Hindus who 'in their conscience found the presence of Untouchábles objectionable' had to be respected, not simply overruled. So Gandhi suggested a roster whereby Untouchables would be admitted for a certain number of hours daily but not at other times. He was even prepared to allow the temple to be ritually purified after their presence (Gandhi 1933: 90–1). When this plan failed he proposed a referendum of temple goers. Some 70 per cent are said to have favoured Untouchable entry, but Gandhi was still not prepared to go ahead until the minority could be persuaded. The whole campaign eventually collapsed in exhaustion. Ambedkar was later scathing about the tendermindedness shown towards people who were nothing but oppressors of the Untouchables (Ambedkar 1945, 1991: 115–17).

The Guruvayur campaign merged with Gandhi's wider 'Harijan tour', which took him to a large number of Indian localities for a period of some nine months in 1933. Gandhi inaugurated the tour with a 21-day fast to 'purify Hinduism', a beginning which signified his intention to engage in moral suasion (and perhaps some browbeating) rather than frontal assault. The tour did raise the salience of the issue of Untouchability but it produced little concrete reform. Gandhi was able to use the tour to promote his new Harijan Sevak Sangh, a service and welfare organisation to supply scholarships, hostels, libraries, lectures on temperance, and so on. The distinctiveness of Gandhi's approach was apparent from his desire that membership of this body be confined to caste Hindus, since it was to be 'an organization of penitent sinners' (Gandhi 1946: 270). In Gandhi's larger campaign of some three years duration the greatest event was the proclamation by the Maharajah of Travancore in 1936 that all public temples in his state were henceforth to be open to Untouchables. Gandhi had been only one of the participants in the struggle for temple entry, but his prestige had made a critical difference. The proclamation in one of the most orthodox regions of India had a shattering impact on the claims of ritual orthodoxy throughout India, and comparable proclamations and even legislation were soon enacted in Madras, Bombay and elsewhere. This is not to say that Untouchables were suddenly allowed into the temples of Travancore, particularly their innner sancta: the now characteristic gap between public principle and everyday practice began to be put in place from the moment the public edifice of Untouchability began to crumble. Thus the Guruvayur temple seems not to have opened its doors to Untouchables until after Indian Independence (Ambedkar 1945, 1991: 117).

By the mid-thirties the character of Gandhi's approach to Untouchability was clear, and Ambedkar and his other critics were correct in pointing to its limitations. His construction of the problem was ameliorative and arguably superficial, and his tactics entailed massive concessions to the enthusiastic practitioners of Untouchability. He was paternalistic towards Untouchables – the only Untouchable of any note to have emerged through his patronage was Jagjivan Ram. He consistently defended the intellectually difficult position that caste was an appropriate moral order for India, and that Untouchability was a mere excrescence to be surgically excised from the sound body of Hinduism. He was even sufficiently committed to the principle of caste to disapprove of marriages across caste, though late in his life he had a change of heart.[8] Gandhi, in short, was very far from a social radical. On the other side, what he brought to the issue of Untouchability was genuine moral passion and the prestige of the greatest and most popular Indian of the twentieth century. No one else could have made such an impact on the caste Hindu mind. His campaign was full of courage and risks: what was insubstantial and

[8] Gandhi eventually allowed one of his sons to marry the daughter of the (Brahmin) leader from Madras, C. Rajagopalachariar.

paternalistic to Ambedkar could be objectionable and inflammatory to an orthodox Hindu. The further Gandhi pushed ahead with his attack on Untouchability, the more resistance and outright hostility he encountered within the ranks of Congress and the wider Hindu community. Even during the 1920s Gandhi had been prepared to scandalise orthodox opinion by engaging in personal contact, including dining, with Untouchables. On his tour of Cutch in 1925 the leader of a reception committee threw the text of his speech at Gandhi, rather than risk pollution by handing the document to so defiled a person (Desai 1953: VII, 231). Gandhi's new Harijan campaign produced a far stronger reaction in proportion to the now greater strength of his commitment. He so alienated party bosses (often landlords) and religiously orthodox Congressmen that he was forced out of the Congress leadership for a time. Gandhi was now disobeying the canon that the unity of the movement against British rule was not be disrupted by pursuit of objectives internal to Indian society (Brown 1977: 330–79).

The crucial test of Gandhi's popularity with the Untouchables themselves was the election of 1937, the first to incorporate the formula agreed at Poona. Congress won just over half the seats reserved for Scheduled Caste candidates, seventy-nine out of 151 (Dushkin 1957: 120). In the United Provinces, Bihar and Madras, Congress won fully fifty-nine of the sixty-five reserved seats. Congress did badly in the large provinces of Bombay and Bengal, and also in the smaller provinces of Punjab and Assam. The explanation for Bombay was the strength of Ambedkar's Independent Labour Party (ILP), which won twelve of the fifteen seats (the other three going to Congress). Congress won only three of thirty seats in Bengal, and this reflected Gandhi's wholesale failure to penetrate this region. And Punjab, where Congress won one out of the eight seats, had been influenced over the previous years by the more radical Ad Dharm and Ambedkarite positions. But clearly Congress had done far better than any other organisation: no other party could command a following across more than one region, and other than Ambedkar's ILP there was no successful party established by an Untouchable.[9] A large proportion of the winning non-Congress candidates were Independents, notably in Bengal (Pradhan 1986: 204). In the next election of 1946, the Congress victory was even more decisive: it won 123 out of 151 seats. The successor organisation to Ambedkar's ILP, the Scheduled Castes Federation (SCF), won only two seats. The other seats were shared between a variety of parties and Independents (Pradhan 1986: 296).

[9] Ambedkar's ILP won three seats outside Bombay, but these were in the neighbouring Maharashtrian region of the Central Provinces.

But there was more complexity behind these Congress victories than is apparent from a simple tally of seats. In 1945 Ambedkar published a detailed analysis of the election of 1937 in which he claimed that Congress had won only 18 per cent of the vote in the reserved seats (Ambedkar 1945, 1991: 156). Congress had maximised the value of its vote by virtue of several factors, including vote splitting between too many non-Congress candidates; the converse of the latter factor, viz. an absence of Untouchable candidates in other constituencies; a caste Hindu vote in some constituencies that went against the preference of the Untouchables; and the benefit of far greater resources than any of the Untouchable organisations could assemble. A study of the 1946 election was even more revealing. Under the formula agreed in the Poona Pact, election to seats reserved for candidates from the Scheduled Castes was to proceed in two stages. In the first stage a primary election of only the Scheduled Caste voters of a reserved constituency was to rank order the Scheduled Caste candidates for the seat; the names of the four leading candidates were then to be put to the whole constituency. In the 1946 election primary polls were held for only forty-three seats; presumably there were no more than four candidates in the other seats. In these forty-three primary elections, Congress won roughly 29 per cent of the vote, Ambedkar's SCF 26 per cent, and other parties and Independents won the remaining 44 per cent (total 99 per cent). Congress topped the primary poll in twenty seats and the SCF in thirteen (Pradhan 1986: 296). But in the overall electorate, the SCF was able to win only two seats. Caste Hindu voters were seemingly unwilling to vote for SCF candidates, even if they were the choice of the Untouchables of the electorate. For Ambedkar this was proof that the Poona formula systematically worked against a party led by Untouchables, and he made a renewed call for the separate electorates that had been rejected in Poona (Ambedkar 1945, 1991: 90–3).

It is doubtful that the mechanical construction of electorates had a major impact on the political success of organisations led by Untouchables. In particular, it is not possible to attribute Ambedkar's declining electoral success to this factor: after all, under the same electoral system, his organisation did much worse in 1946 than it did in 1937. But Ambedkar's analysis does reveal that the hold of Gandhi and Congress on Untouchable sympathies was considerably less than was generally depicted at the time. In 1951, when hagiographic accounts of Gandhi were at their height, Nurullah and Naik were wise enough to observe that

Gandhiji's main work lay among the caste Hindus, and its greatness is to be measured by the extent of change brought about in the minds of the caste Hindus. But however painful, it is a fact of history that he did not have a very large following among the Harijans themselves. (Quoted in Zelliot 1972: 92)

Most of the Untouchable candidates for Congress in the thirties and forties were figures of no prominence and often of little education. Their association with Congress said little about any hold that Gandhi and Congress may have had on the Untouchable imagination. On the other hand, a number of the Untouchable leaders with a base independent of Gandhi came to have an ambivalent relationship with him and with Congress. One of them was M. C. Rajah (1883–1943), perhaps the most prominent pre-Independence Untouchable politician other than Ambedkar. We have noted Rajah's break with the Justice Party in the mid-1920s and his pact with Munje, President of the Hindu Mahasabha, subsequent to the Round Table Conferences. Throughout the 1930s he took an integrationist, anti-Ambedkarite, line and supported Gandhi's Harijan movement. But Rajah became severely disillusioned with Congress, especially the Rajagopalachariar Government that took office in Madras after the 1937 election. He was embittered by the Madras Government's about-face on temple entry legislation, seeing this as a 'gross betrayal' of the Depressed Classes (Rajah Papers: f. 5). On 25 August 1938 he wrote to Gandhi, saying that he was devastated by the shortcomings of the Government in Madras and by the pressure placed on Depressed Classes' Members to toe a party line hostile to the interests of their own communities. He now questioned the principle of joint electorates that he had supported as part of the Poona Pact,

in the full belief that the Congress would really help us in our attempt to secure social and religious freedom. I am forced to think that our entering the Joint Electorate with the Caste Hindus under the leadership of the Congress, far from helping us, has enabled the Congress, led by Caste Hindu leaders, to destroy our independence and to us to cut our own throats. (Rajah Papers: f. 3)

Gandhi responded on 14 September 14 1938 declaring his full confidence in Rajagopalachariar, and urging Rajah to 'trust him' (Rajah Papers). But Rajah was not to be placated. He joined Ambedkar and other Untouchable leaders in supporting the British war effort, and actively opposed the Congress Quit India movement. So having spent much of his political career in opposition to Ambedkar and in support of Gandhi, Rajah ultimately saw himself forced to change sides. This is a substantial comment on Gandhi's lack of rapport with independent leaders of the Untouchables.

Of course, it is clear that the Congress had greater national support from Untouchable voters than did any other organisation in the 1930s and 40s. But it is important not to extrapolate from electoral statistics and any general sense of the congeniality of Gandhi to many ordinary Untouchables, to the proposition that a great mass of enthusiastic

Untouchables were mobilised into the Gandhian and Congress cause in the pre-Independence period. There is simply no evidence of this.

Gandhi and Ambedkar compared

If the Mahatma met stiff resistance to his campaign of the 1930s, the tide that Ambedkar was swimming against was massive. Ambedkar did not bring to the Untouchable struggle any reservoir of prestige with which to support a position that was increasingly threatening to Hindu society. Ambedkar was an object of antipathy for orthodox Hindus and for the nationalist movement, which saw him as a collaborator with the British. Any political movement he created would have had to be drawn almost exclusively fom the ranks of the Untouchables. But even here his prospects were highly limited. While his achievements in London and Poona were of potential benefit to every Untouchable caste in India, he was poorly placed to derive widespread political benefit from this circumstance. Individual Untouchables of varied caste came to see in Ambedkar the pre-eminent Untouchable of his era, but this recognition was not sufficiently widespread or deeply rooted as to allow him to assume a role of mass leadership across India. There was no collective memory of a common Untouchable leadership that could have helped him disarm competitive impulses and suspicions between Untouchable castes. Nor was there a material base of resources and provincial leadership that could have supported such a national enterprise. It is possible to speculate that had Ambedkar first made a general political reputation within Congress, perhaps then he could have carved off the Untouchables as his own special constituency. But just one of the assumptions of this counterfactual is that an Untouchable would have been allowed to rise to the top of Congress in the manner, say, of Nehru. This is dubious in the extreme. Our counter-factual puts the cart before the horse – it was Ambedkar's own efforts that helped open up Indian political life to the influence of Untouchables. At the very end of the twentieth century it may be possible to imagine an Untouchable at the very apex of Indian politics – after all, Jagjivan Ram reached the position of Deputy Prime Minister after a mainstream career of conspicuous caution. But at the beginning of the century the very subordination that so disfigured the lives of the Untouchables would scarcely have allowed one of them to develop a broad constituency cutting across caste, including Untouchable caste, and region. In short, as political figures Gandhi and Ambedkar were highly asymmetrical.

At another level of abstraction, the fundamental differences between the two leaders become still clearer. Gandhi's Harijan strategy was

simple. He would attempt to wean caste Hindus from their sinful discrimination against Untouchables, and in the process he would convince
the Untouchables themselves that they could take their place as equal citizens of an independent India. Acceptance and inclusion would end the
problem of Untouchability – inclusion represented both the means and
the end. Of course, the inclusion that Gandhi actually achieved was to
bind many of the Untouchables to Congress without ending the adverse
discrimination against them. Untouchables had to be content with a
reformism which left in place the syndrome that we have examined in previous chapters. If we turn to Ambedkar, on the other hand, he can be seen
to have developed an analysis of the nature of Untouchability that was
more complex and intellectually more satisfying than that of Gandhi. But
what Ambedkar lacked throughout was a workable political strategy.

The root of Ambedkar's political failure was not of his own making. His
greatest difficulties were inherent in the nature of the Untouchable
population. If Ambedkar aspired to be their pre-eminent leader, then he
had to build a political movement on the basis of the difference between
Untouchables and other Indians. (Gandhi, by contrast, could adopt the
intuitively more attractive position of denying such difference.) But, of
course, the Untouchables were not a single community clearly separate
from the other peoples living under the banner of Hinduism. Ambedkar
was far too astute not to be aware of this. He rejected racial theories of
Untouchability which sought to portray the Untouchables as the original
Indians who had been subordinated by later invaders.[10] Ambedkar was
quite clear that the Untouchables were themselves of diverse origin. His
own position was that what was now called Hinduism was a self-serving
Brahmin invention at odds with the earlier and far more egalitarian order
of the Buddhist period. He recognised that the principal contemporary
link between Untouchables across India was their experience of discrimination at the hands of high-caste society. So, if the Untouchables
were socially diverse but united in their subordination, then it might make
as much sense to try to build a wider class-based coalition of subordinated peoples as to concentrate on the Untouchables alone. This was
precisely Ambedkar's dilemma in the late thirties and forties, as he oscillated between caste and class models of political organisation.

---

[10] Ambedkar developed a complex theory of the origins of Untouchability. The Untouchables were 'Broken Men', fragments of tribes that had lost wars to certain other tribes.
These Broken Men attached themselves as watchmen to settled villages that feared attack
from the same victorious tribes (Ambedkar 1948, 1990: 242, 274–7). Much later, descen-
dants of the Broken Men were constituted as Untouchables by Brahmins who were
seeking to overthrow the Buddhism practised by these people. Ambedkar is careful to
stress that this is not a racial theory of the origins of Untouchables, and that Brahmins
and Untouchables were not of different racial stock.

Although Ambedkar failed to build a strong national organisation, his impact on Untouchable politics in various parts of the country was immense. Venkatswamy's account has given us special insight into the complex situation in the princely state of Hyderabad. Of the two most numerous Untouchable castes of Hyderabad, the Malas were socially, educationally and politically more advanced than the Madigas – there were strong parallels with the divide in Bombay between the Mahars and the Mangs. From early in the twenties there had been intense rivalry between two Mala leaders, Bhagya Reddy Varma and Arigay Ramaswamy.[11] Philosophical differences appear to have been less important than the personal rivalry between the two. In the thirties a third leader, Venkat Rao, emerged on an Ambedkarite platform. Although Arigay had been radical for his time – for example, he had actively pursued inter-caste contacts with the Madigas – he was immediately alienated by the separatism and disrespectful tone of Venkat Rao and his Ambedkarite followers. Arigay had absolutely no inclination to leave Hinduism. But Venkat Rao soon faced his own nemesis in the form of younger, college educated, Ambedkarites who rebelled against his authoritarian style. Internal splits, vindictive press and pamphlet campaigns, a celebrated court case, and even physical violence were enacted between the warring parties (Venkatswamy 1955: I, 192–216). Attempts to bring about unity and to enlist the support of Ambedkar himself only intensified the factionalism. All of this activity was conducted within the hothouse atmosphere of the towns of the State; there was a negligible effort to create a mass movement involving Malas from the villages. In sum, the injection of the hard-edged views of Ambedkar had dramatically increased the intensity of politics among the Malas but had exacerbated rather than resolved the prevailing factionalism. Ambedkar remained a figure of great respect to virtually all the Hyderabad Malas, though by the time Venkatswamy published his account he himself had lost faith in Ambedkar's capacity to show the way.

Despite all the mutual suspicions, Ambedkar managed to gain a limited following from other Untouchable castes within his own Bombay region. In this connection the career of the Chambhar leader P. N. Rajbhoj is instructive as one of the handful of Untouchables to have had some national prominence before Independence. Rajbhoj was an early collaborator with Ambedkar, and was one of the leaders of the satyagraha to open the Parvati temple in Pune in 1929. After the Round Table Conferences

[11] Bhagya Reddy Varma's name was constructed out of his given name (Bhagya), a Brahmin caste name (Varma) and the name of the dominant caste of the region (Reddy). This nominal engineering belonged to the Sanskritising period of Untouchable consciousness.

he swung to the Gandhian side and supported Rajah's pact with Munje against the principle of separate electorates. In 1938 he visited Hyderabad in connection with Gandhi's temple entry movement, and proceeded to belittle Ambedkar as the sectional leader of the Mahars. But on his next recorded visit to Hyderabad in 1944, he was one of Ambedkar's party (Venkatswamy 1955: I, 131, 270–1). Soon after Independence he organised an Ambedkarite satyagraha in Marathwada against the reclamation of land rights ceded to Untouchables. And in 1952 Rajbhoj was the only candidate of Ambedkar's Scheduled Caste Federation to win a seat to the Lok Sabha. But in 1957, a year after Ambedkar's death, Rajbhoj was elected to the Rajya Sabha on the Congress ticket, and he became an insistent spokesman against the extension of reserved employment and parliamentary seats to Mahar Buddhists. Clearly his allegiance had been to Ambedkar, not to the Mahars who sought to carry on the movement in Ambedkar's name.

Ambedkar after the Poona Pact

We now need to lay out in more detail the direction of Ambedkar's movement during the years after the Poona Pact. In the immediate months after Poona Ambedkar had been undecided as to how he should proceed. Although by then he believed that temple admission would flow from broader socio-economic progress and should not be the focus of anti-Untouchability action, his criticisms of Gandhi were for a time moderate. Gandhi was at least taking more action on Untouchability than he had previously. And Ambedkar was able to bask in the achievement of having delivered to his people the promise of a large number of Untouchable legislators. He was not even sure that he would remain a political activist (Keer 1971: 242). He spent much of 1933 in London, and returned in 1934 to the practice of law and to lecturing. But then, again seemingly without warning, he gave a speech which thrust him back into both politics and sectarian controversy.

At a huge conference convened at Yeola in October 1935 to discuss the question of Untouchable conversion, Ambedkar announced that while his birth as a Hindu was beyond his control: 'I will not die a Hindu' (Ambedkar 1969: II, 126–38). From the most prominent Untouchable in India, this was a veritable bombshell. Not only did it attract the opposition of Hindu leaders, Gandhi included, but it bitterly divided the Untouchables themselves. Among his own Mahars, and despite the opposition of some of the older leaders, the direction of Ambedkar's thinking prevailed. There was also some support for conversion in Andhra and Hyderabad (Venkatswamy 1955: II, 81), and in scattered locations in the north. But most communities other than the Mahars showed no enthusiasm for a new round of conversion to some as yet unnamed religion. The Chambhars of Bombay were particularly outspoken in their opposition, and painted the announcement as a stunt to augment the political fortunes of Ambedkar's own community (Gokhale 1993: 167). And there was no doubt that Ambedkar had now drawn a sharper line between his own followers on the one hand, and both caste Hindus and integrationist Untouchables who leaned towards Congress.

With no immediately apparent connection to Yeola, Ambedkar next turned in August 1936 to the formation of what he called the Independent Labour Party (ILP). It was a matter of simple logic to set up a party to contest the election of 1937. But in what ideological form would the party be cast? For the first time Ambedkar sought to establish an organisation that transparently reached out beyond Untouchables to embrace the wider Indian 'labouring classes'. The Party declared itself to be against both 'Brahminism' and 'Capitalism', and defined Untouchability primarily in terms of economy and class. A range of policies was framed on landlordism, public works, exploitative money-lenders, and so on. Interventions were made in industrial struggles. And Ambedkar went out of his way to try to ally the ILP with parties and movements of the left, including the Communists (despite their Brahmin leadership) and the remnants of the Bombay non-Brahmin movement (Omvedt 1994: 207–8). But the distinctiveness of Ambedkar's position remained apparent in his insistence that the Indian working class could not transcend considerations of caste. This was one of his reasons for the rejection of Marxism as a suitable guide for India (Ambedkar 1987a: 441–64). His strategy of the period was to broaden the base of the Untouchable movement, and simultaneously to infuse wider working-class organisations with a sense of the special nature of Untouchability.

Ambedkar's strategy for the ILP had a considerable political logic. Indeed, this approach appears to be a model for Kanshi Ram's Bahujana Samaj Party in contemporary Uttar Pradesh. The first couple of years of the ILP were promising, and we have seen that the party was able to win most of the seats it contested in the 1937 election. It is not clear just how much support was gathered from Untouchable castes other than the Mahars, but seemingly there was a degree of support. And yet a bare five years later Ambedkar wound the party up. The ILP had failed to develop into a national organisation and, crucially, it had not attracted any reliable support from interests representing the caste Hindu poor. It had lost most of whatever ground it had occupied among the Chambhars and Mangs of Bombay. Ambedkar's biographer notes that he had little interest in the hard work of party organisation (Keer 1971: 480), but it is doubtful that better organisation would have allowed the ILP to prosper. The central failure of not being able to attract reliable support outside the Mahar community scarcely arose from weak party organisation.

Ambedkar read the lesson of the ILP with a cold eye, and the Scheduled Caste Federation (SCF) formed upon the dissolution of the ILP in 1942 was an organisation of far more modest ambitions. A new distrust of caste Hindus was evident in the call for formation of entirely separate villages of Untouchables, and the renewed demand for separate electorates (Omvedt 1994: 217). But the actual work of the SCF, particularly after Independence, was

to see that the special treatment provisions were properly used, that the discrimination and injustice still practiced was brought to public attention, and that the seats reserved for Scheduled Castes in legislatures were filled by men under obligation to speak for Scheduled Caste interests. (Zelliot 1969: 55)

In short, the active effort to establish a radical organisation uniting Untouchables and other subordinated Indians was now laid to rest. Ambedkar's own time for political organising was diminished in the 1940s by his official work as Labour Member of the Viceroy's Executive Council and, from 1947 to 1950, as principal draftsman of the Constitution of India. In this context, the SCF failed almost totally in the elections of 1946 and 1952. In his spare time, and substantially freed from the constraint of seeking political allies, Ambedkar wrote his most savage critiques of Hinduism, Gandhi and Congress. *Riddles in Hinduism*, the most daring of all his attacks on Hinduism, was not published in his own lifetime; it was finally published amid violent uproar from fundamentalist Hindus in 1987.

Once his work on the Constitution was over, Ambedkar had one remaining bombshell to detonate.[12] His personal conversion to Buddhism in 1956 was accompanied by the conversion of millions of his Mahar followers – some three-quarters of the whole Mahar population had become Buddhists within a period of several years. There were relatively few converts outside the Mahars, though scattered communities in Uttar Pradesh joined suit. Ambedkar had built a strong connection with the Jatavs (Chamars) of Agra since the time of the Round Table Conferences, and a couple of thousand Jatavs immediately followed him into Buddhism (Lynch 1972: 97–112). Ambedkar had been speaking about Buddhism since the thirties but his first major statement on the religion had appeared in *The Untouchables* (1948), where it is portrayed as the only Indian belief system with an historical tradition of egalitarianism. Buddhism is seen to have been destroyed by a Brahminical counter-

---

[12] For a comment on the several strands of Ambedkar's whole career, see Baxi (1995).

revolution which pushed its most determined opponents to the periphery of society and declared them to be unclean. This was the origin of Untouchability. Although Buddhism was to all intents dead in the land of its birth, Ambedkar set out to reclaim it as both spiritual guide and sharp ideological break with Hinduism.

Clearly Ambedkar's religious conversion represented an approach to the struggle against Untouchability that was strikingly different from his political representations to the British or his activities on behalf of the Independent Labour Party or even the Scheduled Caste Federation. But it would be superficial to discount the common threads that ran through Ambedkar's life. What in a sense unified the different phases of his leadership was impatience with strategies that could be seen to have delivered no substantial benefit after an appropriate trial. He appears never to have been highly committed to the temple entry campaign, so his abandonment of this strategy after a period of only several years was not so significant. His disillusionment with the political regime he had fought for at the Round Table Conferences in London and then in Poona, and with the Left strategy of the ILP period, was more important but scarcely unreasonable. Ambedkar was obviously right to conclude from some years of experience that this strategy would not deliver widespread change in the short term.Meanwhile Gandhi was making great political progress with what Ambedkar saw to be a hollow campaign that would never transform the condition of his people. Nor did the situation improve after Independence. Ambedkar's own popularity did not rise, despite achievements that included drafting the Constitution. And he was disillusioned by routine events such as the failure of the Commissioner for Scheduled Castes and Tribes – the official protector of the Untouchables – to report on what Ambedkar believed to be the rising incidence of violence against Untouchables. The Third Report of the Commissioner was 'absolutely silent over... the tyrannies, maltreatments and oppressions to which they are being subjected almost every day' (Ambedkar 1969: II, 67). How was it possible to rest any faith in a Congress regime of such do-nothing outlook? All of this served to feed Ambedkar's tendency towards systematic, absolutist, thinking in relation to the Untouchables. They could expect no substantial assistance from anyone outside their own ranks. Since it was Hinduism itself that was oppressing them, the Untouchables needed to create for themselves a space in which they were free. They still had to work in the world, but they would be able to do so from a position of inner strength.

4   Public policy I: anti-discrimination and compensatory discrimination

The early years after Independence were marked by a certain optimism about the problem of the Untouchables, which was viewed as part of the larger project of modernisation. Led by the secular and socialist-minded Nehru, official India turned its back on Hindu orthodoxy. Caste was seen as the prime symbol of social difference, the enemy of national unity. Untouchability represented the darkest side of this culture, which would fade away in the light of a new age of national and social freedom. There is no moment when this optimism vanished; it just gradually ceased to be a factor. Certain progress was made, but the problems clearly persisted and could be seen to be long-term. Political attention wandered off to other more pressing or more attractive and soluble issues. This unfortunate outcome is consistent with a general abstractness characteristic of Indian public policy. While the goal of equality for the Untouchables could excite a certain enthusiasm in New Delhi, in Nehru's India such enthusiasm was shallow and thus lacking in sustainable commitment. It was not merely the case that there were gaps between fine policy formulated in New Delhi and weak practice in the States – though practice in the States was indeed weak. The policy itself was abstract and unrealistic. It is this perspective which helps explain the conjunction of appropriately progressive sentiments discernible and genuinely held by leading politicians and civil servants in New Delhi, and an administrative performance that has been massively unequal to the task.

Most of the foundations of post-Independence policy towards the Untouchables were laid ten to fifteen years before Independence, at the time of the burst of political activity described in chapter 3. There have been two broad policies – compensatory discrimination and action against adverse discrimination. The first grew out of Ambedkar's approach, and consists in guarantees of seats in legislatures, positions in public employment, and educational benefits. The second policy more closely reflected Gandhi's position, and has been concerned to bring about a cessation of discriminatory behaviour on the part of caste Hindus.

Of the two policies it is compensatory discrimination that has captured the attention of the Indian public and Untouchables themselves. While Ambedkar conceived of the scheme as a revolutionary political force nurtured in separate Untouchable electorates, its predominant nature has been bureaucratic not political and directed to individuals rather than to Untouchables as a whole people. Administration of the program (popularly known as 'reservation') has developed into a massive, inefficient and highly dispiriting apparatus, and the most sought after benefits are themselves jobs in the bureaucracy. No serious observer now imagines that the scheme is anything so grand as a way of overcoming the overall subordination of the Untouchables. Rather, it has possessed the singular merit of allowing the Congress regime to recognise the claims of Untouchables without having to concede them any important share of power.

Our proposition is not that the state has failed to make a real difference to the lives of Untouchables. Rather, the argument is that any major beneficial impact has tended to arise from policies directed to the whole population and not merely to Untouchables. This is true in relation to the greater life expectancy, increased literacy, and above all the enhanced dignity of Untouchables in the present period. The State of Kerala is the clearest example. Kerala has the best 'social indicators' of any State in India – its literacy and longevity are the highest, and its birth rate the lowest in the country. While Untouchable 'indicators' rank lower than the State average, they are far better than those of Untouchables elsewhere in India. But there has been no special state attention paid to the Untouchables in Kerala. Quite the reverse, there is abundant evidence that a Marxist culture hostile to the 'casteist' dimensions of compensatory discrimination has encouraged delinquency in relation to its requirements. But Kerala Untouchables have benefited from the general welfare policies of the State. They remain at the bottom of Kerala society, but in many ways they are far better off than Untouchables in the other States.

As to compensatory discrimination, its very persistence in a form little changed over a period of sixty years is itself an indication of its fundamental limitations. If the program of action had been more radical, it would have run into greater trouble than it has. Only in recent years, when socially desirable benefits such as entry to medical schools are being taken up in full measure, has the scheme of benefits become more than marginally controversial.

Whether official action against ritual discrimination has done any better remains a question. While we argue that India has been much more successful in the matter of overcoming ritual discrimination than in tackling poverty, the proposition here is that the achievements are less attributable to the state and more to increased resoluteness on the part of Untouchables themselves and also to the emergence of a new civic culture of tolerance. That culture has itself developed partly, but only partly, in response to pressures generated by the state.

Anti-discrimination action

Some years before Independence India already had the rudiments of legislation prohibiting the exercise of adverse discrimination against Untouchables. The first major legislation was a Madras Act of 1938 that made it an offence to discriminate against Untouchables in publicly financed facilities such as roads, wells and transport, and also in 'any other secular institution' (including, for example, restaurants and hotels) to which the general public was admitted (Galanter 1972: 239). This Act carried penalties ranging from small fines to imprisonment for repeat offences, and was widely followed elsewhere in India between the end of World War II and Independence. In 1947 additional legislation was enacted in Madras to prohibit exclusion of Untouchables from temples, and again this was a model followed in other provinces and princely states over the next several years (Dushkin 1957: 133–4; Galanter 1972: 241).

After Independence the *Constitution of India* (1950) purported to abolish Untouchability and make its practice an offence (Article 17), and also prohibited some specific discriminations and exclusions (Articles 15 (2), 23, 25 and 29 (2)). These prohibitions were amplified by the *Untouchability Offences Act* 1955, which set up a regime of offences and punishment for direct discrimination and, for the first time, for the indirect support of Untouchability through mechanisms such as social boycott. The Act had deficiencies and was less than sympathetically interpreted by superior courts (Galanter 1972: 254–61); it was tightened up in a number of respects by the *Protection of Civil Rights Act* 1976. Assessment of its impact is difficult – we will return below to prosecutions under the Act – but it is doubtful that its specific effects have been great. The legislation was framed after decades of political action, and its very passage was a measure of the weakening hold of the ideology of Untouchability. Its impact is probably to be found primarily in further undermining the legitimacy of Untouchability. But before concluding this question, we need first to return to the question of just how much Untouchability is practised today.

Earlier we cited empirical studies by I. P. Desai and others to the effect that Untouchables can now freely walk along virtually any public road, catch a bus or train, use the post office, eat in a café in a major city, and be admitted to a school which will not segregate them within the school-room. But Desai and innumerable other sources also show that in many regions discrimination persists at the water well, barber shop, tea stall and temple, to name some prominent public sites. This discrimination is more to be found in rural rather than urban areas. In the great cities of India, and in the special case of Bengal, there is now a civic culture that does not permit the open practice of ritual discrimination in public space. There are thus three questions to answer. First, why have certain kinds of discrimination disappeared from virtually all environments? Secondly, why has other discrimination persisted in many locations? And thirdly, why have certain places developed a new civic culture that effectively ends all public discrimination on the basis of caste?

If we attend first to the ritual discriminations that have disappeared everywhere, it seems that in most cases they fell away with relative ease once the full weight of orthodoxy began to crumble. Take the case of the prohibition on free use of roads. This was endemic to the south, never the north, and was part of a cluster of specially subordinating structures that included slavery, distance pollution and spittoons. Slavery was the first of these structures to fall, partly under the weight of Christian and then general European disapproval. Access to roads followed within decades – we have noted that by the turn of the twentieth century the Pulayas of Travancore (but not of nearby Cochin) had gained the right to use most roads other than those leading to temples. Although the Pulayas had engaged in protest marches to stake their claim, their victory seems to have come without major battle. Restrictions on movement were probably bound up with the institution of slavery or other severe economic subordination, even if they presented themselves as exercises in Hindu orthodoxy. Once slavery was gone, there was no economic logic for severe restriction of physical movement.

The capacity of an Untouchable to catch a train or bus has not been the subject of much comment, but presumably it came with the general relaxation of separateness inherent in the development of cities and a more mobile workforce. Employers of Untouchables had a clear economic interest in their employees being able to travel to work, and of course the Anglo-Indian state had no desire to exclude Untouchables from its railways. Later, the proprietors of private buses had a strong interest in maximising their customer base. Moreover, except in the ritually strictest regions of the south, physical separateness was not a structure of even notional comprehensiveness. In sum, there was probably little caste Hindu resistance by the time modern travel became a possibility for Untouchables.

The truly radical change is the admission of Untouchable children to schools, and the almost complete cessation of the worst forms of discrimination within those schools. This liberation has been India-wide and has been common to both urban and rural settings. Abatement of discrimination has been a necessary condition for the rapid rise in education and therefore literacy among Untouchables. And since education underpins effective social participation in modern India, the change has been of the first importance. The question, then, is why reform in the matter of education has been so great. We can begin by observing that perhaps it is less problematical to admit a Chamar boy into school than to allow his father to draw water from a well used by Brahmins. Children, not adults, go to school, and perhaps it is easier for a high-caste person to turn a blind eye to the infringements of orthodoxy encountered by children.[1] But more importantly, in most situations in India there has never been any rigorous physical separation of Untouchables. Caste Hindus have always come into close physical proximity with Untouchables – how could a Brahmin landholder direct his Chamar ploughman without talking to him? But sharing food, drink and particular kinds of bodily contact – through a common barber, for example – have generally been treated with greater caution. Clearly the issue of education is rather different. Here the traditional objection has been less about physical contact and more about excluding Untouchables from the holy books and from means of self-betterment.

We have seen that from as early as the middle of the nineteenth century the Anglo-Indian state made formal pronouncements requiring non-discriminatory admission of children to public schools, but that it routinely failed to enforce its edicts. Education became a reality for a small proportion of Untouchable children in the last years of the nineteenth and early years of the twentieth century, and it was variously conducted by Christian missionaries, enlightened princely rulers, Hindu reform organisations, and sometimes the state, including the Indian Army. Despite the severity of its Untouchability regime, Madras Presidency proved to have one of the better records in education when the several provinces reported between 1916 and 1920 on the 'moral, material and educational condition' of the Untouchables; these reports flowed from a resolution moved in the Legislative Council by Dadabhoy, a nationalist leader, in 1916. The (very loose) figures supplied by the Government of Madras in 1920 suggested that over a period of a quarter-century the number of

---

[1] We are aware that adults are sometimes specially sensitive about wrongs done to their children, but it may be that the issue of ritual contamination is viewed through a distinctive lens. To be contaminated by ritual inferiors is, after all, to suffer a particular kind of 'wrong'. At least in the modern period, all Indians know full well that the practice of ritual Untouchability is an official evil.

'Panchama' (Untouchable) pupils had grown from 30,000 to over 150,000. This was still only 2 per cent of the eligible population, and naturally it consisted overwhelmingly of boys (though the number of exclusively female primary schools had grown from eleven in 1892 to 100 in 1920). Fully 100,000 of the 1920 pupils were said to be in Christian mission schools, and the others in a variety of schools including those of Hindu reform organisations. An unstated number were in government schools, but for the future the government had decided that

all schools under public management should be accessible to the Panchamas... But while there can be no doubt that this policy... is the right one from its educative effect both upon the Panchamas and their higher caste brethren, it will also probably be necessary to create and maintain a large number of schools intended chiefly for the Panchamas, field-labourers' schools which are open to all classes but which will chiefly be used by the members of the Panchama class. (Government of India, House Proceedings 1920: 770)

So the Government of Madras was admitting here that it could not integrate Untouchables and caste Hindus within the one classroom. Nor can there have been much integration in the mission schools, given the predominantly Untouchable character of many of the Christian congregations. Christians from high-caste backgrounds regularly excluded Untouchables from their own schools (Isaacs 1965: 77).

Bengal was more liberal than Madras. In its response to the Dadabhoy Inquiry, the Government of Bengal observed in 1917 that

the children of these [Untouchable] classes in Bengal do not suffer from the same disabilities as elsewhere. They are freely admitted into schools and colleges, and have in fact equality of opportunity from the educational point of view. That many of them are not more advanced is due to their own indifference to education. Such apathy is not peculiar to them, but is shared by many of the clean castes. While, however, the depressed classes are under no disabilities as regards admission to colleges and schools, there is a difficulty about hostel accommodation of them; and the Government of Bengal have done their best to remove this difficulty, and have established special Home hostels for Namasudra students at Dacca, Faridpur and Barisal. (Government of India, House Proceedings 1920: 920)

So apart from their admitted difficulty in finding hostel accommodation – hostels involve sharing food, water, toilet and other facilities – the Government of Bengal took the view that Untouchables had no special problems in the schools of Bengal.

The rest of India more closely resembled Madras than Bengal, and in 1920 or thereabouts it seems to have been unusual for an Untouchable child to be admitted to a primary school composed mostly of caste Hindu children. Over the next half-century this situation was quite transformed, but the mechanisms and time lines of the transformation are less than clear. There were occasional set-pieces that provoked conflict (Nayanar 1982: 1–2), but there was never a major campaign for Untouchable entry to mixed schools. Nor did the dam burst with any suddenness. For many years after school authorities began to allow Untouchable boys to receive instruction they were subject to humiliations. One of Isaacs' respondents, a Chamar, recalled being permitted to sit on the verandah outside the schoolroom. He sat there for three years, until an inspector pronounced that this was an infringement of government rules. Thereafter the boy was allowed inside, and he spent his fourth year, 1928, sitting on a chair behind the teacher (Isaacs 1965: 76). Stories like this are commonplace (Aggarwal and Ashraf 1976: 10), and clearly only the most determined child would have had the fortitude to endure the humiliations. By the time of I. P. Desai's research in about 1970 such discrimination was largely absent in Gujarat (1976: 226). A somewhat higher but still low rate of classroom segregation, 8.4 per cent, was reported in a survey of about the same period in Karnataka (Parvathamma 1984: 237). Presumably the residual discrimination in these regions has declined still further over the following two decades.

It would seem that the greatest progress in dismantling discrimination in village-level primary schools took place in the quarter-century after the first Indian governments were elected in 1937. It is known that there was a great increase in literacy and therefore primary schooling between the Censuses of 1931 and 1961, but the absence of separate literacy data for the Scheduled Castes in 1941 and 1951 means that it is not possible to be more precise about the time of uptake. As to the mechanisms of change, these can be seen to consist in a complex of cultural, political and legal factors. Above all, the demand for education was growing fast among the Untouchables themselves. Some of the demand was generated by political developments of the thirties, but it also reflected cultural change that had been working itself through for many years. The long-term impact of of the Christian missions, for example, was more than merely marginal. But certainly Harijan and Ambedkarite politics of the 1930s gave new hope and ambition to Untouchables in many parts of India, though not so much in the populous regions of the north – particularly the present States of Uttar Pradesh and Bihar. The changed political climate slowly began to be translated into public policy favourable to the Untouchables. Scholarships were provided for higher education. And importantly, the legislation pioneered by Madras in 1938 made exclusion of Untouchable children from school a criminal offence. Cases were brought before the courts. All this activity must have put pressure on provincial administrations to enforce the rules regarding admissions. But village schools tended to be the autocratic preserve of the teachers, frequently Brahmins.

While nowadays it is possible to hear fond recollections of teachers well disposed to Untouchable boys of promise, often the teachers were seriously prejudiced and opposed to admitting such pupils. Resistance inhibited new enrolments and made life within the schoolroom miserable for many Untouchable boys, but it was essentially a rearguard action. From the 1940s, and with enhanced vigour after Independence, the pressure for change was welling up from a developmental as well as a reformist ideology. It became an article of nationalist faith that education of the Indian poor, including Untouchables, was a necessity for the development of the nation. In sum, what gradually emerged from these various forces was a new civic culture that accepted the right of Untouchables to go to school. By the 1970s, perhaps even some years earlier, all that was left was a rump of resistance in villages of unusual backwardness. Anti-discrimination legislation had played a part in the emergence of this new civic culture, but it seems not to have been the dominant part.

Thus far we have considered only those areas of social discrimination that have been almost universally abolished. We can now turn to the heart of the old scheme of ritual pollution, viz. issues of water and food. In relation to these issues there is a sharp divide between life in the cities and in the relatively progressive region of Bengal on the one hand, and life in the villages. In the former, such discrimination in places of public resort is now rarely encountered. Indeed, the civic culture we identified in relation to education can be said to have washed away almost all the old practice of public Untouchability. The engine of this culture has tended to be pragmatism rather than egalitarianism. Either people do not care about the traditional values of purity and pollution in the context of Untouchability, or at least they are prepared to go along with the prevailing modern culture while in the city. The same people may revert to 'traditional', more discriminatory, culture during stays in their ancestral village.

The caste of their fellow customers can be of little relevance to ordinary people who buy a glass of iced water from the ubiquitous carts on the streets of Delhi (though it is doubtful that many of the vendors are themselves Untouchable). But at loftier social levels urban segregation asserts itself on the basis of class. Since caste and class tend to run together, this limits the interaction of higher-caste Hindus and Untouchables. A middle-class Untouchable might occasionally eat in the same café as caste Hindus, but for the latter such encounters will usually be anonymous and unknowing rather than personal. Those traditionally minded, perhaps older, people who would find such encounters objectionable are generally able to arrange their life so as to avoid them. But the experience of public eating facilities enjoyed by an Untouchable rickshaw puller, for example, will be limited to outside, makeshift, cafés or at least to very humble indoor establishments. Patronisation of these facilities is more a case of the utilitarian satisfaction of hunger and thirst than of 'inter-dining' with social superiors, to use Shraddhananda's lofty phrase of the 1920s. It is no doubt an advance that Untouchables can now use such facilities (if they have enough money), but we should avoid celebrating this as a great event. There has been no blinding light on the road to Damascus, merely slow change brought about by multiple pressures working against the claims of caste orthodoxy. The new civic culture is one of pragmatism which allows ample scope for compartmentalisation and social hypocrisy.

Avoidance strategies are a useful means of engineering civility in distant social relations, but of themselves they are insufficient to make the former objects of gross discrimination feel comfortable. For example, even now that desegregation of the schools is substantially complete, it is not possible to conclude that all school-based discrimination against Untouchables has disappeared. There remain serious questions about equal treatment in terms of the appropriateness of the curriculum and the sensitivity and diligence of teachers towards their Untouchable students. And there is also the matter of how caste Hindu children treat their Untouchable class fellows. Do they play with them in the schoolyard? And if the discriminatory attitudes of adults are enacted by their children, is this from the earliest years of schooling or only later once they have thoroughly learnt the culture of Untouchability? There is insufficient research on these questions, despite a considerable flow of superficial surveys. Anecdotal accounts are variable – some Untouchable adults report little or no feeling of discrimination from their childhood, while others give less benign accounts. But clearly, in many respects India is still far away from possessing an appropriately democratic and rigorously non-discriminatory system of education.

Although we lack village-by-village data from across India, it is thor-oughly clear that ritual discrimination is now practised to a far greater extent in villages than in cities; provincial towns occupy a middle ground between the two. It is not that Indian villages are islands separate from the influences that have affected the cities. Over a period of many years vil-lages have been progressively integrated into a wider world, such that the idea of the village as a discrete entity is increasingly artificial (Mendelsohn 1993: 820–30). Villages too have experienced the culture of convenience and pragmatism that is the enemy of caste orthodoxy. But discriminatory practices tend to persist where their cessation would cause serious discomfort to their practitioners, and where the punitive consequences of such persistence will not be severe. In the case of schooling, the costs to teachers would have been substantial if they had continued to exclude Untouchable children once the state became serious about enforcing an open admissions policy. But there is no remaining area of frequent discrimination where the state has been equally committed to abolition. It has not been a genuine national priority, though it is law, that Untouchables be given access to village temples maintained by the high castes, or to the regular village barber or the teashop. Untouchables themselves have tended to wax and wane as to how much they have cared about these issues. For instance, the provision of hundreds of thousands of handwells in Untouchable quarters has both masked and softened the force of continuing discrimination in the matter of water supply. In these circumstances, action against abolition of the remaining discrimination has been slow.

We can now return to the question of court enforcement of the legislation proscribing discrimination against Untouchables. In 1953, under various pre-Independence Acts then in force, 362 cases were registered in a total of ten states.[2] Of these cases, 232 were about discrimination in shops, restaurants and the like; fifty were about access to water sources; and twenty-two were about temple admission. These three categories constituted 84 per cent of the cases of that year, and Galanter suggests that the breakdown may be broadly representative of actions taken under the subsequent *Untouchability Offences Act* (UOA) 1955 (Galanter 1972: 305). When the Act was amended in 1976, the ground of 'insulting' Untouchables was added to the list of offences: this has become the leading complaint under the renamed *Protection of Civil Rights Act* (PCRA) 1976. But the greatest total of cases under the Act in any one year during the 1950s was a mere 693 in 1956. This was the year after the new Act came into operation, and presumably reflected relative enthusiasm for the new provisions. By the end of the 1960s the pattern of utilisation had settled down to fewer than 300 cases a year. At the beginning of the 1970s the number of cases began to rise quite steeply, and seemingly the highest figure ever – 5,108 cases registered with the police – was reached in 1976. This was the first full year of Indira Gandhi's Emergency, when action against Untouchability was given fresh Government emphasis; it was also the year the Act was strengthened. The latest available figure is for 1985, when 3,332 cases were registered.

---

[2] The statistics in this paragraph are drawn from the *Reports of the Commissioner for Scheduled Castes and Scheduled Tribes* (RCSCST) 1953: 244–5; 1979–80 and 1980–1: 213; 1977–8: 118; 1986–7: 223; and the Elyaperul Committee 1969: 49.

Of course, all these figures are ludicrously small relative to the quantum of unlawful behaviour. Clearly very few Indians have been directly affected by the anti-discrimination legislation.

When we turn to the outcome of the cases and the scale of punishment, the record becomes even less impressive. In the early years derisory fines of 3 and 4 rupees were quite common (Galanter 1972: 273, 278). There were low rates of conviction too, and these fell rather than rose over time – in 1962, for example, the conviction rate had declined to 23 per cent of prosecutions (itself a smaller figure than registration of cases with the police).[3] The problem was compounded when the Act was amended in 1976: the latest figures show that some 10 per cent were convicted in 1982 and 12 per cent in 1983. Explanation of this low rate of conviction revolves around institutional failure and the social power of defendants. Take this official statement:

The main reason behind such acquittals, as far as the Commission understand, was delay in the disposal of cases during which the contending parties came to compromise behind the court, either of their own accord or as a result of intimidation and inducement offered by the accused to the aggrieved. Besides, the quality of investigation may itself be faulty, but nothing definitely can be said about this aspect in the absence of a scrutiny of the police records.

It is clear that the pressures on complainants grew worse after 1976, when punishment for offences was seriously toughened:

Since imprisonment is compulsory under the PCRA, the accused often arrives at a compromise with the complainant, as a result of which the witnesses turn hostile and do not support the prosecution ... Most of the SCs [Scheduled Castes] work under the non-SCs, and as such, they are pressurised not to support the prosecution.

In an early study of the legislation Galanter concluded that 'the question, then, is not why so few cases were brought, but rather why any cases are brought!' (Galanter 1972: 281). A quarter-of-a-century later this remark continues to hold good. Manifestly, court enforcement of the anti-disabilities legislation has not been a powerful force in bringing about an abatement of the practice of Untouchability. It is highly doubtful that another piece of legislation with even stronger penalties, the *Scheduled Castes and Scheduled Tribes (Prevention of Atrocities)* Act 1989, will greatly alter the situation. The best one can say is that perhaps the whole volume of legislation has contributed to stripping away the legitimacy of Untouchability, but it is difficult to measure such an effect.

[3] The statistics in this paragraph are drawn from RCSCST 1963–4: 22; and 1983–4 (new): 98. The quotation is from RCSCST (new) 1981–2: 73. The quotation in the next paragraph is from RCSCST (new) 1983–4: 99.

Compensatory discrimination

The origins

Guaranteed seats in national and provincial legislatures were provided to the Scheduled Castes after Ambedkar made his case to the British that his people should be treated as a social minority comparable with the Muslims.[4] The road to preferential treatment in public employment and education was not so straightforward. Seemingly the first case of preference in employment was taken as far back as 1902. Under the influence of the non-Brahmin movement of Maharashtra the Maharajah of Kolhapur issued an order that half of all government positions in his princely state were to be filled from castes other than Brahmins (Omvedt 1976: 127). Theoretically this opened the public service of the state to the Untouchables as well as to other backward castes, though it is doubtful that many of them were able to qualify.

The non-Brahmin movement continued to be the main force working for state action to offset social inequalities. Thus the second and more significant case of official preference was instituted in the princely state of Mysore, this time under the influence of the non-Brahmin movement in neighbouring Madras. In 1918 the Miller Committee (named after its British chairman, a judge) was convened in Mysore to consider 'special measures which may be taken to increase the representation of the backward communities in the public service' (Government of Mysore nd: 1). Backward 'communities' or 'classes' were defined by the Committee as everyone in the state other than the Brahmins (and the few Anglo-Indians and Europeans). The Committee's recommendation – accepted in slightly modified form in 1921 – was that within a period of seven years not more than half the higher appointments and one-third of the subordinate appointments were to be held by Brahmins.[5] This was to be accomplished through preferential enrolment in schools, colleges and hostels, and relaxation of entry standards into the state service. There was no thought of making the 'depressed classes' (Untouchables) a separate object of preference. Indeed, it was conceded that these classes were 'not expected to enter the superior service in any numbers for some years to come' (Government of Mysore nd: 2). This somewhat dismissive view reflected the identity of the group that had been instrumental in the Committee's establishment. They were 'urban notables' of non-Brahmin but certainly not Untouchable caste, led by a professor with a prior

---

[4] The experience of reservation of seats in legislatures is discussed in chapter 8.
[5] The Committee's statistics showed that, in 1918, 9,712 of the 13,946 jobs in the state service were occupied by Brahmins.

involvement in the Madras non-Brahmin movement (Manor 1977: 188). Even when the movement later developed a popular base, there is no evidence that it ever seriously concerned itself with the Untouchables.

The Justice Party Ministry in Madras must have had the Mysore model firmly in mind when it was given a share of power by the British after the election of 1920. One of the new Government's early acts was to pass the First Communal Government Order of 1921, requiring all heads of government departments to classify recruits under the following communal labels: Brahmin, non-Brahmin, Hindu, Indian Christian, Muslim, European, Anglo-Indian. This was followed by arrangements designed to secure enhanced appointment and promotion of 'non-Brahmins'. The Justice Party had entered the election with something of an alliance with the emerging leaders of the Untouchables, who constituted about one-fifth of the population of the province (Arnold 1977: 19). But from the beginning the Party had been dominated by professionals and business men from the most advanced of the lower castes, and the preferential arrangements were intended to benefit people from these communities and not the Untouchable castes (Irshick 1969: 368–78). We have noted above that the alliance between the two groupings did not last more than a couple of years. It foundered on the perceptions of M. C. Rajah and other Untouchable leaders that the interests of their constituents were not being taken seriously by the leaders of the Justice Party.

Congress was not enthusiastic about communal reservation for any group. Gandhi and Congress had been forced to accept the reservation of parliamentary seats for Untouchables, and they had to be pushed into any extension of the principle of preference to other institutions. But whatever Gandhi's own views his Harijan campaign of the thirties had helped legitimate special measures for the advancement of Untouchables. When Congress Governments were formed after the elections of 1937 they were impelled to do something towards the enactment of anti-discrimination and preferential arrangements for Untouchables. Their most distinctive achievements in a short period of office were legislative rather than administrative – we have drawn attention above to their anti-discrimination legislation in Madras and elsewhere. The various Congress Governments also pushed ahead with the extension of facilities for educating the Scheduled Castes and for their greater representation in government employment. But since a larger quota of jobs was set aside for the Scheduled Castes in the non-Congress, Muslim majority, province of Bengal, it was clear that Congress could claim no special virtue in this matter. Fee waivers for education and special scholarships were also being increased, though the beneficiaries were still very few – sixty scholarships were provided for the whole of Punjab (Dushkin 1957: 128, 130–1).

Essentially, then, the Congress administrations merely carried on in an evolutionary way from measures already put in place by the British and non-Brahmin administrations.

The period between the resignation of the Congress Governments in 1939 and the achievement of Independence in 1947 was even less eventful in terms of public policy towards the Untouchables. The major development of the period is attributable to Ambedkar, who was then serving as a member of the Viceroy's Executive Council: in 1943 orders were adopted to reserve places in the central government service in exactly the same proportions (8⅓ per cent) as had already been adopted in Madras. This quota replaced a policy of general preferment which had been in place since 1934 but which had been officially pronounced in 1942 to be ineffective. In June 1946 the quota of positions reserved for the Scheduled Castes was raised to 12½ per cent, roughly proportional to their population in undivided India (RCSCST 1951: 24ff). This figure was ultimately raised to 15 per cent in 1970.

After its victory in the first post-war election in 1945–6 Congress was able to dominate the Constituent Assembly formed to draft a Constitution. Although Ambedkar's Scheduled Caste Federation had been routed even in his own province – he only gained a position in the Assembly through the good offices of the Muslim League – Nehru appointed him Law Minister in the first Independent Government formed in 1947, and he was chosen as chairman of the drafting committee of the Assembly (Galanter 1984: 37). It is difficult to estimate the precise significance of this appointment in terms of the ultimate Constitutional outcome for the Untouchables, but they could scarcely have hoped for a more favourable result.

Initially and in conformity with its twentieth-century history, the issue of the Untouchables was approached in the Assembly on the basis that they constituted one of a number of Indian minorities – the other significant ones were the Christians, Sikhs and Muslims. But in the course of the Constituent Assembly the very concept of 'minority' was dropped as inappropriate to Independent India, thereby depriving Muslims of their protected electoral status in British India. Ultimately this did not disadvantage Untouchables. In a previous resolution they had implicitly been declared to be Hindus, but Hindus who needed the same protections enjoyed by non-Hindu minorities. When the Assembly dropped protections for minorities, it did not proceed to do the same in relation to Untouchables (Kananaikil 1982: 15–16). They, and Scheduled Tribes, thus emerged as the only groupings (apart from the tiny community of Anglo-Indians) to have legislative seats reserved for them.

Jawaharlal Nehru, by then Prime Minister, supported the emerging position on the Untouchables in the Constituent Assembly:

Frankly I would like this proposal to go further and put an end to such reservations as there still remain. But again, speaking frankly, I realise that in the present state of affairs in India that would not be a desirable thing to do, that is to say, in regard to the Scheduled Castes. I try to look upon the problem not in the sense of a religious minority, but rather in the sense of helping backward groups in the country. I do not look at it from the religious point of view or the caste point of view, but from the point of view that a backward group ought to be helped and I am glad that this reservation also will be limited to ten years. (CAD 1947-9: VIII, 331)

So the Scheduled Castes emerged from the Constituent Assembly as a backward group deserving of special assistance for a strictly limited period of time. Nehru was unhappy about the retention of an arrangement that was intellectually untidy and premised on considerations of caste that seemed to belong to an earlier era. But given the already long history of preference for the Untouchables and to a lesser extent the tribals, there was no way out. An acceptable gloss could be put on the arrangement by insisting that it was directed to eliminating special backwardness in the country.

The Constitution of 1950 (Article 330) required the Scheduled Castes and Tribes to be given parliamentary seats proportional to their population, and Article 331 limited the period of this reservation to twenty years (not Nehru's ten years); this period has been extended by amendment three times, and now runs until the year 2000. Article 335 did not go so far as to require reservation of public service jobs, but stated that 'the claims of the Scheduled Castes and the Scheduled Tribes shall be taken into consideration, consistently with the maintenance of efficiency of administration'. The Constitution did not provide a direct basis of special provision for the Scheduled Castes in the matter of education, but Article 15(4) provided that the general declaration of non-discrimination in state action (Article 15(1)) did not prevent the state making special provision for the Scheduled Castes (and Tribes and 'socially and educationally backward classes'). A special officer was to be appointed to report to the President and the Parliament on the working of the Constitutional measures (Article 338).

In a sense it is curious that the the Scheduled Castes and Tribes emerged from the Constituent Assembly with their compensatory concessions effectively consolidated, while the politically far more powerful 'backward classes' were not similarly successful. The 'backward classes' did not lose what they had gained: the Constitution permitted their preferential access to bureaucratic positions, and this paved the way for a great expansion of this preference at the State level in the succeeding decades. But they continued to be shut out of reservation in the central government. It was only with the adoption of the Mandal Committee's recommendations by the V. P. Singh Government in 1990 that the principle (not yet the practice) of reservation of government jobs for the 'backward classes' was accepted in relation to the centre.

In scrambling for preferential treatment the 'backward classes' suffered several handicaps. First, they were in a sense too strong both in numbers and politically to be treated as disadvantaged. Depending on the method of calculation, their numbers could total many tens, even some hundreds, of millions. The high-caste leadership of Congress was thus almost bound to be unwilling to concede them a privileged status. And secondly, they had not been able to marshal their political resources in the way that Ambedkar had contrived to do at the beginning of the 1930s. Prior to Independence the backward classes movement had really only existed in the form of the non-Brahmin movement, and its crucial limitation was that it failed to develop a national presence. The non-Brahmin movement began and ended its life as a regional movement, albeit a movement of several regions; there was never a non-Brahmin leader of all-India stature. Ambedkar, by contrast, had first established his radical Mahar movement within Maharashtra and then succeeded in becoming a national figure through capturing the attention of the British on behalf of Untouchables throughout India.

Reservation of public jobs

In the mind of both the public at large and also Untouchables themselves, reservation of government jobs is the most important of the various public concessions to the Scheduled Castes. For great tracts of Indian society a government job is the greatest imaginable good. Competition for government jobs is a national obsession: hundreds of thousands of educated Indians present themselves in the annual competitive examinations to enter the higher rungs of the public service. For Untouchables, with their centuries-old heritage of poverty and subordination, the idea of reputable, well-paid and secure employment by the state was beyond imagination until the advent of an inflexible quota of employment.

It is possible to sum up in brief quantitative terms the experience of job reservation for the Scheduled Castes, and this will be done below. What is more difficult to encapsulate is almost half-a-century of bureaucratic and political labour by beneficiaries, sympathisers and open or covert opponents. The social and governmental system of India changes with creaking and resisting slowness, the more so if it is asked to lift weights that hold down its most despised people. Compensatory discrimination may have been designed as a scheme of liberation, but clearly the liberation had to proceed by way of redistribution of public benefits. The problems the scheme has encountered arise both from its modesty and from its redistributive implications.

The problems can be listed under a number of heads. First, even if the scheme had been impeccably administered from the beginning, only a small proportion of India's Untouchables could have been rescued from poverty: the number of potential claimants is huge and the availability of jobs drastically inadequate in comparison. Secondly, the scheme has been far from impeccably administered: non-performance has sprung from an habitual lack of bureaucratic performance in India, reinforced in this instance by the traditional discrimination practised against Untouchables. So the number of beneficiaries of the scheme has been far less than it should have been, though the situation is now changing quite fast. Thirdly, there has been a backlash. This has ranged from the ubiquitous stigmatisation of occupants of public office who have gained their position by competing for a position within a quota rather than in open competition, to violent protest such as the Marathwada riots (see above, pp. 73–4). There are signs that the backlash is growing in intensity, partly because of opposition to extension of reservation to further elements of the 'other backward classes'. Finally, and only partly connected with the backlash, there are now doubts in a number of quarters about the value to be derived from maintaining compensatory discrimination. For example, it is often said that the benefits have been captured by an hereditary class within the Scheduled Caste grouping, thereby defeating the redistributive thrust of the scheme. And within Untouchable circles there is considerable disappointment about the performance and relevance of Scheduled Caste MPs and bureaucrats to the great body of Untouchable society.

The figures in Table I require some interpretation. First, the best results have been achieved in the lower two rungs of the public service. From the very beginning reservation targets were reached and exceeded in relation to Class IV, the most menial grade (encompassing peons, for example). If sweepers are included in this category, the proportion of Scheduled Castes is further increased.[6] Representation in Class III, the clerical grade, also started from a relatively high base and increased quite

---

[6] On an early occasion when the Commissioner attempted to quantify the proportion of Scheduled Caste persons among the sweepers, they constituted 90.35 per cent of the 59,052 sweepers in the Central Government service (RCSCST 1961–2: 279). The proportion seems to have fallen somewhat: in 1987, 77.51 per cent of sweepers in public sector undertakings and only 49.11 per cent in the public sector banks were said to be from the Scheduled Castes (RCSCST 1986–7: 508).

Table 1. *Scheduled Caste employees of central government*

	1953	1963	1974	1980	1987
Class I	20 (0.35%)	250 (1.78%)	1,094 (3.2%)	2,375 (4.95%)	4,746 (8.23%)
Class II	113 (1.29%)	707 (2.98%)	2,401 (4.6%)	5,055 (8.54%)	7,847 (10.47%)
Class III	24,819 (4.52%)	84,714 (9.24%)	161,775 (10.3%)	235,555 (13.44%)	307,980 (14.46%)
Class IV	161,958 (20.52%)[a]	151,176 (17.15%)[b]	230,864 (18.6%)[b]	247,607 (19.46%)[b]	234,614 (20.09%)[b]

Sources: Government of India 1955: I 134; RCSCST 1963–4: 165–6; RCSCST 1974–5: 82; RCSCST 1986–7: 508.
Notes:
[a] includes sweepers
[b] excludes sweepers

rapidly. At the very apex of the public service, the fulfilment of quotas was also relatively good. Thus by 1964 the quota of annual appointments to the Indian Administrative Service – an elite category within Class I – was reached, and this record has been maintained in the subsequent years. Recruitment to the other (slightly less elite) All India Services within Class I (the Indian Forest Service etc.) also reached their quotas from at least the early 1970s (Government of India 1983: 17). The two categories which responded most slowly to reservation were Class I (apart from the elite services within it) and Class II. For Class I the big surge in representation was only in the 1980s, while in Class II there was already a strong improvement at work in the 1970s.

By 1987, the last year for which there are figures, Scheduled Castes should have reached their quota of representation in all classes of government service. This can be concluded from the fact that reservation has been in place for the entire period of a service career – some 33 years (Galanter 1984: 93). The actual percentage of representation should be between 12.5 per cent and 15 per cent, since the quota was raised to the latter level in 1970. So the above table reveals that there is a considerable shortfall in representation in Classes I and II, while the level is at or above expectation for Classes III and IV.

At the present period it would appear that virtually all reserved positions are being allocated to members of the Scheduled Castes. So the shortfall arises from failures to appoint in earlier periods, particularly the first two decades after Independence. It was often said at the time that there were insufficient qualified candidates among the Scheduled Castes, particularly in the technical areas. There was also the situation that many positions were filled by promotion rather than appointment from outside the service, and before 1957 there was no reservation of positions filled by promotion. Now it is only in the higher levels of Class I that such reservation does not apply. Beyond such technical factors, it is clear that the shortfall in representation arises both from a lack of sufficient commitment to the task by hiring authorities and also from overt and covert discrimination against Scheduled Caste persons. For example, there is persistent comment in the Commissioner's Annual Reports to the effect that hurdles such as the oral interview are used to discriminate against Scheduled Caste candidates (e.g. RCSCST 1965–6: 16).

The record of representation is worse in all areas of government employment other than the regular departments of state: this includes the public banks, public sector undertakings, the armed forces and the universities. Reservation was introduced later in these bodies than for the ordinary departments of administration – indeed there is still no reservation in the armed forces, merely advisory policy – and before such mandatory practice there were devastatingly few Scheduled Caste employees. For example, as late as 1973 only twenty-nine out of 3,582 (0.81 per cent) Class I officers in the Reserve Bank of India were from the Scheduled Castes.[7] It was only after Indira Gandhi's nationalisation of many private banks in 1969 that any serious efforts were made to extend reservation to the banking sector. By 1987 the situation had improved markedly: 7.29 per cent of officers, 13.77 per cent of clerical and 22.30 per cent of subordinate positions (excluding sweepers) in the banks were occupied by Scheduled Caste people. But in 211 public sector undertakings in 1987 there were still only 4.86 per cent and 6.17 per cent of Scheduled Caste persons in the two highest grades.

The latest figures for the armed forces are for 1981, when only 0.44 per cent of officers in the army and 0.16 per cent in the air force were from the Scheduled Castes. The figure is better for junior commissioned officers in the army: 10.62 per cent. Of enlisted men, 7.3 per cent in the navy and 2.57 per cent in the air force were from the Scheduled Castes; there are no figures for enlisted persons in the army.[8] Clearly these figures are far below population percentages. The situation in the universities is much worse still. As late as 1986 only thirteen out of 2,133 professors at forty-one universities, thirty-four out of 3,261 readers and 169 out of 5,341 lecturers were from the Scheduled Castes. No doubt there are special

[7] Statistics in this paragraph are drawn from the RCSCST 1973–4: 147; 1971–2: 110; 1986–7: 499, 491.
[8] Statistics in this paragraph are from the RCSCST 1979–81: 66; and 1986–7: 502.

difficulties in recruiting lecturing staff who meet the threshhold criteria of appointment, but after all the years of compensatory discrimination these are poor figures indeed.

Statistics on employment in the various State bureaucracies are far less reliable than those for the central government, and they are therefore not specifically cited here. But the figures provided in the High Power Panel Report (Government of India 1983: II, 38) are sufficient to reveal a patchy performance which is overall considerably inferior to that of the centre, particularly in the higher levels of service. States with very high numbers of Untouchables, including Uttar Pradesh, Bihar, West Bengal and Tamil Nadu, are below the overall average. On the other hand Maharashtra and Punjab perform considerably better. Such disparities reflect a number of factors, including the diligence and capacity of the State administration to achieve nominated targets and also the variable strength of Untouchable organisation in different States.

In sum, patterns of recruitment and promotion of Scheduled Caste persons now approximate to the designated quotas far more closely than they did in the immediate post-Independence years. The continuing shortfalls are largest in the States as opposed to the centre, and in the authorities that are relatively distant from regular departments of state and therefore from politicians (the banks and so on). Improvements in meeting targets cannot be attributed to an increasing public and political acceptance of the reservation system: quite the reverse, resistance is growing in proportion to the uptake of benefits by the Untouchables. Presumably the improved performance derives from cumulative pressure exerted by politicians, by bureaucratic oversight bodies and most of all by the many Untouchable aspirants who are fully aware that a particular proportion of positions must in law go to them as a class. The room to manœuvre on the part of interests who would wish to divert such positions to themselves has been drastically reduced by the growing assertiveness of Untouchables. Discrimination no doubt continues, but once procedures of recruitment and promotion have been regularised it probably exists only at the margins. Conversely, the worst shortfalls in employment arise from the slow and still patchy regularisation of procedures.

The total of Scheduled Caste persons employed in Indian government is now quite impressive in sheer numbers – the 1987 figure for employees in the various departments, public sector undertakings and public banks of the central government was 1,069,477 (plus 77,790 sweepers in the banks and public sector undertakings, and an unknown number in the departments). To this figure we must add the unknown number of State, municipal and public sector employees – it is doubtful that the sum total of all public employees comes to more than one million-and-a-half. If we assume this figure, the proportion of the total Untouchable population thus employed would be of the order of 1.25 per cent. In 1985 there were an estimated 17.3 million jobs in the whole public sector of India: 38 per cent were in the central government, 49 per cent in State governments, and 13 per cent in local government (Desai and Desai 1988: 71). Even if Untouchables had attained their statutory 15 per cent of all these jobs, their numbers would have been less than 2.6 million or just over 2 per cent of the whole Untouchable population. It is abundantly clear, then, that only a tiny proportion of the Untouchable population has directly benefited or theoretically could benefit from reservation of public employment, though the figure looks somewhat better if one factors in the family members of the employee. The impact of this employment has been significant for the Untouchable population, while at the same time being quite insufficient as a primary strategy for combatting Untouchable poverty. It is only because of the absence of a credible general strategy and the sheer desirability of government employment that job reservation has been accorded such prominent status.

The actual experience of Scheduled Caste employees in departments and other public institutions is highly variable, given the huge numbers of employees in question. In the early years after Independence it seems to have been possible to practise quite gross discrimination so as to block appointments and promotions. Such blatant discrimination has tended to abate over time, in line with general social developments. This is not to say that the life of Scheduled Caste employees is an easy or happy one. We have listened to many stories of bitterness and sadness. The jealousy or contempt of caste Hindu colleagues often constitutes a great burden, the more so in a sophisticated environment like one of the good universities. But we have also talked to senior officials who have no personal experience of discrimination; such people often come from relatively wealthy and privileged backgrounds within the Scheduled Castes, and from States (like Kerala and West Bengal) where active discrimination in the modern sector has not been a general practice for many years. It was also in Kerala that a Scheduled Caste bank employee observed that although it was no longer possible to discriminate in a blatant way, 'they practise discrimination in their hearts'. The key to Untouchables' feeling comfortable in institutional settings would generally seem to be the presence of a supportive network of caste fellows.

If the experience of reservation has not always been easy for its beneficiaries, the appropriateness and fairness of the program are matters of increasing controversy. One persistent criticism is that the benefit of public employment is monopolised by a small, prosperous and self-perpetuating 'Harijan elite' (Sacchidananad 1977). This view has most often been put by high-caste critics, but on a number of occasions the

Commissioner for Scheduled Castes and Scheduled Tribes has complained that the benefits are insufficiently delivered to the weaker caste communities among the Untouchables. It is possible to find variations of this view among Dalit intellectuals themselves. The issue will be taken up in chapter 8. For the moment it can be said that the uptake of reserved positions does tend to reflect the relative prosperity of different castes and of the individuals within those castes. This is particularly true of the higher positions, which require commensurate educational attainment. Even with reduced levels of entry it would be quite impossible for persons from the lowest socio-economic situations to attain to such levels.

Another major criticism of the reservation system is that the Untouchable occupants of bureaucratic positions have been entirely self-directed and have not used their influence for the benefit of Untouchables as a whole. The question of just what difference Untouchables in the public sector have made is difficult to answer. It would be reasonable to expect, for example, that Untouchable policemen might be less inclined to engage in the mistreatment of poor people than has been widespread in rural India. The Government of India accepted this logic at the time 'Harijan atrocities' became a national scandal in the late 1970s, and it took steps to boost Untouchable numbers in the police force and to post them to areas where such violence was a particular problem. On the other hand there is much anecdotal evidence to the effect that dominant interests in the countryside are still able to control the local machinery of the state. Precisely the same issue has been debated in relation to the higher levels of the bureaucracy. A senior member of the bureaucracy in Bihar (high caste but deeply concerned with the underprivileged) has come to the conclusion that it is almost impossible even for quite senior Untouchable officers not to feel cowed by their caste superiors within the bureaucracy. The capacity of such people for innovative policy formation will usually be insignificant, and their ability to implement policy so as to provide favourable outcomes for the poor will be hedged about by all the severe obstacles that arise from the original subordination. There are often unusually severe pressures, not least of a domestic nature, that weigh down Untouchables in relatively high office.[9] Only the most resolute of Untouchable officials will be able to overcome personal burdens and the

[9] One of our informants, a lecturer at one of India's leading universities, spoke feelingly about the personal torment suffered by a number of Untouchables who had risen far beyond the cultural horizons of most within their community. Often they felt themselves to be saddled with their mate, to whom they had been married when very young and who had attained to only a highly modest degree of education. Such people were often terribly lonely at home, and also widely looked down upon in a career where the line between work and social life is blurred. There also tend to be unusually heavy economic burdens placed upon high achievers from Untouchable castes: often they have to support more of their extended family than do persons from higher-caste background in comparable positions.

frequently hostile bureaucratic and external environment sufficient to make a difference. We encountered one such legendary official in Bihar, but this man's background and personality are so singular that there can be few such officials throughout India. On the other hand the advent of the Mayawati Government in Uttar Pradesh showed that it was indeed possible to mobilise Scheduled Caste officers so as to make a collective impact. But hard evidence of the wider effectiveness of Untouchable officials remains almost impossible to gather. Of course, precisely the same kinds of questions are asked in western countries about representation of women and minorities in structures such as the judiciary.

The major threat to the system of compensatory reservation of employment arises from less subtle criticisms than those of the 'Harijan elite' school. In a word, what is compensatory discrimination for one community is unjust discrimination to others. There is no doubt that any scheme of compensatory preference is a denial of strict equality of opportunity, though it may be justified on grounds of seeking to bring about a more substantial equality in the future. Everywhere such policies have provoked a backlash from other communities, who complain that they are unjustly denied access to scarce and valuable public goods. Our own view is that the sheer subordination of the Untouchables represents one of the strongest possible cases for compensatory discrimination in public employment, but surely even this case cannot be maintained forever. The benefits to the Untouchables will presumably at some point become so deeply resented that arguments in favour of restoring strict equality of opportunity will win the day (Galanter 1984; 1991: xxii). Given this likelihood it seems crucial that the system of preference be vigorously implemented while there is still opportunity.

As a final note on employment, we can observe that there has been no advance in the private sector comparable with gains in public employment. In 1976 the *Protection of Civil Rights* Act was amended to prohibit discrimination in relation to private employment, but in the absence of any workable enforcement procedure the prohibition remains academic. There is simply no movement strong enough throughout Indian society to insist that out-groups be adequately represented in private employment. In the longer term, the question of employment in the organised private sector will become a matter of great moment to the Untouchables. For the moment, anything but menial employment in the private sector is generally beyond their reach.

Education

Literacy The most optimistic aspect of the contemporary situation of the Untouchable community is the extent to which education has

Table 2. *Literacy of the general population and of the Scheduled Castes*

	General	Scheduled Castes
1901	5.35	0.10#[a]
1931	9.50	1.00#
1961	24.02	10.27
1971	29.45	14.67
1981	36.23	21.38
1991	52.10	37.41

Note:
[a] Before Independence there was no attempt to aggregate the literacy of the different Untouchable castes into a national average. The figures given for 1901 and 1931 are the literacy rate for the Chamars of Uttar Pradesh. The Chamars are the largest and one of the most advanced Untouchable castes in India. Even in the case of the more advanced Mahars of Maharashtra, the literacy figure was only 0.4 per cent (4 literates per 1,000) in 1901 and 2 per cent in 1931.
Source: Census of India

become a driving ambition. This is partly measurable in the figures on literacy in Table 2, which show an extraordinary and accelerating improvement over the post-Independence period. The rising graph of literacy is paralleled by the rise in school enrolments. Recent figures suggest that the Scheduled Caste enrolment in primary school grades is coming close to being proportional to population.

Untouchable literacy now lags behind that of the general population by about a decade: at the time of the 1981 Census the lag was two decades. If the recent trend persists, literacy among the Untouchables may reach the national average at the time of the 2001 Census. But of course the literacy of the general population is still drastically low, particularly for women. And among women from Untouchable communities only 23.76 per cent were literate in 1991 (though this was up from some 11 per cent in 1981). Since low literacy is associated with high mortality, high fertility and generally poor economic prospects, the cost of persisting illiteracy among Untouchables remains enormous.

There is no basis for attributing any great part of the rising graph of literacy to the scheme of compensatory discrimination. It is true that assistance towards education was the earliest and is still the largest of all the programs of financial assistance to the Scheduled Castes. Moreover, prior to the anti-poverty programs of the 1980s such assistance was often the only form of aid enjoyed by individual Untouchable families. But overwhelmingly this educational aid was directed to post-matriculation studies. The acquisition of literacy as measured by the Census – the test is capacity to read and write a postcard – is something acquired in primary school studies. Over a period of years the supply of government aid has filtered down to secondary school studies and has now reached a point where a number of States – there is great variation between them – promote the primary education of Scheduled Caste children through small inducements (such as the supply of hot lunches to the children, or 'stipends' for attendance ranging from 2 to 5 rupees per month). But such assistance remains minor compared with support of higher levels of education. And there was almost a complete absence of assistance in the first decade after Independence, a decade of considerable uptake of basic education by the Scheduled Castes.

Higher education The position of higher secondary and particu-larly tertiary education is more complicated. Post-matriculation scholar-ships have risen from a total of 114 in 1944–5 to many hundreds of thousands today. In addition to cash transfers, some 5,000 special hostels now accommodate about half of the post-secondary school population of Scheduled Caste students and many of the upper secondary students too (RCSCST (new) 1979–80: 158–9). The hostels have been built with public money and are heavily subsidised. Engineering and medical stu-dents get access to expensive texts through special book loans. This eco-nomic assistance is buttressed by formally guaranteed access to colleges, including highly desired undergraduate and graduate education in elite engineering and medical faculties. There is no doubt – unlike the case of primary school education – that this subsidisation and the guarantees against adverse discrimination have constituted some of the wherewithal for Untouchables to realise their ambitions for higher education. But the assistance is too limited and too flawed in delivery to warrant being called 'compensatory discrimination'. And again it is Untouchables themselves, not government, who have conceived the ambition to educate themselves.

There remain great problems in the experience of higher education by Untouchables, some of them arising from general difficulties in Indian education and some that are particular to the Untouchables. As to enrol-ments, in 1978–9 Untouchables represented only some 7 per cent of all tertiary students – just below half their proportion of the population.[10] This proportion may now have risen – there are no later figures available. In 1978–9 more than half Untouchable undergraduates were in the least

[10] Statistics in this and the following paragraph are from the RCSCST 1986–87: I, 309; II, 171.

prestigious Arts Faculty. Their lowest representation was in the highly prestigious Engineeering Faculty (less than 2 per cent of places). But in undergraduate Medicine, the most sought after Faculty of all, the figure was said to be almost 10 per cent. The disparity between the latter two figures is not self-evident, especially since we can assume that most Untouchables within both faculties had gained their place through reservation (which effectively lowers the necessary entry score). Some regions were particularly laggard in enforcing reserved quotas for the most prized faculties: by 1980 not one of the seven medical colleges in Uttar Pradesh had admitted a single Untouchable student. If one turns to postgraduate enrolments, still more disturbing patterns become apparent. In 1978–9 less than 4 per cent of enrolments in postgraduate Medicine courses were of Scheduled Caste students. The significance of this is that postgraduate education in Medicine consists in the acquisition of a (usually lucrative) speciality discipline. But efforts to redress such under-representation have begun to be met with some of the worst opposition to educational reservation that has been seen in India. By far the worst of a number of violent incidents surrounding access to medical education was the Gujarat riot of 1981. This was sparked by the failure of a high-caste student to gain admission to a postgraduate course in pathology, allegedly because the one available seat was reserved for someone from the Scheduled Castes. The ensuing riot lasted for some seventy-eight days, and tens of people died (Gavai 1981: 17; Wood 1986: 10).

In terms of competitive achievement, it seems to become more rather than less difficult for many Scheduled Caste students as they climb the educational ladder. Reduced standards of entry and positive assistance in the form of money and facilities can assist students through the lower branches of tertiary education, but in many instances these do not offset the original economic and social disadvantage. These findings are reinforced by the fragmentary data we have on dropout rates in higher education, which suggest that these are higher for Untouchable students than for the general population. To speak, for example, to a Valmiki (Bhangi) student in an engineering college is to be made aware of a world of terrible hardship and anxiety. One such young man at Kurukshetra University in Haryana was having to contend with the difficulties of his personal background – his father drank a lot, abused his wife and was a poor provider to the family – and the daunting demands of both academic study (though he was particularly bright) and the social milieu (Interview: 27 April 1985). 'Harijan hostels' have helped – this particular student lived in such a hostel – but many of the more ambitious Scheduled Caste students do not want to cut themselves off from the mainstream by living in a separate hostel. Some of them are sufficiently self-confident and bold to have little difficulty with integration, but often such young men come from the most privileged among Scheduled Caste families. One study reports a finding that highly educated people of Scheduled Caste background enjoy less social acceptance among their caste Hindu peers than do their less educated caste fellows (Malik 1979: 86). It is one thing to let Untouchables into the everyday world of modest advancement, and quite another to ease their progress into a world of high achievement and comparative comfort which is unavailable to most Indians of even high-caste background.

Financial assistance may be available as of right to students from the Scheduled Castes, but uptake of the benefits has been heavily concentrated in the somewhat better off and more progressive elements of these communities. The spread of Untouchable students between the States does not conform to the spread of the whole Untouchable population. For example, the Untouchables of Andhra Pradesh, Maharashtra and Gujarat receive a greater proportion of the national total of scholarships than would be justified by their share of the Untouchable population of India. Bihar, Tamil Nadu and West Bengal receive a disproportionally small number, whereas Uttar Pradesh receives about its correct proportion (Government of India 1984: 3, 31). This reflects varying levels of cultural progressiveness between different caste communities and between whole regions.

There are great differences in the literacy of different Untouchable communities, and of course this must be reflected in divergent representation in higher education too. For example, 21 per cent of the Chamars and the Dusadhs of Bihar were literate in 1981, but only 4 per cent of the Musahars of that State. Again, 48 per cent of the Bhangis of Gujarat were literate, but only 26 per cent of the Bhangis of Rajasthan: this is probably explainable by the generally higher levels of education in Gujarat.

Within individual Untouchable communities – particularly where the community is not among the more socially progressive – it will be the wealthier elements that are best able to carry the burden of leaving their children in school and then university. This is partly because of the disgraceful and heartbreaking manner in which the scholarship scheme has been administered in most areas of India. Scholarship monies arrive chronically late and often with significant (not merely marginal) deductions made by corrupt middlemen in the administrative process. When the money does finally turn up it is inadequate to sustain a person even at a basic level, let alone to enable them to study in some comfort. During the thirty-year period 1945–75 the annual value of post-matriculation scholarships did not change, despite a threefold increase in the cost of living over this period. In these circumstances, clearly only the unusually motivated and/or the relatively better-off Untouchable families will be able to tolerate the burdens sufficient to make a serious commitment to education. If a member of the family has a secure job or if there is a plot of land there may be the regular source of income necessary to sustain extended study by one or more members of the family. We even came across a Chamar family that had enrolled its eldest son in an MA at Patna University on the basis of the dowry delivered to him in marriage. What is notable about this case is that Chamars have traditionally paid bride-price rather than dowry; perhaps recent emulation of the higher castes' dowry practices produced a progressive outcome here.

Even after the hurdles have been jumped, the value of a tertiary degree in India is highly variable. A degree, particularly a postgraduate degree, in Engineering from one of the Indian Institutes of Technology or a degree in Medicine is likely to be the basis of a fine career. But a basic degree in Arts from a mediocre college in Bihar will not by itself lead to any decent job at all. To the extent that the Untouchables are concentrated in the weaker disciplines and the weaker colleges, their best chance of a job will often be the limited number of low-level reserved posts in the public sector. Realistically, a great many of them will further swell the ranks of the graduate unemployed.

Conclusion

In this chapter we have considered the two major policies specifically directed to ending the disabilities suffered by Untouchables, viz. legislation and bureaucratic action to end adverse discrimination, and the program of compensatory discrimination. Judged narrowly by their own terms, it could be argued that compensatory discrimination is the more successful of these policies. The ground for such a conclusion would be the knowledge that targets of public employment are now by-and-large being met, and that some of the special benefits in the educational sector are also being delivered. On the other hand, the failure of anti-discrimination action is measurable in the continuing discrimination against Untouchables throughout large parts of Indian social life. But such a conclusion would be altogether artificial.

We have argued that the scheme of compensatory discrimination is much less impressive than it might superficially appear to be. It has been an arduous and an important achievement to earmark bureaucratic positions for Untouchables in proportion to their share of the Indian population. But this achievement does not begin to address the overall problem of Untouchable poverty or social disadvantage. This is simply because the availability of public employment is so small relative to the size and needs of the Untouchable population. Obviously the higher education sector will also engage the energies of only a fragment of the Untouchable population, and this sector could scarcely qualify as a major force for transformation of the Untouchable condition. Moreover, there is ample evidence that the program of assistance to Untouchables in higher education does not even warrant being classified as compensatory discrimination: it is too limited and too flawed in delivery to warrant such description.

It should not be concluded that the Government of India need not have bothered with measures specially directed to the welfare of the Untouchables. Important benefits have indeed been provided to many thousands of individual Untouchables, and much unwarranted discrimination in public employment and higher educational institutions has been overcome. Moreover, the emergence of quite large numbers of accomplished and professionally experienced Untouchables cannot be discounted as a leavening agent for the larger Untouchable population. Our own view is that these accomplishments have been substantial and that they justify the continuance of policies of compensatory discrimination for some time yet. But manifestly such policies will not transform the Untouchable condition. A realistic understanding of the limitations of compensatory discrimination can help refocus the debate, such as it is, on the problems of the Untouchable population and on the interventionist measures that might help resolve these problems.

Despite the dreadful shortfall in liberating Untouchables from ritual subordination, the waning of some of the worst discrimination constitutes the greatest change in their circumstances during the period under review. The rolling back of adverse discrimination affects the whole Untouchable population of India; it is the basis upon which special policies to do with public employment and higher education can be pursued. But the progress that has been made is not primarily an achievement of the state or of 'public policy'. The miserable failure of enforcement under the *Protection of Civil Rights Act* 1976 is one indicator of the state's incapacity to provide specific protections in the face of socially powerful recalcitrance. On the other hand the transformation of access to schools is in part attributable to benevolent state action. This change is clearly of great importance, but it was able to be accomplished precisely because there was no committed and sustained opposition. The revolution brought about by the spread of education is a slow transformation that involves no immediately discernible redistribution of physical assets or social power. It is only where redistribution is more apparent that the full weight of social opposition can be mobilised, and the next chapter discusses precisely such a circumstance.

5   Public policy II: the anti-poverty programs

Our consistent argument is that the condition of the Untouchables can only be adequately conceived by reference to two interlocking forms of subordination: ritual, cultural and broader social debasement on the one hand, and poverty on the other. This chapter examines thinking and programs directed specifically to the economic condition of the poor, among whom the Untouchables represent a large chunk. Our preoccupation is with the failure of measures that might have led to markedly less poverty than there is in India today, but we also consider the relative successes. We examine health and food policy, and the meaning of the phrase that 'India can now feed itself'; the relative absence of modern social welfare; the implications of the failure to pursue land redistribution more vigorously; the inability of the Indian state to deliver fully on anything other than crisis management; and the weaknesses of the anti-poverty programs that were eventually introduced in the 1980s. We look at how different States have dealt with poverty, and how Untouchables have fared in these varying circumstances. Finally, we consider the question of the overall progress of the Untouchables.

The post-Independence regime has failed to bring about a systematic redistribution of resources in favour of those at the bottom of society, and it has also failed to pursue a consistent, albeit non-radical, strategy of supplying 'basic needs' (health, education and simple welfare) to the poor. Supplying basic needs would not have transformed the condition of the Untouchables – the evidence from Kerala tends to prove this – but it would have made a powerful difference. In failing to overcome or sufficiently ameliorate poverty the regime can be said to have failed the Untouchables. This is by no means to deny that over the last half-century Indian government has undertaken a large number of activities that have benefited the poor. It is just that these various policies and programs have been neither systematic nor always appropriate.

The roots of this post-Independence failure can be traced back to at least the 1930s. While there was no single orthodoxy about national development within the leadership of the nationalist movement at the

time, not one of them took the position that the needs of the poorest
Indians were to to be pre-eminent. This is easily demonstrated in the
case of Gandhi, whose agrarian vision was to be realised through a social
consensus that would have left the traditional elites in full control of
economy and society. But by the 1940s Gandhi was a lonely figure whose
vision was not shared by his nationalist colleagues. On the face of it,
Nehru's socialism should have been more compatible with programs of
radical redistribution. But Nehru was never a radical in that sense. His
conception of development was one of industrialism framed in the twin
contexts of the neglect of industrialisation by the colonial state and the
Soviet example of a massive heavy industry sector built by the state.
Nehru's interest in village India, where most people lived, was almost
marginal. He knew, though from little direct experience, that village
India was an unequal world, and he looked towards a 'democratic social
transformation' of that world (Frankel 1978: 3). But the idea that radical
restructuring of economic and social relations might have to be a pre-
cursor and foundation for industrialisation and modernisation seems
never to have been seriously contemplated. Certainly, radical land
reform of the kind conducted in China or even in South Korea and
Taiwan was not framed as a specific objective either before or after
Independence. Nehru reposed his hopes for broader modernisation in a
remarkably abstract sense of the civilising energies to be released in the
post-colonial era. And prior to the recent policy of economic liberalisation, it was Nehru's vision that largely held sway among Indian policy
makers.

Arguably the most powerful ideological lens focussed on the Indian
poor was a distinctive version of Malthusianism. Well before Independence the Indian leadership was deeply seized of the calamity represented
by the Indian birth rate. Every Census from 1921 on provided quantification of the rising population. It was not merely that the population as a
whole was growing but that the lower-class elements were multiplying
more rapidly than the classes seen to be more refined and more valuable.
Far from celebrating the rise in longevity of those at the bottom of the
order, the Congress leadership was growing ever more frightened and
pessimistic. In 1947 the Sub-Committee on Population – this had been
established in 1938 by the National Planning Committee chaired by
Nehru – reported on the gathering 'mispopulation' of India:

[T]he disparity in the natural increase of different social strata shows a distinct
trend of mispopulation. Throughout India, the backward sections are more progressive demologically than the rest of the population . . . The general increase of
population is more in evidence among the more fertile but less intellectual strata
of society. (Shah 1947: 64–5)

The report's eugenics were specially roused in relation to the growing power of low-caste agricultural workers:

[H]igh castes who own good landed property, but disdain to drive the plough, are going down in face of the unequal economic competition of lower agricultural castes who are proving superior in land utilisation and whose very numbers will in future add to their economic and political advantage. Thus the social attitudes as regards manual toil aggravate the effects of dysgenic customs and practices in bringing about a gradual predominance of the inferior social strata. As education has spread contraceptive practice has been adopted by the advanced castes, and in the absence of birth control propaganda, the mispopulation will be more manifest. No doubt birth control is being adopted by the upper classes in the towns of the major Provinces, and this demands all the more the diffusion of its knowledge among the masses to prevent the deterioration of the racial make-up. (Shah 1947: 66)

Here is a statement that has all the racially based certitude that Annie Besant displayed a generation earlier, though in the context of the new democratic politics the racialism is more clearly joined to fear. When the 'lower castes' (presumably a majority of the population) are not the objects of fear, they are to be patronised: the nation's progress demands that the socially inferior practise 'thrift, prevention of waste and extravagance of all kinds and control of the size of the family'. These habits of sobriety, together with technical and scientific reform of farming practice, would sound the death knell of poverty in the countryside (Shah 1947: 61–2). Such writing suggests that there was little except a bit more optimism to distinguish Congress thinking about rural development from the periodic parliamentary reports of the British raj on the 'Moral and Material Progress of India'. Both were imbued with an Orientalist zeal for the reform of an Indian population deemed to be mired in social waste and obscurantism. Much of the history of policy and program making after Independence can be seen to flow from attitudes such as those expressed by the Population Sub-Committee in 1947. There has been a lot of activity, but much of it has been marred by the spirit in which it has been undertaken. Lack of generosity towards the poor is scarcely an Indian invention, but the elaboration of this spirit in a nation that contains so many poor people has had particularly unfortunate consequences.

Epidemic, famine and fertility control, and the delivery of social welfare

The most basic indication of declining poverty in India is increased longevity, and this has been going up for the entire Census period of more than a century. Untouchables have benefited disproportionately from the change. Thus in Bihar, now perhaps the poorest State, population growth rates since late in the nineteenth century have been higher for Untouchables than for all castes above them in the caste hierarchy (Vicziany 1984: 17). The explanation for this would appear to be quite simple: famine relief and epidemic control have removed the greatest single causes of death, and these measures have disproportionately bene-fited the poorest groups that had been the most numerous victims of famine and epidemic. Improved famine relief and protection against epi-demics became feasible with the elaboration of a transport and communications infrastructure and the growth of a more integrated market. This process began during the nineteenth century. The railways enabled food to be distributed from surplus to deficit grain areas, and thus made villagers less dependent on the capriciousness of a monsoon that rarely failed everywhere. Railways also allowed public health officers to move around more quickly and intervene in the early stages of epi-demic outbreaks. Epidemic control strategies began to produce a marked decline in death from cholera during the twenties and thirties (Vicziany 1986: 10–15). The British also put in place the rudimentary features of modern famine relief by employing labour on public works, supplying soup kitchens, and giving loans and tax remissions to relieve the distress of farmers (McAlpin 1983: 176–85). While the dominant motivation for these measures may have been humanitarian, the raj was always deeply aware of the political instability that could attend famine. On the other side it was precisely these life-saving measures that provoked the concern of high-caste nationalists as to the resulting 'mispopulation' of the country.

The style of both famine relief and epidemic control in colonial India was coercive, and some of this outlook has persisted after Independence. In the smallpox eradication campaign of the period 1973-5, the search, surveillance and isolation procedures reached new levels of invasiveness. Perhaps these methods can be defended on the ground that the campaign was successful. On the other hand success did not crown the mass vasec-tomy campaign conducted during Indira Gandhi's Emergency of 1975-7. This drive was launched just as the smallpox campaign ended. The coer-cive crisis spirit inherited from the raj was here yoked to the old Malthusianism. Key decision makers in the medical profession, bureau-cracy, Congress Party, police and panchayats were mobilised into a cam-paign unique in the degree of its unpopularity. The 'bad' sterilisation campaign and the 'good' smallpox fight had in common an arrogant cer-tainty on the part of the governing class that *they* knew what was best for the poor. Sometimes the governing class has been right, but always it has failed to take its beneficiaries into its confidence. Where the human issues are endemic rather than episodic, as in the case of reproduction, the underlying social contempt of the crisis approach will produce failure. This was certainly the case in the vasectomy campaign: the graphs demonstrating impressive hit rates were more than offset by the flow of adverse publicity once free speech was restored after the Emergency. Indira Gandhi's loss of power in 1977 not only served to undermine the legitimacy of her government's coercive style; for many years the legitimacy of family planning was destroyed altogether. Even now there is a hangover from this period, though more recently there has been some official recognition that 'development is the best contraceptive'. For this valid understanding to be operationalised, officials and health workers must treat their clients – including their poor clients – as responsible human agents. Only when death, morbidity and malnutrition levels have been significantly and securely reduced over historical levels, and when there is a diffused awareness that family welfare is best served by increased public and private expenditure on health, education and general welfare, can there be both enlightened and effective programs of family planning.

Family planning is not a major subject here, and we refer to it only because of its connection to Malthusianism and the coercive spirit that underpins a great deal of twentieth-century Indian thinking on the poor. We do not subscribe to the simple view that if only India had limited its population better mass poverty would not be the problem that it is. This proposition is meaningless without entering into the whole question of why human beings procreate and when they desire to limit their own fertility. In any case, greater fertility control could not possibly have 'cured' the poverty of a category such as the Untouchables. Their poverty arises from causes quite apart from the size of their population.

The colonial state's concern with poverty was exhausted by the emergency of famine, and did not extend to the relief of routine, albeit desperate, Indian poverty. This could also be said of the post-colonial state, though not to the same extent. There is no doubt that Independent India has been far better than the colonial state at coping with the consequences of drought. To this end it has greatly increased stocks of food and also the mechanisms for distributing food to prevent famine. And it has also undertaken large programs to provide food for work during the droughts that have in the past tended to lead to famines – these are discussed below. In a few regions and in limited situations – the school lunch program in Kerala is a leading example – authorities have gone a step further and tried to feed the poor on a regular basis. But by-and-large Indian governments have not tried routinely to deliver food to the needy.

The paradoxes of the Indian state's approach can be seen from the larger context of food policy.

One of the strongest imperatives after Independence was a determination to avoid human disasters such as the Bengal famine of 1943, rightly attributed to the failures of the British raj. To this extent Malthusianism has been set aside following Independence. The mechanisms adopted to this end were a willingness to build buffer stocks of grain by intervention in the domestic market and import of grain for cash or by way of foreign aid; and establishment in the early 1950s of a new public distribution system capable of delivering the grain stocks to regions threatened by famine (Singh 1975: 269–73). But over time the objects of public grain procurement became both more ambitious and more ambiguous. Government of India purchases initially amounted to about 6 per cent of the annual crop, but this gradually increased to between 20 and 30 per cent with increased availability arising from the Green Revolution. Only a part of this procurement has been kept aside for buffer stocks; the rest has been pumped into the retail market through a network of Fair Price Food Shops. Since the whole scheme is heavily subsidised, it is logical to imagine that the intended and actual beneficiaries have been the poor. This is not the case. The Fair Price outlets have been expressly open to everyone without regard to economic level. They have tended not to stock the coarser grains and pulses that the poor can afford; the better-quality, albeit subsidised, food they sell has been more expensive than poorer qualities available in the open market. Moreover, access to the shops is usually quite difficult. In most of India – West Bengal and Kerala are exceptions – they open their doors only once a month, and the poor lack the resources to buy in bulk for a month ahead (Kabra and Ittyerah 1992: 138–9). In sum, the Fair Price Shops are not set up to cater to the poor. Their subsidised customers have tended to be relatively well off people in the cities. And, of course, a good part of the organisation's stock has also found its way on to the open market. A scheme that had its origins in famine relief has ended up as a scheme of middle-class welfare.

Malnutrition is the sometimes forgotten context for the everyday observation that 'India can now feed itself': it will be recalled that Indian poverty is measured in calorie intake. True, India has built impressive buffer stocks of food so that people will not usually die of sudden starvation arising from famine. Further evidence of the increases in food production comes from the regular export of Indian fruit, shrimp, condiments and even grain. The McDonalds hamburger chain is now planning to source the lettuces for its South-East Asian operations in Poona. Altogether, enchanced food output is the great economic achievement of the last half-century. And yet, poor Indians remain among the worst fed of the world's people.

In a poor country like India it is inevitable that 'welfare' measures will still be dominated by a discussion of food policy. More ambitious schemes of social welfare are still in their infancy, and again Kerala has tended to lead the way. For example, in 1980 the Government led by the Communist Party of India (Marxist) (CPI(M)) introduced a modest aged pension (Rs. 45 monthly) for both male (65 years and over) and female (60 years) retired agricultural labourers. While it was no accident that the Agricultural Labourers' Union had been a strong supporter of the CPI(M), the scheme was later subjected to a means test and separated from partisan considerations (Kannan 1988: 286). By now there is a national aged pension scheme of strictly limited scope, and a number of welfare schemes for persons suffering disabilities of various kinds. But the amounts supplied by these pensions tend to be far too little to sustain life, let alone provide for a modicum of dignity in old age or disability. And, of course, the perennial problem of 'leakage' to third parties bedevils their administration. As yet the impact of these schemes is probably only marginal in most States, and for this reason they are not discussed in detail. But we do return to the special case of Kerala below. By far the most important schemes have been the various programs of public works and the asset formation program known as IRDP, and after a short discussion of land reform we shall examine these in some detail.

The question of land reform

Nehru's 'democratic social transformation' was to be a controlled and peaceful revolution accomplished through the mechanisms of parliamentary democracy. Changes to agrarian structure would arise organically from the pressures exerted by a newly enfranchised rural population. Indeed, important social change *has* taken place: the richest agrarian interests have gradually lost ground to the old peasant classes. But this has left the landless or near-landless communities in a substantially unaltered structural position. Once this realisation set in among the national leadership, they were left with no strategy for combatting deep poverty. Nor has an alternative strategy established itself in the succeeding years, though just now we may be on the cusp of a new orthodoxy to the effect that a liberalising market will ultimately supply the jobs necessary to employ the rural poor.

With the clear gaze of hindsight we can now see that redistributive land reform was never likely to take place in post-Independence India. This was not because such reform was impossible to accomplish but rather because the governing elite was not convinced that it was desirable. The example of West Bengal suggests that if the national leadership had thought otherwise, a quite different outcome could have been engineered. During the early 1950s West Bengal accomplished significant resumption of land under the *Estates Acquisition Act* 1953, probably more than anywhere else in India (though curiously, 'feudal' Rajasthan also resumed considerable amounts). This was done simultaneously with the abolition of the intermediary system of administration – so-called 'zamindari abolition' – at a time when there was widespread fear and therefore a cooperative spirit among landlords. In order to buy peace, the landlords of West Bengal were prepared to surrender some of their lands. Later, when they became emboldened by the timorousness of even Communist governments, they were less cooperative and also far more knowing about how to limit the gains of reformism.

As it was, and simplifying a long and detailed story, land was by-and-large not given to the tiller. Rather, India got rid of those arrangements that interposed a third party between the effective owner of land and the state. This meant that secure tenants under the British administration were able to acquire proprietorship (by whatever name) in preference to high-caste landlords who did not work the land with their own hands. But mere sharecroppers, other legally insecure tenants, or perennial and occasional labourers were unable to assert their claims as against the same landlords. The tillers were thus denied the land. A State like Bihar, for example, contrived not to acquire a single hectare of land for redistribution to agricultural labourers until Indira Gandhi's Emergency of 1975–7. This was a feat of quite stunning conservatism on the part of the old landlords of Bihar.

The great losers in this failure of redistributive land reform were the Untouchables. Throughout India, in their tens of millions they tilled the land of others. They did so in a great variety of relationships but usually without any security of tenure under Anglo-Indian land law. In Bihar, for example, it was overwhelmingly they who performed the physical labour for high-caste landlords to whom ploughing the land was an actual sin. Following land reform they simply continued doing what they had done before. But this is not to say that land reform did not make significant changes. In Bihar it liberated the middle stratum of agrarian society which was positioned between high-caste landlords who did not cultivate the land by their own hand and labourers like the Chamars, Dusadhs and Musahars. This middle stratum tended to be low- or 'backward'-caste cultivators who often had the status of legally protected tenants unable to be ejected from their land. Along with the urban middle class, this is the most successful grouping of post-Independence India. Bit-by-bit they have been acquiring land by way of purchase from the high-caste ex-land-lords. This redistribution in the marketplace has to a large extent closed off the agrarian prospects of the Untouchables.

The Untouchables did not merely lose economic prospects with this failure of redistributive land reform. They also lost the opportunity to become a more powerful political force in the countryside. Throughout this work we have been stressing the lack of neutrality in the apparatus of the state, and how it often operates against the interests of poor people. So Untouchables have all too often received harsh and oppressive treatment from the police and from local officials. Such treatment would have been harder to sustain if their position in the village had been stronger, and acquisition of land would have been the basis of a new strength. The persistence of often oppressive and exploitative dependence has been the single greatest limitation on the Untouchables' capacity to enjoy progress.

In the decades after the crucial 1950s when most of the land reform was done, there have been flickers of official interest in carrying the task further. The most promising development has been 'Operation *Barga*' in West Bengal, whereby during the 1970s and 1980s more than a million sharecroppers (*bargadars*), a large proportion of them Untouchables, had their tenancy legally recorded for the first time. This entitled them to the enhanced share of production that the law laid down – basically, three-quarters of the crop rather than half. The Communist Party of India (Marxist) Government of West Bengal has not gone on to the next step of vesting ownership of the land in these sharecroppers. Such a step would have a drastic effect on high-caste, middle-class proprietors of small holdings – some of them poorly paid schoolteachers, for example – many of whom are members or at least supporters of the CPI(M). So even in the case of this positive example the reforms have been far less than complete (Mallick 1993: 50–61). By now it is impossible to be optimistic about land reform in India as a whole. The old middle stratum of the countryside has gained greatly in power, and their grip on the land which they tend to work with their own hands is strong. Indeed, there is increasing tension in various parts of India between these rising middle castes – the Yadavs are the best known north Indian example – and the Untouchables who remain at the bottom of the agrarian hierarchy.

The above is essentially a broad-brush approach to land reform, as befits the design of this book. But it is appropriate to add a qualification to the general picture of Untouchable landlessness we have painted. Thus despite the overall failure of redistibution by the state it is not correct to say that Scheduled Caste persons have received no land in the post-Independence reforms. Most States have responded to the pressures exerted from New Delhi by taking the easy opportunity of distributing portions of government land, including village commons, to landless families. More often than not the selected beneficiaries are persons from the Scheduled Castes. A considerable proportion of this allocation took place during the Emergency from 1975 to 1977. The amount of land in question may not be great relative to the total land in cultivation but it is not altogether inconsequential. So throughout India one now finds quite large numbers of Untouchable families who have acquired very small plots by way of this privatisation of public lands. But a major problem with the approach is that it has caused serious, even violent, disruption almost everywhere it has occurred. In many cases the Untouchable beneficiaries have been physically prevented from cultivating the land that has been given to them. Often – we have personally encountered examples of this in Rajasthan and Bihar – Scheduled Caste beneficiaries have been forced into expensive litigation to try to hold on to the land. In other cases the land has found its way into the hands of peasant caste operators, a particularly unjustified form of privatisation of public land.

No reliable figures are available as to total Untouchable ownership of land, but an official report has claimed that the area of operational holdings in the hands of Scheduled Caste operators in seven particular states, expressed as a percentage of total operational area, was as follows for the year 1985–86:

Haryana	2.0
Gujarat	3.1
Bihar	5.5
Tamil Nadu	7.1
Karnataka	7.2
Madhya Pradesh	8.0
Rajasthan	11.8

(Calculated from Government of India, *Agricultural Situation in India* 1988–9: XLIII).

The favourable figures for Rajasthan are consistent with other reports on the relatively strong redistributive performance of that State. But all the figures must be treated with caution. One reason is that 'operational holdings' comprise land that is leased in as well as owned by the cultivator, so the figures are not to be equated with ownership. It is even possible that some sharecropped land has found its way into the figures. And, of course, the figures do not discriminate as to the quality as opposed to quantity of land; anecdotal evidence suggests that land held by Untouchables tends to be relatively poor in quality. Even if the land is potentially fertile there is the question of whether the Scheduled Caste operator has the means to irrigate or otherwise work it productively. The very smallness of most Untouchable landholdings presents problems – usually oxen or tractors will need to be hired in, and this cannot always be easily arranged. In short, we cannot conclude from the figures above that landholding other than on a sharecropping basis is a major factor in the contemporary economic makeup of Scheduled Caste agricultural workers. It still makes sense to talk of the Untouchables as characterised by a general condition of landlessness.

The anti-poverty programs

If we leave aside famine relief and the scholarships and subsidies entailed in compensatory discrimination, it was not until the 1980s that India introduced targeted anti-poverty programs. It is possible to see these programs as part of a third wave of post-Independence policy. The initial push from New Delhi was towards rapid development of heavy industry. But the disastrous droughts of 1966–7 sharpened the realisation that agricultural potential had been drastically neglected over the first two decades of Independence. Increase of agricultural production now became a major focus. This entailed not only a shift away from the dominant emphasis on industrial development but also the quiet abandonment of considerations of equity in agrarian policy. The latter considerations had already been dealt a fatal blow by the prior discarding of land redistribution as a serious national objective. So the vastly enhanced public assistance to agriculture was channelled to large capitalist farmers on irrigated tracts, and by the early 1970s the reward was 'national self-sufficiency' and a discontinuance of food imports. Assistance was then broadened to include smaller farmers on less fertile lands, and many of these people were given cheap access to new seed strains, water, fertilisers and other inputs. But despite Indira Gandhi's winning slogan of *Gariibi Hatao* (Banish Poverty!) in the 1971 election, none of this touched the vast population of landless labourers. Only after the trauma of the Emergency and the subsequent upsurge of 'Harijan atrocities', was fresh attention paid to the needs of the landless poor. Both the Janata Government of 1977–80 and then Indira Gandhi's new Congress Government after 1980 responded to the violent unrest by taking a fresh interest in moderate measures to benefit the poor and the Untouchables in particular.

The highpoint of the anti-poverty strategy was the period of the Sixth Plan, 1980–5. But despite the considerable resources devoted to them, the several programs were never seriously regarded as an instrument of social transformation by either government or its critics. The left side of Indian politics has tended to pour scorn on them as mere palliatives designed to divert attention from the 'real' issue of land reform. And enthusiasm for the approach always seemed more intense in the New Delhi bureaucracy than among politicians of any persuasion. By the early 1990s enthusiasm had all but trickled away, and there is no longer any serious belief that the several anti-poverty measures will actually effect a major and permanent reduction in Indian poverty.

The food-for-work schemes – the Maharashtra EGS, NREP and successors

The first major anti-poverty program had its roots in old anti-famine policy. For most of the twentieth century national and provincial governments have sought to alleviate food shortages by providing food in return for work. As early as 1877 the British had sought to meet a famine in this way (Clough 1914: 253–5). The Bihar drought of 1966–7 was the first major test of Independent India's enhanced capacity to cope with acute and widespread crop loss, and by-and-large the test was passed. Some 740,000 persons – half a million more than before the crisis – were employed on public works that were small (mostly having to do with improvements in irrigation) and close to home or workplace (Brennan 1990: 203). The workers were paid in cash but the (largely imported) food they purchased mostly came from the subsidised public distribution system (Brennan 1990: 204). A similar response was later made to crop failures in Maharashtra. In 1972–3 that State adopted a much more ambitious Employment Guarantee Scheme (EGS) which created labouring positions on a perennial basis and not merely in times of agricultural crisis (Herring and Edwards 1983: 578). The object was to guarantee casual labourers a certain amount of paid labour during the off-season, which typically lasts at least half the year. At the national level it was another decade before the Government of India turned at all seriously to the problems of agricultural labourers in normal times rather than droughts.

The Sixth Five Year Plan of 1980–5, with its special emphasis on the rural poor and thus the Untouchables, turned its attention for the first time to a national scheme of employment for agricultural labourers during the off-season. The model for this National Rural Employment Program (NREP) was the Maharashtra Employment Guarantee Scheme.[1] But while no one now doubts that the Indian state has a responsibility to feed its people in times of severe crop failure, the

---

[1] During the Seventh Five Year Plan NREP was augmented by the Rural Landless Employment Guarantee Scheme. This program purported to guarantee 100 days of employment to the landless. In 1989 the illogical coexistence of the two schemes was ended and they merged to become the Jawahar Rozgar Yojana.

appropriateness of routine public works to feed the chronically poor remains a matter of intense controversy. Before we discuss the impact of the schemes themselves the positions in the debate can usefully be canvassed.

The most basic objection comes from the ideological position that continuing schemes of public works will create a permanent class of 'wage slaves' working for 'masters' who benefit from the works that the slaves create (Dantwala 1985: 475–6). The illiterate, unskilled, psychologically and economically dependent poor will build up the country's infrastructure not for common benefit but for the highly specific benefit of rich and middle peasants, whose production and marketing opportunities will increase along with the value of their property. This effect comes about from the nature of public works, which are predominantly the improvement of minor irrigation and roads. Improved irrigation will increase the output of land and thus benefit its owners, and improved roads will facilitate marketing opportunities for the same people. Any 'trickle-down' effect from increased income for landowners will be minimal, while relations of subordination and dependency are further increased.

Even from a less committed position against routine programs of public works there are serious concerns about the physical nature of the works. If the object is genuinely to build up national capital, then it is far from easy to devise a vast number of appropriate schemes. Whatever the intrinsic merits of giant projects – and nowadays projects like major dams are increasingly suspect on social and environmental grounds – they are inappropriate as routine public works because by definition they will often be distant from the homes of many of the employed labourers. So appropriate public works will need to be local and therefore small-scale. Inevitably, small irrigation works – generally the construction and repair of water channels – will be a favourite task. But even if these works benefit a considerable number of farmers, they do tend to look more like a private than a public good – though it has to be said that the line between the two is difficult to draw. Moreover, on a physical level the usually mud-lined water channels tend to be highly impermanent and often unable to withstand a single monsoon season. They scarcely represent even a semi-permanent increase of national capital. This sort of problem has led some supporters of public works to argue that the employed labourers should be allowed to work on improving their own private property – their house, a small piggery, and so on. But clearly this approach would entail the abandonment of any intention to create 'public' works of benefit to the national economy, and no Indian government has embraced such a position.

Another problem of public works is that by now it is difficult to find projects which benefit all the affected parties. In irrigation projects, for example, an improved flow to one party will usually produce an adverse effect for another. This then tends to set up a demand for fresh state intervention in order to redress the effect. One academic commentator suggests that this has been a major problem in India since the 1950s, when most of the value-neutral public projects were carried out (J. Krishnamurty interview: 26 March 1985). The projects that remain 'on the shelf' are inherently conflictual.

A further objection to the way in which public works have been done in India is that they are always performed in the agricultural off-season. Of course, it makes sense to provide work when people need it most. But if one takes the view that a major agrarian task is to increase the labourers' share of agricultural output, then the availability of work in the off-season scarcely affects this. The argument is that only when employers have to compete for labour with public authorities will they be prepared to raise wages. Without such competition a public works strategy will have no capacity to bring about structural change, as opposed to merely increasing family income. Again, no Indian government has shown any willingness to accept this argument and compete for labour at times of peak demand.

There are other more practical difficulties in managing public works. In a word, cheating and corruption have tended to reign. In perhaps the most common situation, labourers are paid piece rates for excavating a stipulated quantum of soil in order to build irrigation channels or roads. The contractor measures the extent and depth of the excavated hole, and thereby calculates the cubic content of the excavation. This method is scarcely an exact one and it is in the interest of the contractor to err on the low side, thereby depriving the labourers of their due and enabling the contractor to pocket the margin; this seems to be a perennial occurrence. And, of course, bureaucratic superintendence of the contractors is especially ripe for collusion of contractor and bureaucrat to their joint benefit. There is persistent observation that supervision of public works is chronically slack.

These problems have meant that public works programs have never commanded the loyalty of a large proportion of policy analysts. But Professors Dandekar and Rath have been long-time supporters of the approach as the basis of an Indian anti-poverty strategy (Rath 1985). Their argument has as its premise that land reform, even if it were politically possible, is no longer capable of satisfying the employment needs of the vast rural population. Nor do they have any faith in asset formation schemes such as IRDP (Dandekar interview: 2 April 1985). For Dandekar and Rath, large-scale public employment emerges by a process of elimination as the strategy most likely to attack rural poverty in India. They point to an outstanding need for infrastructure projects in rural India (Rath 1985: 246). And they dismiss as unimportant the outcome whereby public money is expended to enable landless labourers to create assets which disproportionately favour landed interests. This is simply an inevitable outcome which fails to vitiate the benefit of increasing the income of the rural poor (Rath interview: 2 April 1985; Dandekar 1986: A-100).

At its high point the Maharashtra scheme was a large one. In the early 1980s more than 500,000 people were employed daily, and the scheme was consuming some 10 per cent of the State budget (Herring and Edwards 1983: 579). Early reviews of its operations concluded that it was an important source of income for the families of agricultural labourers but that it had not lifted a large proportion of its beneficiaries out of poverty and that it had failed to bring about any structural change (Herring and Edwards 1983: 581–3). Curiously, once the scheme went national there was no credible attempt to evaluate its impact. Food-for-work schemes remain an indispensable part of the national response to agricultural failure, but they cannot be regarded as the primary policy instrument against rural poverty. As liberalisation takes increasing hold of Indian policy there is even less chance that there will be support for a giant army of rural labourers routinely working for daily wages on public works. This particular approach to job creation in the countryside has simply lost its appeal.

Integrated Rural Development Program (IRDP)

The term 'Integrated Rural Development' first achieved prominence during the Janata Government of 1977–80, when it was a neo-Gandhian aspiration to turn back towards a village-centred Indian society where new employment opportunities would be created by locally based industry. But as it developed during the 1980s under the re-elected Congress Government, IRDP became simply one of the anti-poverty programs – albeit the most distinctive and novel of these. What made IRDP different was that it sought to create assets for its beneficiaries, who were then to manage their assets without substantial assistance from the state. The new asset was to be the functional equivalent of land. Here, then, was a genuinely fresh approach to poverty that confronted the reality that radical land reform was not a possibility, and posited an attractive alternative. Poor people would be empowered to take control of their own lives and would be liberated from the permanent dependency characteristic of other schemes such as food-for-work. They would become, in short, small business people. Their asset was not a public gift – it was structured as part grant (about 33 percent) but greater part loan (66 percent) repayable to the public banks that determined eligibility.

Rath calculates that during the Sixth Plan period 1980–5 close to 16 million households benefited from IRDP; the total number of poor Indian households was some 90 million in 1981. Even though perhaps 15 per cent of the beneficiaries were not really 'poor' and so should not have qualified, Rath calculates that some 34 per cent of poor rural households actually received benefits under the scheme. In 1982–3 alone total government expenditure on IRDP was some 3.6 billion rupees (Rath 1985: 240–1). Whether or not the figures are perfectly accurate, it can be seen that IRDP has constituted a very large project indeed.

The idea of IRDP was attractive for several reasons, not the least being that it promised to liberate poor people from the clutches of public officials dedicated to their own rather than their clients' cause. But implementation of the scheme has been little short of a nightmare. The core failure has been the false assumption that very large numbers of habitually poor, usually illiterate, people could become in effect mini-entrepreneurs. This assumption overestimated the skills typically at the command of poor people, and underestimated the hostility of people capable of blocking their progress. But even without this unrealistic and damaging optimism, there would have been other difficulties sufficient to render the scheme highly problematical. One of the central issues was the nature of the assets themselves. The planners' favourite asset, particularly early in the life of the program, was a milch animal – usually a buffalo, sometimes a cow. Many thousands of these animals were supplied to people who qualified for an IRDP loan. The idea was that the buffalo would be farmed so as to provide milk as a saleable commodity. Other assets were later financed in considerable numbers, including sewing machines and rickshaws. By the earlier 1990s 48 per cent of IRDP assistance still involved agricultural projects such as the buffalos, 33 per cent was given to households involved in the services sector and only 19 per cent to projects in secondary industries (Eighth Five Year Plan 1992: II, 48).

A number of the deep problems of IRDP can be discerned in the story of the cows and the buffalos. First, the sudden new demand for these animals could not be met by an adequate supply of good crossbreed stock. It seems that often the demand was superficially satisfied by the supply of poor-quality animals incapable of supplying appropriate levels of milk. Indeed, anecdotes suggest that quite often the animals were altogether barren; the 'beneficiary' had no choice in the matter. But even if the cow turned out to be a good one, what was one to do with the milk? In some areas there is a regular milk marketing scheme into which a new producer can enter, but this situation seems to be comparatively rare. Often the necessary roads and transport are quite lacking, and milk sales can be no more than a haphazard affair. In a great many instances the problem was 'solved' by the owner and his family drinking the milk themselves. Now, enhanced consumption could be of real nutritional benefit to poor families. But IRDP was not set up to produce such a direct effect. If the product created out of the asset is not sold, then there can be no income sufficient to repay the loan. Accordingly, cases were reported of the poor turning to local moneylenders in order to borrow money to pay off the loans from the banks. By 1990 the Government of India was itself worried by figures showing that some half of all beneficiaries were overdue in their loan repayments. In the words of the Eighth Five Year Plan, this raised 'doubts about their ability to come out of the debt syndrome' (Eighth Plan 1992: II, 36). With more than a hint of desperation, a new scheme with a new acronym – TRYSEM or Training of Rural Youth for Self-Employment – was devised to instil business skills in the poor.

The whole object of IRDP was to make poor people more independent, but management of an asset like a milch animal can in fact induce a new dependence. Given that the beneficiaries of IRDP loans tend to be landless, they are faced with negotiating a source of fodder for the animal. Presumably the most common arrangement is the exhange of unpaid labouring work for a landowner in return for access to cattle fodder. But such arrangements are not always easy to achieve, particularly if there is a shortage of fodder around the village. And even if there is enough fodder to go around in a good year, in drought times naturally the landowner will satisfy the requirements of his/her own animals first. Earlier (pp. 69–71) we discussed a 'Harijan atrocity' case in Karnataka whose proximate cause was the grazing of an IRDP buffalo on land belonging to the assailants. And in another Karnataka case (pp. 71–2) the issue of entitlement to fodder was a major cause of poisonous relations between the Untouchables of the village and the high-caste landowners.

If the enterprise is to be viable in the longer term, the owner of the cow or buffalo also needs to be able to pay for occasional veterinary treatment. Otherwise the asset may die, leaving only a debt in its place. But it will be the rarest of very poor people who is able to produce a stream of income from his/her cow sufficient to meet such eventualities. The problem is compounded if the requirements of the animal are unusual. Thus we encountered a man in Bihar who was struggling not with a cow but with pigs which had been given to him through IRDP. These were no ordinary Indian pigs, but special pigs designed to be slaughtered for the pig meat market. But what the keeper had not sufficiently realised was that these pigs were unable to process and derive nutrition from excrement and other waste in the manner of ordinary country-style pigs. So the man was forced to buy expensive food for them against the comparatively distant time when he might be able to sell them for a reasonable profit. This profit was considerably hypothetical, since he was not sure of the management of these pigs or of the demand for their meat once they reached maturity. To cap it off the pigs were paler and less hairy than the country variety, and were thus proving susceptible to sun-stroke. Altogether the venture looked suspiciously headed for disaster.

It has become abundantly clear that those who can make a success of IRDP loans are located not very far below the poverty line, especially those with access to land (Sundaram and Tendulkar 1985: 20–3). These are the people who may have enough knowledge and all-round resilience to be able to work and maintain the asset and to repay the loan. The banks themselves soon and correctly realised that it was futile to lend money to the very poor under the terms of IRDP. This did not mean that such people were not given loans; rather, they tended to get significantly smaller loans than they needed. This may have limited the losses of the banks but it also ensured the failure of the enterprise and thus made a mockery of the whole rationale of IRDP. This is simply a scheme that is unsuitable for the very poor.

Accurate quantitative assessment of IRDP is difficult to achieve. But in 1985 Rath suggested that some 3 per cent of the poor households in rural India had been lifted out of poverty during the then seven years that IRDP had existed. Others had had their income increased but not sufficient to carry them over the official poverty line. Rath was further sceptical that even these beneficial effects would be able to be maintained (Rath 1985: 243). These figures do not have the status of being generally agreed, but nor are there markedly higher figures that are plausible.

The program continues in the 1990s, albeit in a wounded way after the barrage of criticism and doubt that it has suffered. The government has made a number of adaptations.[2] Some of them try to confront what had become notorious problems in the administration of IRDP; others seek to scale down the expectations excited for the scheme, so that it does not have to be abandoned as an abject failure. Along the latter course, IRDP is no longer officially justified only by its capacity to 'carry' people over the 'poverty line'. It is now seen to have a role in the augmentation of family income, even if this is not sufficient for the family to make a permanent exit from poverty. The deserving character of the beneficiaries is

---

[2] For a discussion of these see Concurrent Evaluation 1987; Bandyopadhyay 1988: A77–A88; Hirway 1988: A89–A96.

demonstrated by pointing out that almost half of them are Untouchables or tribals (Eighth Five Year Plan 1992: Appendix I, 48). And changes have been made. There is now less enthusiasm for farm animals, more for establishing small businesses of a non-agricultural nature. An attempt has been made to substitute elected panchayats for District officials as the decision maker on prospective beneficiaries of IRDP funds. This is an effort to answer the objection that District officials had no way of rationally selecting just which families in a District were appropriate beneficiaries. But since panchayats tend to be dominated by large landowning castes, the value of the change is not self-evident. Essentially, then, the government has been tinkering with the main design of the program, rather than engaging in creative thought (Thimmaiah 1988: 331–2). There is now an abundance of evidence to challenge the Government of India's rosy assessments of the impact of IRDP and the other anti-poverty programs on the experience of poverty in India (Minhas, Jain and Tendulkar 1991: 1,673–82). The government maintains something of a bold front, but there is no doubt that it too has lost faith in its favourite policy of the early 1980s.

Special Component Plan

The Special Component Plan was the last of the major anti-poverty initiatives instituted during the Sixth Plan period. Unlike food-for-work and IRDP the Special Component Plan does not constitute a specific bundle of projects. It proceeds from an awareness that despite the special programs the 'weaker sections' continue to be denied a fair share of development funds. So the Special Component Plan simply required that the Scheduled Castes and Tribes share in all relevant development outlays according to their proportion in the local population. For example, the Scheduled Castes should benefit from road construction according to their population share.

On the face of it this is an appropriate and sensible measure. The Plan has the merit of drawing public attention to just how limited a share of public outlays is allocated to poor people. On the other hand it is doubtful that such a blanket approach can ever be much more than a noble aspiration. The planning and implementation mechanisms for such a policy are simply not in place. It is true that Scheduled Caste Development Corporations were set up in the States in order to oversee the flow of development funds through the Special Component Plan and other schemes, but implementation was largely left to the regular District administrative machinery (as opposed to the public banks, in the case of IRDP). This was another way of condemning the initiative to death. The

District administration is overburdened, often grossly inefficient, and always subject to the intense pressures of local notables who tend to oppose the transfer of benefits to Untouchables. In short, it is highly doubtful that any significant flow of funds occurred through the operation of the Special Component Plan.

An index of the current thinking of New Delhi is evident in the movement of bureaucrats. During the 1980s some of the brightest and most committed bureaucrats were in the Department of Rural Development, which devised and supervised the most significant anti-poverty measures. In the 1990s this is no longer a Department at the cutting edge, and some of its talented bureaucrats have migrated to the Department of Finance. This Department is now the bureaucratic powerhouse of economic liberalisation, whose thrust is the very antithesis of massive state intervention on behalf of the poor.

Two regional approaches to development

To conclude – as anyone must – that the targeted anti-poverty programs have failed to deliver large proportions of Indians from poverty is not to have made any substantial comment on the extent to which poverty in India, or among Untouchables in particular, is either abating or intensifying. Indeed, any serious observer finds it difficult to make sweeping comments on the general experience of poverty over recent years. Even the data on calorie intake are unclear. Thus, there are figures to suggest that the number of poor Indians (measured by calorie intake) fell quite sharply from the late 1970s but again rose after the advent of economic liberalisation in 1991 (Gupta 1996:150). But despite such figures it is clear that in some parts of India substantial economic progress has been enjoyed by the great majority of people, even those at the bottom of society. Increasingly the experience of poverty varies with region as well as with social position. But to complicate the situation further there is the particular example of Kerala. This State has developed a complexion markedly different from the rest of the country. By reference to some indicators that everyone regards as important, Kerala is the most 'developed' State in India. But the people of Kerala – particularly those at the bottom of its society – are ranked low by reference to individual patterns of consumption. A rehearsal of the circumstances of Untouchables in Kerala and the Green Revolution region of Punjab-Haryana and adjacent areas will point up the ambiguities and inconclusiveness of the debate about models for development and their relation to the poor. If the anti-poverty programs have failed then it is also true that India has discovered no other agreed way of combatting poverty.

Kerala

Kerala is the leading example of a State committed to supplying what we have called the 'basic needs' of its population. In this respect it is an important exemplar for all the other States of India. But a closer examination of the Kerala record suggests that its successes are not quite so towering as they are sometimes represented, while on other scales its failures are notable. And in so far as Kerala's successes are real and important they cannot easily be emulated in the rest of India.

Kerala's progress has not been made from the 'targeted anti-poverty programs'. The performance of the State in relation to these programs has been no better – indeed it has been worse – than that of many other States. Kerala's genuinely important achievement has been in literacy – in 1991 the rate of literacy reached 90 per cent against a national average of 52 per cent (Census of India 1991: 1 (2), 53). This achievement very largely accounts for the other indices for which Kerala is rightly celebrated. The educated women of Kerala (86 per cent literate in 1991) have quickly seen the benefit of reducing their own fertility in the face of levels of mortality which declined from 16 to 7 per thousand between 1960 and 1980 (State Planning Board 1984: 102). Educated women also learn to discard traditional physical practices that injure rather than promote health. For example in India it has been widespread practice to treat diarrhoea in babies and small children by stopping liquids. Unfortunately this leads to dehydration and possible death. With education, the women of Kerala have learnt to maintain liquids even during bouts of diarrhoea. This is one reason for the decline in infant mortality from 55 to 39 per thousand between 1964 and 1980 (State Planning Board 1984: 97). Of course there is an intermediate step between education and changed practice in the matter of treatment of diarrhoea. This step is acquisition of knowledge. Kerala has a profusion of modern health clinics, and the importance of these facilities in promoting the health of the population has to be recognised. But given the willingness to change that tends to come with education, the women of Kerala have not needed to attend clinics *en masse* to learn how to change life-threatening behaviour.

The superior education and health facilities of Kerala have come at a price: in the year 1982–3 (the latest for which we have figures), the State spent 39 per cent of its total outlays on 'social services' (State Planning Board 1984: 23). The major part of this expenditure was on education and health, including sanitation and clean drinking water. While this proportion will not seem large to observers of provincial budgets in western countries, it seems quite unusual by Indian standards. And given Kerala's impressive 'social indicators' on mortality, life expectancy, literacy and fertility, there will be a tendency to assume that there must be a causal connection between the quantum of outlays and the indicators achieved. In fact, this connection is far from complete.

In the mid-1980s the State's own planning body attacked health expenditure as being wrongly biassed towards clinical and curative as opposed to preventive medicine (State Planning Board 1984: 26–8). It pointed out that a large quantity of expensive, western-style, medical equipment had been purchased by the State, and that this reflected an approach to medicine that was of little relevance to a poor society such as Kerala. Worse still, the equipment was insufficiently maintained and therefore tended to run down in value. The review went on to argue that the reduced mortality of Kerala could not be attributed to a health system which was plagued with problems (State Planning Board 1984: 28). Literacy, the higher status of women in Kerala, and the flow of monies from Kerala people working in the Gulf, were cited as more potent factors in bringing about the gains. Even where clinical medicine could be ceded an important role it had often been private rather than state-run clinics that had been the major suppliers of services. This perspective suggests that it will not be easy to transfer the Kerala successes to other States with quite different circumstances.

Nor is the Kerala story of education so straightforward as the splendid figures on literacy might suggest. First, it is not possible to attribute the literacy levels merely or even predominantly to the emphasis of progressive governments over the last forty years or so. Explanation of the Kerala propensity towards education is a complicated historical task. Material factors include the influence of maritime geography, the strong presence of Christianity, the background of matrilineal Nayar culture, the hold that Marxism gained during the 1930s, and so on. Secondly, the closer one looks at education in Kerala, the less of a panacea it appears. The now standard account of contemporary Kerala takes the line that the State has not performed nearly as well in industrial and general economic terms as its superior social indicators would suggest it should. But the existence of a population and workforce marked by literacy is a necessary rather than sufficient basis for the development of modern and dynamic industries. There are a variety of reasons – they need not be canvassed here – why Kerala has not enjoyed industrial development that could have made appropriate use of the State's comparatively well-educated population. Conversely, there are particular factors that have made Bangalore, Bombay or Delhi more encouraging to modern industry than, say, Cochin. It has been no substitute for industrialisation that a large number of Kerala people have found (now dwindling) employment in the Gulf, since this employment has had only a limited multiplier effect (in the domestic construction industry, for example) within Kerala. Quite tragically, Kerala leads the nation in educated unemployment.

While this problematic economy affects all communities in Kerala, it has obvious relevance to the Untouchables. They are poorly equipped to acquire the hotly competed for jobs that are not earmarked for them by way of reservation; their overall literacy rate (80 per cent in 1991) is only 10 per cent less than the average for Kerala, but Untouchables often fail to complete higher levels of study. And Untouchables who are literate but not highly educated tend to be trapped in menial labouring jobs. True, Untouchables have benefited greatly from the relaxation of overt discrimination on the basis of caste; and like the rest of the population they have taken to better health practices and family planning. But in the mid-1980s their infant and child mortality was still almost double that of Kerala Hindus in general. And there were large disparities in mortality figures between agricultural labourers and other manual workers on the one hand, and owner-cultivators and non-manual workers on the other (Bhat and Rajan 1990: 1961). Both Untouchables and tribals continue to have a grossly disproportionate share of the Kerala poor (Kannan 1995: 710–11). Clearly, then, the admirable 'basic needs' strategy has not solved the economic problems of these communities. They remain at the bottom of the social and economic heap.

Punjab-Haryana and adjacent Green Revolution regions

The economy and overall situation of the twin states of Haryana and Punjab – and, more recently, of adjacent areas in Rajasthan and Uttar Pradesh – are at the other end of the scale from Kerala. These are among the most prosperous regions of post-Independence India, but their progress is measurable in family income rather than superior 'social indicators'. Prosperity here has derived overwhelmingly from agriculture. Punjab was the first Green Revolution zone in India, and in the 1960s it became a major exporter of wheat and later of rice to the rest of the country. For the present purposes the question is just how much of the wealth has accrued to the Untouchables. This is far from a marginal issue, since Punjab's Scheduled Castes are proportionally more numerous than their counterparts in any other state: 28.31 per cent (5,743,000 persons) in 1991. The Haryana proportion is also high: 19.75 per cent (3,251,000 persons).

If we look first at social indicators, the difference between Kerala and these northern states is clear. The literacy figure for the Scheduled Castes of Punjab was 41 per cent in 1991, and 39 per cent for Haryana. This was almost exactly half the Kerala figure. And whereas the Kerala

Untouchables were only 10 per cent less literate than the general population, in both Punjab and Haryana the gap was 17 per cent. As to fertility – the Census measures this by isolating the population aged between 0 and 6 years old – in Kerala the figure was 13 per cent, Punjab 19 per cent and Haryana 21.5 per cent. Clearly the Kerala Untouchables practise more birth control than do their counterparts in Punjab and Haryana.

But on measures of poverty Punjab and Haryana do far better. In calculations for the period 1983–4 Punjab emerged with the least poverty of all states among both the general population and the Scheduled Castes (Mendelsohn and Vicziany 1990: 258). Whereas 22 per cent of the rural Scheduled Caste population in Punjab was 'poor', the figure for Kerala was exactly double. The Haryana figures are close to those of Punjab. Field observations in Haryana and bordering areas of Rajasthan – a Green Revolution area too – confirm the view that living standards of even those at the bottom of rural society have tended to rise quite considerably in this region.

It remains a telling comment on differences in regional prosperity that many thousands of Bihari agricultural workers have been attracted to labouring positions in Punjab and Haryana from the late 1970s. Most of this migration has taken place in the context of the second wave of the Green Revolution in Punjab and Haryana, during which rice as well as wheat has been planted over considerable acreage. It has largely fallen to Bihari labourers to transfer the technology of padi to a region that had never grown it before. While this Bihari migration has been widely condemned as part of the larger phenomenon of bonded labour, this approach is rejected below because of its tendency to lump together workers of highly variable prosperity. There can be no doubt of the exploitation of migrant workers by their employers and labour middlemen, but it is also true that many of the migrants earn multiples of what they would be paid in Bihar.

Our own best field-work on this region comes from the village of Behror, the administrative centre of a division of Alwar District in Rajasthan that is close to the border with Haryana. This is a Green Revolution area, though not one that has moved on to the second phase of rice production. It is equidistant, about 120 km, from Delhi and Jaipur and has become a local hub for bus transport. Over the last twenty-five years Behror has enjoyed great economic progress, and the Untouchables have shared in this. We can see this by looking at several of the major Untouchable communities in the village.

When we first encountered Behror in 1971 only one of the houses occupied by the Bhangis – ritually the lowest caste in Behror – was of the preferred *pukka* (brick or stone) construction. By 1985 fully fifty-five of the sixty Bhangi houses were pukka and so more durable and less demanding of maintenance. The Bhangis' economic success has come about primarily through the expansion of opportunities to perform the sweeping work scorned by everyone else. For many years – in some cases almost half-a-century – Bhangi men of the village have been employed in secure jobs outside the village; in 1985 the total of such workers was thirty-two, twenty of them working in the one city of Poona. Sweeping work has greatly increased within Behror itself, particularly after establishment of the new bus stand. The Bhangis have also been able to diversify into other labouring work: fifteen men now pedal rickshaws carrying goods and people between the bus stand and the markets inside and near the village. Five of these men have taken out loans to buy their rickshaw, while the rest hire their vehicle on a daily basis. Other men are involved in the construction industry in various capacities, though not as highly skilled tradesmen. And the leading spokesman for the community has worked for decades as a tailor, mainly to his own community and other Untouchables. (It was his house that was already pukka in 1971.) Bhangi women are exclusively employed as sweepers for private households and also for the municipality.

While all this new income has markedly increased the prosperity of the Bhangi community – all of them agree on this – there has been no rapid change in attitudes towards education and fertility control. About 30 per cent of the boys of the community are now said to go to school. As yet few girls have received any education, but this is predicted to change since there is now a belief that a girl's marriageability is enhanced with at least a modicum of education. Despite all this economic progress the Bhangis remain the most scorned community in Behror – not least by the other Untouchable castes, who will generally not take water, eat or share the *hookah* with them. Traditional attitudes of superiority are now joined to a superciliousness about the Bhangis' new prosperity, derived as it is from their monopoly of work that no one else will do. But this sense of superiority is not usually exhibited by the grosser practice of ritual Untouchability. Since the Bhangis have their own water pump, drawing water from a common source is not an issue. And since Behror is an administrative and commercial centre as well as a large village, there can be no ban on the Bhangis' using the teashops open to the general public. But as a matter of practice, they do not frequent the teashops closest to the residential areas of the village. They are unlikely to feel comfortable there.

The Chamars of Behror – there are some ninety households in the village – are occupationally more diversified than the Bhangis, and have proceeded further down the path of education. For the last fifteen years or so most boys, but only a minority of girls, have attended at least the early years of school. A handful of men have studied up to the level of MA, and the oldest of these is a schoolteacher already in his late 50s. In 1985 six men from the village were teachers, two of them in primary and four in middle schools. There were three sepoys in the army, thirteen fourth-class government officers (the lowest rung of service), an overseer in the Public Works Department, and a 'computer' in Rajasthan Roadways (the public bus company). The highest placed officer was an Inspector with the Food Corporation of India. In the private sector there was a compounder (technical assistant) in an X-ray unit, a couple of assistants in a veterinary hospital, and several workers in a nearby yarn factory.

Most other male Chamar workers in Behror are either labourers or are engaged in the shoe industry. In contradistinction to the Bhangis, not a single person has taken up the option of plying a rickshaw between the village and the nearby bus terminal – this they regard as a demeaning occupation. Five Chamars were skilled tradesmen in the construction industry, and a half-dozen more were simple construction labourers. The making, repair and polishing of shoes occupied some twenty-five people, including children. Four of this group worked in Delhi, one of them in Chandigarh. None of the Chamar men will now do field labouring, not even during the period of peak demand at harvest when rates of pay are high. They abandoned this work in about 1980 when they came to regard it as beneath their station. But Chamar women are still prepared to do harvesting work, and in 1985 some thirty of them were thus employed. This was the only paid work that Chamar women of the village performed. About thirty of the families had a plot of land, in all cases only a fraction of an acre. Most of them had been given the land in 1975 during Indira Gandhi's Emergency. As usual in such cases, the land had previously been common to the landholders of the village. In 1985 some fifty families owned a cow or buffalo, and twenty families had goats.

The third large Untouchable community of Behror is the Dhanaks. This is a relatively small caste found in several States of the north; like the Mahars or Paswans the Dhanaks' traditional involvement in ritually polluting work was only marginal. In the past the Dhanaks of Rajasthan were associated with Rajputs, for whom they often acted as watchmen (Singh 1993: 428). There are some sixty Dhanak households in Behror, ten in one colony and fifty in another. The two colonies are markedly different in ambition and patterns of employment. In the smaller colony, people are less educated and less ambitious. Twelve men of this colony pedal rickshaws – all owned by their operator – but all these men, and several more, also perform as bandsmen for weddings and other events. One man is a skilled construction worker. Most of the women are not in regular paid employment but three of them work as dyers in a local yarn factory. Five women go into the fields at harvest time. As to education, most of the young men have spent some years in school. In 1985 there was one matriculant in the colony. Only a few girls have so far gone to school. Seven families were given a small plot of land during the Emergency but ten years later only three still had the land; the others had sold their plot to Ahirs, the dominant peasant community of the area. As with most of the Bhangis, all these Dhanaks' houses are now pukka.

The other Dhanak colony in Behror is quite different in its aspirations. Here, five men are already in positions of 'service': two schoolmasters, two policemen, one fourth-class (junior) official, and one *patwari* (junior revenue officer). Most of the men are involved in construction, twenty as skilled workers and about thirty as ordinary labourers. If there are public works in the area, they also turn out for this. Like the men of the Chamar community Dhanak men have also given up field labour as beneath their dignity. Few of the women are prepared to do this work either. No resident of this Dhanak colony plays in a band – they gave this up in about 1980. (Band playing is a ritually polluting occupation, presumptively because of its association with the leather of the drum.) The women gather fodder for cattle – a number of the families have a buffalo or cow and goats – and fetch fire wood from the 'jungle'; this is so-called 'small' work. But the great passion of this colony is for 'service' positions. They do not mind what the particular service might be – schoolteaching, medical orderly or whatever. To this end all boys now study at school. But in 1985 only some ten per cent of girls were at school. In common with the other Untouchable colonies of the village, almost all the houses in this large colony are now pukka.

The fourth large Untouchable community of Behror is the Khatiks, and we need say no more than a word or two about this group. The Khatiks' most distinctive work is tending sheep and goats, some of which they own and some of which they manage for others. Five of them are also butchers. Some fifteen Khatiks still go into the fields at harvest time. (Given the high level of mechanisation, there is little field labouring available in Behror other than at harvest.) For the rest, both men and women work as ordinary labourers on construction sites. No one had yet gained a position in service, but one physically imposing young man – the son of the leading man of the community – was about to become a policeman. Although less oriented to education than the Chamars or Dhanaks, for the last couple of years several Khatik girls were said to be going to school. As in the other communities, their houses are now pukka.

The economic and educational progress of the Untouchables of Behror seems broadly characteristic of the situation of many such communities in the Green Revolution regions of north-western India, albeit that Behror's bus terminal has given it a special local boost. There can be no doubt that as a class Untouchables have shared in the growth brought about by the Green Revolution. This is true despite their weak base in landholding. Although the Untouchables are often depicted as mired in a culture of poverty that includes abuse of alcohol, the single most salient sign of their progress in Behror is the conversion of their dwellings to pukka structures. This has involved major and patient investment.[3] The Behror Untouchables are also now clearly persuaded of the material and social benefits of education, and a number of them have already gained employment available only to educated persons.

In material terms they seem to be better off than their counterparts in Kerala. Probably very few of them now fall below the level of calorie intake that would make them officially 'poor'. At the same time their levels of education and therefore worldliness are far beneath those of the Kerala people. And health facilities are much worse. Accordingly, they are at a considerably earlier stage in the process of 'demographic transition' (entailing high levels of education, good health facilities and therefore low fertility), though it seems likely that the gap will be closed more quickly than appeared possible a decade or two ago. These days Behror has a considerably dynamic air. The Untouchables there are determinedly optimistic. They have seen how far they have travelled in the recent past, and they see prospects for their children to be still better. Discrimination on the basis of Untouchability no longer seems any great problem to them.

But like their counterparts in Kerala it will prove greatly difficult for the Behror Untouchables to acquire 'service' positions of sufficient quality and quantity to satisfy their ambitions. Most of the positions they have so far acquired are in the public sector, and on present indications they will have to continue to depend on reservation for any secure employment. But given the swelling number of legitimate claimants, such positions will become ever scarcer. In the long term the Untouchables of Behror can only make substantial professional headway if they are absorbed into the private sector. Otherwise, and despite their growing education, they will tend to be employed in manual capacities or join the growing numbers of educated unemployed. This, it will be recalled, is the other side of the Kerala 'model'.

---

[3] In 1985 the cost of building a pukka room was approximately Rs.10,000, and an average house had two or three rooms. At the time, a skilled construction worker was paid between Rs. 25 and Rs. 28 per day, and an unskilled labourer Rs. 15. Since day labourers are never employed for the whole of the year, as opposed to servants retained on an annual basis – there are now almost none of these left in Behror – the construction of a house will absorb many person-years of income.

Recent studies of Punjab suggest that the problem is even more acute than a projection of the uncertain future of Behror can indicate. These studies show a steep decline in net returns from wheat production (Gill and Gill 1990: 2,507). The profits of rich farmers have fallen and the debts of marginal and poor farmers have risen. There is now a massive over-supply of rural labour and no great increase of industrial employment in urban areas. One indication of this problem is an apparent decline in real wages – not necessarily in daily rates – of agricultural labourers (Jose 1988: A47–8, 50–1). Even worse, it now appears that the success of the Punjab model has not been based on the simple assertion of market forces, as was once believed. Punjab and the adjacent territories have been supported by a large number of critical subsidies. Indeed it is now being argued that if the same level of subsidy had been pumped into Bihar, the profitability of wheat agriculture in that State would be higher than in Punjab (Acharya 1992: 112). If this is so, and in the overall climate of economic rationalism, the Punjab model will come to be seen as too expensive to replicate in other regions of India.

So while we have ended this chapter with a short excursion into two relatively successful approaches to development, these cannot be represented as general 'models' with the aid of which the huge Untouchable population will be able to move permanently out of poverty. Few people now believe that Untouchables and other Indians are poor because they are brutish and stupid, but there has been no discovery of a sure-fire way of rapidly transforming the circumstances of the bottom segment of the Indian population. This is the context for the present popularity of approaches to development that rest their faith in market forces and the transforming power of globalisation.

6   The new Untouchable proletariat – a case study of the Faridabad stone quarries

In recent years another figure of Indian poverty has intruded itself beside that of the familiar poor villager. This figure is one of the great and growing army of men, women and children labouring on roads, construction sites, quarries and brickworks, and living in 'dwellings' made of bits of scrap. These people are most numerous either within or close to the growing cities and towns of India, and they have been present from the beginnings of modern urban life during the colonial period. But the scale of the phenomenon is growing fast, and it represents a kind of distorted reflection of the urbanisation and overall economic growth which India is now undergoing. Urbanisation holds out prospects of a better life for tens of millions of people in the countryside, but for the labourers who build the towns and cities it tends to represent another version of a familiar poverty.

What could be called the new Indian proletariat, sometimes lumpen-proletariat, is not always sharply distinguishable from other categories of poverty within the Indian population. But what we have in mind is people who have a history of migration from their home village, are locked into menial labour, and exist in forms of habitation that are grossly inferior to minimum human standards. This category is broad enough to encompass, for example, a considerable proportion of the great city of Bombay, some half of whose citizens are said to live either in the 'slums' or on the pavements. But it would be wrong to suggest that all those who perform hard labour outside their village can usefully be fitted into such a grouping. We must avoid the fallacy identified below in relation to a companion category, 'bonded labour': this concept has been employed too promiscuously, with the effect that economic situations of no special severity have been quite uselessly condemned. Thus Bihari farm labourers in Punjab and Haryana have often been labelled 'bonded labourers', as if this category of subordination sufficiently summed up their condition. Indeed, as we shall see below, the statutory definition of bonded labour can apply to many such people. But if we attend to the lives of these people rather than to ideological/juridical postulates of dubious progressiveness, we sometimes (not always) find considerable personal benefit to have accrued from their technically 'bonded' employment. Despite these cautions, we are sure we are identifying in this chapter a phenomenon of subordination that is real and quite fundamental to the developing character of Indian society. The process of 'migration' or movement in search of livelihood is crucial to the condition. It scarcely matters whether we account for this migration in terms of people having been pushed or pulled out of their home village; often, the difference between these formulations is merely semantic. The common social background is one of defeating poverty, sometimes even destitution.

The core of the present chapter is a study of some stone quarries near Delhi, a site we take to be broadly representative of the new proletarian labour. Roughly eight out of every ten labourers in these Faridabad quarries are Untouchables, and most of the others are tribals. This social composition is characteristic of the least attractive sites where the new proletariat work. Our point of entry into Faridabad was a struggle over bonded labour and working conditions, expressed in political, industrial and legal forms. What follows is a case study of the struggle, which we use for several interlocking purposes. First, it provides a detailed illustration of the new poverty. Secondly, it represents a rare example of an effort to organise a segment of the poorest Indian labour. And finally, the Faridabad struggle can lead us towards relevant perspectives on the Indian state – in its statutory roles of industrial regulation and welfare provision; in its judicial role through the Supreme Court, labour tribunals and other judicial bodies; and in the functioning relationships between the state (including the police), the quarry owners and the labourers. The largely unsuccessful struggle throws light on the arduousness of inducing reform in so exploited and degraded a situation as the Faridabad quarries.

The pivotal figure in the Faridabad struggle has been Swami Agnivesh, at once Arya Samaj monk and unconventional politician. For Agnivesh the Faridabad quarries have been an important example of what he takes to be the much larger problem of bonded labour in India. In 1980 he had set up his *Bandhua Mukti Morcha* (Bonded Liberation Front) to expose bonded labour throughout India and to work for its liberation. His definition of bonded labour is simply that of the *Bonded Labour System (Abolition) Act* 1976. The Act defines bonded labour as 'any labour or service rendered under the bonded labour system'. This, to paraphrase and shorten the definition in the Act, is the system of forced, or partly forced, labour, whereby in return for an advance a labourer agrees to work for no wage or a nominal wage, or to forfeit freedom of employment or movement. Agnivesh's contention was that the stone quarries of Faridabad operate predominantly as a bonded labour system. His principal object was to have the bonded labourers released, sent home to their place of origin and rehabilitated there by the relevant State government.

The Bonded Liberation Front took up the issue in early 1982 after an earlier involvement with the brick industry workers of Haryana and western Uttar Pradesh and the sand quarry workers of Delhi. It is not difficult to see why a political reformer would find this site compelling. Here, within some 20 km of the capital, workers labour in conditions which can only shock even the most inured observer of Indian industrial conditions. The area has apparently been mined for most of the present century and now appears as a kind of dreadful moonscape. Access is by way of what are now raised tracks between deep canyons of mined rock with jagged cliffsides. At the bottom of the canyons the workers can be seen smashing large quartzite rocks into smaller ones with the aid of sledgehammers up to 13 kg in weight. The large rocks have been produced by blasting the cliffside, a job performed by the same rock choppers. They have to make a fast escape (usually barefoot) once the fuse has been lit, since it is very short for reasons of economy. Smashed or merely injured limbs turn out to be a daily occurrence. Women and larger children work alongside the men, while smaller children play in the dust and dirty puddles. But what gives these quarries their almost surreal horror is the pall of snow-like dust that practically whites out vision when the crushers are operating. These are the large and primitive machines which shiver the small stones produced by the smashing process into still smaller stones for use primarily in road construction. There were in 1983 some seventy crushers operating within the one area and they produced an intense fog and level of noise which made speech difficult. Instinctively one could believe the claims of almost certain respiratory disease, including asthma and tuberculosis, for those who worked and lived here long. The houses of the labourers – some few of them relatively decent, others squat mudbrick structures like piggeries, still others leaky shacks of iron scrap and plastic – are clustered throughout the quarries amid all the noise and dust.

Agnivesh's strategy has been built around a petition to the Supreme Court of India. This central judicial tactic has been buttressed by political action and by organising the workers industrially. Thus almost simultaneous with initiation of the Supreme Court writ, the Stone Quarry Workers' Union was established in Faridabad in January 1982. This was an unusual union in that its primary object was not the improvement of industrial conditions but the liberation of workers so that they could leave the industry. Agnivesh recognised that some workers would freely stay in

Faridabad, so a secondary object was the improvement of health and safety conditions and remuneration. To Agnivesh's surprise, legal research revealed a number of progressive Acts to do with mining, inter-state migration, and health and safety standards; these were apparently being utterly ignored by the employers and by the Haryana and Union governments. Complaints of violation of this legislation and the *Bonded Labour System (Abolition) Act* 1976 constituted the basis of the writ petition to the Supreme Court.

By the end of the 1980s, and despite a spectacular success in the form of the Supreme Court judgment, the Faridabad campaign had to be counted a failure. Very few workers had effectively been rehabilitated from a situation of bonded labour; wages had risen only moderately; and the health and safety conditions were scarcely different from a decade before. Swami Agnivesh concedes this failure himself and has now all but abandoned organising in the quarries, though he persists with the resid-ual litigation. The reasons for the failure are several but they form part of a familiar Indian syndrome, viz. the overwhelming power of large employ-ers and the unreliability of the state as an ally of the poor, despite the good intentions of elements within the judiciary and bureaucracy. But Swami Agnivesh, senior bureaucrats in New Delhi and the Supreme Court itself played a part in the failure by adopting too purist a view of bonded labour on the basis of the superficial *Bonded Labour System (Abolition) Act*. It is now possible to see that the primary emphasis on the bonded nature of the labour rather than its more generally exploitative character was an unhelpful analysis given the real life choices of the labourers. In short, it has not helped the Faridabad labourers to be deemed 'bonded' because there is no realistic hope that government will provide the material basis for a life outside the quarries. It may have been preferable to devote more energy to the more narrowly industrial struggle for improved wages and conditions within the quarries, though it has to be said that this struggle is also scarcely more winnable.

The Supreme Court action and its aftermath

Shortly after his decision to take up the Faridabad case at the beginning of 1982 Agnivesh instituted the Supreme Court writ petition to free the bonded labour and to enforce the welfare legislation (*Bandhua Mukti Morcha v Union of India and Others* or the Quarry Workers Case). From a legal standpoint the case was an important example of what has come to be called 'public interest litigation', a kind of judicial activism inspired but not directly patterned after models in the United States. One of the unorthodox aspects of this litigation in its early period was the Court's willingness to take evidence in the form of research findings of appropriately qualified social scientists. Thus by the time Bhagwati J. delivered judgment in the Quarry Workers Case on 16 December 1983 he had the benefit of a 'socio-legal investigation' of conditions in the quarries specially commissioned by the Court. This device of appointing a fact-finding agent remains controversial by virtue of its creation of what the defence sees as biassed evidence unchallengeable through the regular court procedures.

The socio-legal report of Dr S. V. Patwardhan, an academic, set out a situation of systematic law-breaking by the proprietors of the quarries. He found that there were many bonded labourers, and that the welfare provisions of the *Inter-State Migrant Workmen (Regulation of Employment and Conditions of Service) Act* 1979 among many other pieces of legislation were not being enforced. The bonded nature of the labour flowed from the advances paid to workers prior to their leaving home to come to the quarries, these sums usually being paid through intermediary *jamadars* or labour sub-contractors. The money was strictly repayable prior to the workers' departure from the quarry, so they lacked freedom of movement within the meaning of the Act. Their vulnerability as dependent migratory labour habitually led to general exploitation, including under-weighing of stones for which they were paid on a piece-rate basis. And the benefits they were legally entitled to as migrant labour and miners – proper housing, clean water, washing facilities, schooling for their children, crèches, health facilities, sick pay – were systematically denied to them. The dangerous physical presentation of the site and the lack of safety procedures and equipment were unlawful under the *Mines Act* 1952 and other legislation. Multiple government authorities required to take action under the relevant legislation were almost completely neglectful of their duties. The Supreme Court's investigator concluded that the quarries 'show full signs of a reckless drive for stone extraction... In several places there the quarrying is nothing short of slaughter mining' (Patwardhan 1982: 74).

The Supreme Court agreed, against the claims of not only the quarry owners but also the Governments of India and the State of Haryana. Haryana sought to have the case thrown out on jurisdictional grounds by arguing that even if what was alleged were true, it would not justify a writ petition under Article 32 of the Constitution since no breach of fundamental rights was at issue. Bhagwati J. was scathing in response:

We can appreciate the anxiety of the mine lessees to restrict the writ petition on any ground available to them, be it hyper-technical or even frivolous, but we find it incomprehensible that the State Government should urge such a preliminary objection with a view to stifling at the threshold an inquiry by the Court as to

whether the workmen are living in bondage and under inhuman conditions...
[T]he State Government ... is, under our constitutional scheme, charged with the
mission of bringing about a new socio-economic order where there will be social
and economic justice for everyone and equality of status and opportunity for all...
(Quarry Workers Case 1984: 811)

These are unusually strong words directed from the bench to government
and demonstrate the extent to which particular members of the Court
saw public interest litigation as distinct from ordinary kinds of adversarial
litigation.

The Court also rejected the contention of the Government of India
that the concerned workmen were not migrants under the *Inter-State
Migrant Workmen Act* because they came to the stone quarries 'of their
own volition and they are not recruited by any agent' (Quarry Workers
Case 1984: 21). Bhagwati J. said he would ordinarily be prepared to
accept so serious a contention of the Government of India, but in the face
of an empirical report from Dr Patwardhan he could not. The judge concluded that many of the workers had been brought to the quarries by a
jamadar and as such they were clearly inter-state migrants within the
meaning of the Act and therefore entitled to its protections.

As to whether the labourers named in the petition were bonded
labourers within the meaning of the *Bonded Labour System (Abolition)
Act*, the judge did not feel competent to decide this central issue; he dele-
gated the task to an official who could make on-the-spot inquiries.
Instead, he limited himself to laying down some legal guidlines on the
matter. Regrettably, these guidelines appear to be quite beside the point.
Bhagwati J. seemed to regard the central problem to be the evidentiary
difficulty of discovering whether an advance had been given by the
employer to the worker. To meet this problem he laid down a rule that if a
worker were obliged to provide forced labour, it could be presumed that
the force proceeded from some economic relationship and that the
labourer was therefore bonded. Now there is nothing objectionable
about this presumption – in contemporary Indian conditions the capacity to extract forced labour presumably does usually arise on the basis of
some economic relationship rather than anything else. But this is not the
practical difficulty. The real problem is to decide just what constitutes
force in the relationship between contractor and quarry labourer. Is the
labour *forced* wherever the labourer owes money to his employer?
Bhagwati J. is silent on this question, which is the very core of the
problem.

On perhaps the most natural reading of the Act's very broad definition,
all such loans do give rise to bonded labour. The reason for saying this is
our assumption that no labourer would ordinarily be free to leave his/her

employer for another without having first discharged any debt to that employer. In terms of the language of the Act such lack of freedom could easily be said to constitute an example of 'the bonded labour system'. Is this what the court intended? Bhagwati's judgment gives no answer. Instead, he turned over what he took to be the merely technical task of discovering whether the labourers named in the petition were in fact bonded to the Director-General (Labour Welfare) of the Government of India, L. D. Mishra. It is this official and not the judge who provided the definition of what was 'forced' labour, as we shall see shortly.

If any workers were found to be bonded they were to be asked whether they wished to go back to their home, and if they did the District Magistrate of Faridabad was to make the necessary arrangements for their release and transportation home. Mr Mishra was also to inquire into which particular employers were prima facie bound by the *Inter-State Migrant Workmen Act* and the *Contract Labour (Regulation and Abolition) Act* 1979. The judge went on to observe that:

the problem of bonded labourers is a difficult problem because unless, on being freed from bondage, they are provided proper and adequate rehabilitation, it would not help to merely secure their release. Rather in such cases it would be more in their interest to ensure proper working conditions with full enjoyment of the benefits of social welfare and labour laws so that they can live a healthy decent life. But of course this would only be the next best substitute for release and rehabilitation which must receive the highest priority. (Quarry Workers Case 1984: 829)

This passage suggests that the judge was troubled by the extent to which it would prove prudent to move the workers out of the quarries, in view of the village situation from which they had originally come. This doubt turned out to be realistic.

Finally, the Court ordered the Union and State governments to secure compliance with those legislative provisions requiring the employers to ensure safe working and living conditions. In all, the Court issued twenty-one directives for action into matters including the spraying of water over the crushers so as to reduce dust emissions; the provision of adequate supplies of clean drinking water, latrines, proper medical facilities and crèches; and inspection of truck capacity to ensure that workers were not required to supply the contractor more stone per load than the 150 cu.ft they were paid for.

Clearly this was a great judicial victory for the Bonded Liberation Front. The victory was given substance when L. D. Mishra went on to name 295 workers to be bonded within the meaning of the Act and to order their release by the Haryana government. These workers were among 352 who had been interviewed out of a total working population (estimated by the Regional Labour Commissioner at Chandigarh) to be 4,130 (Mishra 1984: 5). (The union's estimate of workers was up to three times this figure.) Mishra states that he was only able to interview a small proportion of the potentially bonded population and says that constraints of time and resources inhibited a more thorough job. As to the determination of who were 'inter-state workmen' within the meaning of the Act, he found that all his interviewees would qualify.

The approach taken by the Labour Department official was a highly expansive one. His criterion for the existence of 'forced' labour was simple:

If you are working with or under or for me and owe me some advance money, you are tied to me and have no freedom of movement or freedom of choice of alternative avenues of employment until and unless the advance money has been fully liquidated. What better ingredient of the worst form of bonded labour system could there be than this? (Mishra 1984: 15)

This construction is consistent with the definitions in the Act and its effect is to make a very large proportion of migrant workers (and also a very high proportion of agricultural labourers) legally bonded. Most seasonal workers who travel from one part of India to another require an advance from their employer for their expenses. In law at least part of this advance is not repayable but is a legitimate charge against the employer under the *Inter-State Migrant Workmen Act*. In fact, the common practice of employers is to recover advances of all kinds from the employees; without repayment the worker would no doubt find it difficult, perhaps impossible, to leave his employer. The same would apply to the common practice of making occasional loans to employees – this creditor–debtor relationship is endemic in agricultural labour.

What the Labour official L. D. Mishra did was to supply the definition of 'forced' labour which the Supreme Court did not. He did so consistently with the spirit of a judgment highly favourable to Swami Agnivesh's organisation, and in a way that seems to make sense of the Act. But the interpretation is far clearer than the Act and, if it were generally adopted, would convert the legislation into an instrument of extraordinary breadth. *The Department official in effect assumed that all labourers indebted to their employers are bonded labourers.*

So far as the struggle was concerned the matter did not end with the Mishra Report. On 31 October 1984 the Bonded Liberation Front petitioned the Court that seven months after the Mishra Report the 295 labourers had still not been released or rehabilitated. Indeed the Front claimed that the labourers' situation was now worse, in that they were no longer being given work and were being 'terrorised' by the contractors. On 29 November 1984 the Court ordered inquiries into this, and directed that if some of the labourers deemed bonded were still there and desired to go home the District Magistrate was promptly to make arrangements for this at the cost of the State government. This directive brought some action and on 16 December 1984 a total of up to 106 families were put into the charge of the authorities of Barmer District in Rajasthan by the District Magistrate of Faridabad. But on 30 January 1985 the Front was back in the Supreme Court with a petition complaining that many of these families had wrongly been classified as only 'inter-state' and not 'bonded' workers and were therefore stripped of the right to debt cancellation and rehabilitation. There was also a recital of the failure of the State authorities to provide adequate housing or other facilities to the families, such that already three of the children had died in the cold of January. No action seems to have flowed from this petition.

Release of the Barmer labourers at the end of 1984 effectively marked the end of the Front's success in relation to bonded labour. Many of the other labourers deemed bonded by L. D. Mishra seem to have stayed on in the quarries, presumably for want of any satisfactory alternative. Contrary to the instructions of the Supreme Court no further inquiry into bonded labour was undertaken until the Court appointed its own Commissioner once more in 1989; by then it seemed too late to affect the situation favourably. Overall, then, the practical success of all the judicial action was meagre in juxtaposition to the soaring rhetoric and expansive legal definitions of Bhagwati J.'s judgment.

Indeed, the fate of the 'liberated' labourers makes the practical achievement even less to celebrate. We were able to follow the Rajasthan contingent back to where they had been sent in January 1985; our own visit was in April of that year. Ninety-five families had been taken to Barmer District – the other Rajasthanis from Faridabad must have gone elsewhere. These families turned out to be from a single tribal community, the Bhils, and they had been dumped into a place with which they had no more than a casual connection. Before 1947 they had been part of a large nomadic community in what is now Pakistan but on partition they had migrated to India and were arbitarily located in Barmer District. They had had to be fed for some time at public expense but soon a Punjabi contractor had picked them up and taken them to the Delhi area. Over the years they had been moved around various quarries in Haryana. They had not left the quarries since their arrival there and had certainly not been back to Barmer. So they had no roots whatsoever in the area to which they were now 'repatriated'.

The families had been split into two almost equal parties and settled in different locations near the town of Balotra, one 6 km from the town and the other 11 km in a different direction. When we encountered them their condition was deplorable. They had been delivered there some four months earlier, given a sum of Rs. 500 plus some 'building materials' and basically left to fend for themselves. The first settlement was on a sandy windswept plain where no-one would willingly choose to live. The winds of mid-April were already distressingly hot and dusty. Their 'houses' were flimsy *jhopris* made of grass, almost completely permeable to the weather. It had been bitterly cold in this arid desert when they arrived four months previously, and many of the children had fallen ill with pneumonia; one child was diagnosed with this condition in our presence. A TB patient had not received medicine since his arrival here. As to employment, they were able to get a bit of labouring work here and there. One of the sources, ironically enough, was a nearby small quarry. Others found some work at a brickworks, while some travelled the 6 km into the growing town of Balotra to try to pick up some loading or carting work. Everyone was eating poorly and they were unable to purchase the medicines which they now needed more than ever. Bad as their condition was in Faridabad, they were unanimous that it was far worse here in Rajasthan.

The other settlement told similar but worse stories. The major difference was that they were further from the town of Balotra and therefore unable to take advantage of labouring opportunities there. Their major source of income came from the (illegal) collection of sticks from a hill some distance away. They were able to sell bundles of these twigs in Balotra for use as fuel; the going rate was Rs.3 for a head-load. In order to earn this sum they had to walk 11 km to Balotra and 11 km back. They left at 4 am and returned by 1 pm. The bus was far too expensive. One, two or three people from each family made the trek every day, while others went in search of the sticks. Again these people had suffered many illnesses since being brought to Barmer, and they produced large bills for drugs they were forced to purchase. In our presence a doctor in Balotra examined a sick baby of one of the women and pronounced that the illness was 'either simple fever or malaria. I cannot make an exact diagnosis due to inadequacy of facilities.' Good medicine was further from their reach than ever.

These people had been bonded to their employer by virtue of their borrowing from him. The figures they quoted as debts were in the main small sums of around Rs. 1,000. But since they would not have been allowed to leave without repaying these amounts, they were clearly bonded within the meaning of the Act as interpreted by the Director-General (Labour Welfare). Moreover, they presumably received less than their due under prevailing piece rates – the deductions for their loans would have ensured this. But equally clearly, when we saw them rootless out in the Rajasthani desert they had by their own and anyone else's reckoning been positively disadvantaged by having been declared bonded.

We have no direct information on what has become of these Bhils in the succeeding several years. But in a report on the Faridabad situation prepared in February 1989, yet another commissioner appointed by the Supreme Court reports one of his informants to the effect that all the Barmer labourers were back working in the Faridabad quarries (Jain 1989: 179). This information may not be authoritative but it is believable. It is difficult to imagine that even with some sincere effort on the part of the Government of Rajasthan (like the provision of livestock and better housing), the Bhils could have survived let alone thrived in the physical location to which they had been led. The most logical outcome is that they would return to the life they knew in Faridabad.

Undoubtedly the body that has to take primary responsibility for this sad story is government at both central and State levels. But by now we know that attitudes ranging from lukewarm assistance through indifference to callous opposition are characteristic of government performance in matters to do with the socially deprived. This knowledge has simply to be factored into any program undertaken for these people by bodies outside government. We will return to this case after a discussion of several other cases which have not been the subject of judicial action but are useful as a point of comparison.

Some further enquiries into the labourers of Faridabad

The Case of Yad Ram

Yad Ram is a Raegar (or Chamar) and was 38 years old when we talked to him in February 1985. He was born into the quarries – his father worked there too – and he had been breaking rocks for the last twenty-five years. His family is from Jaipur but he does not know the particular locality or when they left for the quarries. He has never been to Jaipur and is therefore no longer really a migrant worker. Yad Ram is married with four children, the eldest of whom was a boy of 12 studying in school. He wanted to send the younger three children to school too – including the one daughter – but this possibility now seemed beyond his economic reach. The reason is that Yad Ram suffers a physical disability following an accident in the quarry. About a year before our conversation a rock fell on him, breaking his leg and smashing his foot. The foot is now permanently and seriously damaged, and he can no longer perform physical labour to the extent that he previously could.

It seems that Yad Ram's employer paid for the operations on his foot and for the drugs and dressings he received during the period of his convalescence. But he received no money at all as compensation for his injury. Accordingly, his economic circumstances were ruined. For seven months he could do no work at all, and he now works with only a shadow of his former vigour. He said that he and his wife together could now earn only Rs. 300 a month, a sum quite inadequate to the family's needs. In order to live during the period he was unable to work, Yad Ram was forced to borrow Rs. 5,000 at the interest rate of Rs. 3 (3 per cent) per month, as he puts it, or 36 per cent a year. His monthly payments are thus Rs. 150. The loan is from a fellow Raegar in Delhi; he was forced into this loan because no other source was available to him. He made the connection with the lender through his wife, who originally comes from Delhi. 'Big people', he noted, do not lend to people of his kind. In fact, the rate of interest is quite standard for loans in the quarries, even for loans made by fellow quarry workers. Indeed, it is not uncommon to find rates of Rs. 5 or 60 per cent on an annual basis.

Some three years before our interview Yad Ram's wife had fallen ill and remained so for about two years. Since she could not work in the quarry – women are mostly employed to excavate earth from the site so as to expose the rock – they were forced to sell all her jewellery, save some light silver anklets and toe-rings. Barely had she recovered from this illness than Yad Ram suffered his accident. After repayments on the loan they had about Rs. 150 a month to live on. This is far too little for anything but the most meagre survival, if that. Yad Ram was very bitter indeed but his wife was more resigned to their lot. The children were well fed and it was easy to believe Yad Ram's statement that he denied himself for the sake of the family. Their one asset was a goat but they were just about to sell this. The goat was bought with money from the Rs. 5,000 loan, and he said it would now fetch from Rs. 300 to 350. The family had themselves consumed the goat's milk as an accompaniment to tea but they could no longer afford to retain the animal. In addition to bits of grass they could collect as green fodder, they had had to purchase millet in the market. When we asked why he had not applied for a bank loan/subsidy under the IRDP scheme, Yad Ram said that none of the Raegars had any knowledge of such schemes.

Yad Ram's case may not be entirely typical of the cases we collected in Faridabad – his situation was more immediately desperate than many, and he had waited impatiently to tell his story. But the case does reliably represent the precariousness of life in the quarries. With good health and strength it is possible to live up to and sometimes even beyond the level of ordinary labourers in villages. But if a rock rolls the wrong way or if the cliff face slips, then life becomes even more of a nightmare than is usual among the very poor of India. And such accidents happen all the time – this is not an occupation of only ordinary danger. Even without catastrophic accident the chance of sustaining good earnings over a long period of time is slight.

Despite the severity of Yad Ram's situation this is *not* a case of bonded labour, simply because Yad Ram borrowed money from a caste fellow in Delhi rather than from his employer. Presumably the employer would not have been prepared to make a loan to someone who could not be relied on to pay the instalments, and Yad Ram's injury made him a dubious proposition. Since Yad Ram was not a migrant labourer he did not receive an annual advance to bring him back to Faridabad. But given the outrageous rate of interest, it can scarcely be said that the source of Yad Ram's loan was advantageous to him.

When we left Yad Ram his outlook appeared to be one of unrelieved misery. More than a year later we learnt that he had become a jamadar or sub-contractor of labour. Since this position is usually an exploitative one, Yad Ram may now be yet another example of those oppressed people who through cunning or necessity connive at the exploitation of their fellows. Yad Ram would not have chosen such a role willingly. He had ambitions for his children; he did not want them to grow up to be as driven down as himself.

The case of Jagdish Prasad

This is a case of no great complexity and is offered as an example of a quarry labourer for whom nothing had yet gone wrong. Jagdish is from the Balai caste of Untouchable weavers, and his home in Rajasthan is only several hours away from Faridabad by bus. He is 29 years old, married for four years, so far without children, and has worked in the quarry for nine years. His father worked here before him for twenty-five or thirty years, he says. Jagdish had already passed tenth standard school before coming to Faridabad. By then there was insufficient money for him to continue studying and he was unable to get a regular job. Although he was very sad about coming to the quarries, there was no alternative.

Jagdish's wife works alongside him, clearing earth to expose the stone. She is paid Rs. 10 a day for this. When we talked to him she had just come back from his village, where she stayed for a month. He himself goes home twice a year for four or five days at a time. Otherwise he works all year round, including the rainy season. He does not need advances from his employer to make these short trips. But he has borrowed Rs. 1,200 in his village at the favourable rate of 30 per cent a year. He took out this loan at the time of his marriage, four years previously. He services the loan at the rate of Rs. 30 a month, which means that he is doing no more than paying interest. Since there are four or five at home, including his mother and father and a young brother who is studying in school, he has to send money back to the village. None of the family at home is earning, though they possess a little bit of unirrigated land which produces some millet if there is rain. Jagdish's 45 year-old father, now retired from the quarry, does the agricultural work.

Four or five of Jagdish's extended family work in the quarry too. It seems that perhaps three-quarters of the able-bodied Balais of his village work outside the village. There are twenty-one Balai houses in the village and most of the people there are either old or children. There is a still a bit of weaving done by the old people. Agricultural work is no longer available in the village since the caste Hindu cultivators 'do their own work'. Tractor cultivation in this region has greatly cut down labouring opportunities.

This, then, is a favourable case. Neither Jagdish nor his wife has suffered major illness or accident. Their position is not improving because of the burdens of the modest debt they incurred for their marriage and the support they provide the remainder of his family. But thus far, and without children, they have not slipped into a decline. Of course this is also a sad case, typical of Untouchable poverty. Jagdish attained a fair measure of education and had hopes. Now he is the most menial of labourers, living in a hut and an environment unfit for human habitation.

The case of Shivaji Bhagwan

This case is again unremarkable except that it appears to be one of bonded labour, whereas the two earlier ones are not. Shivaji is from the Vade community, a Scheduled Tribe in Maharashtra. He is 30 years old, married with three children. He has four brothers, three of whom work in the quarries too; the fourth brother is only 8 years old. Shivaji's wife and the wives of his two married brothers work alongside their husbands. The men are well educated, three of them to matriculation standard. This is the second generation of the family to work in quarries owned by their employer, a man named R. L. Sharma, one of the three major contractors of Faridabad. Their father had worked in a number of the Sharma family quarries in Maharashtra, Andhra Pradesh and Gujarat. Such a career is apparently common, since it is said to be the policy of large-scale contractors to move their workers around wherever possible in order to minimise the chance of labour organisation.

Shivaji and his brothers had hopes of getting a position 'in service' after their schooling and had not expected to be doing the same work as their father did. But there were simply no other opportunities and no agricultural land to fall back on. The youngest brother is said to be very bright and they have high hopes that he will go to college. The next youngest also has active plans to go to college and his brothers treat him as if he is not really working in the quarry at all – he had only been there six months at the time of interview. Shivaji himself had been quarrying since 1973 and in this particular location for three years.

The whole family returns to the village in Maharashtra during the summer and rainy seasons, a total of some four months. They usually take with them a total of about Rs. 1,200 which they have accumulated during the previous eight months; this works out at about Rs. 200 per working person. This is insufficient for their needs during their stay at home and they try to supplement it with whatever labouring work they can find in the village. Shivaji says they can usually manage only ten or fifteen days work throughout the four months. Invariably he is forced to take an advance to come back to Faridabad – this is usually from Rs. 200 to 250. This year he is further in debt to his employer, since he borrowed Rs. 150 to send to his parents in the village. The advance and any loans must be repaid before he can leave for home. In addition to these debts Shivaji and his brothers say they are invariably in debt to Maratha or Muslim money-lenders in their village. This money is borrowed during the rainy season at rates of interest as high as 120 per cent. It is usually about four months after their return to Faridabad before the various loans are repaid and saving can begin. Hand to mouth as the cycle is, Shivaji and his brothers' situation would be far worse if there were serious accident or illness among the workers. They pointed to another man present at the interview who had had to pay Rs. 2,000 over a period of time for treatment of TB in his wife.

A major difference between Shivaji and both Yad Ram and Jagdish Prasad is that Shivaji has to travel a great distance at considerable expense to return home. Yad Ram's home, such as it is, is now in the quarry itself. Jagdish Prasad can be home by bus within a few hours. Also, Shivaji's language and culture are different from that of Haryana and this may prompt his group to spend a longer time at home in Maharashtra. Since there is little work at home, the family group invariably has to take an advance in order to return. And the fact of taking this advance is sufficient to constitute Shivaji and his brothers bonded labourers within the meaning of the Act. By virtue of his debt Shivaji can be assumed to lack the freedom to change employers or to 'move freely throughout the territory of India'. On an ordinary reading of the Act this is sufficient to constitute the state of being bonded. But presumably Shivaji is a bonded labourer for only a portion (usually four months) of the year, the period when he is actually in debt to his employer.

Forfeiture of freedom of action through the advance system is pernicious, though people like Shivaji tend to regard it as so standard as to be unworthy of comment. Some feeling did emerge when we got on to the subject of the jamadar, a man from their own community. This jamadar performs the task of annual recruitment by disbursing sums of money either from his own pocket or – this is more usual – as an agent of the contractor. He has a continuing role in the quarry as the intermediary between contractor and labourer. Usually the contractor pays the jamadar for the crushed rock, and the jamadar then passes the money on to the labourer – less his own deductions for commission and any debts owed to him. The precise relationship between jamadar and labourer varies. In one instance we found a harmonious relationship between labourers from Madhya Pradesh and their jamadar, who professed to be closer to the labourers than to the contractor. He had taken what seems to be the characteristic path to becoming a jamadar, viz. first working as a labourer himself. As this man, Dhurwa, told it, others in his area asked him to arrange employment for them, and his contractor agreed to this. When they came to work for the contractor, Dhurwa was made their jamadar. Dhurwa rather than the contractor provides advances to his workers to enable them to return to the quarries after their period at home. The advance is usually Rs. 400 or 500, which is repaid (without interest, he claims) out of their wages. As jamadar Dhurwa is responsible for managing as well as supplying labour to his contractor, and for this he is paid 10 per cent of the wages bill. He takes and passes on orders from the contractor as to what is to be done; but since the workers know their job, this does not amount to an onerous task. Several years previously Dhurwa had apparently invested his own funds to build some mud brick housing for his workers. He did this in order to make work more attractive in the quarries – since he is paid on a percentage basis he has an interest in maximising his workforce. The houses may be an attraction to the workers but they are so small that one has to stoop low to enter them and sit or lie rather than stand up inside. The land on which the houses are built is owned by a nearby Gurukul (monastery) of the Arya Samaj, which charges the occupants Rs. 5 per month for the privilege of occupying the site.

The question of bonded labour

The above are only three of many cases we collected in the quarries but they will suffice to present a picture of individual labourers. Only one of the three cases can be seen to reveal bonded labour within the meaning of the Act as it was interpreted by the Labour Department official, and an obvious question is whether this is the 'worst' case. Pretty clearly this is not so, at least in the absence of any documentation of particular exploitation arising from the creditor–debtor relationship between Shivaji and his employer. Thus on its own the case of Shivaji Bhagwan would not warrant being placed in a category separate from that of Yad Ram or Jagdish Prasad. Our more general suggestion is that the term 'bonded labourer' as it is defined in the Act and interpreted by the Court and particularly by the Director-General (Labour Welfare) will not always do service in identifying the most downtrodden labour in India. Degrees of exploitation cannot be fixed with the same definitional purity that is the stuff of legal language. The worst examples of bonded labour do constitute some of the very worst labour situations in India. But Shivaji and his brothers work at the margins of what is a very broad category, and it may not greatly advance our understanding of their position to think of them first as bonded labourers rather than as ordinary migrant workers in the quarries.

Behind the questions of technical law lie crucial questions for public policy and political action. Just what is the principal condition which is sought to be cured? If the starting object is not simply the 'liberation' of bonded labourers but rather the more diffuse effort to maximise the welfare of poor and often migrant workers, then the emphasis of action may sometimes shift. Part of the shift may entail a less doctrinaire outlook on the matter of employers lending money to their workers. No doubt exploitation is facilitated where workers borrow from their employers, but it cannot be assumed that the initiative for the loan always comes from the side of the employer as a way of entrapping the dependent and ignorant worker. Often the employer may be the only source of a needed loan. Thus we discovered labourers in the Bhati sand mines of Delhi who responded very warmly when asked whether they were better off following nationalisation of those mines. They claimed they were actually worse off, citing their inability to get loans from their new employer. This was clearly a major issue for them. Undoubtedly they would not be persuadable that expenditure (and therefore borrowing) for marriage, death and other 'unproductive' activities was undesirable and that the government was really helping them by not encouraging such frivolous waste. True, employers do not lend to their employees out of altruism. But the example of Yad Ram shows that outside creditors may be no better. In the absence of cheap institutional credit for necessities (including marriage and death), it is not necessarily progressive to demand a cessation of all credit relationships between employer and employee in the name of ending bonded labour.

The nature of our remarks should not be misunderstood. There is no benevolence to be discovered in the demonstrably exploitative quarry owners discussed here, but we are also raising a caution about 'progressive' stands that turn out to be rooted in elitist assumptions about the way poor people should lead their own lives. Moreover there is a danger that the very concept of bonded labour will be trivialised if it is reduced to the routine case of a credit relationship between employer and labourer.

The larger subject of bonded labour in contemporary India has not been approached at all uniformly by recent scholars. Naturally, most who have written on the subject are appalled by the indebted poverty of many Indians in agricultural labour and other spheres such as quarry labour. And since there is abundant evidence of bonded conditions and even outright slavery in the recent past, there is a tendency to conflate this past with present conditions too. Breman has recently delivered a sharp criticism of such thinking (Breman 1985: 306–13). He wants to distinguish the contemporary condition of the Halpatis of south Gujarat from their historical status as bonded labourers. In return for small sums often taken out at the time of marriage, this community became bonded to their employers for life. Usually the bonded relationship extended to wife and children too, such that the whole family worked without pay for the bondsman. In return they got bare subsistence amounts of food but also a small plot of land and some *noblesse oblige* entitlement to care in adversity.

Breman says that this *hali* system died sometime during the post-Independence period. In his telling the system has been destroyed by the development of a capitalist labour market in the agriculture of south Gujarat. It no longer suits landowners to give labourers security by tying them as they did in the past. Nowadays they play one set of labourers off against another. These developments have actually made the Halpatis worse off than they were under the old order. More generally, Breman wants to distinguish the farm servant tied to an employer for a particular period from the bonded relationships of earlier times in south Gujarat and elsewhere in India. He notes that 'it is the conditions accompanying the debt, rather than the debt itself, which constitutes the coercive character of the service bond' (Breman 1985: 307). The essence of the old order is seen to have consisted in a relationship of personal, not economic, subjection and dominance which now lies in the pre-capitalist past.

Precisely the opposite view is put by Utsa Patnaik, in her introduction to a book of essays on both historical and contemporary examples of the problem of bonded labour and slavery (Patnaik and Dingwaney 1985). Patnaik notes that:

No other society in the world, perhaps, is as burdened by the memories and material survivals of its ancient past, as is the Indian; anachronistic precapitalist social relations and ideology form an incubus on the new society painfully attempting to chart a capitalist path of development. Marx's prescient observation of a century ago remains as true today as then, that Indian society suffers not only from the development of capitalism, but also from its insufficient development. (Patnaik in Patnaik and Dingwaney 1985: 25)

The several essays in this volume proceed on the basis that the contemporary forms of debt bondage – for example, brick kiln workers in Muzaffarnagar, Bihari labourers in Punjab, agricultural labourers and weavers in South Arcot – are instances of a more general and long-standing Indian form of bondage.

This book is not the place to consider the divergent views represented by Breman and Patnaik. Suffice it to say here that Breman is not to be dismissed lightly when he points to the change from non-economic to merely economic coercion as characteristic of labour relations in the countryside. This view coincides with some of our own observations over a number of years in different parts of India, particularly Rajasthan and Bihar. The conditions for the old patterns of subordination are no longer generally present, though there are no doubt pockets of persistence in various parts of India.

Secondly, there is a *naïveté* in many of the accounts of contemporary 'bonded labour' (including perhaps the *Bonded Labour System (Abolition) Act* 1976 itself) which seem to proceed on the basis of too sharp a distinction between tied or long-term contractual labour and more casual labour relations. This distinction may be based on an idealised conception of the possibility of achieving significant wage rises in an open labour market. But overall income for the labourer (as distinct from per diem wages) can fall in the 'free' market too. The contractual arrangements which often bind landowner and field labourer together for a year are, of course, exploitative. Characteristically, the labourer and his family have to work longer hours than they would if they were paid on a daily basis. But the conditions of casual labourers are only marginally rather than dramatically better and they always receive less, usually very much less, work than the tied labourer. The labourers themselves know this. It is beyond question that many labourers deliberately opt for a tied relationship that strips them of their capacity to sell their labour at high rates prevailing during peak periods of agriculture (chiefly harvesting). They choose this option because they value the security of a higher overall income.[1]

But if Breman has touched on a major transformation, we can at least agree with Utsa Patnaik that there are similarities of form and perhaps culture to be discerned in the old schemes of bondage and the contemporary exploitation within ventures like the brick and stone industries. India has not yet been so thoroughly transformed by capitalism as to have consigned all the old culture to the past. Throughout this work we have drawn attention to the 'traditional' exploitation of Untouchable women by high-caste men. Although we have also referred to the resistance to such oppression that is characteristic of our own time, it would be foolish to deny that much sexual exploitation still takes place. Surely it is possible that such practices represents a link between the old order and the new, predominantly capitalist, forms of domination.

As to the action consequences of the different approaches, these are not entirely clear. It may be that the Patnaik approach is more conducive to intervention so as to disrupt the lingering patterns of subordination; certainly the Breman view would be pessimistic about such action. But we do not need to make a choice of theoretical view to come up with an appropriate action response. We have tried to suggest here that any doctrinaire treatment of the problem should be avoided in favour of a more pragmatic approach. Thus our own view is that it is terribly difficult to 'rehabilitate' migrant labourers by sending them back to their home village. The case of the Barmer labourers is admittedly not a fair test, since these labourers did not have a home village to return to. But it seems likely that 'rehabilitation' at home will not often work. First, any reliable observer of village India can see that dynamic forces are at work pushing/pulling people out of villages and into a variety of labouring situations connected with a developing capitalist India. This process of change will clearly continue. And secondly, no government can be relied on to put in place conditions that will guarantee the material wellbeing of large numbers of people selected for rehabilitation as bonded labourers.

[1] In the State of Haryana it is still common, though fast becoming less so, to find one-year labour contracts for field servants. During field-work in Kaithal District in April 1985 we found field labourers among the best paid in India. For example, one labourer was receiving Rs. 2,400, plus some green fodder for a buffalo and 2 quintals of wheat and padi in both the kharif and rabi seasons. In addition, the landowner had supplied advance money of Rs. 5,000 at 'nominal interest' (which amounted to about 18 per cent p.a.) so that the labourer could build his own pukka house. The loan was seen by the landowner as an extra benefit to the employee, who would otherwise have sought to claim a higher wage. Indeed, another labourer of the same owner received Rs. 3,000 because he did not have access to the fringe benefits of cattle fodder and loan. Of course, the loan in question would render the labourer bonded within the meaning of the Act.

In these circumstances it would seem prudent to attempt to rehabilitate only the very worst examples of exploited migrant labour which can reasonably be thought capable of reinstatement at home (with resources such as the provision of land).

The Union struggle

Even before the Supreme Court had handed down its decision at the end of 1983, Swami Agnivesh had broadened his activities in Faridabad to encompass the health and safety conditions, wages and social amenities of the labourers. He took on this role despite a marked reluctance to see himself as union organiser rather than liberator of bonded labour. In Agnivesh's own telling the change came about partly because of the 'moral embarrassment' of not being able to secure proper rehabilitation for labourers released prior to the Rajasthan group (Interview: 12 March 1985). The later experiences of the Rajasthan people cannot have increased his confidence. It is not clear how long-term a role he envisaged for the union; perhaps originally it was conceived as little more than a short-term activity while the main business of discharging labour was proceeding with the aid of the Supreme Court. In the event the Court took almost two years to hand down its decision, and almost another year elapsed before the Barmer labourers finally went home. By then Agnivesh was committed to continuing action on wages and conditions for the labourers who chose to remain in the quarries. This gradually wound down in the late 1980s as solid progress proved elusive.

The Union organisers were badly harassed by the contractors in the early period, but as they achieved legitimacy through their association with the highest court in India and with Agnivesh's flair for publicity the situation gradually eased. Workers became increasingly confident about asserting their rights, and Agnivesh regards dissipation of the 'fear psychosis' in the quarries to be one of the major achievements of the union activity.

By early 1985 there were said to be 1,500 financial members of the Union paying dues of Rs. 12 annually. Four organisers were paid a monthly wage of Rs. 400 out of these dues, but the principal organiser was paid directly by the Bandhua Mukti Morcha (which derives its operating expenses from a variety of sources, including foreign assistance agencies). The total cost of the Union activity was said to be Rs. 30,000, leaving a gap of Rs. 12,000 between dues and expenses. Apparently this shortfall was made up from donations by members of the Union. Some of the workers gave a monthly sum of Rs. 5.

The progress of the Union may more easily be understood by saying a little about the organisers. The principal organiser was a 29-year-old man who had taken for himself the name 'Vidrohi' or rebel. He comes from a peasant caste and village background in Haryana, and was educated to MA standard in Political Science and Hindi. Vidrohi had separated from his family in 1977 and has had little contact with them since – he says his values diverge from those of his father. He first encountered Agnivesh in 1977 and through him got a job managing an Arya Samaj hostel. He joined the Lok Dal, an opposition party, in 1980, and in 1981 he began working for the Bandhua Mukti Morcha. From July 1981 he began organising the Union, which was officially inaugurated in January 1982 with Swami Agnivesh as president and Vidrohi as general secretary. Unlike the other organisers, Vidrohi did not live at the quarry site but at Agnivesh's headquarters in New Delhi. He commuted daily, except when there was work at the Court, on a motorbike.

The other organisers have come and gone – none of them has been an actual quarry worker, though this was an ambition of the leadership. Some have been more and some less likely union organisers, perhaps reflecting the difficulties of attracting outsiders to work and live in such unpropitious circumstances. For example, Prem Bhati is an older man of adventurous spirit. In true Hindu fashion he has now separated himself from his wife and grown-up children – he says he loves them in the same way he loves all humanity. Prem Bhati is a former employee of the Rajasthan Electricity Board, with which he was in bitter conflict for years. He says he would not connive at the corruption that was endemic there. In 1977 he rode his bicycle from Rajasthan to Kanya Kumari at the southern tip of India and later cycled to Kathmandu. In 1978 he became a *saddhu* and wandered around India for six years; he happened to meet Vidrohi, who recruited him for his then position several months before our meeting. When asked why he had abandoned his religious search he explained that he was now engaged in *jan sewa* (service to the people), which he regarded as a branch of religion.

Scarcely surpising, the issue that has caused the greatest conflict with the contractors is wages. The Union's strategy in this area has been a variant of its approach on the issue of bonded labour, viz. to use the appropriate judicial tribunal, which in this instance was an industrial arbitration body. This strategy has reflected Agnivesh's perception that what they had on their side was a body of progressive legislation and procedures and the necessary knowledge to take advantage of them. So in 1984 the Stone Quarry Workers Union made a claim for increased wages before the Central Industrial Tribunal, Chandigarh. The matter started out in the conciliation jurisdiction of the Tribunal with the Union making application for a rate of Rs.100 over the allegedly current Rs.71 to be paid for every 150 cu.ft of broken stones delivered to the contractor. This amount was to be paid in addition to supplying the inputs – explosives, detonators, wicks and so on. It is not clear just what part the contractors played in proceedings, but clearly at best it was minor. Their tactic seems to have been largely one of avoidance. The tribunal made a determination on 10 September 1984 which seemed to be even-handed – it rejected the Union's claim for Rs.100 but decreed that the deductions by the employers for the inputs were unlawful as determined by the Supreme Court in the Quarry Workers Case. In short, the workers were to get Rs.71 nett of all costs.

The Union was jubilant at this result, since the employers were paying amounts far less than Rs.71 (Rs.48 and less was standard) and deducting significant further amounts from this to cover the cost of the inputs. So in thinking to confirm the amount of Rs.71 and also decreeing the cessation of deductions, the Tribunal was actually benefiting the Union twice over. It is not clear just where the figure of Rs.71 came from.

The employers, needless to say, did not accept this result. In a response to litigation initiated in the Supreme Court by Agnivesh's organisation, R. L. Sharma claimed that his company had been disbanded and was no longer working in the Faridabad area. Indeed, Sharma does seem to have taken some legal steps to terminate his company and form a new one. But the object was not to effect any physical change or cessation of operations but to be able to claim that the corporate body against which the industrial award was made no longer existed. This issue does not seem to have reached the stage of decision by the Court. Meanwhile the Pioneer Crushing Company, another of the contractors, moved the High Court of Punjab and Haryana on 3 May 1985 for a writ quashing the award on a number of grounds, including breach of natural justice to the contractors by virtue of having been insufficiently heard. But on 27 July 1985 the Court declared this action premature, since it was available to the contractors to move the Industrial Tribunal itself that the award be set aside.

No further legal action directly on this matter took place, though there is still a matter pending in the Supreme Court which could conceivably overturn the award. But again, the favourable legal outcome did not lead to any large rise in the rates of pay for the quarry workers. The employers simply declined to pay the rates enjoined on them by the tribunal. Agnivesh says that privately the Arbitrator advised them to negotiate and fix on a mid-way point between the prevailing rate and the Rs.71 with no deductions decreed in arbitration. But Agnivesh does not seem to have taken up this suggestion, perhaps for a number of reasons. As we have suggested, Agnivesh has always been uncomfortable in the role of union

leader – despite the other organisers on the ground, all the policy decisions have been made by him. He is not the person to sit down with
employers for whom he has no respect and proceed to hammer out a
compromise. As a lawyer he is also bemused by the near impotence of
even the highest court in the land on the matters he has pursued over such
a long period.

On a number of occasions throughout the years of the struggle there
have been serious clashes between workers and employers. The Union
has staged several strikes and numerous marches. In one clash a worker
was killed early in 1985, and in the ensuing processes Agnivesh himself
was arrested in apprehension of a breach of the peace. Characteristically,
Agnivesh instituted another Supreme Court action following these
events alleging contempt of court on the part of the employers for their
several failures to conform to the orders of the Court. Regrettably,
Bhagwati J. retired before this petition reached judgment; it had to be
started afresh.

By the second half of the 1980s the workers' struggle was slowly disin-
tegrating. The principal union organiser, Vidrohi, left amid recrimina-
tions, and the lack of dramatic improvement has tended to rob the
movement of enthusiasm. Agnivesh noted in an interview in June 1989
that he was not personally going to the quarries because in conscience he
could no longer ask the workers to undertake any action.

From the beginning his most vehement denunciations have been
reserved for government. Early on it seems to have come as a surprise to
him to learn how callously indifferent the authorities appeared to be in
the face of the lawless exploitation of labour in the Faridabad quarries.
His analysis has proceeded on the basis that there was collusion between
the contractors and the highest level of the State government of Haryana,
such that in return for favours to the ruling party the State government
would not cooperate with even lawful directives favouring the workers.
The central government has not been seen to be quite so tightly connected with the contractors, but it has also been negligent in failing to dis-
charge many of the duties it has under national legislation. He has been
critical of even the Supreme Court. Though this body has been favourable to the workers' cause in its judgments, these have often taken so long
that the workers' movement has been robbed of momentum.

For their part, the employers too have been critical of the central
government. Their persistent complaint has been that the system of quarrying rights conspires against good management and the capacity to pay
higher wages. The prevailing system has been to auction quarrying rights
for a period of three years, and this tenure is said to be too short to justify
major investments to improve profitability and therefore amenities in the

quarries.[2] Since there are no figures readily available, such claims are difficult to evaluate. It may well be that a period of three years is too short for economic efficiency, but this is clearly not the root of the problem in the quarries. Agnivesh is likely to be far closer to the truth in his claims about the relationships between contractors and political parties and the awful neglect of legal duties on the part of officials for a number of reasons, including sheer moral indifference.

The concrete achievements

After some eight years of struggle in Faridabad, the gains have been meagre. The latest commissioner appointed by the Supreme Court reported in February 1989 that 'the mine lessees and the crusher owners and others have failed to implement' the original twenty-one directives of the Supreme Court, 'which is reflected in the sub-human conditions in which the quarry/crusher workers of Faridabad find themselves till date' (Jain 1989: 196). This finding stands in the face of evidence submitted to the Court by both the Haryana and Union governments showing substantial compliance with the Court orders. The commissioner reported that there had been little or no improvement on matters like the provision of fresh water, toilet facilities, safety equipment, health facilities, the reduction of dust emissions, and so on. Perhaps the judgment of the commissioner was somewhat too sweeping – there is now, for example, a bit more fresh water available than there was before the struggle. Evidence tendered to the Court by the central government suggests too that sprinkler mechanisms have been installed on the crushers, though it may well be true that these have not actually worked to reduce dust emissions significantly. The commissioner's own report together with information from Swami Agnivesh's organisation shows that there has been a modest rise in wages paid to the labourers over the period – presumably at least partly due to the strenuous activity of the Union. But there is no doubt that these improvements are strictly marginal.

A table reproduced but not commented on in Jain's report of 1989 suggests that none of the above is the major change to have come over the Faridabad quarries during the 1980s. Table 1 of the report shows that the quarry workers have been reduced from 4,050 in 1984 to 1,300 in 1988. These are said to be official figures obtained from the Department of Mines Safety and the Labour Enforcement Office, Ghaziabad. The most

[2] This claim was made in an interview with Kartar Singh, one of the major contractors at Faridabad, and his assistant Mr Ojha: Faridabad, 10 March 1985. It also appears in various representations of the employers. The period of the lease seems later to have been extended to five years.

likely explanation for the reduction is that the old quarries have become increasingly unproductive and that operations have started to move elsewhere. But it is barely possible that the major effect of the union activity and the modest government measures aimed at securing compliance with the Court orders has been to drive the contractors away. Either way, the workers have not gained from the change.

Conclusion

This account of the Faridabad struggle is offered as a case study of some of the conditions of migratory labour – the greater part Untouchable – and also of the difficulty of intervening to ameliorate these conditions. Perhaps the most remarkable aspect of this case is the abject failure of the Supreme Court to have its decrees enforced; nothing much has changed in the quarries as a result of the Supreme Court's decisions. The contractors have had everything but law on their side, and law is simply deficient in the face of that degree of power. The workers may have come closest to some kind of victory when they staged a strike in 1984, but almost inevitably they went back to work without having achieved any solid results. Severe poverty in the context of a State Government favourable to large contractors defeated them. In this and other encounters the Haryana police force was not neutral but rather an obedient servant of the contractors' interests. The workers could be portrayed as disturbers of the peace, and selected workers and organisers imprisoned at strategic moments. Nowadays Swami Agnivesh suggests that the workers will not get anywhere until they administer a 'brushing' (beating) to the employers and their 'musclemen'. But it takes a climactic moment after a long struggle for the workers to reach this point of boldness. The possibility of reaching such a moment is now long past.

   Clearly the actions of the reformers cannot be immune from criticism. Their major institutional success was the release and 'rehabilitation' of the Barmer labourers, but this success was transformed into a pathetic failure by the eventual return to Faridabad. We have come close to suggesting that the Barmer exercise was doomed from the start, given the special nomadic history of this group and their lack of any but a fleeting connection with the area they were sent back to. And throughout we have adopted a severely critical – some might think cynical – stance in relation to government in its dealings with the poor. But, of course, it is too easy to be critical of organisations like that of Swami Agnivesh. He himself was genuinely optimistic that with the support of the Supreme Court in its new 'public interest' jurisdiction, the tide could be turned against a group so powerful as the quarry contractors. And he has had to learn as a painful discovery that government (particularly the bureaucracy) has a severely limited willingness/capacity to intervene decisively in support of the workers. It should be said that Bhagwati J. of the Supreme Court of India seemed to evince the very same optimism that government could intervene effectively.

Organisation of the Faridabad workers was also flawed, as Agnivesh recognises. He attributes part of the problem to the sheer difficulty of organising migrant workers, who are far less secure than workers living at home. Many of them come and go, destroying continuity of organisation. And clearly their capacity to absorb the hardship of loss of income during industrial action is specially limited away from home. But clearly too there were faults that arose from Agnivesh's less than enthusiastic role as union organiser and his pursuit of a wider political agenda as a national opposition figure. Still, it would not be appropriate to dwell on these limitations. What Agnivesh accomplished was to make migrant workers like the Faridabad quarry labourers visible for the first time. And he pursued with admirable energy a strategy of judicial, political and industrial action which looked immensely promising for this particular group of workers. In the end it is highly doubtful that any other organisation could have achieved more.

What stands out above all is the sheer difficulty of intervening in processes like that represented by the Faridabad quarries. Effective intervention entails an elaborate and energetic effort by government to enforce admirably progressive health, safety and labour legislation. The employers must be forced to pay the transport costs of their workers without deducting these costs from future earnings of the workers. Most important, means must be found to provide loans to poor workers so that they can spend modest amounts on life-cycle events such as marriage and death without becoming hopelessly indebted at usurious rates of interest. The mainstream Indian trade unions need to be interested in areas of labour other than the most organised and most privileged; it is not reasonable to expect makeshift organisations such as that of Swami Agnivesh to undertake the long-term task of industrial organising. Such a list is obviously forbidding and represents a corrective to naïve optimism. Clearly the broader task is to build a political culture that places a high value on organising the poor. Nonetheless it is unreasoning cynicism to believe that no useful intervention is possible even in present circumstances.

7   Untouchable politics and Untouchable politicians since 1956

Mayawati, a Jatav (Chamar) woman, became Chief Minister of Uttar Pradesh (UP) in 1995. She is the first Dalit woman to have acceded to the highest office in an Indian state, but gender is not the most remarkable aspect of this accession. Its special importance arises from the uniqueness of a Dalit becoming Chief Minister through the vehicle of a political party centred on Untouchables themselves. The Bahujana Samaj Party, founded and still dominated by Kanshi Ram, seized its unlikely opportunity in UP after the collapse of a Government in which it was junior partner. Mayawati's minority Government was backed for strategic reasons by the right-wing Bharatiya Janata Party (BJP), and it lasted a mere four months. But the very advent of such a Government had an electrifying effect on Untouchables across India. It was as if the world had been stood on its head, so that the bottom ruled over the top. When Mayawati again came to power in April 1997, this time in actual coalition with the BJP, the event was improbable without being unimaginable. The earlier accession had established, perhaps for the very first time, that the Dalits were a central and not merely a marginal political force.

Installation of two Mayawati Governments is not the only event of recent political significance to the Dalits. At the national level a powerful Dalit leader has emerged within the Janata Dal, the party that formed Governments after the elections of 1989 and 1996. Ram Vilas Paswan was Minister for Labour and Welfare in V. P. Singh's Government of 1989–90, and he was one of the driving forces behind the immensely controversial decision to adopt the Mandal Report and thus extend reservation of public employment to a new class of 'Backward' elements. The intention was to try to create an historic coalition of the downtrodden by joining together the Dalits, the Backward Castes and, after the destruction of the Babri Masjid, the Muslims too. While no such secure coalition is yet in sight, its very possibility continues to have political potency. So this aspiration was something of an ideological rationale for the formation of the coalition Government led by Deve Gowda after the inconclusive election of 1996. Ram Vilas Paswan was Minister for Railways in that

Government – he retained the post after the Prime Ministerial change-
over of 1997 – and he was widely regarded as the politician most relied
upon by Prime Minister Gowda. Kanshi Ram and Ram Vilas Paswan, bitterly opposed though they are to each other, represent a new Untouchable politics that is radical and assertive but also ruthlessly pragmatic. For
the first time across large parts of India the Dalits have to be taken seriously rather than viewed as a vote bank to be exploited by their social
superiors.

Still another indication of the new radicalism is the so-called Naxalite
activity that has persisted for a number of years in regions of Bihar and
also Andhra Pradesh. We have briefly discussed the Bihar situation in
chapter 2. In Andhra, the violent activity is centred in the same Telengana
region that produced a major insurrection at the time of Independence.
Untouchable labourers were at the centre of that insurrection (Harrison
1960: 215–16). During the 1980s and 90s the Madigas and also the Mangs
have been a key constituent of the new agrarian resistance, though the
movement has tended to be led by high-caste figures. While the Naxalite
activities of Andhra and Bihar cannot be portrayed as the likely future of
Untouchable politics in India as a whole, nor can these movements be
dismissed as phenomena relevant only to the most backward regions of
India. Like the more widespread and articulate Dalit movement, the
insurrectionary labourers of Bihar and Andhra reflect a deep Untouchable resistance. But for the rest of this chapter we are concerned with
more mainstream political life.

Untouchable politics during the era of Congress dominance

Earlier we suggested that the attachment of Untouchables to Congress
during the 1930s and 40s was far less than is sometimes assumed. In the
years after Independence Untouchable support for Congress clearly
strengthened. From 1952 until 1989, with the exception of the post-
Emergency election of 1977, Untouchables tended to function in both
national and State elections as a 'vote bank' for Congress. Their vote for
Congress was a vote for the party of government, a party that had committed itself to a program of action on Untouchability and poverty. In
rational terms – and here their situation was similar to that of the Muslims
– there was little electoral choice open to Untouchables in most parts of
the country. If the Left had developed more strength outside what
became its strongholds in West Bengal and Kerala, the Untouchable
attachment to Congress might have been less. Thus in the very first post-
Independence election of 1952 the Socialists won a good part of the

Scheduled Caste vote in Bihar.[1] But this was the highpoint of their electoral experience in that State. It is only in the nineties that the logic of class (albeit often dressed in the garb of caste) is again being asserted across large parts of India, particularly the north.

While the Untouchables were a crucial Congress vote bank in India as a whole and in a majority of individual States, even before the recent flux they did not cling to Congress in regions where another party or movement rose to dominance. The major examples of long-term non-Congress dominance are West Bengal, Kerala, Tamil Nadu and Andhra Pradesh. Untouchables in the former two States have for a number of years had a strong identification with the Communist Party in its several divisions – in recent years predominantly with the dominant Communist Party of India (Marxist) (CPI(M)). A number of Ezhavas associated themselves with the fledgling Communist Party from the early 1940s, but with increasing prosperity the caste vote has been split along class lines between the Communists and Congress (Jeffrey 1974: 59). As to the other and poorer Untouchable castes of Kerala, these have been far less influential in the councils of the Communist movement. But in conformity with the class divisions of Kerala politics, the Scheduled Castes have tended to gravitate towards the parties of the Left. In West Bengal, the Communist movement was slower to gain control of the State: the first United Front Government came to power in 1967, a decade after the first such government in Kerala. Support for the CPI(M) in West Bengal has been broadly based and not confined to particular castes, but again the party has done particularly well among poorer voters and therefore among the Scheduled Castes. In short, the Untouchables of Kerala and West Bengal have behaved according to the logic of their class position within a political culture more directed to considerations of class than anywhere else in India. But from another perspective the Untouchables of these two States have been doing little different from their counterparts elsewhere in India. They have simply aligned themselves with the majority party – it is doubtful that most of these Untouchables have been affected with any special passion for Marxism.

In Tamil Nadu and Andhra Pradesh regional parties have come to dominate State politics. The non-Brahmin movement of Tamil Nadu spawned a succession of parties – first the Justice Party and after Independence the Dravida Munnetra Kazhagam (DMK) and Anna DMK. Anti-Brahminism has been joined with Dravidian nationalism to produce a highly distinctive political and popular culture. For decades

[1] Karpoori Thakur drew this to our attention during an interview on 18 May 1985. It is not clear from official statistics for 1952 and 1957 just how the Scheduled Castes voted, but certainly the Socialist and then Praja Socialist Party polled well during these elections.

State elections have largely been fought out between the DMK and Anna DMK, each of which lays claim to the common culture. The Untouchables were relatively slow to embrace the culture, given their break with the non-Brahmin movement in the early 1920s and their subsequent attraction to Congress. But with the dominance asserted by the DMK and then the Anna DMK from the late 1960s, the Untouchables have been rolled up into the prevailing politics of the State. But since Congress has often been able to engineer electoral accommodations with one or other of the three dominant leaders over the last three decades – Karunanidhi and the film star politicians M. Ramachandran (MGR) and Jayalalitha – many Tamil Untouchables have voted for the DMK or Anna DMK at State elections and for Congress in national elections. If we turn to Andhra, the emergence of a dominant regional party is more recent. The Telegu Desam party of Andhra has been built around N. T. Rama Rao, the charismatic Telegu movie star. NTR's style, like that of the Tamil leaders, was best described as populist, and his party attracted Untouchable voters as it moved into a position of dominance. But Telegu Desam has not been so dominant even in State elections as have successive regional parties in Tamil Nadu. In short, and unlike the position in the Communist States, in both Tamil Nadu and Andhra the Untouchables have not been wholly lost to Congress.

Within Congress the importance of the Untouchable vote did not translate itself into great influence for individual Untouchables in either the organisation or the ministry. In particular, the building of the compensatory discrimination system arose more from the arithmetic of elections and the goodwill of sections of the elite than from the efforts of Dalit parliamentarians. Jagjivan Ram was alone as a Scheduled Caste politician in becoming a genuinely national figure through Congress. There have been a couple of Chief Ministers – one of them was Bhole Paswan Shastri, who three times held this position in Bihar for very brief periods in the 1950s. Bhole Paswan was respected for his modesty, dignity and probity, but he made no deep mark on even State politics: his life and career are discussed in the next chapter. A small number of other State and national politicians have gained a measure of ministerial seniority, but none has had either a long period at the apex of ministerial service or any substantial political base. Just why this is the case may require an answer at several levels. Perhaps it is to be expected that a collection of castes distinguished by their overall subordination would not produce the highest crop of educated, experienced and generally talented politicians. Over time the gap in education and sophistication between Untouchables and, say, Brahmins has diminished, and the depth of talent among Untouchable aspirants for high office is no doubt growing. But it will not help the Untouchable cause to deny that there has been a gap at all. On the other hand, issues of talent and preparation for public office can scarcely constitute the primary explanation for the low representation of Untouchables at the highest political levels.

There are persistent suggestions that Dalit politicians have not thrived within Congress if they have too strenuously promoted the cause of their own people. This is an explanation sometimes offered in relation to Yogendra Makwana, a talented and energetic Minister of the early 1980s whose career did not prosper under either Indira or Rajiv Gandhi. Makwana can be contrasted with Buta Singh, a Mazhabi Sikh (converted from a Sweeper caste) who rose to the position of Home Minister under the same Prime Ministers. Buta Singh (later relegated to a junior portfolio under Narasimha Rao) was known for his political *savoir-faire* and his loyalty to the Nehru family, rather than for any particular zeal for the problems of the Scheduled Castes. Of course, as a category Prime Ministers tend to distrust colleagues of whatever community if they have a political base or agenda independent of their own. Yet it remains an important truth that the ideological and social makeup of Congress has made it less than welcoming to highly assertive advocates of the Untouchable cause. Low social standing has also made individual Untouchable spokesmen relatively easy targets for political demolition. Untouchables have therefore tended to construct their political careers as dependants within factions led by high-caste politicians. It is impossible to think of a single example of a substantial multi-caste faction leader who is/was himself a Dalit.[2]

Something more needs to be said here about the career of Jagjivan Ram.[3] Under the patronage of the Nehrus Jagjivan Ram rose to the position of Defence Minister. He climbed a rung higher to the post of Deputy Prime Minister under Charan Singh in 1979, a position that rewarded him for ostensibly having delivered the Untouchable vote to the Janata coalition in the extraordinary election of 1977. Jagjivan Ram's career is notable for its extraordinary longevity, a consequence of both his competence and also his carefulness not to engage in dissent and controversy. On both counts he was the ideal Untouchable for Congress to promote through its ranks.

Jagjivan Ram was the only significant Untouchable to have played a strong part in Gandhi's Harijan movement of the 1930s. He became

---

[2] We are assuming here that Kamaraj Nadar, a highly substantial factional leader of the 1950s and 60s, was not an 'Untouchable'. It will be recalled that the Nadars have a background similar to that of the Ezhavas.

[3] Jagjivan Ram's childhood and education are discussed in the next chapter, alongside the lives of other Untouchable politicians.

President of the All-India Depressed Classes League formed in 1935, and was elected to the Bihar Assembly for Congress in the election of 1937. In 1946 he was appointed Labour Minister in the Viceroy's Executive Council, and from then (with a short interregnum during the Kamaraj Plan) he held Cabinet positions in successive Congress Governments and later the Janata Government until its electoral defeat in 1980. Once he became a Minister he seems not to have made Untouchability a central preoccupation in either speech or action. His most extensive public comment is to be found in a small book published in 1980, *Caste Challenge in India*. This book is neither novel in its analysis nor specially hard-hitting, though clearly its author believed that he could be more expansive now that his career had come to an end. Thus despite the book's mild tone, the preface contains the propitiatory remark that his views are offered 'not to hurt any class or caste but to provide a brief historical account of the Hindu social system... and the miserable condition of the Scheduled Castes and Tribes' (Ram 1980: 5–6).

It is difficult to estimate the power that Jagjivan Ram wielded within Congress. He played an important role at several critical moments in the post-Nehru era: he supported Indira Gandhi's candidacy for Prime Minister in 1966, stayed with her when Congress split in 1969, and quit the party in 1977. Paul Brass observes that he was 'always thought to be able to control 40 to 60 votes in Parliament and was deferred to in the Congress for that reason' (Brass 1990: 208–9). But the quality of this 'control' is not self-evident. It seems likely that he had more power than anyone else in selecting Scheduled Caste candidates for Congress from the reserved seats in Bihar, and he may have exercised some power in neighbouring Uttar Pradesh and perhaps other States too; his qualification was not only his long career but also the fact that his own Chamar caste was by far the largest Scheduled Caste of north India. Presumably Ram's role in the selection of candidates invested him with some influence in relation to the MPs who depended upon his continued support. Thus it is possible that he was able to deliver votes to Indira Gandhi in the succession contest after the death of Prime Minister Shastri and in the Congress split of 1969. But when he left Congress in 1977 he failed to persuade any of the Party's other Scheduled Caste MPs to accompany him. And more importantly, there is no evidence that he either sought or was able to mobilise a bloc of MPs in order to make policy gains for the Scheduled Castes within Cabinet. Any part he may have played in either the development or maintenance of programs and policies favourable to Untouchables was for the most part hidden. It is suggested that when he was Minister for Railways he was successful in rapidly building up the Scheduled Caste (allegedly mainly Chamar) component of the railways workforce. And in his other portfolios too he may have exerted pressure for the legal quotas to be filled. But by far his most potent moment came when he left Congress on the eve of the post-Emergency election in 1977, since his departure seemed to crystallise the first large anti-Congress vote among north Indian Untouchables. This vote was of major significance to the outcome of the election. But the limits of Jagjivan Ram's electoral appeal and the special nature of the 1977 election were revealed when he failed to prevent the return of these same voters to Congress in 1980.

There is no single set of characteristics common to the leadership of Congress over the last half century, but a glance at the background of those at the very apex of Indian politics is instructive. All five Congress Prime Ministers have been Brahmins, including three from the Nehru family. In the non-Congress Governments of 1977–9 and 1989–91 two of the Prime Ministers were Rajputs, one was a Brahmin and the third was Charan Singh, a Jat, and till then the only Prime Minister from a background other than that of a twice-born (upper) caste. Now Deve Gowda, short-lived Prime Minister after the 1996 election, shares that status with Charan Singh. While it is not possible to extrapolate from the caste background of Prime Ministers to the background of Congress leaders in general, high-caste and particularly Brahmin domination of the most senior positions has been characteristic of Congress throughout its long history. Nor is this phenomenon confined to Congress. Atul Kohli has produced figures to show that both Congress and Communist Party dominated Governments in West Bengal have had a strikingly skewed caste composition. The caste of Ministers in Congress Governments in West Bengal between 1952 and 1962 was 23 per cent Brahmin, 31 per cent Kayastha, 24 per cent Vaishya, and only 2 per cent Scheduled Caste. In the case of Governments led by the Communist Party of India (Marxist) between 1977 and 1982 there were even more Brahmins than in the Congress Governments, over 35 per cent; the number of Kayasthas (31 per cent) and Vaishyas (23 per cent) was almost the same as in Congress Governments, while Scheduled Caste representation was marginally lower at 1.5 per cent (Kohli 1990: 374). These figures must be read in the context of a State which has the highest concentration of Scheduled Caste people in the country – now almost 24 per cent (Census 1991). Demonstrably, the many Scheduled Caste members of the West Bengal Assembly have almost no chance of rising to the position of Minister. Their representation is even lower if inferior Ministers – Ministers of State and Deputy Ministers – are left out. In the Governments formed after the elections of 1952, 1957, 1962, 1977 and 1982 there was not a single Scheduled Caste member of the Council of Ministers. Of course, it is not merely the Scheduled Castes that have been grossly underrepresented in West Bengali Cabinets – the same is true for Scheduled Tribes, Muslims and lower-caste Hindus.

A similar, if less pronounced, pattern is true of the organisational wing of the Communist Party of India (Marxist), and given the ideological orientation of the party it is worth attending to this phenomenon more closely.[4] In both Kerala and West Bengal Untouchables are scarcely represented at the highest levels of the Party. In Kerala, those who have risen to leading Party positions from poor backgrounds have almost always come from 'proletarian' unions of the towns. The Ezhava dominated bidi workers' union is one such example. Scheduled Caste workers in Kerala still tend to be agricultural labourers, and they have found it impossible to rise to the top of the Party hierarchy. In West Bengal, until the late sixties the Party was essentially an urban and high-caste organisation. With the later focus on agrarian problems there has been a growing membership drawn from the villages. Scheduled Caste membership is now in double figures, most of it rural in origin (though not usually drawn from the ranks of agricultural labourers, the lowest agrarian category). But even if such people are as likely as anyone else to rise to the top of the Party – a questionable assumption – it would take considerable time before their presence might be felt.

It is not open to infer the whole character of a government or a political party from the caste composition of its senior members. The Communist governments of West Bengal and Kerala have been among the best State governments in India in terms of both probity and service to their poorer citizens. But even these governments are vulnerable to criticism for their insufficient attention to those at the very bottom of the social hierarchy. For example, both governments have frequently been attacked for their failure to meet job reservation quotas. Presumably this failure can be said to arise from an ideological antipathy to programs constructed on the basis of social primordialism (caste). But it can also scarcely be irrelevant that reservation is adverse to the interests of large proportions of the castes that predominate within the government.[5] Even in less intensely caste conscious West Bengal it cannot be assumed that Communist Ministers are effectively without caste (or class). This is not to propose the existence of a caste conspiracy or even a lack of goodwill towards the underprivileged. It is merely to recognise that it is difficult to induce and sustain a sense of urgency about the claims of out-groups in the absence of their own advocates.

[4] This discussion is based on an interview with Prakash Karat, CPI(M) Politburo Member, New Delhi, 18 November 1995.
[5] The Nayars and Nambudiri Brahmins have dominated leadership positions in the CPI(M) of Kerala, though there is also strong representation of the Ezhavas.

A deeper criticism of the Communist governments can be levelled at their agrarian programs. Thus Kerala has one of the poorer records of land reform among the various States. There has been only a slight amount of redistribution of agricultural land, and agricultural labourers (many of them Untouchables) have had to be content with gaining ownership of the land on which their 'hutment' is built within the village. Kerala has done far better in the matter of fixing minimum wages for its agricultural labourers, though here there have been some unfortunate consequences. Partly because of the resulting high cost of labour there has been a radical reduction in the amount of work available to Kerala labourers: mechanisation, leaving land fallow, and employment of out-of-State workers have been options preferred by many employers. The West Bengal experience on the same two issues has been the reverse of that of Kerala. West Bengal has done much better in the area of land redistribution, and it has also accomplished significant reforms for sharecroppers. But the CPI(M) Government has paid little attention to the interests of the army of agricultural labourers in the State. A large proportion of these labourers are, of course, from the Scheduled Castes, and their rates of pay and general living conditions are at the poorer end of the national scale. Nor is Operation Barga (see above, p. 155) beyond criticism. These reforms were abandoned at the highly incomplete point when further action would have directly injured the interests of small, usually absentee, landlords. Many of these mainly high-caste people have been supporters of the CPI(M) regime, and the decision can therefore be painted in tones of political pragmatism. Moreover, in an 'encircled' polity such as West Bengal there are undoubtedly limits to just how much redistribution is a possibility. Clearly we must be careful not to repackage the whole huge problem of Indian poverty and inequality into the receptacle of caste – this will make no analytical sense, nor indicate a way out of the practical condition. Nonetheless, we doubt it can be said that ties of caste and community, wrapped up in positions of class, are of no relevance to the policy and performance of the Government of West Bengal.[6]

The above question can be crystallised by reference to Ambedkar's description of Indian Communists as 'a bunch of Brahman boys' (Harrison 1960: 191). He was referring not only to the number of Brahmins within the Party, but also to discriminatory attitudes and blindness to the problems of the Untouchables. If we discount the hyperbole, the observation contains a (slippery) grain of truth. On the one hand we should not subscribe to the false proposition that only the representatives

---

[6] The most sustained attack on the West Bengal regime from the perspective of the Scheduled Castes has been made by Ross Mallick (1993).

of a particular community are capable of working for the good of that community. But we must also recognise that a community or a people needs to speak for itself if its interests and potential are to be realised to any great degree. This is the dialectic embedded in the issue of Untouchable representation in contemporary politics. Thus it is reasonable to assume that greater Untouchable representation at the highest levels would produce outcomes more favourable to their own people than occurs through government dominated by the high castes. The benefits would no doubt range from individual allocations (such as jobs, licences, contracts) to broader policy. To give one small but important example of possible policy, greater Untouchable presence in government could conceivably lead to the application of more pressure towards the extension of affirmative action into private- and not merely public-sector enterprises. This is exactly the sort of non-revolutionary but quite far-reaching change that is potentially within the realm of government action in India.

The Ambedkarites and the Dalits after Ambedkar

Until the recent emergence of the Bahujana Samaj Party, the only post-Independence example of a party centred on Untouchables was the Republican Party of India (RPI). This was the final political vehicle devised by Ambedkar, though its formation in 1957 reached fruition only some months after his death.[7] The Republican Party was a transformation of the Scheduled Castes Federation, electorally unsuccessful and also judged to be an inappropriate organisational form for Buddhists who had sloughed off *caste* by the act of abandoning Hinduism.[8] Again, as in the days of the Independent Labour Party, Ambedkar planned a party along class rather than caste lines. But almost from the beginning the RPI ran into ideological, organisational and factional problems. The first major division was between an old guard more deeply rooted in the village world of the majority of Mahars, and a younger and more highly educated leadership that increasingly focussed on the opportunities inherent in urban life and the scheme of compensatory discrimination. This generational conflict was connected to a split between those who saw the future of Mahar politics in terms of broader economic and class struggle – some of these were the older village-based activists – and an emerging leadership

---

[7] Our account of the Republican Party and the Dalit Panthers draws heavily on the writing of Jayashree Gokhale (1993).

[8] The SCF had a final moment of glory in the election of 1957, before the change of name to Republican Party had taken effect. On the back of agitation for a Marathi-speaking state and because of its electoral alliances, the SCF won four Lok Sabha seats (two of them unreserved) and seventeen Assembly seats (Dushkin 1972: 198).

less committed to working with caste Hindus and even other Untouchable communities. While Ambedkar himself had been far less concerned with agrarian problems than with broader questions of political and constitutional principle, his stature had been such as to engender loyalty right across Mahar society and thus to blur the divergence of interest within it. After Ambedkar, and in the context of growing social and economic diversity among the Mahars, there was no one who could command this general loyalty. By 1959 division in the RPI was so deep that the two major factions held separate conventions (Gokhale 1993: 224). Inevitably it was the younger, better-educated and more prosperous faction based in the cities that became the more energetic element of the party.[9]

The RPI carried its divisions into the election of 1962, and failed to win a single Lok Sabha seat from the new linguistic state of Maharashtra.[10] It did somewhat better in the State Assembly election of that year, but after that it won only a handful of Assembly seats in Maharashtra. The RPI also put down roots in several States where Ambedkar's influence had been relatively strong – particularly Uttar Pradesh (notably the cities of Agra and Aligarh) and Punjab, but also Haryana, Andhra Pradesh and Karnataka. Extraordinarily, the RPI was electorally more successful in Uttar Pradesh than in Maharashtra. Its success in UP was built around a substantial Buddhist politician of Chamar origins, B. P. Maurya, who drew votes away from Congress by engineering a local coalition of Untouchables and Muslims in the city and District of Aligarh. But the inherent instability of this alliance – there had been no historical sympathy between Chamars and Muslims – and the Congress split of 1969 quickly changed the electoral equation for the RPI in Uttar Pradesh. By 1971 B. P. Maurya and his major opponent within the party, Ramji Ram, were both returned to the Lok Sabha under the banner of Indira Gandhi's ostensibly left-orientated branch of the Congress. This was the effective end of the Republican Party as a force in Uttar Pradesh.

In Maharashtra, the death or eclipse of one Ambedkarite form has been a prelude to the rise of another. Thus in the early 1970s an organisation calling itself the Dalit Panthers was formed with the project of reinstating

---

[9] After a great outpouring of effort, the Mahars and other Untouchables converted to Buddhism finally gained access to reserved employment under the Government of India in 1990 during V. P. Singh's Government. Earlier in 1969 the Buddhists had succeeded in retaining rights to post-matriculation scholarships (Galanter 1984: 321). Individual States have extended the same level of public employment to Buddhists as they have given the Backward Classes, but Maharashtra – the most affected State – has allowed the Buddhists to enjoy the same higher level of job reservation that they previously enjoyed as Scheduled Castes.

[10] For discussion of the RPI's performance in Maharashtra see Dushkin 1972: 198–9; and Gokhale 1993: 250–5. Commentary on its performance in Uttar Pradesh is to be found in Brass 1965: 103–6; Lynch 1969: 111–28; Dushkin 1972: 198–202; and Joshi 1982: 100–7.

class-based Dalit politics following the Republican Party's perceived lapse into narrow self-interest (Gokhale 1993: 264). The name, with its insurrectionist symbolism, was borrowed from the Black Panthers of the United States. At the time India was marked by widespread famine, pervasive student activism and a non-party oppositional politics which later developed into Jayaprakash Narayan's direct confrontation of Indira Gandhi. But the Dalit Panthers proved unable to connect up with broader leftist politics. They were also no more attuned to the Dalit 'masses' – a majority of Mahars were still illiterate villagers – than was the Republican Party, and within a couple of years they were even more riven by ideological and personality differences. The core ideological split was publicly evident by 1974 and was personified in the two pre-eminent leaders of the movement, Namdeo Dhasal and Raja Dhale. For Dhale's faction, the defining moment in Dalit history was the mass conversion to Buddhism under the leadership of Ambedkar; future gains were to be made primarily through a deepening and widening of Buddhist consciousness rather than through secular political action. Namdeo Dhasal, on the other hand, represented a more orthodox leftist, indeed Marxist, position, which gave both Ambedkar and the conversion movement less of a defining role. Abolition of Untouchability was an issue of class and economics more than of caste, religion and consciousness, and the natural allies of the Untouchables were the poor classes of whatever religious or caste community. Consistent with this view Dhasal had seen the CPI as the appropriate overall leader of the Dalits. But within a few years Indira Gandhi's anti-poverty programs of the Emergency period persuaded Dhasal that here was a leader genuinely committed to the poor, and his faction supported Congress in the 1977 election. By then the Panthers were divided into a number of geographically centred factions of little potency, and it was only the riots in 1978 surrounding the Maharashtra Government's decision to add the prefix 'Dr Babasaheb Ambedkar' to 'Marathwada University' that brought them into some prominence again. The Dalit Panthers had failed to define a durable role for themselves – they were political activists without a political party or a clear strategy agreed among themselves. Moreover, they had become scarcely more radical, and certainly no more connected to ordinary Mahars, than the Republican Party. And, of course, they had demonstrated little capacity to reach out to other Untouchable castes.

The void left by the demise of the Panthers has been filled not by another party or other directly political organisation of the Mahar Dalits but, extraordinarily, by a literary movement. A whole new literature has sprung up on the common basis of rejection of varna. The lives and interior world of Untouchables have been explored by a profusion of writers, some of them highly talented. It is tempting, and indeed legitimate, to see this new literature as heir to the great tradition of bhakti, though many of its exponents reject this tradition, Chokha Mela in particular, for its acceptance of inequality in the expectation of a better world in the life-to-come. The resort to literary means of communicating Dalit anger has been consciously adopted in disgust at what is perceived to be the failure of orthodox politics to transform the lives of the Dalits. Clearly the Dalit literature is an intensely political body of writing, some of it infused more with passion than with concern for literary effect. But the best Dalit writers are widely recognised as having created a literature of genuine merit.

Nor is this Dalit literature confined to Maharashtra. There is now a vigorous assembly of Dalit writers in Karnataka too. The immediate origins of this movement can be located in a speech delivered in 1974 by a Minister in the Congress Government of Karnataka. Basavalingappa, an Untouchable, was moved to describe the literature of Kannada, the language of the region, as little more than *boosa* or cattle fodder. He had in mind this literature's lack of attention to the lives of ordinary people, among them the Untouchables (still usually called Adi-Karnataka). It was as if Basavalingappa had put a torch to a pile of tinder, so great was the explosion of both acclamation and repudiation. To the orthodox custodians of Kannada literature the Untouchable Minister had defamed their cultural heritage in the service of a mindless radicalism. But to an astonishingly large number of actual or aspiring Dalit writers, Basavalingappa had opened the door to a palace of opportunity to express their rejection of their own place in Karnataka society (Mahadeva 1989). A conference of Dalit writers was held in 1974, and some hundreds are said to have attended (Indudan Honnapur interview: 10 January 1988). In subsequent years this Dalit literary movement has moved in a number of directions. For example, one group of young Dalits has established a popular weekly magazine, *Sugathi*, which combines the transmission of popular culture (film features and so on) with political and social comment on Dalit affairs. Its readership is mostly drawn from Adi-Karnatakas themselves, and in 1988 circulation was some 65,000 copies.

The literary movement preceded any narrow political expression of Dalit radicalism in Karnataka, and subsequent institutional forms have not followed the pattern of Maharashtra. Without the direct legacy of Ambedkar, the Karnataka Dalits have not sought to establish a Dalit political party. Rather, the *Dalit Sangharsh Samiti* has been set up as something of an umbrella organisation for the various Dalit groups within the State. Dalit activities have been directed to educating the consciousness of Adi-Karnataka adults and children, and staging agitations and demonstrations on matters of particular concern. A special focus has been on Harijan atrocities. Within particular industries – the nationalised banks, for example – there are organisations of Dalit workers. Many of the Dalit activists have embraced Buddhism and are engaged in increasing their knowledge of the literature of this religion and proselytising among the unconverted. But while the Karnataka movement has derived its inspiration from Ambedkar and from the Maharashtra movement in general, there is also a concern to avoid what is seen to be the Maharashtra defect of being too inward-looking and exclusive. Some of these activists have gone so far as to reject reservation of jobs and parliamentary seats as a trap which cuts them off from other progressive elements and also fails to do anything for the larger Dalit community. And there is special scorn for the occupants of reserved seats in legislatures. While there have been no intense ideological splits in Karnataka, there is evidence of the same tensions that have so destructively affected the Ambedkarite movement in Maharashtra. The recurrent choice for radical Untouchables everywhere is between cultivating a separate Untouchable identity or constructing alliances with all oppressed people who are prepared to listen.

Even more than in Maharashtra, the Dalit movement of Karnataka has been an urban phenomenon. The Untouchable castes of village Karnataka have not been drawn into a movement whose main preoccupations have been literary, cultural and religious. During a visit to his ancestral village, one of our Dalit guides – a leader among Dalit bank employees and a Buddhist – spoke scornfully of the backwardness of the Adi-Karnataka there. They lacked ambition and remained locked into a world of drudgery, alcohol and attachment to what he called 'some non-veg god'. To this man there was no point in trying to rouse the consciousness of his caste fellows and relatives in the village. His time was better spent working with young men studying in schools and colleges in the towns, and in staging demonstrations that would catch the eye of the media.

The lack of mobilisation of village Untouchables in Karnataka and even Maharashtra serves to point up the distinctiveness of the rural revolt in Bihar. In so far as there has been an ideological guide to the activity in Bihar, it has been a derivative of revolutionary Marxism. This should not lead us to conclude that Marxism is the appropriate ideology for the Dalits of Karnataka and Maharashtra, or that Ambedkarite principles are inherently incapable of attracting widespread support in rural India. As we shall see, Kanshi Ram has skilfully used the figure of Ambedkar to build a following among rural as well as urban Chamars in Uttar Pradesh. But it is notable that the Bihar mobilisation has proceeded primarily on the basis of several pragmatic issues – social respect, higher wages and access to land – that have had an immediate and powerful resonance with the Untouchable population. These are the same broad issues that were the core of the program of Ambedkar's Independent Labour Party from 1937 to 1942, and in somewhat variant form they were also the foundation of the later Republican Party and Dalit Panthers. But none of these bodies actually pursued their program with any determination, and the post-Independence organisations fell seriously out of step with village Mahars at the same time as they became further isolated from communities other than the Mahars. Part of the problem has been Buddhism: despite its merits as a wellspring of personal empowerment, Buddhism scarcely speaks to the issues that are of immediate concern to poor villagers of Mahar or any other Untouchable caste. In so far as the Dalit leadership of Maharashtra has concentrated on the project of Buddhism, they have tended to abdicate from a position where mobilisation of village and less educated Untouchables is a possibility. Even worse, preoccupation with another religious system has driven a positive wedge between the Mahar Buddhists and Hindus from other poor and subordinated communities.

But despite the limitations of the Ambedkarite movement as an electoral and mobilising force in western India, the thought and life of Babasaheb Ambedkar enjoy a tremendous and indeed fast-growing potency across large parts of India. Within Maharashtra itself one of the recent expressions of this was the demonstrations and counter-demonstrations surrounding the publication of Ambedkar's work *Riddles in Hinduism*. This work is part of a multi-volume set of Ambedkar's writings being published, or usually republished, by the Government of Maharashtra under the direction of Dalit scholars. That the project has gone forward at all is testimony to the weight of Ambedkar's writing and the political passion of his followers. *Riddles in Hinduism* had been considered too inflammatory a work to be published during Ambedkar's lifetime, and tens of years after it was written the work had scarcely become less controversial.

While Maharashtra and neighbouring Karnataka remain the centres where Ambedkar's legacy is taken most seriously, the physical image of the historical figure is now to be found on posters and in the form of statues in countless locations throughout India. The propagation of Babasaheb's image has become both a sacred duty to his followers and also an easily available means for politicians and political hopefuls to position themselves as radical champions of their own communities. Juxtaposition of one's own image beside that of Ambedkar can now be an alternative to statement of a clear political position. But more positively, through the politics of iconography Dalits have been busy reclaiming their own twentieth-century history. The great loser in this struggle of images is Gandhi. Whereas once Gandhi could be portrayed as the great champion of the 'Harijan', now Dalits themselves prefer to ignore or even castigate him for condescension and adherence to subordinating orthodoxy. Now it is Ambedkar who shows the way in thousands of out-of-the-way locations to which his writ did not run during his own lifetime.

The new Dalit politics of north India

North Indian politics are presently in a state of great flux. Whereas the Hindi-speaking region was once the basis of Congress rule of the nation, now the Congress vote has quite disintegrated there. Uttar Pradesh is the most dramatic case. In the general election of 1984 Congress won eighty-three out of eighty-five UP seats with 51 per cent of the total vote. But five years later the party won only fifteen seats with 32 per cent of the vote. In 1991 the Congress vote slipped further to 18 per cent, and it won five seats. This was also its tally of seats in 1996. Congress' dominance had been built on a strong command of the Brahmin, Muslim and Untouchable 'vote banks', together with considerable but variable support from the other upper castes and also the Backward Castes. The latter were the first to desert the party, and since the mid-eighties it has also suffered the fatal blow of having lost its three stable vote banks.

The waning of Congress has coincided with the rise of two other parties – the Janata Dal and its offshoots, including Mulayam Singh's Samajwadi Party, and the Bharatiya Janata Party (BJP). These parties have risen to prominence partly because of the vacuum caused by the waning of Congress, and partly because of their own attractiveness. Thus the leading party in 1989 was Janata Dal, with fifty-four seats and 36 per cent of the vote. But in the next election of 1991 the largest party was the BJP with fifty-one seats and 33 per cent of the vote. The Janata Dal and the Samajwadi Party draw their major strength from the Backward Castes, whereas the BJP has traditionally been strongest among the upper castes of the towns. But each of these two political forces picked up other groups as they gathered momentum. Thus the Janata Dal and Samajwadi parties attracted a large share of the Muslim vote disenchanted with Congress after the destruction of the Babri Masjid. And the BJP has picked up considerable Backward Caste support, partly because it has had a strong Backward Caste (Lodhi) leader in Kalyan Singh.

Another development of the first importance in Uttar Pradesh has been the rise of Kanshi Ram's Bahujana Samaj Party to the point where it was able to form the State government in 1995 and 1997. Although Kanshi

Ram has benefited crucially from the collapse of Congress, his rise is not to be attributed simply to the vacuum effect. Kanshi Ram has spoken directly to the aspirations of the Chamars, and he has also had a radicalising impact on a wider constituency of Backward and other Scheduled Caste communities. Kanshi Ram's mode of operation has been to yoke an aggressive Ambedkarite ideology to hard-headed manipulation of the vote banks of Uttar Pradesh. The indispensable basis of his power is his own community, the Chamars. These constitute not only the largest Untouchable caste in India, but almost certainly the largest single caste in Uttar Pradesh.[11] Kanshi Ram has not had the total support of the Chamars – until recently the Jatavs of western UP have been an important hold-out – but his command in eastern UP has been overwhelming. Kanshi Ram's strategy has been to join his bank of Chamar voters to other Scheduled Caste and Backward Caste voters (particularly the Kurmis) and also the Muslims. He has been careful to cede the non-Chamar communities a majority of Bahujana Samaj candidates – there has been a specially large number of Muslim candidates – in the knowledge that voters will often be attracted by a candidate of their own community. The Bahujana Samaj could offer these communities the prospect that the large Chamar vote would be added to theirs, since the Chamars believed that the party was above all theirs. But before we consider the contemporary situation in some detail, something must be said about the origins of Kanshi Ram and the Bahujana Samaj Party.

Kanshi Ram: from BAMCEF to the Bahujana Samaj Party

Kanshi Ram was born in 1934 as a Raedasi Sikh, a community of Punjabi Chamars converted to Sikhism.[12] The family had 4 or 5 acres of land, some of it inherited and the rest acquired through government allocation after Independence.[13] As we shall see in chapter 8, a small landed background is characteristic of many Scheduled Caste legislators but remains a comparative rarity for Dalits in general. Kanshi Ram's father was himself 'slightly' literate, and he managed to educate all his four daughters

[11] In 1931 – this was the last Census that counted non-Untouchable castes individually – the Chamars of the United Provinces (roughly coterminous with the present Uttar Pradesh) constituted 12.7 per cent of the population of the province. The Brahmins were next largest with 9.2 per cent, while the Yadavs (called Ahirs and Ahars) were third with 8.7 per cent of the population (Census 1931 for UP: 18 (1), 619–20).

[12] The continuing disabilities suffered by Sikhs of Untouchable origin were recognised by their qualification for all the benefits of reservation, including legislative seats, from the inception of the Constitution.

[13] Interview with Kanshi Ram: New Delhi, 10 January 1996. The following details of his early life are also drawn from this interview.

and three sons. Kanshi Ram, the eldest, is the only graduate. He was given a reserved position in the Survey of India after completing his BSc degree, and in 1958 he transferred to the Department of Defence Production as a scientific assistant in a munitions factory in Poona. Kanshi Ram had encountered no Untouchability as a child, and overt discrimination was not a phenomenon within the educated circles of his adult life. But his outlook underwent a sudden change in 1965 when he became caught up in a struggle initiated by other Scheduled Caste employees to prevent the abolition of a holiday commemorating Dr Ambedkar's birthday.[14] During this conflict Kanshi Ram encountered a depth of high-caste prejudice and hostility towards Dalits that was a revelation to him. His almost instant radicalisation was completed soon after by a reading of Ambedkar's *Annihilation of Caste*: he read the book three times in one night, going entirely without sleep.

Kanshi Ram's introduction to the political ideas of Ambedkar – he has never been attracted to Buddhism – was through his Mahar Buddhist colleague and friend at the munitions factory, D. K. Khaparde. Together the two of them began formulating ideas for an organisation to be built by educated employees from the Scheduled and Backward castes. Such an organisation would work against harassment and oppression by high-caste officers, and also enable the often inward-looking occupants of reserved postions to give something back to their own communities. So Kanshi Ram and Khaparde began to contact likely recruits in Poona. At about this time Kanshi Ram abandoned any thought of marriage, largely because it did not fit into a life he now wanted to dedicate to public concerns. He had also quite lost interest in his career, though he continued in the job until about 1971. He finally left after a severe conflict over the non-appointment of an apparently qualified Scheduled Caste young woman. During this conflict he had gone so far as to strike a senior official, and he did not even bother attending most of the ensuing disciplinary proceedings. He had already made up his mind to become a full-time activist, and the movement was by then strong enough to meet his modest needs.

In 1971 Kanshi Ram and his colleagues established the Scheduled Castes, Scheduled Tribes, Other Backward Classes and Minorities Employees Welfare Association, which was duly registered under the Poona Charity Commissioner. Their primary object was:

To subject our problems to close scrutiny and find out quick and equitable solutions to the problems of injustice and harassment of our employees in general and the educated employees in particular. (Anon pamphlet 1972)

---

[14] Much of the material on Kanshi Ram's early career in Poona comes from interviews with D. K. Khaparde: 18 January 1996; and with Mr Dekate: 16 December 1995.

Despite the Association's inclusive reach, its aggressively Ambedkarite stance ensured that most of its members were Mahar Buddhists. Within a year of its establishment there were more than one thousand members and it was able to open an office in Poona: many of the members were from the Defence and Post and Telegraph Departments, and their first annual conference was addressed by the then Defence Minister, Jagjivan Ram. Kanshi Ram's next organisational step was to create the basis of a national association of Scheduled Caste government servants. As early as 1973 he and his colleagues established the All India Backward and Minority Employees Federation (BAMCEF), and a functioning office was established in Delhi in 1976. BAMCEF was relaunched with greater fanfare on 6 December 1978, the anniversary of Ambedkar's death, with claims of two thousand delegates joining a procession to the Boat Club Lawns in New Delhi (BAMCEF Bulletin April 1979). Although the stated objects of the new organisation were essentially the same as those of the earlier body, the rhetoric had grown bolder. It was not merely the oppressors who came in the line of fire, but also many of the reserved office holders too:

As all the avenues of advance are closed to them in the field of agriculture, trade, commerce and industry almost all the educated persons from these [oppressed] communities are trapped in Govt. services. About 2 million educated oppressed Indians have already joined various types of jobs during the last 26 years. Civil Service Conduct rules put some restrictions on them. But their inherent timidity, cowardice, selfishness and lack of desire for Social Service to their own creed have made them exceptionally useless to the general mass of the oppressed Indians . . . The only ray of hope is that almost everywhere in the country there are some educated employees who feel deeply agitated about the miserable existence of their brethren. (BAMCEF Bulletin 2 1974: 2)

By the mid-1970s Kanshi Ram had established a broad if not dense network of contacts throughout Maharashtra and adjacent regions. During his frequent train trips from Poona to Delhi, he adopted the habit of getting down at major stations along the way – Nagpur, Jabalpur and Bhopal, among others – to contact likely sympathisers and to try to recruit them to the organisation (Kanshi Ram Interview: 1996). Once he had moved to Delhi he pushed into Punjab, Haryana and Uttar Pradesh, as well as further into Madhya Pradesh. Parallel to his work among educated employees Kanshi Ram was also contacting a wider audience with simple presentations of Ambedkar's teachings. Thus in 1980 he put together a roadshow called 'Ambedkar *Mela* on Wheels'. This was an oral and pictorial account of Ambedkar's life and views, together with contemporary material on oppression, atrocities and poverty. Between April and June 1980 the show was carted to thirty-four destinations in nine

States of the north. Jang Bahadur Patel, a Kurmi (Backward Caste) and President of the Uttar Pradesh Branch of the Bahujana Samaj Party until late 1995, recalls meeting Kanshi Ram for the first time when he brought his roadshow to Lucknow (Interview: 25 November 1995). Kanshi Ram talked persuasively about how Ambedkar had struggled for all the down-trodden classes, and how the Scheduled Castes, Tribes and also the Backwards and Minorities were all victims of Brahminism. Because of their weight of numbers, these people had the potential to convert them-selves from 'beggars to rulers'. It was all a matter of organisation. Patel immediately joined BAMCEF, though he was in a distinct minority as a non-Untouchable: Untouchables constituted about 90 per cent of the membership, with the other 10 per cent being split between tribals and Backward Caste people.

BAMCEF's motto, 'Educate, Organise and Agitate', was adopted from Ambedkar, and its activities were formally divided into a number of welfare and proselytising objects. But increasingly Kanshi Ram's agita-tional activities were leading him into politics. By the late 70s he was no longer content with being the leader of reserved office holders, a class for whom he had less than complete respect. Kanshi Ram's first attempt to create a radical political vehicle capable of mobilising the larger body of Dalits was the *Dalit Soshit Samaj Sangharsh Samiti* (DS4) formed in 1981. This was conceived as a political organisation parallel to BAMCEF: it shared the same President in Kanshi Ram, the same office, and many of the same members. DS4 was a quasi- rather than fully fledged political party, partly because government servants were forbidden to take part in electoral politics. But DS4 made little concrete progress, and late in 1984 Kanshi Ram took the plunge and formed the Bahujana Samaj Party (a variant on the name of Phule's nineteenth-century organisation). Inevitably, this caused major strains in BAMCEF ranks. Their agitational activities had placed many of his colleagues from the Poona and early Delhi periods in a delicate position as government servants and, in any case, the political loyalty of many of them was to the several strands of the Republican Party. There were also strains arising from Kanshi Ram's will to total domination of all three organisations. And the need for money was rising with the push into politics: one of the Maharashtra workers recalls delivering Kanshi Ram a purse of forty thousand rupees collected from Maharashtra in 1984. These several strains grew more severe over the next two years, and early in 1986 a major split took place. Kanshi Ram announced at that time that he was no longer willing to work for any organisation other than the Bahujana Samaj Party. His transition from social worker to politician was complete.

Kanshi Ram is more an organiser and political strategist than an innov-

ative thinker or charismatic public speaker. While his Ambedkarite ideology has remained constant and lacking in any innovation, there has been a
progressive sharpening of his rhetoric. The early issues of BAMCEF's
monthly magazine, *The Oppressed Indian*, were full of his didactic exposi-
tions of Ambedkar's views on Indian society. These have now given way to
simpler formulations, repeated in numerous newspaper accounts and
both public and private speech. The central proposition is that Indian
society is characterised by the self-interested rule of 10 per cent over the
other 90 per cent (the *bahujan samaj* or common people). Although the
ruling 10 per cent is composed of several castes, they derive their legitimacy and ruling ideology from Brahminism. All the institutions of society
reflect this ruling ideology and distortion, including the press. These
institutions can therefore be termed *Manuwadi* (after the great Brahmin-
inspired text) or *Brahminwadi*. In the marketplace of elections, such
simplicity has been further reduced to crudeness and epithet. A slogan
coined after the formation of DS4 was, '*Brahmin, Bania, Thakur Chor,
Baki Sab Hein DS-Four*'. Loosely translated, this rhyme states that
Brahmins, Banias and Rajputs are thieves, while the rest of society are
their victims. The epithets reached their height during the election campaign for the UP Assembly in 1993, the most notorious being: '*Tilak,
Taraju, Talwar. Maaro Unko Joote Char*'. This slogan, with its insistent
rhythm in Hindi, advocates that Brahmins, Banias and Rajputs, each
identified by a slighting term, be beaten four times with a shoe – a traditionally demeaning form of punishment because of the ritual impurity of
leather. While Kanshi Ram and Mayawati denied authorship of such
slogans, they served as a simple and dramatically offensive marker of the
party's ideological position.

Kanshi Ram's strategy and his larger understanding of social change
are now considerably evolved. He no longer believes in the primacy of
social reform. Rather, expenditure of effort on any object other than the
capture of government is seen to be superfluous. It is administrative
power that will bring about desired social change, not vice versa. So he
declines to spell out policies on basic issues such as the liberalisation of
the Indian economy or on land reforms. His view is that such issues are
irrelevant to the project of gaining power, and that the appropriate policies will fall into place once power is attained. His picture of India is of a
kind of holy war on the part of the bahujan samaj against their
Brahminwadi oppressors. In the context of this war debates about policy
are almost frivolities. This is a stance of pure fundamentalism, but it also
frees him to engage in the most ruthless pragmatism in the name of capturing power.

Consistent with this stance, Kanshi Ram has become increasingly critical of the institution of reservation in government employment. Reservation is a 'crutch' – useful for a cripple, but a positive handicap for someone who wants to run on his own two feet (Kanshi Ram interview: 1996). He now throws off the line that once the bahujan samaj get to power throughout India, it will be they who can condescend to the Brahmins by giving *them* reservation proportional to their own meagre population. There is more than a little bravado in this, but there is no doubt that Kanshi Ram is now hostile to the system of institutional preference that was the indispensable basis of his own personal and political career. It seems that he believes that reservation has now done enough for the Scheduled Castes. He notes that of some 500 Indian Administrative Service (IAS) Officers in Uttar Pradesh, 137 are from the Scheduled Castes. By comparison, there are only seven IAS officers from the Backward Castes, six of them Yadavs (*Hindustan Times*, 6 April 1994). His point is not that there are now too many Scheduled Caste officers – their number conforms strictly to the legal quota – but too few from the Backward Castes. He apparently assumes that the capture of political power will automatically transform the composition of the bureaucratic elite.

The Bahujana Samaj Party first made headway in Punjab, Kanshi Ram's home State, but his primary political task was to wean the Chamars of Uttar Pradesh from Congress. It was Kanshi Ram's fortune that he built the party at the historical moment that the long-term Congress decline became a landslide. The formal entry of his party into Uttar Pradesh was in a by-election in 1985 for the Lok Sabha seat of Bijinor, in which its candidate was Mayawati. She is a Jatav (or Chamar), the daughter of a minor government official in Delhi, and had completed a BA and LLB from the University of Delhi. Mayawati had made contact with Kanshi Ram in 1977 while she was a student, and had gradually been drawn into his organisation. Her opponents in Bijinor included Ram Vilas Paswan – the two have had poor relations since this contest – and Meira Kumar, Jagjivan Ram's daughter, representing Congress. Rajiv Gandhi was at the height of his popularity at the time, and Meira Kumar won the seat easily. But by 1989 the Bahujana Samaj Party had put in five years of solid organising work in UP and also in the neighbouring regions of Madhya Pradesh, Punjab, Delhi, and parts of Haryana. And meanwhile the Congress Party had slumped in popularity. Kanshi Ram had prepared the ground carefully. He had selected organisers and candidates from a variety of social backgrounds. One of his organisers was Dr Mahsood Ahmed, a temporary lecturer in history at Aligarh Muslim University. Mahsood had become disillusioned with Congress when Indira Gandhi made her infamous tilt towards the Hindus in the early

1980s (Mahsood interview: 27 November 1995). He joined BAMCEF and then switched to DS4 in 1983 as a full-time organiser and fund raiser. Mahsood was later put in charge of the whole of eastern Uttar Pradesh for the Bahujana Samaj Party.

The years of organisation bore fruit in 1989 and 1991. In the four State Assembly and Parliamentary (Lok Sabha) polls for Uttar Pradesh between 1989 and 1991 the Bahujana Samaj Party's share of the vote varied only marginally between 8.7 and 9.4 per cent. But this impressive vote produced a disappointing number of seats – in 1989 the party won thirteen out of 425 State Assembly seats, and in 1991 it won twelve. The party won only two Parliamentary seats in 1989, and one in 1991; Kanshi Ram himself subsequently won a by-election from UP in 1992. Both the strength and the weakness of the party is that its primary 'vote bank', the Chamars, are relatively evenly spread across the State. This spread gives the Bahujana Samaj a chance in a large number of seats, but also make it logically impossible to win even a single seat without strong support from other communities. Although it has attracted a measure of Muslim, Backward Caste and other Scheduled Caste support, it has encountered considerable resistance in these target communities. We need to look more closely at this problem.

First, there is the question of why the majority of Jatavs of western UP deviated from their kinfolk in the eastern part of the State, and continued to vote Congress in 1989 and 1991. The answer to this question is not entirely clear. Some have blamed the result on the poor organising capacities of Mayawati – she was in charge of this region – but the deeper reason may be the Jatavs' historical association with B. P. Maurya. In a move of some desperation, Congress resurrected the 70-year-old Maurya as one of four national Vice-Presidents in the run-up to the 1996 elections. But by then Mayawati had become an electorally popular figure in eastern UP. As to the Scheduled Castes other than the Chamars/Jatavs, only Pasis appear to have voted for Kanshi Ram's party in large numbers. The Valmikis (formerly known as Bhangis) voted solidly for the BJP in the 1993 Assembly elections, and the sole Valmiki in the Lok Sabha elected in 1991 represented the BJP (though in 1980 he had been elected for the Janata Party). Mangal Ram Premi MP – his biography is sketched in chapter 8 – accounts for the Valmiki support of the BJP by simply advert-ing to the community's dislike of the Chamars (Interview: 4 November 1995). The Chamars are more numerous, better educated and more successful in acquiring reserved positions than the Valmikis, and this tends to produce resentment. Many of the Dhobis too have recently voted for the BJP. In short, Kanshi Ram's party has not solved the problem of how to mobilise all or even most of the Scheduled Castes. The problem that dogged Ambedkar has thus repeated itself in Uttar Pradesh, though Kanshi Ram's Chamars are both more numerous and numerically more dominant among the Untouchables than were Ambedkar's Mahars in the western part of the country.

Among Backward Castes, Kanshi Ram's strongest support has come from the Kurmis. In Bihar, this is an upwardly mobile peasant community responsible for several of the worst atrocities against Dalits. But in Uttar Pradesh the Kurmis are comparatively low on the scale of prosperity. Moreover, they have had a history of anti-Brahmin radicalism – Shahu Maharaj of Kolhapur remains a source of inspiration to some of them. And a sprinkling of them had been members of the Republican Party. The Kurmis could see advantage in being associated with a party that was not dominated by the more numerous Yadavs (whose firm affiliation is with Mulayam Singh's Samajwadi Party). As to the large number of other Backward Castes in UP, over the last several years there has been an intense three-way tussle between the BJP, the Bahujana Samaj Party and the Samajwadi Party to capture their support. All three have had some success, but perhaps the larger part of this vote is a floating one that will flow with the main political current of the time. The last community to consider is the Muslims. In the aftermath of the destruction of the Babri Masjid the Muslims have been politically leaderless. They have shunned Congress for what they see to have been its culpable failure to prevent the demolition of the mosque, and have given considerable support to Mulayam Singh's Samajwadi Party and some support to Kanshi Ram. Thus in the municipal elections of Uttar Pradesh in November 1995 and in the national and UP elections of 1996 it seems that UP Muslims were prepared to vote for whichever party was locally the strongest anti-BJP force. In short, the politics of post-Congress Uttar Pradesh are currently cast largely in terms of community vote banks. Political strategy is a matter of positioning one's party so as to retain one's core vote bank and also attract others at the margins. At least as much as any other player, Kanshi Ram has adapted to this game with calculating skill.

Kanshi Ram and Mayawati in Government

Before the UP Assembly election of 1993 (held after the dismissal of the BJP Government), Kanshi Ram entered into an alliance with Mulayam Singh. The primary vote banks of the two men were complementary – the Yadavs and the Chamars. This was by no means a 'natural' alliance, since the two communities had engaged in perennial and sometimes violent conflict in the villages. Indeed, the Yadavs had frequently captured voting booths in eastern UP and prevented the Chamars from voting. But each of the leaders could now see that his prospects were poor without the other, and they agreed on a division of seats so as to combine their vote. The alliance produced a dramatically enhanced increase in seats for the Bahujana Samaj Party (67), but its vote rose less dramatically to 11.11 per cent (achieved admittedly in a sharply reduced number of contests). Meanwhile the Samajwadi Party won 109 seats and 25.83 per cent of the vote, making it second to the BJP with its 177 seats and 33.3 per cent of the vote. The Samajwadi Party and the Bahujana Samaj Party were able to form a coalition Government, with Mulayam Singh as Chief Minister. But Kanshi Ram and Mayawati soon came to believe that their party's interests were being infringed by Mulayam – one issue was the alleged kidnapping of one of their candidates during panchayat elections. There was also concern at the number of 'atrocities' perpetrated against Scheduled Caste people, some of them by Yadavs; the belief was that Mulayam was deliberately failing to control his own followers in this matter. But above all Mulayam had brought about the defection of a number of the Bahujana Samaj legislators to his own party – some of them were Kurmis – and was daily seeking to whittle away his coalition partner from above. Accordingly, in June 1995 Kanshi Ram and Mayawati brought the Government down.

Given the overwhelming importance that Kanshi Ram now places on the acquisition of administrative power, his willingness to form a new Government with the support of the 'Manuwadi' BJP becomes more comprehensible. He took the view that so long as he did not have to take orders from the BJP then he was prepared to put up with the odium of being propped up by the party hated by the whole of progressive India. Perhaps conveniently, he argued that the Congress, the Janata Dal and the Communists were as much 'Manuwadi' parties as was the BJP. But there was still an enormous cultural and ideological gulf between his party and the BJP, and it was left to an outsider to play a perhaps crucial role in bridging the gap. Jayant Malhoutra, a prominent industrialist and Member of the Rajya Sabha, did much of the diplomatic negotiation between the leaders of the two parties. He and Kanshi Ram had formed an unlikely friendship several years earlier, and Malhoutra claims that his assistance to Kanshi Ram was motivated by concern to help bring about a 'soft landing' for India after the inevitable clash between the haves and have-nots (Malhoutra interview: 7 November 1995). For its part the BJP knew that neither of the other two large legislative parties would support a minority Government of its own. Since the BJP leaders had come to have a special antipathy to Mulayam's rule, their best option was to allow the third and seemingly less threatening party to form a Government – they saw more to fear from the Yadavs than the Dalits. The BJP leadership had in mind the longer-term goal of permanently splitting the vote banks commanded by the Samajwadi Party and the Bahujana Samaj Party, thereby opening up a path to their own domination of Uttar Pradesh.

In June 1995 Kanshi Ram ceded to Mayawati the task of leading the new Government in Uttar Pradesh, and her period as Chief Minister has been a platform upon which Mayawati has built a now considerable political presence in Uttar Pradesh. Early on the much younger Mayawati was properly regarded as a mere lieutenant of Kanshi Ram, to whom popular accounts suggest she is romantically as well as politically linked. But Mayawati has been able to bring a charisma and liveliness to the hustings that Kanshi Ram himself has lacked. She has represented a novelty – a direct and forthright Dalit woman with courage sufficient to run hard against the powerful institutions that so oppress poor Indians. In short, Mayawati has become both considerably popular and also a force to reckon with.

The Government of 1995 is properly regarded as a joint Kanshi Ram–Mayawati Government – Kanshi Ram continued to reside primarily in Delhi but made frequent trips to Lucknow, the capital of Uttar Pradesh, and was consulted on all major decisions. In terms of new policies or administrative programs, there was little to be seen from the four months of their rule. But this is by no means to say that this was not a signficant or a distinctive administration. Part of its significance resides in the intrusion of a different culture into the machinery of government of the State. Mayawati demonstrated that the Bahujana Samaj's antipathy to 'Brahminwadi' culture was no mere abstraction but was to serve as a guide to the identity of the actual bureaucrats who could be trusted to direct the administration. In a word, Mayawati chose to promote and work through a small coterie of Scheduled Caste officers. For example, the high-caste incumbents in the Chief Secretary and Chief Minister's Principal Private Secretary positions were both replaced by Scheduled Caste officers. Even more controversially, a number of more junior Scheduled Caste officers were favoured with accelerated promotion and positions at the centre of the administration. This change inevitably provoked resentment and the claim that merit had been replaced by casteism.

Within the larger administration of the State Maywati made energetic resort to the device of transfers and disciplinary action against officers found delinquent in one aspect or another. The transfer of senior officials for reasons other than completion of a normal term has become commonplace in a number of States of India, but by common consent Mayawati engaged in the practice more richly than before in Uttar Pradesh. Quite deliberately she created a climate of fear in order to motivate officials to work to her agenda. She dealt particularly severely with officials judged to have failed to protect the most vulnerable people in a particular District, the Dalits above all. Overwhelmingly condemned in the press, her actions appear to have evoked a sense of satisfaction among common people routinely subjected to official arrogance and callousness. And a number of commentators both within the administration and outside believed that Mayawati had administered a powerful and long overdue lesson to bureaucrats that their place was as servant, not master, of the people.[15]

The most persistent complaint about the Bahujana Samaj Government was the degree of illicit money it exacted, particularly in the matter of obliging individual bureaucrats regarding their transfer or non-transfer. Given the habitual misuse of public office to derive funds for party if not personal purposes, it would be surprising indeed if some of these stories were not true. What cannot be established is whether such official wrong-doing was conducted on a scale greater than that of earlier administrations in Uttar Pradesh. Perhaps a good deal of the problem arose from the callowness of Mayawati and her lieutenants – some of the stories suggest that their insufficient knowledge of the system, and also the hurry they were in, made it difficult for them to derive funds efficiently and quietly. Official corruption is something of an acquired art.

It is clear that Mayawati was not an accessible Chief Minister. Apart from the question of the tightness of her bureaucratic team, she was inaccessible to many of her own Ministers and to representatives of the BJP who felt entitled to a hearing in return for their support of the Government. Some of this inaccessibility may have arisen from motives that were not unreasonable. Thus Mayawati and Kanshi Ram were determined not to run a Government that freely granted favours to people for reasons other than the welfare of the party itself. They were particularly suspicious of requests from politicians where the request seemed to arise from personal pecuniary interest. The problem of inaccessibility was compounded by Kanshi Ram's continuing to reside in Delhi rather than Lucknow throughout the life of the Government. There were also issues of personal style. Mayawati's reputation is one of meting out harshness and even humiliation to those with whom she finds fault, though it is also true that many informants report having experienced no such treatment. On the other side, the practice of showing elaborate respect to the leaders became something of a culture within party circles. This sometimes took

[15] One of these people was Dharam Singh Rawat, a retired IAS officer in Lucknow. In both press articles and private interviews, Rawat – not himself a Dalit – celebrated the unprecedented jolt that Mayawati was administering to his old service (Interview: 26 November 1995).

the form of touching the feet of Mayawati and Kanshi Ram, a ritual form of respect that now tends to be seen as demeaning and 'feudal' in origin. The complaint is that the two leaders encouraged this practice. In short, there were problems of both process and style that gave rise to considerable resentment and disaffection in Lucknow. This is one, but only one, reason for the large number of defections from the legislative party that took place after the Government fell.

The public style of the Mayawati Government was more abrasive than radical. Indeed, Mayawati's own most provocative gesture was enacted even before she formed her own Government. In March 1994, during the Mulayam Singh government, Mayawati had somewhat casually condemned Gandhi as 'an enemy of the *dalits* and the Bahujan *samaj* at large' (*The Telegraph*: 15 March 1994). Despite the frequency of previous Ambedkarite attacks on the Mahatma, Mayawati's remarks occasioned a storm of protest in the pages of the press. The extravagance of this reaction was a pointer to the sensitivities aroused by the Dalits' proximity to power in Uttar Pradesh. During her own Government Mayawati curbed her rhetoric – indeed, she felt constrained to lay the customary wreath on the occasion of Gandhi's birth celebration. The most flamboyant gesture of her Government – and here Kanshi Ram's hand is clearly evident – was to build a *Pariwartan Chowk* or Revolution Square in Lucknow that was to have huge statues of the great figures of anti-Brahmin activism: Phule, Periyar, Ambedkar, Shahu Maharaj. In the event, the Government fell before the statues could be completed. Construction of the *Chowk* proceeded around the clock in order to coincide with the staging of a Periyar *Mela*: this was a celebration of the life and works of the great figure of the Tamil non-Brahmin movement, Periyar E. V. Ramaswamy Naicker. The event was less than a resounding success in Lucknow, where Periyar is almost unknown, but the symbolism was probably directed more to Dalits in the south of India.

After the fall of the Bahujana Samaj Government it became fashionable to declare that a great opportunity had been lost by Kanshi Ram and Mayawati: they could have struck a blow for the liberation of the Dalits but they squandered their opportunity in corruption, crassness and the politics of business-as-usual. This is a dubious interpretation. Throughout their brief period of power Kanshi Ram and Mayawati had little room to manœuvre. They had a small minority of MLAs, and they knew they existed on borrowed time from the beginning. At best they could have had about a year in power before elections in mid-1996. There was simply no time to initiate solid administrative or development programs, even if they had the capacity to formulate such initiatives. In these circumstances the politics of symbolism was bound to be the most effect-

ive way to encourage their own constituency. But strong symbolism
breeds savage reactions in contemporary India, and the New Delhi leadership of the BJP found it increasingly difficult to hold State leaders to the
bargain of supporting Mayawati in the name of strategic electoral gain. It
surprised no one when this leadership bowed to the pressures welling up
in Uttar Pradesh and decided to end the life of the minority Government.
President's rule intervened until a new Government could be formed
after the general election of April 1996; in the event it was not until March
1997 that a new Government took office.

The surprising durability of the Bahujana Samaj Party

The last several years have been an exhilarating roller coaster ride for
Kanshi Ram, replete with towering peaks and deep troughs. His ambition
has been to become the kind of national leader the Dalits have never had.
In 1994 he made his most concerted bid to build a national movement by
conducting rallies and meetings in Kerala, Karnataka, Maharashtra, West
Bengal and Andhra Pradesh. The Bahujana Samaj had contested seats in
a number of these States as early as 1989, but Kanshi Ram was now more
serious about taking his message throughout the country. But these
efforts came to little, particularly in the strong Communist States of
Kerala and West Bengal. There, his caste-based analysis failed to cut into
the prevailing ideology constructed out of the language of class. Kanshi
Ram developed a considerable following in Andhra, where he staged a
number of impressive rallies. It seemed for a time that he could have
entered into a governing alliance with NTR's Telegu Desam Party, but
negotiations broke down and the Bahujana Samaj was soon a spent force
in Andhra. After the fall of Mayawati's Government in Lucknow it
became clear that the national and provincial elections of 1996 would be
crucial to the very survival of the party.

   Although candidates were to be put up in a number of States, Uttar
Pradesh was by far the most important arena. Given the close competition between the three leading political forces – Congress, the BJP and the
'Third Front' of leftist and regional parties – Kanshi Ram hoped to be in a
position to dictate outcomes at both State and national levels. But the
whole history of his party suggested that there could be little electoral
success without an alliance with another major force. The logical partner
was the Janata Dal, but Kanshi Ram declared himself against any new
alliance that included Mulayam (Interview: 1996). This stand appeared
tantamount to political suicide. It was clear that Kanshi Ram's movement
could not easily survive a poor result in Uttar Pradesh in 1996. Unlike the
figure of Ram Vilas Paswan, Kanshi Ram had set his sights on great and

rapid victories. His age and ill health seem to have intensified the sense of urgency that had succeeded the patience of his earlier years in politics.

Considering its lack of strategic alliances, the Bahujana Samaj Party did surprisingly well in the Lok Sabha election of 1996. It won a total of eleven seats, six of them in Uttar Pradesh, three in Punjab and two in Madhya Pradesh. (In the previous Parliament its only UP seat was the one occupied by Kanshi Ram himself.) It was clear that Mayawati had become something of a cult figure in Uttar Pradesh. And in order to compensate for its lack of partners the party had energetically sought to woo communities other than its own vote bank of Chamars. The still leaderless Muslims were a particular target, and about one-quarter of the party's tickets in Uttar Pradesh had been conceded to Muslims (*The Pioneer:* 18 September 1996). There were also a number of Backward Caste candidates.

In the subsequent UP Assembly election in 1996 Kanshi Ram and Mayawati reverted to the approach of constructing a strategic alliance. This time their ally was Congress. Amazingly, given its glorious past, Congress was relegated to the position of junior partner, and it was agreed that the combination's candidate for Chief Minister would be Mayawati. Kanshi Ram was reported to have asked Congress to field 100 Brahmins in the 125 seats allotted to it, so as to wean the upper castes from the BJP and attract them back to Congress (*The Pioneer:* 9 July 1996). Again Kanshi Ram was playing the caste game with ruthless application. His own list of candidates was carefully mixed according to the appropriate communitarian formula: of his sixty-seven successful candidates, nine are upper caste representatives, twelve are Muslims, twenty-six from the Backward Castes and twenty Dalits (*The Times of India*: 27 October 1996).

The overall result of the 1996 Uttar Pradesh Assembly election was strikingly similar to the previous Assembly election: the BJP won 174 seats in the Assembly of 425 seats; Mulayam Singh's Samajwadi Party won 110 seats; and the Bahujana Samaj (67) and Congress (33) jointly won 100. Again there was a stalemate. For a time it appeared that Mulayam Singh, now installed as Defence Minister in New Delhi, would be forced by his coalition partners at the centre to back a Bahujana Samaj–Congress Government in Uttar Pradesh. This plan ultimately collapsed under the weight of multiple rivalries and suspicions. President's rule from the centre persisted until finally a Bahujana Samaj–BJP coalition Government took office in Lucknow in March 1997. This time the agreement was that Mayawati would serve as Chief Minister for six months and then give way to Kalyan Singh from the BJP for the same period. Again Kanshi Ram and Mayawati could argue that it did not matter which of the 'Manuwadi' parties they made an alliance with –

Congress or the BJP. Their task was simply to get into government and remake the system from the inside. And second time around their abrasiveness has been even greater. During the drawn-out struggle to form a Government Mayawati was so fearful of her Assemblymen defecting to other parties that she locked them up in the Party headquarters in Lucknow for a period of weeks. They were not allowed out of the building, not even for Diwali, and visitors could see them for no more than fifteen minutes at a time (*The Asian Age*: 1 November 1996). During this same period Kanshi Ram's always strained relations with the 'Manuwadi' media deteriorated to the point that he ordered an attack on a group of journalists outside his official residence in New Delhi. He personally assaulted one of the journalists, and criminal charges are pending.

It is far too early to make a mature assessment of the Kanshi Ram–Mayawati phenomenon. Early on it might have been thought that the two leaders had achieved little more than the transfer of Congress Chamars to their own party in the context of the overall collapse of Congress in the north. It is certainly true that their only stable 'vote bank' is the Chamars, and no doubt a principal reason for the Chamars' support is their understanding that this is 'their' party. The Chamars have also responded favourably to Kanshi Ram and Mayawati's arrogant disdain for orthodoxy and their denunciation of the large and petty oppressions that still characterise the lives of many Chamars. This community is now richer, better educated and bolder than when it gave its support to Jagjivan Ram. But Kanshi Ram and more recently Mayawati have also worked hard to dispel the notion that their party represents only the Dalits, let alone simply the Chamars. They have had considerable success in attracting other groups, including Muslims, to their cause, despite their willingness to cultivate relations with the anti-Muslim BJP. To what extent their approach is more than opportunistic exploitation of the multiple divisions of contemporary Uttar Pradesh society remains a question. Perhaps this question will partly be answered by the impact Mayawati can make on the apparatus of government in Uttar Pradesh, such that a culture of governance less hostile to those at the bottom of the social hierarchy begins to emerge. Undoubtedly Kanshi Ram and Mayawati have their faults, but they do represent a more aggressive attack on the order of social orthodoxy than has previously been seen from participants in the mainstream of Indian electoral politics. Kanshi Ram has shown that a person of Dalit origins can lead a party that wins seats at the ballot box and is not afraid to form a Government that puts the interests of the most subordinated Indians at its very centre. Throughout India it will now be more difficult to ignore the interests of Dalits.

Ram Vilas Paswan

Ram Vilas Paswan was elected to the Bihar State Assembly in 1969 as a member of the Samyutka Socialist Party. At the time he had considerable attraction to the Naxalite movement and no faith whatsoever in non-violence.[16] In 1970 Paswan's confrontationist tactics led to his imprisonment for seven months in Bhagalpur Gaol (later infamous for the deliberate blinding of a number of prisoners). It was only with the advent of the 'JP Movement' that he came to accept the superiority of non-violence. Paswan became a close colleague of Jayaprakash in 1974, and he was of some importance in the movement by virtue of being both an MLA and also a Harijan (the term still used in Bihar). He was arrested at the beginning of the Emergency in 1975, and spent the whole of the Emergency in gaol. In the election of 1977 he won a reserved Parliamentary seat for the Janata Party, and with the exception of the period from 1984 to 1989 has been a member of the Lok Sabha ever since. His party affiliation has changed with the many recompositions of the secular anti-Congress parties – he has variously been a member of the Janata Party, Lok Dal and the Janata Dal. The three leaders he has acknowledged in this time are Charan Singh, Karpoori Thakur and V. P. Singh.

Ram Vilas Paswan had a tumultuous period as Minister for Labour and Welfare in the V. P. Singh Government of 1989–90. He says that this was the portfolio he wanted, because he could simultaneously do work for the Dalits and the Backward Castes (Interview: 27 October 1995). One of his accomplishments was implementation of the long-standing Dalit demand that Dr Ambedkar's portrait be placed in the main hall of Parliament alongside the other greats of the national struggle for Independence. He was also able to persuade the Government to extend reservation in employment to Scheduled Caste persons who had become Buddhists; the primary beneficiary of this change is the Mahars.[17] But, of course, Paswan's most notorious action was to be intimately involved in the decision to adopt the Mandal Report that had lain on the table throughout the 1980s – it was commissioned by the previous Janata Government. This measure was of no value to the Scheduled Castes but of immense symbolic importance to the Backward Castes, particularly

---

[16] For an account of Paswan's earlier life and circumstances, see pp. 242–4.

[17] The mechanism of the change was the *Constitution (Scheduled Castes) Orders (Amendment) Act* 1990. This amended paragraph 3 of the *Order* of 1950, which stated: 'no person who professes a religion different from the Hindu or the Sikh religion shall be deemed to be a member of a Scheduled Caste'. The amendment added the words 'or the Buddhist' after 'Sikh'. Quite illogically, the change leaves Christian Untouchables still outside the scheme of benefits available to the Scheduled Castes.

those of Uttar Pradesh and Bihar. The backlash it created among the upper castes was a major factor in the disintegration of the Government.

Paswan's strategy in opposition remained essentially the same as it was in Government. His object was to be seen as the national leader of the Dalits, while simultaneously promoting himself as a strong leader of other out-groups – the Backwards and also the Muslims, from whom he claims to have particularly strong personal support. To augment his appeal to the Dalits he established a separate organisation called the Dalit Sena. Apparently this was established as early as 1983, but Paswan invested more energy in it after Congress lost its hold on the north Indian Untouchable vote. Of course, the key image placed alongside Paswan on the posters and promotional material of the Dalit Sena is that of Ambedkar. On the walls of the public rooms of his New Delhi residence there are now more likenesses of Ambedkar than of anyone else. But Paswan has come late to Ambedkar. The influences on him have mostly derived from the Lohia socialist movement and from Jayaprakash Narayan. But clearly Ambedkar has become the key symbol for building any all-India Dalit constituency. Paswan cannot afford to surrender any part of the Ambedkar legacy to his principal rival, Kanshi Ram.

There have always been formidable obstacles in front of Ram Vilas Paswan. His own power base is limited: he is the pre-eminent leader of the Paswans, the second Untouchable community (behind the Chamars) of one State, Bihar. For the rest, since clearly he wishes to be Prime Minister, he has to stake his claim to be the overall leader of the disadvantaged. One practical obstacle is that his spoken English is sufficient only for limited private conversation, and he therefore has no real capacity to build a mass following outside the Hindi belt. And, of course, there are a number of other competitors for the same constituency of the disadvantaged. Finally, there remain deep questions as to whether an Untouchable will be acceptable as Prime Minister of India.

Paswan's party, the Janata Dal, has done badly in electoral terms since its triumph in 1989. Its results in the 1996 poll were also poor, but events played into Paswan's hands. After the failure of the BJP to gain defections from other parties, Deve Gowda was able to cobble together an unlikely coalition of leftist, centrist and regional parties to form a Government in 1996. Deve Gowda installed his Janata Dal partyman Ram Vilas as his principal political lieutenant. Always energetic, as Minister for Railways Paswan rapidly turned this classic source of patronage into an instrument to promote the interests of Dalits. He claims, for example, that he has been able to regularise the position of thousands of temporary sweepers in the railways (Interview: 19 March 1997). When Congress brought down Gowda's Government at the end of March 1997, Paswan was one of the names mentioned as a possible replacement Prime Minister. But the position went to an establishment politician, the then Foreign Minister I. K. Gujral.

In terms of actual policy Ram Vilas does not stand for a program greatly different from that of any of the other parties putting up for the Scheduled Caste vote. Despite his inclination towards radicalism, he recognises that structural change will now be difficult to bring about in the short run. It is too late for radical land reform, and the reforms that are possible have to be conducted with due regard to the stance of the courts (Paswan interview: 1995). The major way ahead is to train Dalits so that they have marketable skills. He sees it as important to extend the principle of reservation to the developing private sector. Whatever his youthful origins, Paswan is now far from a social revolutionary. He is against the assertion of any animus against the upper castes – his second wife is an upper-caste Sikh – and Brahmins in particular. Rather, his overall goal is to work towards ensuring that Dalits and other out-groups get their fair share of social goods.

Conclusion

The great change in the politics of the Untouchables is that over large parts of India they can no longer be taken for granted as a dumb vote bank. To a much greater extent than even a decade ago they have begun to shape their own politics. The biggest change has been in the north, and the single most potent factor has been Kanshi Ram. He has given encouragement to Dalits across India, even though he has failed to have a major electoral impact outside a few States of the north. But Kanshi Ram did not fabricate his own political success from nothing. The times have eminently suited him. While the V. P. Singh Government's adoption of the Mandal principles of reservation initially served to displace Kanshi Ram as a strong advocate of the oppressed, the Mandal factor later worked in his favour. The Mandal decision served to create and legitimate a new politics of the disadvantaged, and Kanshi Ram's later electoral alliances were creatures of this new political environment. Meanwhile, the rise of the BJP has obligingly sapped the capacity of Congress to compete for the Dalit vote.

While Kanshi Ram and Mayawati have been spectacularly successful in Uttar Pradesh, the success has been built on dubious foundations and has appeared in danger of collapse at every point. His strategy has been to build an organisation of his own, and to use this body to draw votes and even active support from social groupings beyond his own caste. But major electoral success has depended on the construction of alliances with other parties, and these alliances have lacked both principle and stability. Ram Vilas Paswan, by contrast, has pursued the more cautious route of climbing the ladder in a broader, socially more heterogeneous, party on the mild left of Indian politics. He has projected himself as the special leader of Dalits within this national party. Paswan's fortunes have risen and fallen with the position of his party, but his strategy is eminently more risk averse than that of Kanshi Ram. Like Ambedkar before him, Kanshi Ram has plotted a difficult route to power.

More generally, it is now abundantly clear that there can be no single political strategy for Dalits throughout India. If India had developed a dominant national politics constructed on the basis of class and relative disadvantage, the situation might be different. But it is also a mistake to assume that such a politics would necessarily have taken a form advantageous to the Dalits. In this chapter we have interrogated the record of Indian Marxism in relation to the Dalits, and found that considerations of caste have obstinately clung to its processes (as well, for that matter, to those of the similarly egalitarian faiths of Christianity and Sikhism). The current fragmentation of party politics means that no party can realistically hope to command a national majority of the Dalit vote. But this too is not necessarily unfavourable for the Dalits. It will be recalled that in the era when they voted overwhelmingly for Congress their political and social power was considerably less than it is today. The common political task of the Dalits is to add to their collective power, but there can be no single strategy that will deliver this objective.

The question of reservation – the lives and
    careers of some Scheduled Caste MPs and
    MLAs

During the period of the V. P. Singh Government in 1989–90 the issue of compensatory discrimination moved to the very centre of Indian political life for the first time. The Mandal controversy was about preference for the other 'socially and educationally backward classes' (under Article 15(4) of the Constitution), that is the classes other than the Scheduled Castes and Tribes. It was a contest about power as well as about access to public employment for the 'backward' castes. The assumption was that higher-level bureaucrats possess serious power and status, and that reservation is a short cut to appropriation of these properties. In short, the bitterness of the Mandal affair arose from its construction as a contest over just who is to run India.

By contrast, compensatory discrimination for the Scheduled Castes has never presented itself as a mechanism for redistribution of power in India as a whole. It was not until the advent of Mayawati's first administration in Uttar Pradesh that Scheduled Caste officers were seriously considered a centre of power, and the brevity of that administration curtailed any serious development of the issue. While there is growing opposition to reservation for the Scheduled Castes as well as for the other backward classes – the two are now increasingly connected in the popular mind – there is another level of criticism of the former on the ground of the suggested deficiencies of its beneficiaries. Sacchidananda spoke for perhaps the mainstream attitude within caste Hindu society, when he painted this picture of what he called the 'Harijan elite':

Large numbers of educated Harijan elite both in the towns and in the villages have little active concern with bettering the lot of their less fortunate caste fellows. They overload political processes with petty local issues. Alienated from their own base, they have betrayed an incapacity to apply themselves to the tasks of reshaping the larger society into egalitarian structures. Their major preoccupation appears to be that of meeting the needs of the immediate family and kin. Some of the elite who have risen high in the social hierarchy have snapped their ties with their bleak past. They are largely out of tune from the mass of the community and seek a realignment with status and power groups in the wider society. (Sacchidananda 1977: 170)

Sacchidananda's suggestion is that reservation has created a privileged elite devoted to its own petty advancement and uncaring about the wider Untouchable community. This is the fatal flaw identified in reservation, not its incapacity to redistribute power and resources. In the 1990s there remains a widespread contempt for the Scheduled Caste beneficiaries of reservation, but there is now a tinge of fear too. Officers from the Untouchable castes are seen as inferior in capacity and in morality too: they are said to be specially inclined to take illicit money for performing their duties. Although the 'Harijan elite' school is essentially a high-caste account of reservation, criticism of the system has grown among Dalits themselves. We have seen that Kanshi Ram has simultaneously championed the cause of Scheduled Caste officers and scorned them for their insufficient commitment to radical transformation. Professor Parvathamma, a leading social scientist of Untouchable origins, has attacked the system from a more conservative position. Parvathamma is concerned that a small body of people has captured the great majority of reserved positions and that these people are self-perpetuating – their children too become the beneficiaries of a scheme whose whole rationale is compensation for the disadvantaged (Parvathamma 1984: 289). The occupants of reserved positions are routinely stigmatised as inferior, and this is not in the interest of the wider Untouchable population. Parvathamma believes it would be better if Scheduled Caste people struggled to achieve positions strictly on merit, as she herself did (Interview: 16 January 1988).[1] So, from different ideological positions and with different futures in mind, Sacchidananda, Kanshi Ram (see above, p. 224) and Parvathamma converge in their attack on compensatory discrimination as an appropriate remedy for the disabilities of the Untouchables.[2]

Whatever the considerable merits of these criticisms, there is no likelihood that reservation will be dismantled in the short or even medium term. Indeed, change is quite in the other direction. All the major political parties are now committed to extension of reservation to a broader category of 'backwards', and the Supreme Court has upheld the constitutionality of this policy. Clearly this is not the time to get rid of reservation for still more subordinated people. The present representation of Dalits in the public services and the legislatures would almost certainly fall quite drastically in the absence of guaranteed quotas, and undoubtedly Dalits would punish the Governments that brought this about.

If we return to the merits of reservation, we can see that it is all too easy

---

[1] An account of Professor Parvathamma's own life is presented in Isaacs 1965: 134–6.
[2] There is a considerable literature on the merits and demerits of reservation. For an oppositional view see Kumar (1992b). The literature on reservation of parliamentary seats is not large, but see Galanter (1979) and Baxi (1984).

to provide a one-dimensional and ultimately false view of the occupants of reserved positions. Here we present biographical rather than conjectural material derived from interviews with twenty members of the Lok Sabha and Rajya Sabha (the two Houses of Parliament in New Delhi) drawn from a number of different States, and with twelve Members of the Legislative Assemby (MLAs) in the single State of Bihar.[3] Whereas the picture we drew in chapter 7 is one of rapid political change and the opening of significant new opportunities for certain Dalit politicians, this is a very recent trend. The stories told by the subjects of our interviews are of personal struggle against material and social deprivation, and of limited capacity to represent their own communities in the face of a hostile power structure. In most of these stories it is difficult to recognise the 'Harijan elite' portrayed by Sacchidananda. Of course, such a limited sample is insufficient to permit general conclusions to be drawn about the character of reserved office holders. And we have limited ourselves to a study of parliamentarians, not bureaucrats or lower-level office holders. Nonetheless the voices to be heard here sound a warning against assumptions about just who the beneficiaries of reservation are. The interviews were done in 1982–3, but it is doubtful that much has changed in the social circumstances of most Scheduled Caste parliamentarians – indeed, a number of the interviewees are still in office.

There can be no controversy about the proposition that Scheduled Caste MPs and MLAs are not typical of the general Untouchable population of India. One of our most general findings is that in the present period almost no one rises in a single generation from the ordinary Untouchable condition of poverty to the heights of parliament. No more than one or two of the men interviewed – no female MPs could be interviewed, and there was no Dalit woman in the Bihar Assembly – had risen to such eligibility without an older member of the nuclear or extended family having made a break from the condition of landless labour that typifies Untouchable poverty. In a high proportion of cases a modest plot of agricultural land acquired in one generation has been the basis of a political career in the next. The economic base of an upwardly mobile Untouchable family may be painfully weak by the standards of more prosperous communities, but it constitutes the essential point of leverage for succeeding generations.

[3] The biographies discussed by name in this chapter are based on the following interviews:
Narsing Suryawanshi MP: New Delhi, 17 February 1983
Ram Vilas Paswan MP: New Delhi, 26 December 1982 and 27 October 1995
Suraj Bhan MP: New Delhi, 24 December 1982
K. C. Halder MP: New Delhi, 7 January 1982
Kunwar Ram MP: 30 December 1982
Radha Krishna Kishore MLA: Patna, 25 January 1983

Extended case study 1: Narsing Suryawanshi MP Narsing Suryawanshi (NS) is of the Mang caste (related to the Madiga of Karnataka
and Andhra), and is from a region in Karnataka close to the border
with Maharashtra. NS in effect rode to Delhi on the back of a cow. The
story goes like this. NS and his brothers and sisters are children of agricultural labourers. Their father was of unusually enterprising spirit, and
he managed to save enough money to buy a cow. Now, this cow turned
out to be a prize one. Every year for some nine years it produced a
beautiful calf that could be sold in the market for between Rs. 500 and
700. This income transformed the lives of the younger generation of the
family.

NS is the eldest son, and therefore it fell to him to tend the cow. After
some years of accumulating savings, it became possible to contemplate
new directions for the family. NS says that among the dominant Lingayats
and Marathas of his village there were a number of 'socialist minded'
people who had been busy persuading his father of the value of schooling.
So eventually the cow-minding duties were transferred to a younger
brother, and NS began his school career at the ripe age of 11. At about the
same time, in 1956, the father bought 11 acres of land from a Lingayat
Deshmukh or notable for the sum of Rs. 1,500. But for the next ten years
his father continued to hire himself out part-time as an agricultural
labourer, since initially he had no capital with which to work the land. He
started out by hiring oxen from a neighbour in return for a one-quarter
share of the crop grown in his fields – in those days there were no agricultural banks in the area. Despite the modesty of the family's economic
base, over the years it became the most prosperous of the forty Mang families in the village.

The rest of the story up to the time of interview was relatively straightforward – diligence at school, a reserved place at college, provision of
hostel accommodation, a modest government scholarship, and continuing help from the family. As to the latter, during his high school days NS
was able to bring grain from his father's house to his temporary home
with a sister in the nearby town. So the land was a crucial base to allow
him to study for years on end; for all this time he was a drain rather than a
source of family income. It was only with his election to the Lok Sabha in
1980 that NS began to earn an income.

Jitan Ram Manji MLA: Patna, 28 January 1983
Mangal Ram Premi MP: New Delhi, 6 January 1983 and 4 November 1995
Narsinh Makwana MP: New Delhi, 7 January 1983
A. C. Das MP: New Delhi, 24 December 1982
Bhole Paswan Shastri, Member of Rajya Sabha: New Delhi, 12 December 1982
Jagjivan Ram: New Delhi, 5 January 1983
Krishna Wada (pseudonym) MP: New Delhi, 17 February 1982

NS completed a BSc degree, but from the beginning he was more interested in politics than science. From his second year of study he involved himself in Sanjay Gandhi's Youth Congress movement. When he graduated in 1974 he became a 'social worker' advising his fellow Harijans (his term) on approaches to government and on education. NS got the Congress ticket in 1980 by initially applying through the mail. He had no patron, and made no trips to Bangalore, Delhi or anywhere else. It was his education and local reputation that won him the ticket, he says. At the time of interview NS saw himself as a party man without ambition to make a mark in the Lok Sabha itself. He thought of himself simply as a young Indian leader, not a leader of the Untouchables in particular. In 1979 NS married a woman educated up to university level. His own father and mother were still working in their fields in 1982, but they had managed to educate all their children other than the eldest daughter.

Comment: None of the cases we collected can be termed 'typical', but the example of Narsing Suryawanshi is broadly representative of the background of a young Untouchable politician of his period. What comes through is the fineness of the line between overwhelming poverty and, as in this case, hopeful poverty. Here it was a fabulous cow that enabled Suryawanshi's family to make the crucial break from the condition of all the other Mangs of the village. At this early stage in his political career NS was less preoccupied with the issues of the Scheduled Castes than external critics might wish to prescribe. His desire to be seen as a general leader was partly a matter of personal style, but it also reflected the politics of the period. NS saw himself as a follower of the Nehru family and of Sanjay Gandhi in particular. For him the prospects of the Untouchables were tied up with the fortunes of Congress. We have noted that in more recent years there has been a considerable radicalisation of Dalit politics throughout India. Nowadays it may be that a Scheduled Caste MP is more likely to portray him/herself as primarily committed to the welfare of the Scheduled Castes, though the demands of their political party may not allow them much opportunity to act on this commitment.

Extended case study 2: Ram Vilas Paswan MP We have sketched the important career of Ram Vilas Paswan in chapter 7. His early circumstances have elements in common with Narsing Suryanwanshi, and they are not the circumstances of a person who could reasonably have expected to achieve national prominence. Paswan was born in 1947 into an isolated Bihari village, some 15 kms from the nearest road and only to be approached on cycle or foot. The village consists of a handful of high-caste families – apparently they migrated from elsewhere in Bihar earlier this century – and the rest of the population is from Backward and

Untouchable castes. What set Paswan's family apart from the other Dusadhs was its relative prosperity – the common link with the situation of Kanshi Ram and many other Dalit politicians is unmistakable. Paswan's grandfather had managed to acquire 2 acres of land, and his father and uncles were able to build this up to some 30 (mostly flood prone) acres. The land had come on to the market when the high-caste owners were short of money, and the family was in a position to buy it because of the unusual industriousness of Paswan's father and the earnings of an uncle employed as servant to a businessman. Ram Vilas was also assisted by the unusual character of his father. He had been something of a 'saddhu' from childhood, and had learnt to read and write a little during his devotional wanderings over half-a-dozen years. When he finally came back to the village to settle down, he was too worldly for anyone to get the better of.

Paswan's father conceived a desire to educate the sons of the family, at the time a unique ambition for the local Dusadhs. There is no school in the village, so his father hired a tutor to teach four boys from the joint family. The tutors – first a Bania, then a Kayastha, both from poor families in other villages – were retained for three years. At the fourth class level he and his three cousins were admitted to a school several kilometres from his own village: to reach it they had to cross two rivers, one by boat and the other by wading up to the waist. Untouchability was not an issue in the school, since there were no upper-caste students. He graduated after two years to a middle school, again some kilometres from his own village. Paswan was able to proceed to the next level of schooling because the nearest high school had a Harijan hostel attached to it. He survived in the hostel by taking grain from home and tutoring younger boys. And he also had the benefit of a scholarship of Rs. 10 a month, mainly expended on fees.

Paswan eventually went to college in Patna, completing his BA but not his LLB. Again he lived in Harijan hostels, and somehow managed to survive despite the gross dilatoriness of the scholarship system – he received his last instalment when he had already been elected an MLA. But despite all the hardship, he says he grew up self-confident because of the love showered on him in the family and because he scarcely came into contact with high-caste people. At college he applied himself more to politics than to study, but he can date his politicisation to an incident that happened earlier in his own village. An ailing Chamar had gone into debt to his Brahmin employer for the sum of Rs. 50 that the Brahmin claimed he had expended on four medicinal pills for the Chamar. For the next ten years the Chamar paid interest on this 'debt', and he is said to have paid some Rs. 300. Meanwhile the Chamar had borrowed Rs. 75 from the

Brahmin against the security of his tiny plot of land, in order that he might arrange the marriage of his daughter. He was duly forced to forfeit the land to the Brahmin, and had gone to work as a labourer in Purnea District. He eventually returned with Rs. 350 of savings, which the Brahmin immediately demanded. When the Chamar refused to part with the money, he seized the man and had him bound hand and foot. The Brahmin was about to beat the Chamar in front of a crowd of people when Paswan turned up. He proceeded to untie the Chamar, and in a fit of fury he struck the Brahmin. This, of course, was a shocking event. His own father was deeply shocked that his son would strike a Brahmin. But the younger generation of Dusadhs stood behind him, indeed joined in the beating. Eventually the Brahmin was forced to leave the village, so great was the humiliation he had suffered.

Before completing his LLB Paswan appeared for the State Public Service Examination, and was offered a position as Deputy Super-intendent of Police within the category reserved for Scheduled Castes. His father was overjoyed that his son had attained to so unimaginably high a position for a Paswan. But before he was to take up the position, he happened to meet some socialist political workers in the village of his aunt. They were caste Hindus and were on the lookout for someone to run in the local reserved constituency against the Congress incumbent, a man who had held the seat continuously since 1952. Paswan agreed to think it over, and soon decided to take up the suggestion. Ram Manohar Lohia's Samyutka Socialist Party (SSP) was active and popular at the time, and he decided to apply for a ticket there. Meanwhile he bought a bicycle and for several months made himself known in numerous villages in the electorate. This proved of enormous help to him. When the SSP finally determined ticket allocation for the 1969 poll, he was the only applicant. He went on to beat the incumbent Congressman by a narrow margin.

Comment: Ram Vilas Paswan had the great advantage of coming from a family that was considerably better off than the other Dusadhs of his village. It was this circumstance and the progressive and enterprising outlook of his father that provided a base for him to achieve the education necessary to make a political career.

The economic background of Scheduled Caste MPs and MLAs – some other examples

In two other cases among our sample the family 'fortune' derived from its hereditary occupation as priest to families denied Brahminical rites by virtue of their Untouchability. Seemingly every Untouchable jati has such priests, and they tend to be better off and more respectable than the rest of the community. Even before modern education became a possibility for Untouchables these priests sometimes acquired a rudimentary literacy. And once literacy is acquired, it tends to be passed on to the next generation. In one of the above two cases the father of the MP was also an aryuvedic doctor, and a third MP – Suraj Bhan, now the leading Untouchable within the BJP – described his father and grandfather before him as 'quacks' who sold medicines to the people of their community. In the former two cases the priestly families had used their cash flow to acquire some land.

A more common background is one of more or less steady income flowing into the family from shoe-making/repairing/selling in the case of Chamars, clothes washing for dhobis in a city like Calcutta, or rickshaw pulling, as in the case of the brother of a Musahar MLA and Minister in Bihar. A toddy business established by a Pasi family – hereditary brewers of toddy in Bihar – was the basis of another MLA's career. In most of these cases the family was also able to acquire a small amount of land along the way, and this tended to underpin the break from abject poverty.

Several of the politicians in our survey were from considerably more comfortable backgrounds. K. C. Halder, a CPI(M) MP from West Bengal, is of the Sunri caste, many of whom work as brewers, agricultural labourers and small businessmen. Halder lives in the town of Burdwan, close to his ancestral village. Reasonable prosperity is quite common among the 2,000 or so Sunri families of Burdwan town, but Halder's family is the leading one. He was one of the older MPs in the study, but literacy in his family goes back to his grandfather. In the present generation the family's fortune is bound up with the business activities of Halder's brother, who possesses a range of distributorships (including Eveready batteries). Although the great majority of Bengalis from the Scheduled Castes are very poor, examples such as that of Halder seem not to be quite so remarkable as elsewhere.

Of greater rarity is the case of Kunwar Ram, since his Chamar family has built its considerable business in the unpromising location of Bihar. Kunwar Ram's father and mother established a charcoal supply business in Patna in about 1919, initially serving the needs of British officials including the governor of the province. He claims that for three decades after the establishment of the business there was not a single Untouchable business man in all Bihar to rival his father. The efforts of his parents and those of the next two generations have created a substantial and diversified business that now includes truck and bus transport, retail shops and brick manufacture. The family's standing has led to the acquisition of reserved positions in government service and to suitable matrimonial alliances. In 1947 Kunwar Ram married a woman educated up to ninth class, a most unusual achievement for the period. One of his daughters is married to a Deputy Superintendent of Police. Clearly this is for Bihar a highly exceptional Untouchable family. But Kunwar Ram rightly points out that his house is modest by Patna standards, and Patna standards are not as high as those of the great cities of India. There must be many members of the Lok Sabha and State Assemblies who are wealthier than Kunwar Ram.

Radha Krishna Kishore (RK), a Dusadh, is another Bihari of unusually privileged background for a Scheduled Caste MLA. He was only 28 at the time of interview, and his early success was achieved on the coat-tails of his great-uncle – this man had been elected to the Assembly in 1957 and had also been the prime engine of the family's economic rise. In earlier times Dusadhs often had close associations with Rajput zamindars, and in this case RK's great-uncle was able to acquire some education and land from his connection to a particular Rajput. The family now has some 40 or 50 acres of land – admittedly most of it not highly productive. Their strong base enabled various members of the family to study to quite high levels, to gain reserved government positions, marry educated partners, and generally enjoy economic progress. RK himself had a very smooth path into the Assembly – his family's standing made him a natural choice for any party. The achievements of RK's family are not unusual by the standards of the Backward communities – the Kurmis, Koiris, Yadavs and the like – but there are still relatively few such families among the Scheduled Castes.

Extended case study 3: Jitan Ram Manji, the (almost) perfectly self-made man In contrast to all the cases discussed thus far, we encountered only one case of a legislator whose father had remained a landless labourer throughout his working life. Jitan Ram Manji is a Musahar, a caste associated in the public mind with rat eating because of their occasional consumption of field rats that they dig out of burrows during the rainy season. These rats are a delicacy for the Musahars, but the high castes are appalled by the practice. Jitan Ram is a from a village in Gaya where eight Bhumihar families own most of the land. He and his brother, a police inspector, are freakish success stories. Their two sisters are married to agricultural labourers.

Jitan Ram's father and mother were agricultural labourers attached (bonded) to a large Bhumihar family, and from the age of five he himself was required to tend this family's animals. The family retained a tutor, since there was no school in the village at the time. One day, after he had finished his work, Jitan Ram sat down outside the circle of children receiving their instruction. This became something of a habit with him, and on one occasion he intervened to give a right answer to a question wrongly answered by one of the boys (for which error the boy was beaten by the tutor).

The tutor, a Kayastha by caste, regularly encountered Jitan Ram's father at the village toddy shop. One day he mentioned the boy's interest in learning, and suggested that he formally join the circle. His father thought the matter over, and decided there would be no harm in approaching his Bhumihar masters to allow Jitan Ram to join the class after his daily tasks were complete. The response was a sound beating for the presumptuousness of even asking. Education was no business of a Musahar. But one of the Bhumihar brothers was of more humane disposition, and eventually resistance crumbled. Jitan Ram was duly issued with a board and piece of chalk. The concession was crucial to Jitan Ram, but it caused no financial loss to his masters – he continued to feed and drive to water their fourteen or fifteen oxen and the several cows and buffalo. Jitan Ram participated in the informal schooling up to the equivalent of seventh standard, by which time his father was so impressed with his son's diligence that he decided to release him from most of his duties and allow him to go to a regular school. The facility of a scholarship worth Rs. 10 a month made all the difference. So Jitan Ram began walking the 7 km to and from the local school. He passed his matriculation there, and then proceeded to an intermediate college at Gaya. This town was some 40 km from his village, but he was able to stay at a very good Harijan hostel there. By then his government scholarship had risen to Rs. 50 a month, and some of this he sent home so his brother could go to school. He also undertook some tuition to augment his income. In 1967 he passed his BA and went on to Magadh University to enrol for an MA.

Circumstances conspired against his completing the MA. Bihar suffered a severe drought in 1967, and his mother and father were thrown into great difficulties in the village. They were in any case coming to the end of their working lives. His own family responsibilities were growing too: he had been married at the age of 11, and from the age of 13 began living with his wife. Their third child was born in 1967. So in that year Jitan Ram took up a reserved position as clerk in the Post and Telegraph Department. He occupied this position until his election to the Assembly in 1980. From his college days he had it in mind to enter politics, but he knew he could not do this until his brother had been educated and had acquired a job. He got the Congress ticket in 1980 after travelling to Delhi and contacting the 'high command' of the party. He pointed out to these people that there was no Musahar representative from Gaya District, despite the large number of Musahars in the population.

Comment: This life history is unique among those we collected, in that Jitan Ram Manji had nothing but a bit of ordinary decency to get him started. His father could give him nothing more than moral support. But once he was able to acquire the beginnings of an education, the system of scholarships, Harijan hostels and reserved public employment provided the base from which he could launch a political career. Without these, he would have lacked any opportunity to rise.

Political discrimination between the Scheduled Castes

One of the conventional attacks on the reservation system is that its beneficiaries are overwhelmingly drawn from the most prosperous elements among the most prosperous Scheduled Castes. Since our own data are drawn from MPs and MLAs rather than from the far larger category of government servants, we are not in a position to throw more than a little light on this question. But it is clear that a person from one of the lowliest castes tends to have a more difficult path into the Parliament or Assembly. There were at the time five Musahar MLAs in addition to Jitan Ram Manji, and we interviewed only one of these. This man was a Minister, but his early circumstances had also been weaker than those of most other Scheduled Caste legislators. In this case there was a small plot of land – about an acre shared between his father and two uncles – though in the grandfather's generation there seems to have been considerably more land. Importantly, an elder brother was working as a rickshaw puller at the time when education became a possibility for the future Minister. And finally, his father had worked for zamindars and had developed some mildly progressive attitudes towards education. This was the slender but crucial support for his education and advancement.

The only other person of particularly low caste in our sample was Mangal Ram Premi, a Valmiki MP from Uttar Pradesh. In ritual terms the Valmiki are traditionally regarded as the lowest Untouchable community of northern India, but opportunities arising from urbanisation have sometimes given them a greater cash flow than agricultural labourers like the Musahars. Mangal Ram Premi's early circumstances were weaker than many of the legislators we interviewed. But what distinguished his family from other Valmikis was that his father had become a farm manager for a zamindar prior to Independence; he was earning Rs. 7 a day by 1947, a sum far greater than could be gained from sweeping. Mangal Ram's elder brother also turned out to be a better than usual keeper of pigs – at any one time the family kept between twenty and thirty animals. And consciousness about the desirability of education had filtered into the family from a number of relatives employed as sweepers for the British. In short, Mangal Ram Premi undertook a measure of education. This led to the acquisition of positions at various embassies in New Delhi, and finally to a Parliamentary seat. At the time of first interview Premi represented Congress, but he now holds the same seat for the BJP. As we have noted in chapter 7, the Valmikis of Uttar Pradesh are now solidly aligned with the BJP.

It may well be true that there is some tendency for the more prosperous castes – and, as we have argued, more prosperous individuals within these castes – to be overrepresented in the various legislatures throughout India. In Bihar, castes with some 10 per cent of the population were unrepresented in the Assembly at the time of our study. Some of these castes had quite large numbers, particularly the Doms and the Haris, Mehtars or Bhangis (the latter three tend to be lumped together as cleaning and scavenging castes). These are ritually the lowest castes in Bihar. But neither the Doms nor the other grouping individually met the 'quota' obtained by dividing caste population by total number of reserved seats. And any claim of systematic discrimination would have to contend with the fact that at the time there was a Bihari Mehtar in the more prestigious Lok Sabha, and that in 1985 a Dom was elected to the Assembly – though this was said to be the first time this had happened.

Two castes, the Dusadhs or Paswans and the Pasis, were significantly overrepresented in the Bihar Assembly. The Paswans are the second largest caste with some 27 per cent of the Scheduled Caste population, but they occupied 37 per cent of reserved seats. The Pasis had 3.8 per cent of the SC population and 6.25 per cent of the seats (three in number). Conversely, the Musahars (including for this purpose the Bhuinyas) had 21 per cent of the population but 15 per cent of the seats: their 'entitlement' would have been ten seats, rather than the six they had. As the largest caste the Chamars enjoyed exactly their due: they had 30.5 per cent of the population and 31.25 per cent of the seats. Although it is not possible to generalise on the basis of figures for one Assembly, these several figures seem intuitively understandable. The Paswans are the boldest of the Scheduled Castes of Bihar, though it is not clear that they are any wealthier than the Chamars. Presumably, extroverted character can be counted an asset in politics. In the case of the Pasis, their traditional occupation of toddy tapping has sometimes given them a better than usual cash flow. This has tended to lead to higher levels of educational attainment and greater social prominence. The Musahars, by contrast, are by far the poorest and least educated of the three major Scheduled Castes of Bihar. Given the importance placed by all parties on education, the more advanced communities and individuals will naturally be favoured. Of course, there is some tension between this outcome and the whole rationale of reservation.

Preparation for office – education and prior careers

A college education has become a virtual prerequisite for selection as a candidate for a reserved seat. All but three of the thirty-two MPs and MLAs had attended college, though not all had graduated, and a number of them had completed Master's and Law degrees. One of the other three had done a four-year technical course, while the remaining two were both of an older generation and had made careers in labour and social reform work. Narsinh Makwana, a Vankar or weaver by caste, left school at the age of 9 or 10 after a series of fights with rich boys. He became a bootblack in Ahmedabad, where several years earlier his father had gone to work in a textile mill. After about a year-and-a-half he became a bearer in a hotel, and then by the age of 15 or 16 a textile worker. What gradually followed was an interest in union affairs and in the Socialist Party. In 1954 he became a full-time union worker, fifteen years after entering the mill. He contested a number of elections for the Socialist Party (in its several appellations) and, after 1969, for Congress. In 1975 he won a seat in the Gujarat Assembly and in 1980 he became an MP. Makwana's career parallels the experience of a great many unionist politicians in western countries, but this kind of figure is rare for India with its small modern industrial sector.

The second politician without a college education was A. C. Das, at the time Secretary of the Parliamentary Committee for the Welfare of Scheduled Castes and Scheduled Tribes. On completing his school education Das joined Vinoba Bhave's *bhoodan* movement for voluntary land surrender and he had worked among tribals for seventeen years. At one point he thought of going to college but Vinoba persuaded him that he was getting a better education through the life he was leading. It was only after leaving the movement in 1971 that he joined Congress, and he was immediately given a ticket for the Lok Sabha. He was successful at his first attempt, and has remained in Parliament for all the succeeding period. Again, Das stands out sharply from his parliamentary colleagues. Many of the latter claim to have been 'social workers' before entering politics, but for the most part this is a synonym for involvement in extra-parliamentary party politics.

It is now very common for Scheduled Caste politicians to have first made their career in a reserved position of government service. Such a position can be used to build a financial base for their family, and also to make useful contacts. Suraj Bhan, then a Jana Sangh (forerunner of the

BJP) MP for Punjab, said that he was stopped from trying to enter politics directly after college by the sudden death of his father and brother. As it was, he first served for sixteen years in the Post and Telegraph Department. We have seen that Jitan Ram Manji was obliged to follow the same route in Bihar.

Only three of the interviewed politicians had begun their career before Independence. This is no basis on which to generalise about changing career patterns, but it is clear that there is now a regularity to political recruitment that was not present before Independence. Take the case of Bhole Paswan Shastri, who was born in Purnea District of Bihar in 1914. His family had possessed a modest holding of land, but this was lost in 1923 or 1924 after his father fell into financial difficulties; thereafter, his father was an ordinary labourer and sharecropper. It was Bhole Paswan's mother who was the dominant force in the family. She conceived the idea that Bhole Paswan, her only surviving child, should be educated so that he would not have to work in the manner of his father. She died in 1926, before she could see the fruits of her ambition. Bhole Paswan started his education in the village school, and was then awarded a free place in high school. He was not able to take up this offer because he had no money for his living needs. Meantime a nationalist school had been established in Purnea in the name of Mahatma Gandhi, and for four years he was able to study there with the support of the School Management Committee. His future education was combined with work for the nationalist movement, and was supported by progressive elements within that movement. He studied at a college in Banaras for four years, and by the end of this period he felt: 'I have learned something. I can fight. I can make my life. I have no inferiority complex as a Scheduled Caste person. I am a free man.' As a free man he was gaoled by the British in the period 1942–4, which he says was later a qualification for Ministerial office.

Bhole Paswan Shastri was three times Chief Minister of Bihar, though for very short periods – less than a year in total. He observes that he took his opportunities when the high-caste men were disunited. For years before his death in 1984 he had lived in a single room in a hostel in New Delhi – he was then a member of the Rajya Sabha – his reputation for uprightness and honesty unimpeached. Clearly he had not accumulated any wealth, despite having been Minister for Excise in Bihar! Although he had a good income there were always lots of expenses – particularly at election time. His wife, to whom he had been married as a child, lived almost all her life in the village with her brothers. Only for a short period when he was a Minister in Patna did she live with him. Although he did not tell it quite like this, clearly the gap in sophistication between the two was too great to allow a normal married life. There were no children.

Jagjivan Ram's path was far easier than that of Bhole Paswan, since along with most of our other respondents of a later period his generation was not the first to make the break with relentless poverty. Jagjivan was born in Arrah District of Bihar in 1908, into a village which he says did not practise Untouchability in the matter of deriving water. The best water in the village happened to be had from a well within the Chamar quarter, and Brahmins are said to have freely resorted to this well. Jagjivan's family had a considerable parcel of agricultural land – in his grandfather's time it amounted to about 7 acres, and this had grown to some 17 acres at the time of his father's death early in his childhood. His father had joined the army as a paramedical, and his and an employed brother's steady income was the basis of growing prosperity for the family. Jagjivan was sent to school in the village, along with several other Chamar boys at the time, and says he experienced no discrimination there. By the time he went to high school in the nearby town of Arrah he was the only Chamar in the school. Again he encountered no discrimination – he could walk there and back every day, so there was no question of participation in common eating facilities or housing. The first discrimination he suffered was at Banaras Hindu University, to which he had been invited by the Principal after meeting him during a visit to Arrah. In common with the other young men from outside Banaras he was admitted to the university hostel, but he immediately encountered the refusal of kitchen staff to clean his dishes. In order, he says, not to cause inconvenience to the other students he decided to withdraw from the hostel. A teacher of the college put him up in his own house for a time, and after the first vacation he set up house with his mother as housekeeper. But this experience seems not to have greatly scarred Jagjivan, and immediately after graduating from Banaras he commenced his political career in Gandhi's Harijan movement.

The question of 'the Harijan elite'

Before we return to Sacchidananda's thesis, it is appropriate to review one more extended study of an MP. Here the career is essentially city-based and has certain affinities with that of Narsinh Makwana. At the same time, this case has elements of the kind that have led to pejorative judgments by critics of reservation.

Extended case study 4: Krishna Wada Krishna Wada (KW) was elected to the Lok Sabha from Maharashtra in 1957 and 1962, but lost the ticket in 1967. He regained Congress support in 1980. KW's father was originally an agricultural labourer, but shortly after his son's birth he had become a textile factory worker in nearby Nagpur. His mother took up bidi making as an outworker. Although both parents were unable to read or write, KW began school at the regular age; his Mahar family had already been touched by Ambedkar's insistence on the value of education. KW has a BA degree but did not complete his LLB studies. His younger brother is also educated, though he did not complete college and is now in business.

KW was aware of Untouchability in the immediate post-Independence period, but it did not affect him personally. He explained that as a 'city man' he escaped the rigours of the caste system. Immediately after graduation he took a job as headmaster in a school, and soon married one of the teachers – a Brahmin. The marriage caused difficulties in his wife's family, but her parents were eventually mollified. They were 'a little bit liberal but not really liberal'. KW did not remain a teacher but made his career in the Maharashtra trade union movement. His introduction to the movement was through his father, and he was a union activist even during his college days. He has been associated with various unions including the Bidi Workers and Textile Workers Unions. His parliamentary career had been built with the support of the early Ambedkarite unions, but he has not been active in the unions for many years. The rebirth of his career came about after he associated himself with Sanjay Gandhi.

KW has never lived in his constituency, which was given him simply because it was a Maharashtrian reserved seat. His own house is in Nagpur, but he has lived in Delhi since his first daughter was admitted to medical college there. All three of his children are 'identified 100 per cent' with Scheduled Caste people. The second daughter was also in medical college, and the son was doing his MBA, MA and LLB simultaneously. The father's status as a Scheduled Caste person had governed their eligibility for reserved positions. KW sees reservation as the key to the rise of the Scheduled Castes. With appropriate public employment the Scheduled Castes will eventually gain social respectability, and this will be enough to end Untouchability.

Comment: The remoteness of KW from his Mahar roots will inevitably raise questions as to his fitness to occupy a reserved seat. While a perfectly agreeable person, KW seemed to lack political passion or realism in his assessment of the problems of Untouchables. And clearly his children were not from the disadvantaged background that reservation of educational places was designed to combat. Indeed, no one could argue that KW represents the kind of person who ought to be assisted by compensatory discrimination at the stage of career he had reached at the time of interview. But KW is far from a characteristic case among Scheduled Caste legislators. To the extent that such cases do become characteristic, the rationale for reservation will crumble.

An example such as that of KW fuels the tendency to impose higher moral standards on Scheduled Caste parliamentarians than on parliamentarians occupying general seats. The much indulged temptation is to prescribe from the outside what an Untouchable politician ought to be. He – there are no female stereotypes – is supposed to have risen from the mainstream of Untouchable society and thus be able to represent his own kind, but not to the extent that he is biassed against his other constituents and the general Indian population. While required to remain true to his humble roots, he will be looked down upon unless he is a good operator in mainstream politics. His own family will expect him to carry them from rural subordination to educated middle-class status. But the outside world will judge him harshly – more harshly than others who do the same – if he accomplishes this without conspicuous honesty. Such an ideal man can rarely be encountered among ordinary mortals.

What we have found in practice is that there is no one type of Untouchable politician, though there are regularities of several kinds. The most striking regularity is that Scheduled Caste legislators do not come from the characteristic Untouchable situation of landless labour, but tend to be at least the second generation of a family somewhat superior to this condition. There is only one man in our sample – two if you count the rather different case of Bhole Paswan Shastri – from a family that was entirely landless and also without any income from outside the village. But just how comfortable were the early circumstances of the subjects of these interviews, and how prosperous have they become as a result of their careers? Our broad conclusion is that they do not represent a privileged minority when measured against the standard of urban India or of caste Hindus in general. While we have no detailed comparative data, it is safe to suggest that the circumstances of parliamentarians from both the peasant and the upper castes will tend to be greatly superior to those from the Scheduled Castes. What will almost certainly distinguish the latter from other representatives of rural constituencies is the smallness of any landholding they have.

In the sample discussed here, the highest reported parcel of land was some 50 acres of relatively poor land spread over a large extended family. Only two politicians came from business families, and demonstrably their business interests were of minor stature. Most of the group were much less wealthy than any of the above people, many of them being initially only marginally above the level of the general Untouchable population in the countryside. But what happened to them and their families in the course of a political career? By and large, and no doubt unsurprisingly, the answer is that their conditions have improved in proportion to the strength of their initial base – the originally more prosperous men have managed to consolidate this status, whereas those from a weaker background have struggled to carry their family into self-sustaining middle-class status. A number of the families now have members in reserved places in government service, but these positions are often not in the first or second grades. But many Untouchable politicians have only with the greatest difficulty succeeded in carrying their family from rural semi-poverty to lower-middle-class status. While there is a tendency for the families to have been urbanised in the wake of the politician's career, sometimes the transition is only from a village to a sub-district centre. This is a modest transformation by the standards of India in general, but a much rarer and more notable one among the Untouchable castes. The case of Krishna Wada can be seen as quite exceptional. Although his parents were poor and illiterate, two of his children – girls at that – went on to study medicine. A key factor in this transformation is the fact that he married an educated Brahmin woman: this woman's input into the education and motivation of her children must have been a significant factor in their academic success. The other families discussed here have not benefited from sophisticated guidance of this sort.

There is no evidence, then, of great enrichment of the subjects of this study. Indeed, what can be argued with considerable vigour is that many Dalit politicians are not sufficiently comfortable to play the strong and independent political role which might more effectively promote their community's interests. To turn Sacchidananda's argument on its head, the argument might be that the creation of a more privileged group among Untouchables could well be of benefit to the general Untouchable population. Certainly, Sacchidananda's conception of 'the Harijan elite' derives no confirmation from the results of our own study. Admittedly the two samples are different, since Sacchidananda's group included government servants and social workers as well as politicians. But this is unlikely to make a major difference to the findings. Our own conclusion is that it is at best strained to talk of an 'elite' of people who turn out to have the economic characteristics described here.

The Dalits and reservation

The lives and issues discussed in the present chapter provide rich illustration of the complexity of analysis that needs to be brought to bear on the subject of reservation for the Scheduled Castes. We have found little merit in the proposition that reservation has created a particularly selfish and uncaring community of Scheduled Caste politicians. There are undoubtedly danger signals – Krishna Wada's remoteness from 'his' people illustrates one problem quite neatly. And the longer the system of reservation persists, the greater will be the tendency towards concentration of its benefits in the hands of relatively few families. Such an outcome can be predicted from general knowledge of the hereditary character of culture and advantage in any society. But many of these problems are still in the future. The more pressing aspects of reservation are quite other than those raised by the 'Harijan elite' school.

Reservation of parliamentary seats for candidates from the Scheduled Castes is perhaps the most problematical part of the whole scheme of compensatory discrimination. In the past there is abundant evidence that Scheduled Caste Members of both State Assemblies and the national Parliament had little capacity to represent the interests of Dalits. Perhaps the situation would have been different if the concerns of Untouchables had been a central preoccupation of national and State government, but we have seen that this was not the case. The usually high-caste leadership of the major parties actively discouraged the occupants of reserved seats from developing too much of a following among the Untouchable population. In Congress, the task of retaining the support of Untouchables was largely assumed by Indira Gandhi herself during her long tenure as Prime Minister. And as the party's most senior Harijan, Jagjivan Ram could be displayed as living proof that the Party was sympathetic to such people. Given her notorious concern to centralise power in her own hands, Indira would simply not have tolerated anyone – caste Hindu, Muslim or Untouchable – developing a political base genuinely independent of herself. This can be seen to have had a particularly strong impact on an out-group like the Untouchables. Their 'representatives' – if this is what the occupants of seats reserved for Scheduled Caste candidates are – were almost constitutionally disqualified from taking too active a political interest in issues of greatest relevance to their own people. The younger Scheduled Caste MPs and MLAs now actively chafe under this too-constraining control, and a number of them despair at their own ineffectiveness. Several of our interviewees went so far as to recommend cessation of the whole scheme of reserved constituencies. And numbers of young Dalit activists are now disgusted with what they see to be the timidity of Scheduled Caste parliamentarians.

Abolition of reservation would undoubtedly entail a great reduction in the number of Scheduled Caste MPs and MLAs. This follows from the kind of biographical evidence discussed here: very few of these persons could have hoped to compete successfully for a party ticket against their social superiors. If we fully accept the above criticisms, it could be said that this will be no great loss. Kanshi Ram and others have been busy arguing that the Dalits will learn to struggle when they no longer have any institutional guarantees. Our own view is more cautious. We are no enthusiastic supporters of reservation, and we recognise that the greatest engine of Dalit power is their capacity to vote in elections rather than their number of 'representatives' in parliaments. But we are also wary of dismantling a system in which Dalits can come to some prominence as MPs and MLAs. There are signs that in the new fluidity of Indian politics it may be possible for these parliamentarians to make a bolder showing in support of their people.

9   Subordination, poverty and the state in modern India

The heart of this work is an attempt to assess the condition and prospects of a large number of specially subordinated Indians. We did not begin our inquiries with the object of writing about a particular category of people, though this is what the book has become. Initially we were interested in certain dynamic problems, above all the matter of agrarian violence. These beginnings still colour the work. In order to develop explanations for the seemingly high level of violence suffered by one category of victims, the Untouchables, we began to uncover layers of what it means to be Untouchable in India today. It does not mean what it meant fifty, and certainly not one hundred and fifty, years ago. The need to unpack the condition of being an Untouchable has drawn us into a variety of processes, programs, structures and patterns of thought. We have tried, in short, to compose a work that provides a relatively comprehensive account of the lives of Untouchables today, and just how these lives have been historically constructed. In order to balance the inherent superficiality of generalisation we have also engaged in more intensive investigation of particular situations and communities.

While the objects of this work have been firmly rooted in practical problems of Indian life today, they have also been framed by an end-of-century interrogation of the appropriateness of designating a large segment of the Indian population to be 'Untouchables' (or some synonym such as 'Harijans' or 'Dalits'). This interrogation proceeds from a couple of apparently quite distinct sources. One of them is a post-colonial scholarship which has increasingly taken the view that the world created by the British raj was a new world masquerading as 'traditional India', and that the structure of caste was the epicentre of this colonial imagination. It follows that the Untouchables were to a large extent invented by the British. The second doubt arises from the amelioration that has undoubtedly taken place in the condition of people from the castes in question. On this view, any past distinctiveness of the Untouchables has tended to wither away.

While there is a measure of truth in both these views, what they leave out is the crucial perspective of the people themselves. There appears to be a broadening and deepening, not a waning, of the consciousness of these people as to their subordinated condition within Indian society. This development is taking place simultaneous with their gathering sense that they now have opportunities and amenities historically denied them. Surely, then, this enhanced consciousness dictates that we be slow to abandon the use of analytical structures that make sense to the affected people themselves. This is not to make the mistake of taking the idea of Untouchability or Dalitness out of history, by suggesting that it is some kind of immutable essence of Hinduism.

There are several histories to be distinguished in relation to the Untouchables. One of them is a pre-colonial history, the precise contours of which will remain beyond our understanding. Thus it is not possible to say with any precision just when or how all the varied people now called 'Untouchables' or 'Dalits' were pushed into moulds of deep subordination. No assumption can be made that all these people are descended from the most disreputable persons identified either in the classic texts of Brahminical Hinduism or in the poetry of the medieval bhakti movement. But it is clear from the latter texts that there were people in medieval India who were scorned for their lack of ritual fitness, and it is highly likely that these people were among the most menial of the population in terms of their employment and rewards. But a major source of ignorance for the entire pre-modern period is just how numerous the ritually debased people were, and how sharply distinguished they were from other communities – particularly other communities that were also low on the scale of wealth and status.

The second relevant history is that of European colonialism, during which the idea and the experience of Untouchability was powerfully and quite visibly shaped. This history has been explored at considerable length here. Thus it is often said that the British act of inquiring into the nature of the 'Depressed', 'External', 'Exterior' or 'Untouchable' castes served to sharpen their very distinctiveness within Indian society. This is probably true, partly in the sense that it tended to refresh a Brahminical orthodoxy that was always under challenge from untidy practice. But the direct European impact on the Untouchables was slow to develop, much slower than for more privileged communities such as the Brahmins themselves. The great change in Untouchable circumstances during the colonial period was political rather than social, and it occurred at one highly defined moment some fifteen years before the end of British rule. Separately but with combined effect, the British, Ambedkar and Gandhi helped give birth to a new conception of the Untouchables. Out of different motives these several interests helped construct a unitary or aggregated social category – whether it was expressed as 'Untouchables', 'Harijans', or even 'Scheduled Castes' – that covered the whole of India. The basis of this construct was the cultural principle of purity and pollution. It could be said that the construct was artificial, since the personal identity of Untouchables had apparently flowed more from caste (Chamar, Bhangi, Paraiyan, Paswan and so on) than from location in any overarching category of Untouchability. On the other hand, there can be no doubt that the dichotomy of purity and pollution was a central motif of Indian civilisation. In short, it is not really true that 'the Untouchables' were 'invented' during the colonial period. Rather, their description was simplified and objectified at a particular political moment so as to fit them into a bureaucratic and welfare model understandable to the modern Indian state.

The third history of the Untouchables is post-colonial, and undoubtedly its leading characteristic is the blunting of many of the most oppressive aspects of the Untouchability system; a substantial part of this book is devoted to consideration of these improving circumstances. But our conclusion is that that what remains of the *ancien régime* is far from merely residual. This is the context for the upsurge of Dalit representations as to their historic and persisting oppression. A rising incidence of violence involving Dalits – the so-called 'Harijan atrocities' – is the most accessible evidence that their subordination is a continuing interest of many elements within Indian society. Much of the violence is new rather than 'traditional' in character, and is provoked by Untouchables' own efforts to emerge from their subordination.

Despite our argument that it still makes sense to talk in terms of a grouping called 'Untouchables' or 'Dalits', this work has been concerned to develop perspectives that go beyond narrow conceptions of caste. This is a work about the Indian poor as much as it is about a category defined according to ritual criteria. Indeed, our argument is that more progress has been made in relation to the abatement of adverse discrimination than in reducing poverty. If this continues to be the case, the justification for retaining categories that derive from the practice of ritual Untouchability will progressively decline. The politician Kanshi Ram already prefigures this situation by preferring to talk in terms of the *bahujan samaj* or 'common people' rather than 'Dalits'. With an eye firmly pointed towards Muslim and lower-caste voters, his argument is that the now primary divide in Indian society is between the exploiting upper castes – he estimates their numbers to be roughly 10 per cent of the population – and all other Indians. While there is something in what Kanshi Ram says, our own view is that there is still a relatively sharp divide that places the Untouchables in a unique position. But to the extent that Kanshi Ram and other politicians are able to build coalitions uniting elements from the greater bahujan samaj, they will be breaking down the barriers that have made the Untouchables uniquely subordinated.

The Untouchables and change

The change in the situation and outlook of Untouchables over the period of the present century has been monumental. This can be illustrated by recalling a simple event of 21 February 1913.[1] On that day a group of perhaps one hundred Pulayas, the most polluting caste of Cochin, met to form an organisation for the betterment of their community. The meeting was to be held in the southern part of the town, near the house of a sympathetic Nayar man. But the problem was just how the Pulayas would get there. Pulayas were not authorised to use the roads in this part of Cochin, lest they pollute the Nayars and Nambudiri Brahmins who lived there. So the Pulayas devised the strategy of paddling to the meeting along the backwaters. When they arrived, they moored their boats together to form a kind of floating platform on which the speakers could be seen and heard.

Now in a sense there was nothing extraordinary about the circumstances of this meeting in Cochin. There was no atrocity, nor even any substantial unpleasantness. The Pulayas were simply making do in the very circumstances they sought to change. But already by this time there had been considerable amelioration in the Pulayas' condition: the presence of the friendly Nayar is one clue to this. Fifty years earlier the Pulayas had still been slaves. At the beginning of the nineteenth century the French missionary Abbé Dubois had said:

[The] *Puliahs* . . . are looked upon as below the level of the beasts which share this wild country with them. They are not even allowed to build themselves huts to protect them from the inclemencies of the weather. A sort of lean-to, supported by four bamboo poles and open at the sides, serves as a shelter for some of them, and keeps off the rain, though it does not screen them from the wind. Most of them, however, make for themselves what may be called nests in the branches of the thickest-foliaged trees, where they perch like birds of prey for the greater part of the twenty-four hours. They are not even allowed to walk peaceably along the high-roads. If they see anyone coming towards them, they are bound to utter a certain cry and to go a long way round to avoid passing him. A hundred paces is the very nearest they may approach anyone of a different caste. If a Nair, who always carries arms, meets one of these unhappy people on the road, he is entitled to stab him on the spot. (Dubois 1906: 60–1)

[1] This account is drawn from an interview with K. K. Madhavan, former Member of the Rajya Sabha and long-time Pulaya leader, 26 January 1988.

If there was great change from these circumstances to those of the Pulayas who assembled in 1913, the change between the latter date and the present is far greater. Today, one can hire a boatman to row across the bay in Cochin. The boatman may well be a Pulaya. If he is, he will be unrecognisable from the account of the Abbé Dubois. There is not a chance that he will humiliate himself by displaying over-eagerness to acquire the small fare payable for the trip, no matter that he undoubtedly needs every rupee he can get. None of the boatman's customers will make the mistake of treating him as less than an ordinary person offering a needed service. Given the special character of Kerala one is likely to sense a vigorous air of proletarian consciousness in this man. And while waiting for customers at the other side, he may well pull out his newspaper to read. This Pulaya boatman is simply a citizen of a modern democracy, albeit that we can tell from his clothes and his job that he is poor.

It might be objected that the case of the Pulayas is uniquely dramatic, given the severity of their historical condition and also the special degree of change that has marked Kerala society. But against this, a broadly comparable transformation has been taking place throughout India. Everywhere Untouchables are now bolder and less deferential to the high castes than they were even twenty or thirty years ago. They are no longer prepared to be socially invisible or the object of do-gooding pity from high-status reformers. Dalits now demand their rights. This is a matter of great discomfort for many high-caste people, though increasingly they have to recognise that here is a situation that will not go away. The governance of India is no longer a monopoly of the socially respectable.

Contemporary Dalit resoluteness has come at the end of a long history, much of which is discussed in chapter 3. The one great watershed in more than a century of change is the late 1920s and early 1930s. Before this, Untouchable organisations were substantially inward-looking and concerned to rid their communities of habits that were allegedly the basis of their lowly social position. The mood had begun to shift even before the emergence of Ambedkar in the late 1920s. But it was Ambedkar who seized the opportunity presented by a British government prepared to listen to an argument for Untouchable representation along lines already conceded to the Muslim population. In the constitutional settlements of the 1930s and 40s the now 'Scheduled' Castes were provided with parliamentary and employment advantages in the name of righting an historic wrong. But to Ambedkar and even to a moderate like M. C. Rajah, it appeared that the great victories wrung from the British and Gandhi had brought about little change on the ground. In despair Ambedkar turned his back on his life's work in the worldly arenas of law, government and politics. His last significant act was religious. As if Hinduism was simply an optional religion, Ambedkar abandoned it for Buddhism in the company of millions of his followers. But religious rejection has not been a meaningful path to many non-Mahar Untouchables. Dalit striving is now firmly cast in the mould of worldliness.

Unless we count the emergence of Kanshi Ram and Mayawati in the 1990s, there has been no dramatic moment for the Untouchables in all the years after the Poona Pact. In particular, the glow of optimism at the time of Independence proved to be a false dawn. The overall change we can now recognise to be profound has been slow and generational, brought about by the seeping nourishment of the franchise, education, urbanisation, favourable political rhetoric, the waning of orthodoxy, and no doubt other factors too. But two factors stand out above all others – education and the franchise. Formally educated people tend to be different. Education engenders a kind of self-confidence. In the case of Untouchables, this is bound to have made them less tolerant of behaviour that oppresses them. This is not to say that only those who are formally educated resist their own oppression. Ayyankali, the great Pulaya reformer, was illiterate. And the Musahar activists in Bihar today, most of them presumably illiterate, are just one of many historical examples of agrarian resistance by the unlettered. But the spread of education to large numbers among the subordinated Untouchables has tended to infuse them with a new and more ambitious culture. Even where formal educational qualifications do not deliver the desired employment – unfortunately the rule rather than the exception in India today – a multitude of other benefits has been created. Above all education tends to invest a person with a sense of entitlement to equal treatment in matters of common human concern.

But education does not necessarily lead to any special Dalit consciousness. An intriguing full circle can be discerned in the case of the Dalit writers' movement. As we have seen in chapter 7, the Dalit movement of Maharashtra and Karnataka has given birth to a significant corpus of creative writing. The early writing of the mid-1970s tended to be angry and often crude in its denunciations of caste Hindu oppression. But over time a genuine literary culture has developed, to the point that the most talented writers see writing rather than Dalit activism as their occupation. Their stories are sufficiently crafted to be widely published in Marathi or Kannada outlets, and they are now unhappy to be judged by standards other than those applied to creative writers in general. Of course, this brings down criticism from their own communities and also from caste Hindus. Both these critics charge the too-good Dalit writer with having sold out. For the high-caste critic, Dalit artists, unlike artists from more privileged circumstances, are supposed to be eternally suffused with the most pitiable aspects of the Dalit condition. But from a more reasonable perspective, it is a powerful triumph that widely admired writers have emerged from a literary movement whose roots are in Dalit protest. The triumph is one of learning, imagination and art over the tyranny of oppressed ancestry.

If education can liberate the individual, the franchise is the basis of making a difference in politics. In Behror of the early 1970s the sarpanch of the elected panchayat, an upper-caste Bania, counted the Untouchable castes among his supporters. There was no evidence that these people had any special regard for the sarpanch, or he for them. They voted for him because he represented Congress and because they felt more comfortable if the dominant landowning community, the Ahirs, did not control the panchayat. For his part, the sarpanch knew that the price of maintaining Chamar, Dhanak and Bhangi support was to pay them respect and give them whatever paid employment was in his gift. To the faint disgust of his family he was to be seen visiting these people, even the Bhangi colony, on virtually a daily basis, as a way of demonstrating his solidarity. In this simple situation in Behror is the seed of a large part of Dalit potency today.

By the mid-1990s the Indian political process had considerably evolved. The change was neatly encapsulated in one of the Bahujana Samaj Party's slogans in 1994: *Vote hamara, raj tumhara. Nahin chalega, nahin chalega.* (We vote, you govern. Not any more, not any more.) Every political operator, particularly in north India, knows that the long subordinated communities are now a political force that must be addressed and not ignored. This lesson has most dramatically been learned in Uttar Pradesh. In the last couple of years the upper castes that control the BJP and Congress have respectively been forced into government and an electoral alliance with the aggressively anti-Brahminical Bahujana Samaj Party. The leadership of the BJP and Congress may believe that they can ultimately coopt the fire-eaters of the Bahujana Samaj – this is undoubtedly their motivation in moving into such alliance. But this leadership will also find that their own pragmatic politics chip away at the ideological foundation of high-caste dominance. There can be little doubt that transforming social change will be the long-term outcome of the new political assertiveness of vast chunks of the Indian population.

One of the best indicators of the changed outlook of Untouchables is their increasing status as the victims (less often the practitioners) of violence. The 'Harijan atrocity' has been a staple of newspaper reportage since the late 1970s. While this violence is undeniably ugly, its increased incidence is a pointer to new social forces at work in India. Violence seems to have increased in rough proportion to the increased assertiveness of Untouchables themselves. Change does not always lead to violence. But there is more truth in the converse proposition that violence is often a response to unwelcome change.

What has changed far less is the position of Untouchables in the economy. A very large proportion of them are poor, and they also represent a disproportionate share of the total Indian poor. Their poverty arises from the menial nature of their typical employment. The modal Untouchable employee is still the rural labourer who owns either no land at all, or only a very small plot quite insufficient to support his/her family. A scattering of Untouchables have owned land for as long as there are records, and post-Independence reforms have delivered small plots to a significant number of others. But all too often these lands are poor in quality and also the subject of bitter dispute with the dominant landholders of the village: they tend to have been hived off from traditional commons. In short, land ownership cannot be the major source of livelihood for any but a small proportion of Untouchables. The major income of rural Untouchables comes from tilling the soil of others. Untouchables perform this work in a great variety of relationships with their employers, but increasingly they are free rather than tied or bonded labourers. Although the free labourer has less security than the tied labourer, he or she is far less subject to oppression (including rape) by the employer.

But the countryside is decreasingly able to employ its growing population, even at poverty-level wages. Widespread mechanisation of agriculture – the tractor – has displaced labour in wheat and even to some extent in rice zones. So Untouchables have joined the great post-Independence exodus – albeit often a revolving exodus – to the towns and their fringes. Urbanisation has become the greatest avenue of upward mobility in contemporary India, and statistics document the lower incidence of poverty endured by urban Indians. But for communities like the Untouchables and the tribals, urbanisation tends to be an exchange of one form of poverty for another. Our study of stone quarry workers in chapter 6 is a detailed illustration of this developing and disturbing phenomenon. In short, Dalits are fast being transformed into a proletariat and sometimes a lumpenproletariat. Conversely, the number of well-to-do Untouchables is insufficient to constitute an Untouchable middle class of any weight.

The debate on Indian poverty is inconclusive as to whether it is rising, staying constant or declining. For what it is worth, the present writers take the position that its severity is declining. We are less sure about the incidence of poverty. But even the decline in severity is measurable only by reference to the most fundamental indices such as mortality, and not by marginally less basic criteria such as calorie intake. On the latter index the data seem too unreliable to permit a firm conclusion. All of this makes depressing reading at the end of the twentieth century, and it has special implications for the Untouchable population. On the other hand the new engines of pauperisation are also driving whole populations other than the Untouchables too. So in the context of declining ritual discrimination it may be that the Untouchables will become decreasingly differentiated from other Indians by reference to economic prosperity. But this may prove little to celebrate.

The emergence and limits of the new civic culture

In chapter 4 we discuss at some length the waning of discrimination against Untouchables, and the emergence of what we call a new 'civic culture' in contemporary India. This change has been undeniably crucial in easing the burden of the condition of being Untouchable, though in both a logical and a causal sense it is secondary to the trans-formation of consciousness among Untouchables themselves. The new civic culture consists in a pragmatic lack of attention to considerations of ritual purity. This is a fragmentary rather than a comprehensive culture, a quality that reflects the piecemeal way it has developed. Orthodoxy first began to crumble in relation to some of the worst discriminations, notably those that underpinned the slavery formally abolished in the middle of the nineteenth century. So access to roads was opened up, and presumably so too was train and bus transport quite soon after their appearance in at least north India. In the crucial matter of schooling it was Christian missions and a few maverick princely states that first threw open their doors to the Untouchables. Admission to ordinary public schools came much later in most regions, and was attended by appalling discrimination in the schoolroom and the playground. But most of this gross discrimination has now faded away. It is now generally accepted that Untouchable children have the same right to education as do any other children.

Despite this progress, it is highly doubtful that there has been any general change of heart on the issue of caste hierarchy and Untouchable inferiority in particular. What has tended to drive the new culture is a sense of convenience, rather than anything more profound. The change is far more pronounced in urban areas: the larger the urban settlement, the less likely it is to practise ritual discriminations. People in the large cities are simply too hedged about with the pressures and challenges of urban life to attempt a high degree of orthodox purity in their life outside the home. But in private, or if they return to their village, they often adopt a more orthodox cast of mind. Life in the villages, still the home of some 70 per cent of the population, is far less governed by the new civic culture. In the matter of schooling, villages have recognised the rights of Untouchables as much as towns have. But adults have been markedly less willing to let orthodoxy go in relation to sharing facilities for food, water and worship, let alone inviting traditionally polluted individuals into their own homes.

Compartmentalisation, hypocrisy and avoidance strategies are the external face of a major waning of oppression of Untouchables, but in the absence of more rigorous internalisation they are of limited utility in more intimate situations. It is one thing to turn a blind eye to the infiltration of traditionally undesirable people into places of ordinary commerce and intercourse, and quite another to welcome them into the cherished centre of secular, let alone spiritual, life. Reservation may have imposed admission quotas on important public institutions, but it has not been able to guarantee that Untouchables will feel wanted and comfortable in these institutions. Conversations with Dalits in various institutional settings reveal a forbidding world of deprecation and exclusion from the otherwise common culture of the institution. As a generalisation, it can be said that Scheduled Caste men (there are very few women) find particular difficulties if they aspire to positions in the better universities or the elite professions.

Perhaps the best off are Scheduled Caste officers in the Indian Administrative Service (IAS), the elite of the public services of India. By now, the numbers of Scheduled Caste officers in the IAS are so considerable that they can form their own 'network' quite separate from the long-established networks of high-caste officers. This became evident during the period of the short-lived Mayawati Government in Uttar Pradesh. Scheduled Caste officers may also have been helped by the self-consciously civilised culture of the IAS that frowns upon the coarser displays of primordial discrimination. But even in the IAS most Scheduled Caste officers have laboured under considerable difficulties and discomfort until the very recent past. They face the perennial devaluation of being assumed to have entered the service with less merit than that displayed by caste Hindus. And at least until recently they found it notoriously difficult to stand up for themselves in the context of the dominance of high-caste networks both within the service and amongst politicians and local dominants. A Scheduled Caste officer in charge of a District has often possessed very little power or standing.

Some of the best evidence that the new civic culture is pragmatic and superficial rather than transformational can be discerned in the almost complete absence of Dalits from areas of private employment other than the menial or manual. Given a choice, it would seem that employers will ordinarily opt for a caste Hindu over a Scheduled Caste person. It might be argued that the caste Hindu is likely to have a stronger record of academic achievement and greater social presence as a result of the usual disparity in family background. But it is highly doubtful that this is a sufficient explanation. There are now considerable numbers of Dalits who can compete equally with high-caste people for at least middle-level positions. As yet, private employment in the white-collar sector is only a relatively minor source of overall employment in India. But if India is to prosper, it will become perhaps the most important sector. Unless attitudes change, or unless reservation is extended to the private sector, the lack of a Dalit presence there will reinforce their lowly social position.

The ambivalent state

There may be no better illustration of the ambivalent, even contradictory, character of the Indian state than the case of the Untouchables. On the one hand, the state has put in place laws and programs without which deep change in the overall situation of the Untouchables could not have taken place. On the other hand, these measures are too limited in scope and far too poorly implemented to have overcome the pervasive subordination and poverty of these people. The scope is too limited precisely because there was an insufficient understanding of, or solidarity with, the overall condition of Dalits. A progressive consensus had formed itself on the issue of the Untouchables well before Independence, but this consensus was neither sufficiently informed nor sufficiently intense to be the basis of an appropriate national program. For example, as we show in chapter 5, these progressive views had to find their place alongside accounts of the Indian poor as inferior and prolific human stock whose progeny were ruining the moral and economic temper of the nation. Were these the people for whom the now governing elite would undertake arduous programs such as land confiscation in the name of social justice? Such a program would have taken resources away from their own kind – indeed, from themselves.

As to measuring the impact of the schemes actually undertaken, we have divided the activities into several categories: compensatory discrimination; action against adverse discrimination; and anti-poverty measures. All these measures have conferred important benefits on the Untouchable population of India, but none of them has been genuinely transformational. They have been less important than the emergence of the new civic culture of pragmatic disregard to ritual orthodoxies. Of course, the state has played a part in engineering this new civic culture, but it is not the major part. The prime engine has been a diffuse pragmatism, not a specific fear of legal consequences or other penalisation by the state. Legal fiat was certainly one lever in opening the doors of government schools in the pre-Independence period, as was bureaucratic pressure applied to high-caste teachers. But the more decisive factor was a pragmatic accommodation of caste Hindu parents in the face of strong movements from both Untouchable and reformist sources, Gandhi included. The accommodation was not always non-violent, but in the end the principle of excluding Untouchable children from education ceased to be a cause worth fighting for.

This patchy, even weak, performance of the Indian state in a crucial area of social reform will no longer strike any serious observer as exceptional. At the end of the twentieth century, in contrast to the hopes of mid-century, there is a realism bordering on cynicism about the capacities of the state as an instrument of social reform. There are several independent strands to this new realism. First, there is an understanding that redistributive reform cannot usually be accomplished by purely bureaucratic means – unless, that is, there are particularly favourable circumstances. Such circumstances were responsible for the successful Allied imposition of significant land reform in post-war Japan. On a lesser scale, the circumstance of widespread fear among landlords enabled considerable land reform to take place in the State of West Bengal soon after Independence. Later, the fear in these landlords abated and they learnt to defend their interests more effectively. Atul Kohli has rightly contrasted the top-down approach practised in examples such as these with situations where bureaucratic action is buttressed by a strong political campaign from below (Kohli 1987: 223–4). But organised movements of this kind have generally been lacking in India, and the task of reform has been left to an inadequate bureaucracy.[2]

Secondly, we now know that the institutions of the state are not a value-free apparatus directed to the steady enforcement of whatever measures its masters might charge it with. The state is a collection of people as well as a bundle of laws and principles. These people are drawn from particular social strata and have views and associations that naturally reflect their social position. Even if they take on an appropriately professional and institutional character in their official capacity, people do not divorce themselves from their social origins. Unfortunately, the Indian case suggests that the bureaucracy has been decreasingly 'professional' over time. Not only has it failed to support the poor against the rich and powerful of

---

[2] Where we part company with Kohli is in his belief that the government of West Bengal got it right in the 1970s and 80s. Kohli is right about the strong CPI(M) organisation of the countryside which backed the government's efforts at reform of sharecroppers' rights in Operation Barga. But our view is that Operation Barga is very far from a radical program of land reform, important though it is.

the countryside, but it has tended to become a corrupt and unlawful instrument of the latter. One of the saddest realisations of post-Independence India is that the state is often the biggest enemy of the poor. The state apparatus fails to deliver the welfare benefits it is lawfully charged to distribute, and its policemen are a routine source of bullying, extortion and outright violence against the poor.

But beyond these moral and political deficiencies of the Indian administration, there is a still more fundamental weakness in the whole apparatus of the Indian state. Public institutions in India have not proved equal to their tasks in almost every area of administration – tax collection, industrial and commercial ventures, the judiciary, and the distribution of welfare, to name some. The task of building and sometimes rebuilding these institutions is now a major national task. So if we expect the present administration to engage in the always arduous task of systematically pursuing social justice, we are simply expecting too much. It is only when the surrounding political and social circumstances change that we can anticipate a more satisfactory performance on the part of the machinery of government.

Conclusion

In view of the great improvement in the circumstances of Untouchables over the last century or so, it would be illogical to be pessimistic about their further progress. The simplest measure of this future progress will be our inability to apply to these people a categorical term such as 'Untouchable' or 'Dalit', and this is a prospect within contemplation. This is not to minimise the degree of vicious discrimination that still exists against Untouchables today, only to recognise that there are forces at work that will make this increasingly problematical for its practitioners. The chief of these forces is the increasing resoluteness of Dalits themselves. Their spirit of resistance, rooted as it is in a consciousness of inherent equality, is the great change to the lives of Untouchables in the twentieth century.

The most worrying issue is now the economic future of people from the Untouchable castes. Economic liberalisation offers no prospect of early advantage to such people. This is not to say that the present writers have any nostalgia for the now dwindling regime of central planning and its commanding public sector: we have detailed the extent to which this regime has failed to provide employment for poor Untouchables or given 'land to the tiller'. But the idea that the now liberalising economy will rapidly generate enough jobs in the private sector for those at the bottom of Indian society is illusory. If the present emphasis is on raising gross levels of growth, an equal value must continue to be placed on equity. At the very least this means that the 'safety net' of public welfare – food for the needy, pensions, scholarships and so on – must be improved, and certainly not allowed to decline from its present low level. It will be a hollow victory indeed if liberation of the spirit is attended by perpetual poverty.

Bibliography

GOVERNMENT DOCUMENTS

PRE-INDEPENDENCE

Census of India, 1871–2. General Report
  1881. General Report
  1891. General Report
  1901. General Report
  1911. General Report
  1921. General Report
  1931. General Report and Appendix I: 'Exterior Castes'
  1931. V(I) Bengal
  1931. XVIII(I) United Provinces of Agra and Oudh
  1931. XXVIII Travancore
Government of Great Britain 1918. *Report on Indian Constitutional Reforms.* Cd. 9109. London.
  1919. *Indian Constitutional Reforms, Report of the Franchise Committee* (Southborough Committee). Calcutta: Govt Printing Office.
  1932. *Indian Round Table Conference (Second Session) 7 September 1931–1 December 1931,* Proceedings of Minorities Committee. London: HMSO.
Government of Mysore nd [1919?], *Report of the Committee Appointed to Consider Steps Necessary for the Adequate Representation of Communities in the Public Service* (Miller Committee Report).
Indian Franchise Committee 1932. *Report of the Indian Franchise Committee,* I. London: HMSO.

POST-INDEPENDENCE

CONSTITUTION

Constituent Assembly Debates (CAD) 1947–9. 12 vols. New Delhi.
Constitution of India 1950.

ACTS OF PARLIAMENT (AND DELEGATED LEGISLATION)

Union of India
Bonded Labour System (Abolition) Act 1976
Constitution (Scheduled Castes) Order 1950

Constitution (Scheduled Castes) Orders (Amendment) Act 1990
Contract Labour (Regulation and Abolition) Act 1970
Inter-State Migrant Workmen (Regulation of Employment and Conditions of Service) Act 1979
Mines Act 1952
Minimum Wages Act 1948
Protection of Civil Rights Act 1976
Scheduled Castes and Scheduled Tribes (Prevention of Atrocities) Act 1989
Untouchability Offences Act 1955

West Bengal
Estates Acquisition Act 1953

CASES

Bandhua Mukti Morcha v Union of India and Others (Quarry Workers Case): AIR 1984 SC 802.

GOVERNMENT OF INDIA

1988–9. *Agricultural Situation in India.* New Delhi: Directorate of Economics and Statistics, Department of Agriculture and Co-operation, Ministry of Agriculture, XLII–XLIV.

1955. Backward Classes Commission, I [Kalelkar]. *Report,* 3 vols. Delhi: Manager of Publications.

1971. *Census of India 1971. Union Primary Census Abstract,* I, II–A (ii).

1993. *Census of India 1991: Union Primary Census Abstract for Scheduled Castes and Scheduled Tribes, Paper 1 of 1993.*

1990. *Concurrent Evaluation of IRDP: The Main Findings of the Survey for January 1989 – December 1989.* New Delhi: Ministry of Agriculture.

1987. *Concurrent Evaluation of IRDP: The Main Findings of the Survey for October 1985 – September 1986,* and *January–June 1987.* New Delhi: Ministry of Agriculture.

1992. *Eighth Five Year Plan, 1992–1997,* 2 vols. New Delhi: Planning Commission.

1983. *High Power Panel on Minorities: Report on Scheduled Castes, Scheduled Tribes and Other Weaker Sections.* New Delhi: Ministry of Home Affairs.

1978–84. *Reports of the Commission for Scheduled Castes and Scheduled Tribes.* Reports 1–4. (RCSCST (new).)

1951–87. *Reports of the Commissioner for Scheduled Castes and Scheduled Tribes.* (RCSCST.)

1969. *Report of the Committee on Untouchability, Economic and Educational Development of the Scheduled Castes and Connected Documents* (Elyaperul Committee). New Delhi: Department of Social Welfare.

1985. *Report on the Eighth General Election to the House of the People 1984.* New Delhi: Election Commission.

1984. *Selected Statistics on Scheduled Castes.* New Delhi: Ministry of Home Affairs.

GOVERNMENT OF KARNATAKA

1975. Karnataka Backward Classes Commission. [Havanur] *Report*, 4 vols. in 5 parts. Bangalore.
1986. Second Backward Classes Commission. [Venkatswamy] *Report*, 2 vols. Bangalore.

GOVERNMENT OF KERALA

1984. State Planning Board. *Report of the High Level Committee on Social Infrastructure and Services*, 6 vols. Trivandrum.

ARCHIVAL DOCUMENTS

Papers of M. C. Rajah, Nehru Memorial Museum and Library.
Government of India, Home Department Proceedings, 1920. India Office Records, London. P/9956 [Dadabhoy] and P/10842 [Reports for Madras and Bengal].

NEWSPAPERS AND PERIODICALS

The Asian Age, 1 November 1996.
BAMCEF Bulletins 1973–80.
The Daily Telegraph, 3 February and 15 March 1994.
The Hindustan Times, 6 April 1994.
The New York Times, 14 September 1989.
Outlook, 1 November 1995.
The Oppressed Indian (monthly magazine).
The Pioneer, 18 September 1989.
The Times of India, 27 October 1996.
The Tribune (Lahore), November–December 1910.

BOOKS, CHAPTERS AND ARTICLES

Acharya, Serthi 1992. Rates of Return in Indian Agriculture, *Economic and Political Weekly*, 27(3), 111–19.
Aggarwal, Partap C. and Mohd Siddiq Ashraf 1976. *Equality Through Privilege: A Study of Special Privileges of Scheduled Castes in Haryana*. Delhi: Shri Ram Centre.
Aiyappan, A. 1944. 'Iravas and Culture Change', *Bulletin of the Madras Government Museum*, new series, 5 (4), 1–195.
Ambedkar, B. R. 1944, 1989. *Annihilation of Caste*. In Vasant Moon (ed.), *Dr Babasaheb Ambedkar: Writings and Speeches*, I. Bombay: Government of Maharashtra (reprint).
    1945, 1991. *What Congress and Gandhi Have Done to the Untouchables*. In Vasant Moon (ed), *Dr Babasaheb Ambedkar: Writings and Speeches*, x. Bombay: Government of Maharashtra (reprint).
    1946, 1990. *Who Were the Shudras?* In Vasant Moon (ed), *Dr Babasaheb*

Ambedkar: Writings and Speeches, VII. Bombay: Government of Maharashtra (reprint).

1948, 1990. *The Untouchables*. In Vasant Moon (ed.), *Dr Babasaheb Ambedkar: Writings and Speeches*, VII. Bombay: Government of Maharashtra (reprint).

1969. *Thus Spoke Ambedkar – Selected Speeches*, ed. Bhagwan Das, II. Jullundur: Bheem Patrika Publications.

nd (*c* 1980) *Thus Spoke Ambedkar – Selected Speeches*, ed. Bhagwan Das, IV. Bangalore: Ambedkar Sahitya Prakashana.

1987a. 'Buddha or Karl Marx', in Vasant Moon (ed.), *Dr Babasaheb Ambedkar: Writings and Speeches*, III. Bombay: Government of Maharashtra.

1987b. 'Riddles in Hinduism: An Exposition to Enlighten the Masses', in Vasant Moon (ed.), *Dr Babasaheb Ambedkar: Writings and Speeches*, IV Bombay: Government of Maharashtra.

Anon nd *The Depressed Classes: An Enquiry into their Conditions and Suggestions for Their Uplift*. (Articles reprinted from *The Indian Review*.) Madras: G. A. Natesan and Co.

Anon 1986. *Report from the Flaming Fields of Bihar*. Calcutta: Prabodh Bhattacharya.

Ansari, Ghaus 1960. *Muslim Caste in Uttar Pradesh*. Lucknow: Ethnographic and Folk Culture Society.

Arnold, David 1977. *The Congress in Tamilnad: Nationalist Politics in South India 1919–37*. Delhi: Manohar.

Banerjee, S. 1980. *In the Wake of Naxalbari: A History of the Naxalite Movement in India*. Calcutta: Subarnarekha.

Bandyopadhyay, D. 1986. *A Study on Poverty Alleviation in Rural India through Special Employment Creation Programmes*. New Delhi: ILO/ARTEP.

1988. 'Direct Intervention Programmes for Poverty Alleviation', *Economic and Political Weekly*, 23(26), 1, 977–88.

Baxi, Upendra 1984. 'Legislative Reservations for Social Justice: Some Thoughts on India's Unique Experiment', in R. B. Goldmann and A. J. Wilson (eds.), *From Independence to Statehood: Managing Ethnic Conflict in Five African and Asian States*, pp. 210–24. London: Frances Pinter.

1995. 'Emancipation as Justice: Babasaheb Ambedkar's Legacy and Vision', in U. Baxi and B. Parekh (eds.), *Crisis and Change in Contemporary India*, pp. 122–49. Sage: New Delhi.

Bayly, Susan 1989. *Saints, Goddesses and Kings: Muslims and Christians in South Indian Society 1700–1900*. Cambridge: Cambridge University Press.

Berreman, Gerald D. 1979. *Caste and Other Inequities: Essays on Inequality*. Meerut: Folklore Institute.

Bhat, P. N. Mari and Rajan S. Irudaya 1990. 'Demographic Transition in Kerala Revisited', *Economic and Political Weekly*, 25 (35 and 36), 1, 957–80.

Bhowmick, P. K. 1980. *Some Aspects of Indian Anthropology*. Calcutta: Subarnarekha.

Brass, Paul R. 1965. *Factional Politics in an Indian State: The Congress Party in Uttar Pradesh*. Berkeley: University of California Press.

1990. *The Politics of India since Independence*. Cambridge: Cambridge University Press.

Breman, Jan 1985. *Of Peasants, Migrants and Paupers: Rural Labour Circulation and Capitalist Production in West India*. Delhi: Oxford University Press.

Brennan, Lance 1990. 'From Famine to Scarcity to Drought: Food Crisis Management in India, 1947 to 1987', in Jim Masselos (ed.), *India: Creating a Modern Nation*, pp. 199–221. Delhi: Sterling.

Briggs, George W. 1920, 1975. *The Chamars*. Delhi: B.R. Publishing (reprint).

Brown, Judith 1972. *Gandhi's Rise to Power: Indian Politics 1915–1922*. Cambridge: Cambridge University Press.

   1977. *Gandhi and Civil Disobedience: The Mahatma in Indian Politics 1928–1934*. Cambridge: Cambridge University Press.

   1985. *Modern India: The Origins of an Asian Democracy*. Delhi: Oxford University Press.

Cadell, Sir Patrick 1938. *History of the Bombay Army*. London: Longmans Green.

Chakravarti, Anand 1975. *Contradiction and Change: Emerging Patterns of Authority in a Rajasthan Village*. Delhi: Oxford University Press.

Clough, John E. 1914. *Social Christianity in the Orient: The Story of a Man, a Mission and a Movement*. New York: Macmillan.

Cohen, Stephen P. 1969. 'The Untouchable Soldier: Caste, Politics and the Indian Army', *Journal of Asian Studies*, 28 (3), 453–68.

Dandekar, G. N. 1983. *Durga Bhraman Gatha*. Bombay: Majestic Book Stall.

Dandekar, V. M. 1986. 'Agriculture, Employment and Poverty', *Economic and Political Weekly*, 21(38 and 39), A-90–A-100.

Dangle, Arjun 1992. *Poisoned Bread: Translations from Modern Marathi Dalit Literature*. Bombay: Orient Longman.

Dantwala, M. L. 1985. 'Garibi Hatao: Strategy Options', *Economic and Political Weekly*, 20 (11), 475–6.

Das, Arvind N. 1983. *Agrarian Unrest and Socio-Economic Change in Bihar 1900–1980*. New Delhi: Manohar.

Das, Veena 1977. *Structure and Cognition: Aspects of Hindu Caste and Ritual*. Delhi: Oxford University Press.

   1995. *Critical Events: An Anthropological Perspective on Contemporary India*. Delhi: Oxford University Press.

Deleury, Guy A. 1960. *The Cult of Vithoba*. Pune: Deccan College Postgraduate Research Institute.

Desai, Ashok and E. Desai 1988. 'India', in G. Edgren (ed.), *The Growing Sector: Studies of Public Sector Employment in Asia*, pp. 67–97. New Delhi: ILO/ARTEP.

Desai, I. P. 1976. *Untouchability in Rural Gujarat*. Bombay: Popular Prakashan.

Desai, Mahadev 1937. *The Epic of Travancore*. Ahmedabad: Navajivan.

   1953. *Day-to-Day with Gandhi: Secretary's Diary*, VI and VII. Varanasi: Sarva Seva Sangh Prakashan.

Deshpande, Anirudh 1996. 'Hopes and Disillusionment: Recruitment, Demobilisation and the Emergence of Discontent in the Indian Armed Forces after the Second World War', *Indian Economic and Social History Review*, 33(2), 175–207.

Dirks, Nicholas 1987. *The Hollow Crown: Ethnohistory of an Indian Kingdom*. New York: Cambridge University Press.

Dubois, Abbé J. A. 1906. *Hindu Manners, Customs and Ceremonies*. Oxford: Clarendon Press.

Dumont, Louis 1970. *Homo Hierarchicus: The Caste System and Its Implications*. Delhi: Vikas.

1972. 'Scheduled Caste Politics', in J. Michael Mahar (ed.), *The Untouchables in Contemporary India*. Tucson: University of Arizona Press.

Dutt, N. K. 1965. *Origin and Growth of Caste in India*. Calcutta: Firma K. L. Mukhopadhyay.

Frankel, Francine R. 1978. *India's Political Economy, 1947–1977: The Gradual Revolution*. Delhi: Oxford University Press.

1989. 'Caste, Land and Dominance in Bihar: Breakdown of the Brahmanical Social Order', in Frankel, Francine R. and M. S. A. Rao (eds.), *Dominance and State Power in Modern India: Decline of a Social Order*, vol. 1, pp. 46–132. Delhi: Oxford University Press.

Freeman, James M. 1979. *Untouchable: An Indian Life History*. London: George Allen and Unwin.

Galanter, Marc 1972. 'The Abolition of Disabilities – Untouchability and the Law', in J. Michael Mahar (ed.), *The Untouchables in Contemporary India*, pp. 227–314. Tucson: University of Arizona Press.

1979. 'Compensatory Discrimination in Political Representation: A Preliminary Assessment of India's Thirty-Year Experience with Reserved Seats in Legislatures', *Economic and Political Weekly*, 14: 437–54.

1984 [pb 1991 with new preface]. *Competing Equalities: Law and the Backward Classes in India*. Berkeley: University of California Press.

Gandhi, M. K. 1933, 1934, 1946. In B. Kumarappa 1954. *The Removal of Untouchability*. Ahmedabad: Navajivan Publishing House.

Gavai, R. S. 1981. *The Caste War Over Reservations: A Case Before the People's Bar*. Bombay: Maharashtrian State Republican Party.

Ghurye, G. S. 1957. *Caste and Class in India*. Bombay: Popular Book Depot.

Gill, Kanwaljit Kau and Sucha Singh Gill 1990, 'Agricultural Development and Industrialisation in Punjab: Some Issues Related to the Pepsi Model', *Economic and Political Weekly*, 10 November, 2, 507–9.

Gokhale, Jayashree 1993. *From Concessions to Confrontation: The Politics of an Indian Untouchable Community*. Bombay: Popular Prakashan.

Gokhale-Turner, Jayashree 1979. 'The Dalit Panthers and the Radicalisation of the Untouchables', *Journal of Commonwealth and Comparative Studies*, 17(1), 77–93.

1981. 'Bhakti or Vidroha: Continuity and Change in Dalit Sahitya', in Jayant Lele (ed.), *Tradition and Modernity in Bhakti Movements*, pp. 29–42. Leiden: E. J. Brill.

Guha, Ranajit 1983. *Elementary Aspects of Peasant Insurgency in Colonial India*. Delhi: Oxford University Press.

Gupta. S.P. 1996. 'Recent Economic Reforms in India and their Impact on the Poor and Vulnerable Sections of Society' in C. H. H. Rao and H. Linnemann (eds.), *Economic Reforms and Poverty Alleviation in India*, pp. 126–70. New Delhi: Sage.

Gupta. S. P., K. L. Datta and Padam Singh, 1983. 'Poverty among the Weaker

Sections: A Regional Study', in *Regional Dimensions of India's Economic Development*, pp. 349–58. Allahabad: Planning Commission of India and of Uttar Pradesh.

Hanumanthan, K. D. 1979. *Untouchability: A Historical Study up to 1550 A.D. (with Special Reference to Tamil Nadu)*. Madurai: Koodal Publishers.

Hardgrave, Robert L. 1969. *The Nadars of Tamilnad: The Political Culture of a Community in Change*. Berkeley: University of California Press.

1977. 'The Mapilla Rebellion, 1921: Peasant Revolt in Malabar', *Modern Asian Studies*, 11 (1), 57–99.

Harrison, Selig 1960. *India: The Most Dangerous Decades*. Madras: Oxford University Press.

Hauser, Walter 1993. 'Violence, Agrarian Radicalism, and the Audibility of Dissent: Electoral Politics and the Indian People's Front', in Harold Gould and Sumit Ganguly (eds.), *India Votes: Alliance Politics and Minority Governments in the Ninth and Tenth General Elections*, pp. 341–75. Boulder: Westview.

Herring, Ronald J. and R. M. Edwards 1983. 'Guaranteeing Employment to the Rural Poor: Social Functions and Class Interests in the Employment Guarantee Scheme in Western India', *World Development*, 11(7), 575–92.

Hess, Linda 1983. *The Bijak of Kabir*. San Francisco: North Point Press.

Hirway, Indira 1988. 'Reshaping IRDP: Some Issues', *Economic and Political Weekly*, 25 June, A89–96.

Hjejle, Benedicte 1967. 'Slavery and Agricultural Bondage in South India in the Nineteenth Century', *The Scandinavian Economic History Review*, 15(1 and 2), 71–125.

Hutton, J. H. 1963. *Caste in India: Its Nature, Function, and Origins*. London: Oxford University Press.

Ilaiah, Kancha 1996. *Why I Am Not a Hindu: – A Sudra Critique of Hindutva Philosophy, Culture and Political Economy*. Calcutta: Samya.

Inden, Ronald 1990. *Imagining India*. Oxford: Basil Blackwell.

Irshick, Eugene 1969. *Politics and Social Conflict in South India: The Non-Brahman Movement and Tamil Separatism, 1916–1929*. Berkeley: University of California Press.

Isaacs, Harold R. 1965. *India's Ex-Untouchables*. Bombay: Asia Publishing House.

Jeffrey, Robin 1974. 'The Social Origins of a Caste Association, 1875–1905: The Founding of the SNDP Yogam', *South Asia*, 4(1), 39–59.

1976. 'Temple-entry Movement in Travancore 1860–1940', *Social Scientist*, 44, 1–27.

Jones, Kenneth W. 1976. *Arya Dharm: Hindu Consciousness in Nineteenth Century Punjab*. Berkeley: University of California Press.

Jordens, J. F. T. 1981. *Swami Shraddhananda: His Life and Causes*. Delhi: Oxford University Press.

1987. *Dayananda Sarasvati: His Life and Ideas*. Delhi: Oxford University Press.

Jose, A. V. 1988, 'Agricultural Wages in India', *Economic and Political Weekly*, Review of Agriculture, 23(26), A46–58.

Joshi, Barbara R. 1982. *Democracy in Search of Equality: Untouchable Politics and Indian Social Change*. Delhi: Hindustan Publishing Corporation.

Juergensmeyer, Mark 1982. *Religion as Social Vision: The Movement against Untouchability in 20th-Century Punjab*. Berkeley: University of California Press.

Kabra, Kamal Nayan and Anil Chandy Ittyerah 1992. *The Public Distribution System of India*. New Delhi: Eastern Books.

Kananaikil, J. 1982. *Scheduled Castes in the Constituent Assembly*. New Delhi: Indian Social Institute.

Kannan, K. P. 1988. *Of Rural Proletarian Struggles: Mobilization and Organisation of Rural Workers in South-West India*. Delhi: Oxford University Press.

    1995. 'Public Intervention and Poverty Alleviation: A Study of the Declining Incidence of Rural Poverty in Kerala, India', *Development and Change*, 26, 701–27.

Karve, Irawati 1988. '"On the Road": A Maharashtrian Pilgrimage', in Eleanor Zelliot and Maxine Berntsen (eds.), *The Experience of Hinduism: Essays on Religion in Maharashtra*, pp. 142–71. Albany: State University of New York Press.

Keer, Dhananjay 1971. *Dr Ambedkar: Life and Mission*. Bombay: Popular Prakashan.

Khairmode, D. B. 1955. *Dr Bhimrao Ramji Ambedkar*, 2 vols. Bombay: Pratap Prakashan.

Kohli, Atul 1987. *The State and Poverty in India: The Politics of Reform*. Cambridge: Cambridge University Press.

    1990. 'From Elite Activism to Democratic Consolidation: The Rise of Reform Communism in West Bengal', in Francine R. Frankel and M. S. A. Rao (eds.), *Dominance and State Power in Modern India: Decline of a Social Order*, vol. 2, pp. 367–415. Delhi: Oxford University Press.

Kolenda, Pauline 1978. *Caste in Contemporary India: Beyond Organic Solidarity*. Menlo Park: Benjamin/Cummings.

    1981. *Caste, Cult and Hierarchy: Essays on the Culture of India*. Meerut: Folklore Institute.

    1986. 'Caste in India since Independence', in D. K. Basu and R. Sisson (eds.), *Social and Economic Development in India since Independence: A Reassessment*, pp. 106–28. New Delhi: Sage Publications.

Kumar, Dharma 1992a. *Land and Caste in South India*. Cambridge: Cambridge University Press.

    1992b. 'The Affirmative Action Debate in India', *Asian Survey*, 32(3), 290–302.

Levtzion, Nehemia 1981. 'Conversion Under Muslim Domination: A Comparative Study', in D. N. Lorenzen (ed.), *Religious Change and Cultural Domination*, pp. 19–38. Mexico City: El Colegio de Mexico.

Lorenzen, David 1981a. 'The Kabir Panth: Heretics to Hindus', in D. N. Lorenzen (ed.), *Religious Change and Cultural Domination*, pp. 151–71. Mexico City: El Colegio de Mexico.

    1981b. 'The Kabir Panth and Politics', *Political Science Review*, 20, 263–81.

Lynch, Owen 1969. *The Politics of Untouchability: Social Mobility and Social Change in a City of India*. New York: Columbia University Press.

    1972. 'Dr B. R. Ambedkar – Myth and Charisma', in J. M. Mahar (ed.), *The Untouchables in Contemporary India*, pp. 97–112. Tucson: University of Arizona Press.

280   Bibliography

McAlpin, Michelle B. 1983. *Subject to Famine: Food Crises and Economic Change in Western India, 1860–1920*. Princeton: Princeton University Press.
Malik, Suneila 1979. *Social Integration of Scheduled Castes*. New Delhi: Abhinav.
Mallick, Ross 1992. 'Agrarian Reforms in West Bengal: The End of an Illusion', *World Development*, 20(5), 735–50.
     1993. *Development Policy of a Communist Government: West Bengal since 1977*. Cambridge: Cambridge University Press.
Manor, James 1977. *Political Change in an Indian State: Mysore 1917–55*. Delhi: Manohar.
Manu 1884 (1971). *The Ordinances*, trs. A. C. Burnell. London: Trubner and Co.
Marriott, McKim 1971. 'The Feast of Love', in M. Singer (ed.), *Krishna: Myths, Rites, and Attitudes*, pp. 200–31. Chicago: University of Chicago Press.
Marriott, McKim and Ronald Inden 1974. 'Caste Systems', *Encyclopaedia Britannica*, vol. III, pp. 982–91.
Masselos, Jim 1983. 'Jobs and Jobbery: The Sweeper in Bombay under the Raj', *The Indian Economic and Social History Review*, 19(2), 101–35.
Mendelsohn, Oliver 1981. 'The Pathology of the Indian Legal System', *Modern Asian Studies*, 15(4), 822–63.
     1988. 'Last Interview with Karpoori Thakur', *The Times of India*, 18 February 1988.
     1993. 'The Transformation of Authority in Rural India', *Modern Asian Studies*, 27(4), 805–42.
Mendelsohn, Oliver and Marika Vicziany 1990. 'The Untouchables Today', in Jim Masselos (ed.), *India: Creating a Modern Nation*, pp. 254–86. New Delhi: Sterling.
     1994. 'The Untouchables', in Oliver Mendelsohn and Upendra Baxi (eds.), *The Rights of Subordinated Peoples*, pp. 64–116. New Delhi: Oxford University Press.
Mill, James 1820. *The History of British India*, 6 vols. London.
Minhas, B. S., L. R. Jain and S. D. Tendulkar 1991. 'Declining Incidence of Poverty in the 1980s: Evidence versus Artefacts', *Economic and Political Weekly*, 26 (27 and 28), 1,673–82.
Moffatt, Michael 1979. *An Untouchable Community in South India: Structure and Consensus*. Princeton: Princeton University Press.
Morris, Morris D. 1965. *The Emergence of an Industrial Labour in India: A Study of the Bombay Cotton Mills*. Berkeley: University of California Press.
Muhammed, Shah 1980. *The Indian Muslims: A Documentary Record*, 2 vols. New Delhi: Meenakshi Prakashan.
Mukerji, U. N. 1909. *A Dying Race*. Calcutta: Mukerjee and Bose.
Mukherjee, Kalyan and Rajendra Singh Yadav 1980. *Bhojpur: Naxalism in the Plains of Bihar.* New Delhi: Radha Krishna.
Mukherjee, Prabhati 1988. *Beyond the Four Varnas: The Untouchables in India*. Delhi: Motilal Banarsidass.
Namboodiripad, E. M. S. 1977. 'Castes, Classes and Parties in Modern Political Development', *Social Scientist*, 63, 1–25.
Natarajan, S. 1962. *A Century of Social Reform in India*. Bombay: Asia Publishing House.
Nayanar, E. K. 1982. *My Struggles: An Autobiography*. Delhi: Vikas.

O'Hanlon, Rosalind 1985. *Caste, Conflict and Ideology: Mahatma Jotirao Phule and Low Caste Protest in Nineteenth-Century Western India*. Cambridge: Cambridge University Press.

Omvedt, Gail 1973. 'Development of the Maharashtrian Class Structure 1818 to 1931', *Economic and Political Weekly*, 8(31, 32 and 33), 1,417–32.

1976. *Cultural Revolt in a Colonial Society: The Non-Brahman Movement in Western India 1873 to 1930*. Bombay: Scientific Socialist Education Trust.

1994. *Dalits and the Democratic Revolution: Dr Ambedkar and the Dalit Movement in Colonial India*. New Delhi: Sage.

Oommen T. K. 1985. *From Mobilization to Institutionalization: The Dynamics of Agrarian Movement in Twentieth Century Kerala*. Bombay: Popular Prakashan.

Parvathamma, C. 1973. 'Ambedkar and After: The Position and Future of Indian Scheduled Caste Masses and Classes', *Eastern Anthropologist*, 26(3), 221–34.

1984. *Scheduled Castes and Tribes: A Socio-Economic Survey*. Delhi: Ashish Publishing House.

Patnaik, Utsa and M. Dingwaney 1985. Introduction to Patnaik and Dingwaney (eds.), *Chains of Servitude: Bondage and Slavery in India*. Madras: Sangam Books.

Pradhan, Atul Chandra 1986. *The Emergence of the Depressed Classes*. Bhubaneswar: Bookland International.

Pradhan, G. R. 1938. *Untouchable Workers of Bombay City*. Bombay: Karnataka Publishing House.

Prasad, Pradhan 1987. 'Agrarian Violence in Bihar', *Economic and Political Weekly*, 22(22), 847–52.

Punalekar, S. P. 1981. *Aspects of Class and Caste in Social Tensions: A Study of Marathwada Riots*. Surat: Centre for Social Studies.

Ram, Jagjivan 1980. *Caste Challenge in India*. New Delhi: Vision Books.

Rao, S. L. and I. Natarajan 1994. *Markets for Consumer Products in India*. Delhi: Global Business Press.

Rath, Nilkantha 1985. '"Garibi Hatao": Can IRDP Do It?', *Economic and Political Weekly*, 20(6), 238–46.

Rizvi, S. A. A. 1981. 'Islamization in the Indian Subcontinent', in D. N. Lorenzen (ed.), *Religious Change and Cultural Domination*, pp. 39–60. Mexico City: El Colegio de Mexico.

Robertson, Alexander 1938. *The Mahar Folk*. Calcutta: YMCA Publishing House.

Sacchidananda 1977. *The Harijan Elite*. Delhi: Thomson Press.

Saradmoni, K. 1980. *Emergence of a Slave Caste: Pulayas of Kerala*. Delhi: People's Publishing House.

Scott, James C. 1985. *Weapons of the Weak: Everyday Forms of Peasant Resistance*. New Haven: Yale University Press.

Searle-Chatterjee, Mary 1981. *Reversible Sex Roles: The Special Case of Benares Sweepers*. Oxford: Pergamon Press.

Shah, K. T. 1947. *Population: Report of the Sub-Committee, National Planning Committee Series*. Bombay: Vora and Co.

Shraddhananda, Sanyasi 1926. *Hindu Sangathan: Saviour of the Dying Race*. Delhi: Kurukshetra Gurukula.

Singh, K. S. 1993. *The Scheduled Castes*. Delhi: Oxford University Press.
Singh, K. Suresh 1975. *The Indian Famine 1967: A Study in Crisis and Change*. New Delhi: People's Publishing House.
Srinivas, M. N. 1955. 'The Social System of a Mysore Village', in McKim Marriott (ed.), *Village India*, pp. 1–35. Chicago: University of Chicago Press.
  1959. 'The Dominant Caste in Rampura', *American Anthropologist*, 61, 1–16.
  1984. 'Some Reflections on the Nature of Caste Hierarchy', *Contributions to Indian Sociology*, 18(2), 151–67.
Stokes, Eric 1959. *The English Utilitarians and India*. Oxford: Clarendon.
Sundaram K. and S. D. Tendulkar 1985. 'Integrated Rural Development in India', *Social Action*, 35, 19–23.
Thimmaiah, G. 1988. 'Concurrent Evaluation of IRDP', *Economic and Political Weekly*, 23 (7), 331–2.
Ventkatswamy, P. R. 1955. *Our Struggle for Emancipation*, 2 vols. Secunderabad: Universal Art Printers.
Wolpert, Stanley 1967. *Morley and India 1906–1910*. Berkeley: University of California Press.
Yagnik, Achyut and Anil Bhatt 1984. 'The Anti-Dalit Agitation in Gujarat', *South Asia Bulletin*, 4(1), Spring.
Zelliot, Eleanor 1972. 'Gandhi and Ambedkar – a Study in Leadership', in M. Mahar (ed.), *The Untouchables in Contemporary India*, pp. 69–95. Tucson: University of Arizona Press.
  1992. *From Untouchable to Dalit: Essays on the Ambedkar Movement*. Delhi: Manohar.

UNPUBLISHED PAPERS, DISSERTATIONS AND PAMPHLETS

A. N. Sinha Institute of Social Studies, Harijan Cell nd. 'The Pipra Carnage: An Interim Report', Patna.
Anon., 1972. Scheduled Castes, Scheduled Tribes, Other Backward Classes and Minorities Employees Welfare Association, Pune.
Anon nd 'The Pipra Carnage – An Interim Report'. Patna: A. N. Sinha Institute for Social Studies.
Cohn, Bernard S. 1954. 'The Chamars of Senapur: A Study of the Changing Status of a Depressed Caste'. PhD thesis, Cornell University (University Microfilms, Ann Arbor).
Dushkin, Lelah 1957. 'The Policy of the Indian National Congress towards the Depressed Classes – An Historical Study'. MA thesis, University of Pennsylvania.
Friedlander, P. G. 1987. 'An Introduction to Ravidas', SOAS seminar, December.
Graham, James R. 1942. 'The Arya Samaj as a Reformation in Hinduism with Special Reference to Caste'. PhD thesis, Yale University.
Jain, Mahaveer 1989. Unpublished Report for the Quarry Workers Case.
Karnataka Dalitha Sangharsha Samiti nd (*c.* 18 January 1988). Press handout by the State Convenor, B. V. Chandraprasad Tyagi, Bangalore.
Kumar, Ravinder 1985. 'Gandhi, Ambedkar and the Poona Pact', Occasional Papers on History and Society, 20. Delhi: Nehru Memorial Museum and Library.

Mahadeva, Devanura 1989. 'Excerpts from *Kusumbal'*, International Writing Program, University of Chicago, 21 September.

Mendelsohn, Oliver 1981. 'The Indian Courts and Radical Redistribution: The Problem of Land Reform', Department of Legal Studies, La Trobe University.

Mishra, Laxmi Dhar 1984. Report for the Quarry Workers Case.

Parvathamma, C. 1974. 'The Crisis of Scheduled Caste Leadership and Karnataka Politics: Interplay of Constitution, Caste, Religion and Politics', World Congress of Sociology, Toronto.

Patwardhan, S. V. 1982. Report for the Quarry Workers Case.

People's Union for Civil Liberties nd. 'Report of the Bihar PUCL Fact Finding Team on Arwal Massacre', Patna.

Vicziany, Marika 1984. 'The Demography of Untouchability: Bihar 1872–1971', Asian Studies Association of Australia Conference, University of Adelaide.

1986. 'Population Growth and British Imperialism 1921–51', Asian Studies Association of Australia Conference, Griffith University.

Wood, John R. 1986. 'Reservations in Doubt: The Backlash against Affirmative Action in Gujarat, 1985'. Conference: 'What's Happening to India – the Last Ten Years?', Melbourne.

Zelliot, Eleanor 1969. 'Dr Ambedkar and the Mahar Movement'. PhD thesis: University of Pennsylvania.

Index

abolition of slavery, 82
achuta, 5
Ad Dharm movement, 79, 102
Adi-Andhra, 3
Adi-Dravida, 3
Adi-Karnataka, 3, 215–16
Agnivesh, Swami, 177–9, 196–202
Ambedkar, B. R.
  his analysis of the 1937 and 1946
    elections, 109
  assessment of stategies, 13–14, 79–80,
    117, 262–3
  on Brahminism, 115, 117, 211
  burning of Manusmriti by, 101
  career after the Poona Pact, 114-15
  on caste, 20–1
  on the Commissioner for Scheduled
    Castes and Tribes, 117
  compared with Gandhi, 77, 79, 111–14
  and the Constituent Assembly, 79, 116,
    131–2
  as a contemporary symbol, 73–4, 217–18,
    221–3, 234, 235
  conversion to Buddhism, 77, 79, 81,
    114–17
  early life and career, 100
  impact in Agra, 116
  impact in Aligarh, 213
  impact in Hyderabad, 113–14
  Independent Labour Party, 108, 115–16
  and the Mahad satyagraha, 101-2
  and Marxism/Communism, 77, 115, 211
  on origins of Untouchability, 14, 77, 112,
    116–17
  Poona Pact with Gandhi, 105
  and M. C. Rajah, 110
  and P. N. Rajbhoj, 113–14
  and Republican Party of India, 212–13
  at the Round Table Conferences, 79–80,
    104–5
  and Scheduled Castes Federation, 108–9
  and separate electorates issue, 99, 106,
    109

  and the Simon Commission 1929–30,
    104
  on temple entry, 79, 100, 102–3
  Yeola declaration by, 79, 114–15
Andhra Pradesh (inc. Hyderabad), 75, 85,
  102–3, 113, 114, 204–5, 231
anti-discrimination legislation
  assessment of, 145–6, 121, 266–71
  Constitution of India, 120
  convictions and fines under, 127–8
  implementation of, 127–8
  Protection of Civil Rights Act 1976, 120,
    127, 140, 146
  Scheduled Castes and Scheduled Tribes
    (Prevention of Atrocities) Act 1989,
    128
  Untouchability Offences Act 1955, 120,
    127
anti-poverty programs
  assessment of, 147–9, 164–6, 175,
    268–71
  in Bengal, 154
  employment (Food for Work) policy,
    158–65
  Fair Price Food Ships, 152–3
  famine policy, 150–2
  'Garibi Hatao', 157
  and health policy, 150, 167–8
  IRDP, 160–5, 187
  in Kerala, 35, 153, 166–9
  land reform, 31–2, 60–1, 153–7, 236,
    269
  literacy policy, 168–9, 141–5
  in Maharashtra, 158–9
  Operation Barga, 155
  pensions, 35, 153
  Special Component Plan, 165–6
  see also compensatory discrimination;
    poverty
Arwal, 64–9
Arya Samaj, 92–3, 177, 197
Aryans, 7
Ayyankali, 86, 97, 263

LaVergne, TN USA
26 November 2010

206268LV00005B/1/A